ALL PURPOSES
ITALIAN FOR ADULTS

ALL PURPOSES
Italian for Adults

A comprehensive Course on modern lines
designed for beginners and others;
for self-tuition or classes; and
graduated progressively to
university standard

by

CHARLES DUFF

*Formerly Lecturer at the Institute of Education,
London University; General Editor, Basis and
Essentials Series of Text Books on
Modern Languages*

THE ENGLISH UNIVERSITIES PRESS LIMITED

102, NEWGATE STREET
LONDON, E.C.1

*Printed in Great Britain for the English Universities Press Ltd.,
by Richard Clay and Company, Ltd., Bungay, Suffolk*

INTRODUCING THE COURSE

THIS is a comprehensive " All Purposes " Course in Italian, similar in method and scope to *French for Adults* and other books in this Series from the same publishers. It has been prepared on modern principles, evolved from long practical experience, and is arranged so that it can be used by adult learners, and used in more ways than one, including class tuition. It is *not* intended for children or juveniles—not because it is insufficiently simplified but because they cannot be expected to have an adult knowledge and appreciation of many of the phases of life with which the book deals. An adult comprehension of these is assumed.

Those adults wishing to learn Italian come under these broad headings:

(1) Absolute beginners, many of whom may have some knowledge of another modern language.

(2) Those who may have acquired a smattering of Italian and now wish to achieve a good working knowledge of the language.

(3) Those who are interested in the Italian contribution to civilization, which includes the fine arts, literature, science, architecture, painting, sculpture, philosophy, religion and music, and wish to approach this contribution through the medium of Italian.

(4) Those who wish to acquire the language for an essentially practical purpose such as travel, commerce, amusement, and so forth, including the tourists who wish to " get off the beaten track " in Italian-speaking areas where any language but Italian would be of little help.

(5) Those who wish to have Italian as a " second " foreign language, an extra for examination or academic purposes.

All these categories of learners have been carefully borne in mind while preparing the Course, which has not been prepared with any particular examination in mind, or any particular purpose other than that of providing a good foundation for all the practical purposes that are likely to arise. Nevertheless, one may state with some confidence that the person, including the absolute beginner, who works through this Course should be able to satisfy the examiners for the General Certificate of Education in Britain, or its equivalent in the United States of America or elsewhere. The standard of knowledge aimed at here is that required for entrance to a university. In fact, it goes a little farther than that.

Italian is an extremely attractive language and one which offers to the novice many encouraging features. The pronunciation is not only delightful but also, to the English-speaking learner, it presents no such difficulties as the French nasal sounds, the German glottal stop and gutturals, or even the Spanish *j*. The Italian vocabulary has innumerable words greatly resembling many in English which are derived from the same Latin roots, whether directly or through French. The grammar, though more extensive and more complex than our uniquely simple English grammar, is on the whole straightforward and demands only a reasonable persistence combined with practice— and a normal but not exceptional intelligence—to enable the average learner to make his way competently in everyday affairs without either shocking native speakers or letting himself down in effectiveness. Here a word may usefully be said of the Italians, of their almost invariable good-nature, patience and tolerance in dealing with the stranger who may not be very well equipped with their language. They have always struck me as among the best people in the world in this respect: always willing to help, to explain intelligently and, above all, incomparable in that they never look down or even seem to look down their noses at the poor struggler with their language. Hence, my advice to every beginner, in this most pleasant effort, is never to miss an opportunity of speaking the language with native speakers. They will seldom be found wanting in this royal road to fluency of speech.

One of the difficulties of Italian lies in knowing which syllable to stress when pronouncing a word: for, although in most words this stress is either regular or indicated by a grave accent in standard orthography, there are many words in which no provision is made for indicating stress. The difficulty is overcome in this Course by printing in italic a stressed vowel when this stress does not follow the rules. As it is important to pronounce correctly, this help leaves the learner in no doubt. Apart from stress, Italian orthography is an almost perfect guide to pronunciation: excepting irregular stress, all words in the language are pronounced as they are written.

This Course can be used for self-tuition, for individual tuition, or for class-work. It is highly desirable for the self-taught (and all others) to start from the outset with a good pronunciation, and this can rarely be achieved without some help from a good native speaker, especially in the whole of Lesson I. A bad pronunciation at the start is difficult to eliminate afterwards and *may not be understood*. By following the instructions in Lesson I, it should be possible to acquire something better than a merely passable pronunciation. A good accent will come with practice and by constant listening to native speakers, whether in everyday life or on the Radio. The latter is the best possible help for the self-taught and those who do not meet Italians fairly often. Remember the dictum of that great linguist and teacher, Otto Jespersen, who wrote: " Language cannot be separated from *sound*; and that is the sum of the matter."

The learner will notice that I have provided few " set " or " made-up " exercises, but that very quickly he finds himself dealing with " living " practice: in Italian written for Italians. Much of this kind of practice is given, and it is the best of all. Nevertheless, in a few instances, where the English-speaking learner is apt to encounter some special difficulty or difficulties, a modicum of " set exercises " is given. For the rest, the learner must rely on the well-annotated *Lettura*, to which a translation is added up to the end of Lesson IX. He is advised to go over it again and again until he has completely absorbed the Italian. This, the making up of his own sentences after memorizing words and phrases in " Situation Material ", and listening to Radio or, if possible, speaking with Italians, proves to be not only more interesting and encouraging, but it has also proved to be as quick and effective and a much more interesting method of learning than by pouring over those " set " exercises so familiar to and so greatly disliked by the modern learner. In this Course he is dealing with Italian that has, in the first instance, been written or spoken by Italians: the *natural* material of the language.

The Course is divided into ten Lessons, each one consisting of five sections. Each Section is intended for a minimum of one hour's class-work. The self-taught make their own pace. But, in order not to split up some parts of the language which logically should be stated together in sequence, some Sections contain more material than others. In such Sections, much of the material is given to show principles with examples of their working, and the remainder is for reference, to be revised or finally memorized later, or on a second perusal. A smaller type is used for this reference or revision material.

I have relied throughout on grammars written by Italians for Italians and, in the end, depended on them entirely. I have had most help from the *Grammatica Illustrata della Lingua Italiana* (1955), by Vicenzo Palumbo, and *La Lingua Nazionale* (1955), by Bruno Migliorini. These sound grammars have been my authorities though not my models in my presentation of Italian grammar for English-speaking learners, which demands a different approach and presentation.

Grateful acknowledgments are due to the writers and publishers of the extracts I have used here for Reading Material. Whenever possible the names are given with the text. The names of those to whom I am specially grateful are as follows: my friend Paul H. Stamford, for reading the galley proofs; Fr. D. Valente for permission to use material from *La Voce degli Italiani*; Mr. John Greenwood and *Ente Nazionale Industrie Turistiche* for permission to use material of use and interest to visitors to Italy; The Italian Institute, London; Radio Italiana and *Radiocorriere* of Rome for relevant information and material; to Mrs G. L. Compagnone for help and material; and to Carlo Doglio for reading the page proofs. Finally to the publishers and printers for making this book so typographically attractive.

CHARLES DUFF

London, 1958

TABLE OF CONTENTS

PART I: First Principles

LESSON I

PART II: Framework of the Language

LESSON V

WHY LEARN ITALIAN?

Because:

In its central area it is spoken to-day by over 50,000,000 people —in Italy, Switzerland, South-east France, West Austria, Trieste, etc.

It is spoken by some 10,000,000 people on the American continent, with heaviest concentrations in the United States, Argentina, Brazil, and Chile, in all of which countries there are Italian-language newspapers, cultural and other societies. It is estimated that there are from two to three millions of Italians in other countries.

The Italians have shown quite remarkable capacity in pioneering and originality not only in the fine arts but also in many branches of science, technology, and invention—in all of which the modern world is greatly interested. In this respect, theirs are often the original records.

It is the language of the fine arts which in the Middle Ages flourished in Italy as nowhere else and which, during the Renaissance, sprang ahead, giving to those arts and culture the broad impetus which developed into what we call Western Civilization. From Florence, Bologna, Siena, Venice, and other centres of the " new learning " came much of our enlightenment. Rome—" eternal Rome ", with the Città del Vaticano, is the spiritual headquarters of the Roman Catholic Apostolic Church.

In Italian Literature are many names that are landmarks in the history of European as well as Italian culture.

It is pre-eminently the language of music: an international language in musical education generally, and one which those interested in music can ill afford to ignore. Italian is one of the most melodious and sonorous languages in the world, by its nature beautifully adapted for singing, and the dominant language of opera.

It is the most direct and closest descendant of Latin, an important element in the evolution of our English vocabulary. Whoever knows Italian is never far from Latin.

It is not a difficult language to learn for most practical purposes, and it is in every sense a very rewarding language, one well worth learning for itself alone. It is rewarding to the tourist, to the person with cultural leanings, and to all who are capable of appreciating one of the most attractive ways of life in the present world.

PART I

FIRST PRINCIPLES

> Language cannot be separated from
> *sound*; and that is the sum of the matter.
> *Jespersen*

HOW TO STUDY PART I

1. Take one Section or part of a Lesson at a time. First read it through carefully so as to *understand* everything. When it is understood, go over it again, *learning* the principles. See how they work in the examples given, learn the examples and all new words as you go along. Then revise the whole lesson before proceeding.

2. In Lesson I and afterwards you are provided with " Situation Material " of an essentially practical nature. You must memorize as much as possible of this material as you progress through the course. Learn all new words and phrases as you go along. It is with this, plus Reading Matter, that you test your knowledge; and practise as you go along.

3. In Lessons I, II, and III some Practice based on the material given in each Lesson is provided. It is necessarily rather artificial. You will also be provided with Italian written by Italians for Italians. This will have explanatory notes wherever necessary. In this Reading Material you will see the grammar " in action ".

4. After Lesson III you should begin to listen to Radio Broadcasts in Italian. You may not understand much at first, but listening will train your ears to the *sounds* of the language. Listening to speech and mimicking the speaker is the royal road to fluency in speaking. See pages 143–145 for List of Radio Stations.

5. *Speak to Italians in Italian* whenever you can. You may be shy at first, but, with knowledge and practice, the shyness will disappear.

6. All that has been said above applies particularly to the self-taught. When a teacher, or a friend who knows Italian well, is available, most things become easier. Nevertheless, make your own effort to follow the instructions given above, and in time you will achieve a good working knowledge of the language.

NEVER MIND SLOW PROGRESS SO LONG AS YOU KEEP GOING!

LESSON I

§ 1. *Alphabet—Accent—Stress—Rule for Stress—Exceptions—Pronunciation of Consonants—Double Consonants—Practice*

THE Italian alphabet consists of the following twenty-one letters, below which their names in Italian are given:

a	b	c	d	e	f	g
a(h)	*bi*	*ci*	*di*	*e(h)*	*effe*	*gi*
h	**i**	**l**	**m**	**n**	**o**	**p**
acca	*i(h)*	*elle*	*emme*	*enne*	*o(h)*	*pi*
q	**r**	**s**	**t**	**u**	**v**	**z**
cu	*erre*	*esse*	*ti*	*u(h)*	*vi*	*zeta*

The letter *h* is placed here after the vowels to indicate that they are pronounced long, as will be described below. **q** is pronounced as *coo* in English. **z** is pronounced *tseta*.

ACCENT: There is one accent (`) which is placed on a vowel to indicate that it must take the principal stress (also called the " tonic " accent) in a word, when this does not occur where it would be normally expected. Thus: **perchè, verità**—words which, without the accent, would be pronounced with the stress on the vowel before the last.

This accent is also used in some small but important words to distinguish them from similar words written without the accent. Thus:

dà, gives; **da**, by
dì, day; **di**, of
è, is; **e**, and
lì,
là, } there; **la**, the

sè, oneself; **se**, if
sì, yes; **si**, self
nè, neither, nor; **ne**, of it, of him, of her, of them

3

and in certain diphthongs to show the vowel stressed:

già, already	**più,** more
giù, up	**può,** can

but not in

qui, here	**qua,** hither

Note: There is, strictly, no other accent written in Italian, but one often finds the acute (ʹ) in text-books, dictionaries, news-papers, and maps as a useful way of showing the stressed syllable that is not otherwise indicated. One also finds the circumflex (ˆ) to indicate the omission of the letter **i** in plurals ending grammatically in **ii.** Thus:

olio, oil; **olî,** oils (= **olii**)   **ampio,** ample; **ampî** (= **ampii**)

J with the sound of **Y** is sometimes seen in proper names: **Jugoslavia.** And **X** is found in **ex-** before such words as **ex-ministro,** *ex-minister.*

STRESS: Every Italian word has one syllable which is more strongly stressed than the others. The general rule throughout the language is that this stronger stress is given to the *syllable before the last.* Thus: **fratello,** *brother*: **e** is stressed. **caro,** *dear:* **a** stressed. **parola,** *word*: **o** stressed. This rule embraces the majority of words in the language. But there are two groups of exceptions: (1) words in which the last syllable is stressed, and this is indicated by the grave accent (ˋ)—**bontà,** *goodness*; **attività,** *activity*; and (2) a large group in which the stress is given to a syllable other than either the last but one or the last. Italian orthography does not provide any accent or other indication of this stress, which is nevertheless important. In this book we shall indicate the stress in words of this group (2) by printing the stressed vowel in italic type. Thus: **u***l*timo, *last*: **u** stressed. Similarly:

perdere, to lose	**umido,** moist, humid
t*i*mido, timid	**zucchero,** sugar
apprendere, to learn	**andandomene,** going out of it

(Latin scholars will note that an Italian word which follows the Latin nearly always has the stress on the same syllable as the Latin original. Thus: Latin adjective *carus, -a, -um.* Italian **caro, cara,** *dear.* Latin noun *castellum,* Italian **castello,** *castle.* And so forth.)

THE LEARNER MUST MEMORIZE THE STRESS WITH EVERY NEW WORD, PRONOUNCING IT ALOUD SEVERAL TIMES UNTIL WORD AND STRESS ARE KNOWN AS A WHOLE.

PRONUNCIATION OF CONSONANTS: Italian consonants are pronounced as in English with the following exceptions: **C, G, H, R, S, Z,** and certain combinations which will be given below:

c before **e** and **i** is pronounced like the English *ch* in *church, cheap.* Thus: **città,** *city.* The English word *cello* (short for **violoncello**) has been taken by English in its Italian pronunciation: **cello** = chello (but we do not usually pronounce the Italian **ll** correctly, for which see Double Consonants, below).

cc before **e** or **i** is pronounced like a double *ch* in English. Thus: **accento,** *accent* = ach-chénto.

ch is pronounced like English *ch* in *chemist.* **perchè,** *why* = pairkay'.

g before **e** and **i** is pronounced like English *j* in *jam,* or soft *g* in *gem.* Thus: **gelo,** *frost* = jaylo.

gg before **e** and **i** is a similar sound but more clearly made, as if it were our *dj.* Thus: **oggi,** *to-day* = od-jee.

gh is always pronounced like hard *g* in *go.* Thus: **ghirlanda,** *garland* = g(h)eerlanda.

gl has two sounds in Italian: (1) hard like our *gl* in *glow, glade,* and (2) a soft sound like liquid French *ll* or Spanish (Castillian) *ll,* and akin to our *lli* in *brilliant, million.* Thus: **egli,** *he,* **gli,** *to him* = aylyee, lyee. This is the usual sound of Italian **gl,** but it is pronounced hard as (1) when followed by an **i** that is followed by another consonant, as in **negligente,** *negligent.* This also happens

in a few little-used words such as **ganglio,** *ganglion.* The
hard **gl** sound is not often met.

gn is like our *ni* in *union, onion* and is equivalent to French
gn in *Boulogne,* or Spanish *ñ,* in *Señor.* Thus: **incognito,**
unknown, " *incognito* ", eencony′eeto; **bagno,** *bath* =
bahnyo.

gu is always pronounced like English *gw.* Thus: **guerra,**
war = gwerra; **guida,** *guide* = gweeda.

h is always silent in Italian. Thus: **ho, hai, ha,** *have,
hast, has* = oh, ahee, ah.

qu is always pronounced like *kw* or English *qu* in *quick.*
Thus: **questo,** *this* = kwáysto.

r is well trilled and pronounced with the tip of the tongue
against the upper front teeth. Thus: **raro,** *rare* =
rráhrro.

s has two sounds, " pure " and " impure ": " pure " when
it is followed by a vowel; " impure " when followed by
a consonant, except *p,* especially at the beginning of a
word.

> **s** " pure " = English hard *s* in *some, such.*
> **s** " impure " = English soft *s* in *rose,* or *z* in *zero.*

Thus: **spedire,** *to despatch* = sspaydee′ray; **svelto,**
quick, nimble = zvelto. This will be further dealt with
under Articles.

sc before **e** and **i** is pronounced like English *sh* in *ship,* but
before **-a, -o, -u** is like our *sk.* Thus: **scena,** *scene* =
shayna; **scelta,** *choice* = shaylta; **scusare,** *to excuse* =
skoosáhrey.

sch is always pronounced hard like *sch* in *school.* Thus:
schiavo, *slave* = skeeah′vo.

z at the beginning of a word usually sounds like *dz* in *adze.*
Thus: **zero,** *zero* = dzayro; **zelo,** *zeal* = dzaylo. Otherwise it is pronounced like *ts* in *bits.* Thus: **scienza,**
science = shéentsa.

zz is generally pronounced like *ts* in *bits.* Thus: **bellezza,**
beauty = bel′láytsa. But in the following words, which
must be memorized, the double-*z* is pronounced like *dz:*

mezzo, half, middle   **dozzina,** dozen
in Verbs ending in **-azzare:**
analizzare, to analyse   **fertilizzare,** to fertilize
scandalizzare, to scandalize
all *dz* sound.

DOUBLE CONSONANTS: Apart from what has been given above, the general rule is that each Italian consonant has a fixed value and each consonantal sound must be pronounced clearly, even when two similar consonants come together. When this happens, remember to pronounce the consonant, and then begin to pronounce it again, so that the two sounds are heard as in English *book-keeper*. Thus: **fratello,** *brother* = frahtel´lo; **fiamma,** *flame* = feeahm ma.

This book gives standard Italian pronunciation, but the learner will find that in almost every district of Italy there are local variants, not only of pronunciation but also in the use of words. Your rule must be: KEEP TO STANDARD ITALIAN. If correct, and correctly pronounced, it will rarely be misunderstood.

PRACTICE

First concentrate on pronouncing the words given as examples up to now. If you can remember the meanings, so much the better. But, as they will all come up again, pronunciation at this stage is of more importance. If you can find a good speaker of Italian, for preference a native, to help, this will be a great advantage. Here are the words:

perchè—verità—dà—da—dì—di—è—e—lì—là—la—sè
—se—sì—si—nè—ne—chè—che—già—giù—più—può
—qui—qua—olio—olî—ampio—ampî— Jugoslavia—ex-
ministro—fratello—caro—parola—bontà—attività—
ultimo— perdere—umido — timido — zucchero — apprendere—andandomene—città—violoncello—accento — perchè — gelo — oggi — ghirlanda — egli — gli —
negligente— ganglio—incognito—bagno—guerra—ho,
hai,   ha,—questo—raro—spedire—svelto—scena—

scusare — schiavo — zero — zelo — scienza — bellezza — mezzo — dozzina — analizzare — fertilizzare — scandallizzare — fratello — fiamma

When in doubt, refer below for vowel sounds.

Revise when you know the vowel sounds well.

§ 2. *Italian Vowel Sounds—Diphthongs—Triphthongs—Euphony: Elision; Shortening—Addition of a Letter—Practice— Situation Material: Greetings, etc., Words and Phrases— Practice*

All Italian vowel sounds are pure. Open the mouth well, carry the voice well forward and each vowel must be given a clear value—even when two or three come together. First learn their simple sounds, as follows:

> **a** is pronounced like English *a* in *father*: **la sala,** *the hall* = lah sahlah.
>
> **e** has two sounds, " close " and " open ". The close sound is like *a* in *late*: **cera,** *wax* = chayra. The open sound is like *e* in *men*, *let*: **sella,** *saddle* = sel'la.
>
> **i** is like *i* in *machine*: **timido,** *timid* = teem'ido, the second *i* being unstressed is shorter than the first.
>
> **o** has two sounds, " close " and " open ". Close *o* is like *o* in *hope* or *rope*. Open *o* is like *o* in *croft*, *soft*. Example of close *o*: **voce,** *voice* = vohche. Example of open *o*: **cosa,** *thing* = cawsa, the *aw* being short.
>
> **u** is like *-oo-* in *moor*, *moon* (never like *u* in *mute*). Thus: **luna,** *moon* = loona.

*Note on " close " and " open " **e** and **o***: Good speakers attach importance to correct pronunciation of these vowels, and it can be learnt only from constant listening to good speakers. But the foreigner who always pronounces Italian **o** like our *o* in *hope* or *rope* will not be misunderstood. There are rules governing the correct pronunciation, but they are complicated and uncertain, all except this one: " The distinction between **e** and **o** open and close is made only in the accented (stressed) syllable, while in the unaccented syllable the **e** and **o** are always close."—

Bruno Migliorini in *La Lingua Nazionale*, an authoritative work on Italian for the use of Italians.

DIPHTHONGS: When two vowels come together in Italian, each is pronounced clearly, but one of them has more stress than the other.

> *Stress on second vowel:* **ie, io, ia, iu, ue, uo, ua, ui**— which means that these are pronounced rather like *yeh, yoh, yah, yoo, weh, woh, wah, wee.*
>
> *Stress on first vowel:* **au, eu, ai, ei, oi, ui**—which means like *ahoo* (= *ow* in *cow*), *ehoo, ahee* (= *i* in *fight*), *ehee, ohee, wee*; but always with the stress on the last vowel-sound.

TRIPHTHONGS: These present no difficulties, nor do combinations of more than three vowels, if what is given above is remembered. One of the commonest combinations ends in **-uolo, -uola,** with a vowel combination before it as in:

> **fumaiuolo,** *chimney-top*, pronounced *foomaheewóhlo ; -uolo* is a diminutive ending (see page 310)

The "imitated pronunciation" given here must not be regarded as anything more than a makeshift. Pronunciation of any language can be learnt accurately only by listening to native speakers and mimicking their speech. A book cannot *speak*! Every letter and combination of letters in Italian represents Italian sounds which seldom have a close resemblance to our nearest English equivalents. As Italian is a beautifully soft language and our sounds are usually hard or even harsh to Italian ears, it is worth the learner's while to have a teacher in this first stage so that the sounds can be accurately *heard*. The Italian sounds are *all* easy to learn, and there is no reason why a few hours' practice with a native speaker should not teach pronunciation well enough for practical purposes. The self-taught must not expect the same results, but they should be able to "get along" with what has been provided in §§ 1 and 2.

EUPHONY: In few languages is greater importance attached to sound than in Italian. The written language is often slightly altered to make the sounds more pleasing to the ear and in the spoken language such slight changes are even more numerous.

All this is a matter of custom or usage, and very often writers
and speakers make their own use of the freedoms that are
willingly granted in the interests of speech-sounds which are
easier to utter or fall more pleasantly on the ears of the listener.
There is nothing very difficult in such changes from the foreign
learner's point of view, but it is important for all such learners
to get used to them and to be able to use them. This is a matter
of experience and practice, but careful note should be taken now
of the few principles on which the changes are based. They
come under three headings, as follows: (1) elision of a letter;
(2) cutting a word or phrase short—**troncamento** or **stronca-
mento** this is called; (3) adding a letter for euphony. Thus:

(1) *Elision:* In the next Section, dealing with the Articles,
you will find that the Italian words for *the*—**lo, la, gli** and
le—and the feminine form for *a, an*—**una**—lose the last
vowel (which is then replaced by an apostrophe) in certain
circumstances: **lo, la, le** when the next word begins with
e; **gli** when the next word begins with **i**; **una** when the
next word begins with any vowel. Thus:

l'amico, the friend	**l'asta** (*not* **la asta**), the rod
gl'indigeni, the natives	**un'anima** (*not* **una anima**),
l'erbe (*not* **le erbe**), the	a mind, soul
grass	

The apostrophe always indicates elision.

(2) *Shortening:* In this, not only the last vowel but the
last syllable is dropped. Thus: instead of **fare,** *to do,*
make, we find **far;** instead of **hanno,** *they have,* we find
han, instead of **bello** we find **bel,** etc. You see that not
only is the vowel dropped, but also the consonant preceding
it when this is doubled. In this shortening the apostrophe
is regarded as unnecessary. But often words ending in a
consonant drop this consonant, and again many words such
as **poco,** *little;* **modo,** *manner;* **voglio,** *I wish,* etc., are
shortened to **po´, mo´, vo´.** With some authors and
speakers this happens very frequently, and in so many words
that they are learnt only by experience.

You will find many examples of both (1) and (2) in the Reading Matter and Situation Material which will be given. But meanwhile note the general principles, and refer back to this question of euphony from time to time until you have become used to it.

(3) *Addition of a Letter for Euphony:* The common words **e,** *and,* and **o,** *or,* become **ed** and **od** in the following circumstances:

> **e,** *and*: before a consonant. Thus: **il padre e la madre,** *the father and the mother*
>
> **ed,** *and*: before a vowel. Thus: **la madre ed il padre,** *the mother and the father*
>
> **o,** *or*: before a consonant. **il padre o la madre,** *the father or the mother*
>
> **od,** *or*: before a vowel. **la madre od il padre,** the *mother or the father*

PRACTICE

(1) Say the following words slowly at first, paying great attention to the vowels, then saying them more quickly until the words come easily. Concentrate first on sound, referring to the equivalents given above:

la—pane—bello—timido—la cosa—la voce—la cera— la sella—unione—la manutenzione—l'uomo—fumaiuolo—tutto—altro—tutt' altro—degli—della—il padre —la madre—il padre e la madre—la madre ed il padre —la madre od il padre—il padre o la madre

(2) Now go over all the words on page 7, which, with the above, have the stressed vowel marked in italic. This is to help you at this stage, until you are familiar with the Rules for stress on pages 4–5.

SITUATION MATERIAL

To learn grammar and vocabulary is important, but it is not enough. One must be able to use both for the practical purposes of everyday life, that is, to deal with the situations which are constantly arising. Every language has its own ways, its own words and turns of phrase for this purpose, which is the commonest and most essential. From now onwards you will be given this material, beginning with the simplest, and one cannot do better than start with those everyday greetings and exchanges which prepare the way for further conversation. The learner will find that words which have already been given will often reappear in this " Situation Material ", which is intentional: because it helps to drive them home. At first, the difficulties will be explained, but later the learner will find that, as he knows his grammar and vocabulary, it all becomes clear.

Greetings, etc.: Words and Phrases

BUON GIORNO, SIGNORE. Good morning, good day, good afternoon, sir.

BUONA SERA, SIGNORA. Good evening, madam.

BUONA NOTTE, SIGNORINA. Good night, miss.

It is customary to use the words **signore, signora, signorina,** unless you know the person very well. One says **Signor Locatelli** when speaking *of* him; or **il signor Locatelli.** But when addressing the person use **signore.**

COME STA LEI? How are you? (**LEI** is polite form for *you*.)

MOLTO BENE, GRAZIE. Very well, thanks.

E LEI? And you?

COME SI CHIAMA QUESTO IN ITALIANO? What is this called in Italian? **COME,** how; **SI CHIAMA,** calls itself.

QUESTO SI CHIAMA UN COLTELLO. This is called a knife.

Note: With the last two sentences you can go over all the nouns you have learnt up to this point.

PARLA LEI ITALIANO? Do you speak Italian? (**INGLESE,** English)

NON PARLO BENE ITALIANO. I do not speak Italian well. (**BENE,** well)

CHE COSA DICE LEI? What do you say? (**CHE COSA,** what thing)

A RIVEDERCI. *Au revoir*. "Till we see one another again."

ADDIO. Good-bye. Mostly used when unlikely to meet again soon.

PERDONI. Pardon. I beg your pardon.

MOLTE GRAZIE. Many thanks.

MILLE GRAZIE. Very many (a thousand) thanks.

PARLI PIÙ FORTE. Speak louder.

NON LE PARE? Doesn't it seem (so) to you?

CREDO DI NO. I don't think so.

PRACTICE

Go over these words and phrases several times, at first concentrating on pronunciation, and then to learn the meaning.

Once you begin to learn meanings, you should try to learn words both ways. For example:

> **il padre,** the father; the father, **il padre**
> **la madre,** the mother; the mother, **la madre**

DO NOT PROCEED UNTIL YOU FEEL QUITE CONFIDENT OF THE PRONUNCIATION OF ALL ITALIAN WORDS AND PHRASES. A bad pronunciation learnt at this stage is difficult to eliminate afterwards. The importance of having a good speaker of Italian at this first stage will therefore be realized.

§ 3. *The Articles—Gender: Indefinite Article—Definite Article—Definite Article with Prepositions—***AVERE,** *to have—***ESSERE,** *to be—***TU** *and* **VOI**—*Polite form for YOU—How to Practise—Situation Material: Everyday Words and Phrases—Practice—Vocabulary—***LETTURA:** *Reading*

DEFINITE AND INDEFINITE ARTICLES: *the* is called the " definite " and *a, an,* the " indefinite " article.

GENDER: There are two genders in Italian, masculine and feminine. Every noun is either masculine or feminine and, as there is no neuter gender as in English, what we should regard as neuter will be either masculine or feminine in Italian. A masculine or feminine form of either article accompanies a masculine or feminine noun, respectively.

THE INDEFINITE ARTICLE: a, an

Masculine

un before a consonant or vowel:
  un treno, a train
  un ufficio, an office
  un console, a consul
  un turista, a tourist
  un portiere, a door-keeper
  un passaporto, a passport

Feminine

una before a consonant, **z** and impure **s**:
  una bandiera, a flag
  una tavola, a table
  una stazione, a station
  una settimana, a week
  una donna, a woman
  una figlia, a daughter
  una casa, a house
  una zampa, paw, claw
  una scatola, a box

uno before **z** or impure **s**:
  uno zero, a zero
  uno sportello, shutter
  uno scherzo, a joke

un' before a vowel:
  un'ombra, a shadow
  un'acqua, a water

There are no plural forms for the indefinite article, but equivalent to plural is the word "*some*", for which see pages 79, 112.

THE DEFINITE ARTICLE: the

Masculine

Singular

il before a consonant: **il console**
lo ⎰ before **z**:
       lo zio, the uncle
      ⎱ before **s** impure:
       lo studio, study
l' before a vowel:
  l'uomo, the man

Plural

i before a consonant:
  i consoli, the consuls
gli ⎰ before **z, s** impure, or a vowel except **i**:
       gli zii, uncles
       gli studi, studies
       gli uffici, the offices
      ⎱ **gli uomini,** the men
gl' before the vowel **i**:
  gl'Italiani, the Italians

Feminine

<table>
<tr><td align="center">*Singular*</td><td align="center">*Plural*</td></tr>
</table>

la {
before a consonant:
la casa, the house
before **z** or impure **s**:
la zia, the aunt
la scuola, the school
}

l' before a vowel:
l'amicizia, friendship

le before a consonant, **z, s** impure, or a vowel:
le case, houses
le zie, aunts
le scuole, schools
le amicizie, friendships

Note: Custom has sanctioned a few departures from what is stated above as the general use of the articles before nouns. Learn these exceptions:

gli Dei, the gods
per lo meno, at the least

per lo più, at the most
lo gnocco, dumpling, blockhead

ARTICLES SUMMARY

Indefinite

Masculine

> **UN:** use with all masculine nouns not beginning with **s**-impure and **z-**.
>
> **UNO:** use with masculine nouns beginning with **s**-impure and **z-**.

Feminine

> **UNA:** use with all feminine nouns: drop **-a** before a vowel, and use '.

Definite

Masculine

> **IL,** plural **I:** before masculine nouns beginning with consonant except **s**-impure and **z-**.
>
> **LO,** plural **GLI:** before masc. nouns beginning with **s**-impure and **z**. **L'** is plural of **LO** before a vowel.

Feminine

> **LA,** plural **LE:** before all fem. nouns.
> **la** drops **a** before vowels.
> **le** drops **e** when confusion is not created.

VISUALIZATION: It is important as soon as possible to get into the habit of thinking of persons and things in Italian rather than by translation. Thus, when you meet the word **il coltello** or **la casa** or **lo zio,** try to form in your mind a picture of *knife, house, uncle,* instead of thinking of these English words. When you visualize persons and things in this way with their Italian word you are *thinking in Italian.* There is no process of translation. You may begin to practise visualization now, and you can continue to do so throughout this Course. Fluency in speaking will depend on your ability to think in Italian. So practise it assiduously with all the nouns you meet. In time you will be able to do it with other words as well as nouns. Your ultimate goal must be to be able to think in Italian as easily as in English.

Visualization has many advantages: it helps those learners who find it difficult to memorize words in lists. It is particularly helpful for the self-taught. Reading, speaking, and listening to Italian Broadcasts will finally drive words home in the best way.

The indefinite and definite articles must be mastered before proceeding. They are best learnt with nouns. Here is a short list of nouns in almost everyday use:

il coltello, knife	**i coltelli,** knives
il sarto, tailor	**i sarti,** tailors
il libro, book	**i libri,** books
la casa, house	**le case,** houses
la scena, scene	**le scene,** scenes
l'ambizione, ambition	**le ambizioni,** ambitions
uno zio, an uncle	**gli zii,** uncles
una zia, an aunt	**le zie,** aunts
una camera, bedroom	**le camere,** bedrooms
un'attrice, actress	**le attrici,** actresses
lo stato, state	**gli stati,** states

Signore, Mr.   **Signora,** Mrs.   **Signorina,** Miss

These words are used when addressing a person, but when speaking of somebody the definite article is used before them:

il Signor Toscanelli   è arrivato da Firenze.
La Signora   „   } *has arrived from Florence.*
La Signorina   „   } è arrivata da Firenze.

DEFINITE ARTICLE WITH PREPOSITIONS: The following Prepositions, when used with the Definite Article, form contractions for euphony:

a, to, at   con, with
da, from, by   di, of
in, in   per, for, by
su, on

Thus:

	IL	LO	LA	I	GLI	LE	
A	al	allo	alla	ai	agli	alle	to the
CON	col	con lo	con la	coi	con gli	con le	with the
DA	dal	dallo	dalla	dai	dagli	dalle	from, by the
DI	del	dello	della	dei	degli	delle	of the
IN	nel	nello	nella	nei	negli	nelle	in the
PER	pel	per lo	per la	pei	per gli	per le	for, by the
SU	sul	sullo	sulla	sui	sugli	sulle	on the

There are two other Prepositions with which there are no contractions: **TRA,** *between, among*; **FRA,** *between, among*. They are synonyms whose use is governed by euphony. **Fra il, fra lo, fra la, fra i, fra gli, fra le.** And: **Tra il, tra lo, tra la, tra i, tra gli, tra le.**

The learner need not allow himself to be held up here mastering the above table. But, as the forms are of frequent occurrence, the sooner they are known the better.

Some less common contractions may be found in reading:

collo = con lo   colla = con la
cogli = con gli   colle = con le

Also:

pello = per lo   pella = per la
pegli = per gli   pelle = per le

AVERE, to have   **ESSERE,** to be

io ho   I have   io sono   I am
tu hai   thou hast *   tu sei   thou art *

egli }   egli }
ella } **HA** she } **HAS**   ella } **È** she } **IS**
esso }   it (*m.*) }   esso }   it (*m.*) }
essa }   it (*f.*) }   essa }   it (*f.*) }

noi abbiamo we have   noi siamo   we are
voi avete   you have *   voi siete * you are

essi (*m.*) } **hanno** they have essi (*m.*) } **sono** they are
esse (*f.*) }   esse (*f.*) }

B

LEI HA, you have (*singular*)   **LEI È,** you are (*singular*)
LORO HANNO, you have   **LORO SONO,** you are
(*plural*)   (*plural*)

---

* **TU HAI, TU SEI; VOI AVETE, VOI SIETE: TU,** *thou*, is used by
Italians to address children and animals, among relations, intimate friends,
also among artists; and to address the deity, the Virgin Mary, or saints.
The foreigner is advised not to use it until he knows the language and
people well.   **VOI** (second person plural) is used in commercial correspondence, speechmaking, preaching, and addressing a number of people.
It is admissible in ordinary speech, and is so used in some parts of Italy.

The foreigner is advised to use always the polite forms **Lei** and **Loro**:

POLITE FORM FOR YOU: by implying the word **Signoria
Vostra,** *your lordship* (or **eccellenza,** *excellency*) and using the
third person singular (**Lei**) or plural (**Loro**) pronouns, with the
corresponding form of the Verb, a polite form of address is
made. As **Lei** and **Loro** mean *her* and *their*, they must be
written with capital letters when used for the polite form for
you.   **Ella**, *she*, can similarly be used for **Lei.**

In this book the full tenses of Verbs will be given, but the
learner must not forget that he is learning the forms with **TU** and
VOI merely to be able to recognize but not to use them.   He
will keep to **LEI** and **LORO** for **YOU**, singular and plural,
both genders, and these words will be always used in the Situation Material given for practice.   **TU** and **VOI** will be found
in many of the extracts given for Reading.

HOW TO PRACTISE: In the next and in all Situation Material
to follow, you must learn all new words and phrases.   Note that,
in Italian, one can say **io sono** or simply **sono** for *I am*.   And
note that you need not always use **Lei** for you, because the third
person of the verb will indicate where *you* is intended.   Thus:
È occupato? *Are you busy, occupied?* Or: **È occupato Lei?** the
Lei here emphasizes *you*.   You will also notice that, instead of
saying *give me*, the objective pronoun comes first: **mi dia**.
This is a little strange at first and, until you come to rules about
it later, just memorize the phrases.   When you know the words
and phrases in the Situation Material, try making up others with
all that you have learnt before.

SITUATION MATERIAL

Useful Everyday Words and Phrases

SI, yes   **NO,** no   **NON,** not (*before a verb*)

Note again that **Signore,** Mr., **Signora,** Mrs., and **Signorina,** Miss, are generally added to questions and replies.

PER FAVORE, by (your) favour = please. (*Add to the end of questions for politeness.*)

DIRE, to say, tell.   **MI,** me.   **PUÒ,** can you (*polite form*)

MI PUÒ DIRE, PER FAVORE? Can you tell me, please?

QUANDO? When?   **QUANTO?** How much?

QUANTO TEMPO? How long?

OGGI, to-day   **È,** is

È MOLTO OCCUPATO? Are you very busy?

IO NON SONO MOLTO OCCUPATO. I am not very busy.

APERTO, open   **QUANDO È APERTO?**
                                        When is (it) open?

CHE COSA. What (thing)?   **INTENDO DIRE,** I mean.

CHE COSA INTENDE DIRE? What do you mean?

MI DIA, give me

MI DIA UNA SIGARETTA, PER FAVORE. Give me a cigarette, please.

E (ed before vowel), and   **UN FIAMMIFERO,** a match

MI SCUSI, excuse me

DOVE? where?   **VA,** he goes, she goes

LEI, you (*used with third person of the verb*)

DOVE VA LEI? Where are   **VADO,** I go, am going you going?

DOV'È? Where is?   **Dov'è la sigaretta?**

IO SO, I know   **IO NON SO,** I don't know

NON IMPORTA, it does not matter

PRACTICE

Buon giorno, signore. Dove va (Lei)? Where are you going?

Vado al teatro. I'm going to the theatre.

Dov'è il teatro? Where is the theatre?
(io) non so, I don't know.
È aperto? Is it open?　　　　　**Sì, signore,** Yes (Sir).
Lei è molto occupato oggi? You're very busy to-day?
Oggi non sono occupato. To-day I'm not busy.
Lei parla bene italiano. You speak Italian well.
No, Signorina, non parlo bene italiano. No, Miss, I don't
speak Italian well.
Parlo bene inglese. I speak English well.
Como si chiama questo? What is this called?
Si chiama un coltello. It's called a knife.

Now use the following words, with all that you have learnt
above and until now, to make up sentences of your own. At
first this may be a little difficult, but with persistence you'll be
able to do it.

Il proprietario, owner, landlord
il palazzo, palace
la porta, door, gate
la porta della casa, the door
of the house
la scatola, box

la casa, house
il contenuto, contents
il portiere, porter, door-
keeper
l'ascensore, the lift
il fumo, the smoke
di, of

Examples:

　Dov'è il palazzo? Where is the palace?
　Non so, e non è aperto oggi.
　Como si chiama questo?
　Questo è l'ascensore.
　Che cosa dice Lei?
　Questo si chiama l'ascensore.

Now continue.

READING MATTER: It is important to begin reading Italian as
soon as possible, especially Italian that has been written for
Italian readers and is not "made up" specially for beginners.
It is possible to do this even now by learning the necessary
vocabulary first, with explanations of difficulties. In this
Lesson every word will be explained; and the Reading Matter

itself will be provided with a literal translation placed interlinearly. With the first three short pieces a free translation will
also be given. The learner is strongly advised to study these
pieces very carefully and to read the Italian text several times
after he has mastered the meaning of every word. In this way
a "feeling" for the language can be acquired and quickly
developed. Reading, with "Situation Material", should be
regarded as the finest outlet for practice in the language, especially
for the self-taught.

Vocabulary and Notes

UNO, UN, one, a
DUE, two
UN INGLESE, an English-
man
DUE INGLESI, two Eng-
lishmen
ADDETTO, attached, *plural*
ADDETTI
A, to
LA, the (*feminine form*)
ALLA, to the
LA MANUTENZIONE,
maintenance, upkeep
DI, of; **d'un,** of one, a
UN FARO, a lighthouse
NOTARE, to note; **nota-
rono,** noted, observed
UNA BARCA, a boat, row-
boat
CHE, which
veniva, came, was coming;
from **VENIRE,** to come
VERSO, towards (*preposition*)
LORO, they, them; **verso di
loro,** towards them
MA, but
a, to, *also means* at
UN CERTO, a certain
(UN)PUNTO, (a) point

acqua, water; **in acqua,** in
(the) water
correndo, running (*from*
CORRERE, to run)
AIUTO, aid, help; **in aiuto,**
(in) to (the) help
della (dell' *before a vowel*), of
the
UNICO, UNICA, unique,
only
(LA) PERSONA, (the) per-
son
A BORDO, on board
GRAZIE, thanks
PER, for
AVERE, to have; **AVERMI,**
having me
SALVATO, saved
disse, said (*from* **DIRE,** to
say)
LO, the (*before impure* s *or* z)
SCONOSCIUTO, un-
known
APPENA, hardly
raggiunse, reached (*from*
RAGGIUNGERE, to
reach, attain
VENIVO, I came (*from*
VENIRE, to come)

incominciò (*past tense, third person singular*); *from* **INCOMINCIARE,** to commence

ad (= **a** *before a vowel*), to **AFFONDARE,** to sink

e, and (**ed** *before a vowel*) **L'UOMO,** the man; **UOMINI,** men

degli uomini, of the men (*for* **degli** *see page* 17)

GETTARE, to throw; **si**

gettò, threw himself (**si,** himself)

RITIRARE, to withdraw, collect

da voi, by you, here to you **PER,** for, in order to **LA VOSTRA,** your (*see page* 106)

(**LA**) **RATA,** instalment **delle,** of the **LA TASSA,** tax, income tax; **LE TASSE,** taxes

LETTURA: READING

DUE INGLESI ADDETTI ALLA MANUTENZIONE
Two   Englishmen   attached   to   the   maintenance
D'UN FARO, NOTARONO UNA BARCA CHE
of   a   lighthouse,   noted   a   boat   which
VENIVA VERSO DI LORO, MA A UN CERTO
was   coming   towards   them,   but   at   a   certain
PUNTO LA BARCA INCOMINCIÒ AD AFFON-
point   the   boat   began   to   sink,
DARE, ED UNO DEGLI UOMINI SI GETTÒ IN
and   one   of   the   men   threw   himself
ACQUA CORRENDO IN AIUTO DELL'UNICA
in   (the)   water   running   in   help   of   the   only
PERSONA A BORDO.
person   on   board.

— GRAZIE PER AVERMI SALVATO — DISSE LO
" Thanks   for   having   saved   me,"   said   the
SCONOSCIUTO APPENA RAGGIUNSE IL FARO.
unknown   (man)   hardly   arrived   (at)   the   lighthouse.
— VENIVO DA VOI PER RITIRARE LA VOSTRA
" I   was   coming   by   (to)   you   to   take   your   instalment
RATA DELLE TASSE.
of   the   taxes."

FREE TRANSLATION: Two Englishmen who were looking after a lighthouse saw a boat that was coming towards them, but at a certain point the boat began to sink, and one of the men threw himself into the water, hastening to the help of the only person on board.

"Thanks for saving me," said the unknown man when he had hardly reached the lighthouse. "I was coming to you to collect the instalment due on your Income Tax."

> From: TEMPO of Milan, an illustrated weekly which provides excellent reading matter.

DO NOT BE SURPRISED IF YOU HAVE TO SPEND MORE TIME THAN YOU THINK IS JUSTIFIED ON THIS FIRST LESSON. THE BETTER IT IS KNOWN, THE QUICKER YOU WILL PROGRESS LATER.

§ 4. *Nouns: Rules for Gender—Exceptions—Practice—Test and Practice—Situation Material: Everyday Words and Phrases —Practice—***LETTURA:** *Vocabularies, Texts, and Translations*

See page 13.

RULES FOR GENDER OF NOUNS: (1) Names of men and male animals are masculine, names of women and female animals are feminine.

(2) Nouns ending in **-o** or a consonant are masculine, those ending in **-a, -udine, -u,** and **-ione** are feminine.

Rule (1) is a good general guide, but, in regard to (2), note the following words:

> **la mano,** the hand; **le mani,** hands
> **il muro,** wall; **i muri,** walls; but **le mura** (*f.*) external walls or walls of a city
> **il paio,** pair; **le paia** (*f.*), pairs
> **il riso,** laugh; **le risa** (*f.*), laughs, laughter
> **il centinaio,** hundred; **le centinaia,** hundreds
> **il migliaio,** thousand; **le migliaia,** thousands
> **l'uovo,** egg; **le uova,** eggs (*f.*)
> **il miglio,** mile; **le miglia** (*f.*), miles

The main difficulty is with Nouns which end in **-e,** as some are masculine and some are feminine, and the gender must be learnt by using an article with them.

In regard to genders generally, it is best for the learner to memorize the gender of each Noun as it is met. For this reason, every Noun when first met will be given with its appropriate Article in the Lessons, though not in the Vocabulary at the end of the Course.

SUMMARY OF THE GENDER OF NOUNS: FOR REFERENCE

Exceptions

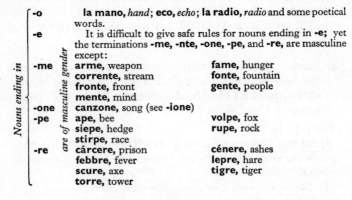

Nouns ending in — *are of masculine gender*

-o	**la mano,** *hand*; **eco,** *echo*; **la radio,** *radio* and some poetical words.
-e	It is difficult to give safe rules for nouns ending in **-e**; yet the terminations **-me, -nte, -one, -pe,** and **-re,** are masculine except:

-me   **arme,** weapon   **fame,** hunger
      corrente, stream   **fonte,** fountain
      fronte, front   **gente,** people
      mente, mind

-one   **canzone,** song (see **-ione**)
-pe   **ape,** bee   **volpe,** fox
      siepe, hedge   **rupe,** rock
      stirpe, race

-re   **cárcere,** prison   **cénere,** ashes
      febbre, fever   **lepre,** hare
      scure, axe   **tigre,** tiger
      torre, tower

Exceptions

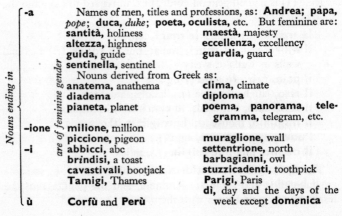

Nouns ending in — *are of feminine gender*

-a   Names of men, titles and professions, as: **Andrea; pápa,** *pope*; **duca,** *duke*; **poeta, oculista,** etc. But feminine are:
      santità, holiness   **maestà,** majesty
      altezza, highness   **eccellenza,** excellency
      guida, guide   **guardia,** guard
      sentinella, sentinel
      Nouns derived from Greek as:
      anatema, anathema   **clima,** climate
      diadema   **diploma**
      pianeta, planet   **poema, panorama, telegramma,** telegram, etc.

-ione   **milione,** million
      piccione, pigeon   **muraglione,** wall
-i   **abbicci,** abc   **settentrione,** north
      brindisi, a toast   **barbagianni,** owl
      cavastivali, bootjack   **stuzzicadenti,** toothpick
      Tamigi, Thames   **Parigi,** Paris
        dì, day and the days of the week except **domenica**

ù   **Corfù** and **Perù**

Names of fruit-trees are usually masculine. When they end in **-o**, this often changes to **-a** for the fruit. Thus:

il melo, apple-tree	**la mela,** apple
il ciliegio, cherry-tree	**la ciliegia,** cherry
il pero, pear-tree	**la pera,** pear

But note:

il fico, fig-tree	**il fico,** fig
il noce, walnut-tree	**la noce,** walnut
il dattero, date-tree	**il dattero,** date
il limone, lemon-tree	**il limone,** lemon
il pomo, apple-tree	**il pomo,** apple

Because the word **città,** *city* (*f.*), is usually understood with the names of cities and towns, they are treated as feminine. **Torino è bella.** *Turin is beautiful.* But **Cairo** is masculine: **Cairo è famoso.**

There are some fairly common words of which the genders should be memorized, as they do not correspond to rules:

il fiore, flower	**la canzone,** song
il latte, milk	**la gente,** people
il piede, foot	**la fame,** hunger
il clima, climate	**la crisi,** crisis
il sistema, system	**la metropoli,** metropolis
il brindisi, toast (to one's health)	

ENDINGS **-a, -u:** Most words of foreign origin and words representing scientific or geographical terms are masculine.

It will be seen that in some respects the gender of Italian Nouns is not always easy, but what has been given above should help the learner in memorizing. It must be repeated that it is best always to memorize the Article with each Noun, and use it with the Noun. Thus, the word for " apple " should be memorized as **il pomo,** and not just as **pomo.**

The feminine of masculine Nouns for persons ending in **-o** is made by changing the **-o** to **-a.** Thus:

il ragazzo, boy	**la ragazza,** girl
il bambino, baby boy	**la bambina,** baby girl
il cuoco, cook (*m.*)	**la cuoca,** cook (*f.*)

GENDER OF NOUNS: SUMMARY

MASCULINE: Names of male persons or animals.

Names of things: Fruit-trees; names of rivers ending in a consonant or in **-e, -i, -o, -u;** some divisions of time, such as **inverno, autunno, secolo.**

FEMININE: Names of female persons or animals.

Names of things: Most fruits of trees; cities and regions; names of rivers ending in **-a;** letters of the alphabet; some divisions of time, such as **domenica, settimana.**

EXCEPTIONS: As there are many exceptions, the safest rule for the learner is that which has been given: to learn the article with each noun as it is met.

PRACTICE

First learn all the words given to illustrate gender.

Then practise by reading the following sentences, noting the genders of Nouns, those met before this Section being repeated here:

TEST AND PRACTICE

You should be able to recognize the following phrases and their meanings. Where necessary, fill in the relevant article, paying attention to gender and number.

Buon giorno, signorina. Come sta? Molto bene, grazie, e Lei? Che cosa dice? Come si chiama questo in italiano? Questo si chiama —— mano. E questo? —— coltello. Dove va Lei? Vado al teatro. —— muro. Mi può dire, per favore, quando va al teatro? Oggi, io vado al cinema. È aperto oggi? Sì, signore, tutt'il giorno. Lei parla bene Italiano. Ma, no! Che cosa intende dire? Intendo dire che parlo bene inglese, ma ancora (yet) non parlo molto italiano. È molto occupato? Oggi non sono occupato. —— mano. —— mani. —— mela. —— melo.

Vuole fumare. Desidero fumare —— sigaretta. Mi dia —— fiammifero, per favore. Andiamo a fare —— passeggiata. Vuole bere —— tazza di caffè? Come si chiama questo. Questo si chiama —— fiore, —— latte, —— noce. Può ballare? Non posso ballare. Desidero comprare due francobolli.

Now continue, with the words and phrases you have learnt, to make your own sentences. If you find in the above test that you do not know all the words and phrases, refer back and note down everything of which you are doubtful.

SITUATION MATERIAL

Everyday Words and Phrases

VUOLE (or **vuol**)? *Do you wish to, would you like to? Is usually followed by the Infinitive of the Verb. Thus:*

    ballare = to dance. **Vuole ballare?** Would you like to dance?

    bere = to drink. **Vuole bere?** Do you wish to drink? Do you want a drink?

ANDIAMO, we are going. **Andiamo!** Let's go! **Andiamo a ballare.** Let's go dancing.

POSSO, I can; **posso ballare,** I can dance; **posso bere,** I can drink.

DESIDERO, I want, wish to have; **Desidera,** he, she, wishes; **Lei desidera,** you wish; **desidera Lei,** do you wish?

FUMARE, to smoke. **Desidera Lei fumare una sigaretta?** Would you like to smoke a cigarette?

COMPRARE, to buy; **un francobollo,** a postage stamp. **Desidero comprare un francobollo.** I want to buy a stamp.

DETTO, said; **HO,** I have; **HA,** (he, she) has; **NON HO.** I have not; **NON HA,** he, she has not

HO DETTO, I have said; **CHE,** what? **Che ha detto?** What have you said?

CAPISCO, I understand; **CAPISCE,** he, she understands. **Lei capisce?** Do you understand?

SICURO, sure; **sono sicuro,** I'm sure. **È sicuro Lei?** Are you sure?

DEVO, I must; **DEVE,** he, she must; **LEI DEVE,** you must

ANDARE, to go; **(io) devo andare,** I must go; **(Lei) deve andare,** you must go

MANGIARE, to eat; **Devo mangiare,** I must eat

FARE, to do, to make; **una passeggiata,** a walk; **FARE UNA PASSEGGIATA,** to go for a walk

Andiamo a fare una passeggiata. Let's go for a walk.

Devo fare una passeggiata. I must go for a walk. **Andiamo!** Come along.

il tè, tea	**lo zucchero,** sugar
il latte, milk	**il caffè,** coffee
la tazza, cup	**il pane,** bread
il burro, butter	**mi piace,** I like (it pleases me)
non mi piace, I don't like	**Le piace?** Do you like?

PRACTICE

Andiamo a fare una passeggiata, a bere una tazza di caffè. Let's go for a walk, and have a cup of coffee.

Devo comprare un francobollo. I must buy a stamp.

Bene, (very) well

Le piace il caffè? Do you like coffee?

Mi piace molto. I like it very much.

Come si chiama questo? **È il burro.** It's (the) butter.

Vuole mangiare il pane ed il burro? Would you like to eat the bread and butter?

No, grazie, desidero bere questo caffè. No thanks, I wish to drink this coffee.

È molto buono (good). It's very good.

FROM NOW ONWARDS, TRY TO USE AS MANY OF THE WORDS AND PHRASES THAT YOU HAVE LEARNT, WHETHER NOW OR IN PREVIOUS PAGES

Continue to make up sentences of your own.

LETTURA: *Reading*

Vocabulary for Reading

RIMASTO, remained (*from* **rimanere,** to remain)

RISENTITO, resented (*from* **RISENTIRE,** to resent)

EGLI, he

HA, has

DETTO, said

OGNI, each

(la) FAMIGLIA, family

c'è, there is

uno scemo, a half-wit

PERCHÈ, because. **Perchè?** Why?

POI, then

bene, well; **BENISSIMO,** very well

SA, (he, she, you) know(s)

(il) FIGLIO, son

UNICO, only

sono rimasto, I have remained

molto risentito, much resented = full of resentment, offended

— **SONO   RIMASTO   MOLTO   RISENTITO**
" *I   am   (have)   remained   very   resentful*
QUANDO EGLI HA DETTO CHE IN OGNI
when   he   (has)   said   that   in   each
FAMIGLIA C'È UNO SCEMO!
family   there's   a   half-wit! "
— **PERCHÈ, POI?**
" *Why, then?* "
— **PERCHÈ EGLI SA BENISSIMO CHE SONO**
" *Because   he   knows   very   well   that   I'm   an*
FIGLIO UNICO.
only son. "

FREE TRANSLATION: " I am most resentful because he said that in every family there's a half-wit (*or* that every family has its half-wit).
" Why so? "
" Because he knows perfectly well that I'm an only son."

Vocabulary

LO SO, I know (it)

TANTO, so much, so

BELLO, beautiful, good-looking

di *before infinitive* **ESSERE = che,** that

diceva, said (*from* **DIRE,** to say)

IL GIOVANE, the young man

LA FIDANZATA, fiancée, betrothed

FARÒ, I shall make; **ti farò,** I'll make thee

FELICE, happy

LA BRUTTEZZA, (the) ugliness

la tua bruttezza, your (*familiar form*) ugliness

LA MAGGIOR PARTE, the greater part

tu la passi, you pass, spend

L'UFFICIO, office

alla sua, to his, to hers

vedrai, thou shalt see (*intimate form, 2nd person singular, future of* **VEDERE,** to see)

io non ci farò caso, it won't matter to me (idiom), I won't bother about it

tanto, so much that, seeing that

IL GIORNO, day; **del giorno,** of the day

in ufficio, in the office

—LO SO DI NON ESSERE TANTO BELLO—
" *I know (myself) not to be so good-looking,*"
DICEVA IL GIOVANE ALLA SUA FIDANZATA.
said the young man to his fiancée.
— MA VEDRAI CHE TI FARÒ FELICE!
" *But you'll see that (how) I make you happy.*"
— OH, MA IO NON CI FARÒ CASO ALLA TUA
" *Oh, but I won't mind*
BRUTTEZZA, CARO. — RISPOSE DOLCEMENTE
your ugliness, dear," *replied sweetly*
LA RAGAZZA. —TANTO LA MAGGIOR PARTE
the girl. " *In so much as the greater part*
DEL GIORNO TU LA PASSI IN UFFICIO.
of the day you spend (*it*) *in* (*the*) *office.*"

FREE TRANSLATION: " I know I'm not a beauty," said the young man to his fiancée. " But you'll see how happy I'll make you."
" Oh, but I won't bother about your ugliness," the girl replied sweetly. " Because most of the day you'll spend in the office."

§ 5. *Nouns: Formation of Plural—Miscellaneous—Nouns with two Plurals: List for Reference—Defective Nouns: For Reference—Everyday Words and Phrases—***LETTURA:** *Vocabularies, Texts, and Translations*

The majority of Italian Nouns form their plural in accordance with principles and rules to which there are few exceptions,

apart from some irregular plurals that are quite outside the rules.
The rules are:

I. Masculine and feminine Nouns ending in **-o** or **-e** and
masculine Nouns ending in **-a** (**-o, -e, -a** unaccented), form
the plural in **-i**. Thus:

> **il farmacista,** chemist, druggist; **i farmacisti,**
> chemists
> **il libro,** book; **i libri,** books
> **la madre,** mother; **le madri,** mothers
> **il papa,** pope; **i papi,** popes

II. Feminine Nouns ending in **-a** (unaccented) form the
plural by changing **-a** to **-e**. Thus:

> **la riviera,** sea coast; **le riviere,** sea coasts
> **la ragazza,** girl; **le ragazze,** girls
> **l'ora** (*f.*), hour; **le ore,** hours

III. Masculine Nouns ending in **-io** form the plural by
dropping the final **-o**. Thus:

> **il figlio,** son; **i figli,** sons
> **il viaggio,** voyage; **i viaggi,** voyages, trips

If the **-i** of **-io** is stressed, then the **-o** is changed to **-i.**
Thus:

> **l'addio,** farewell; **gli addii,** farewells
> **lo zio,** uncle; **gli zii,** uncles

IV. Masculine or feminine Nouns ending in a consonant, in **-i, ie, u** or an accented vowel, do not change in
the plural. Thus:

> **il re,** king; **i re,** kings
> **la difficoltà,** difficulty; **le difficoltà,** difficulties
> **il lapis,** pencil; **i lapis,** pencils
> **la città,** city; **le città,** cities
> **la virtù,** virtue; **le virtù,** virtues

In addition to the changes or otherwise which occur in accordance with these rules, there are other changes which are made for euphony. For example:

(1) Nouns ending in **-ca, -ga, -co, -go,** add **h** after the **-c-** or **-g-** and thereby preserve the hard **c** or **g**. Thus:

> **il duca,** duke; **i duchi,** dukes
> **il fico,** fig; **i fichi,** figs
> **il collega,** colleague; **i colleghi,** colleagues
> **il lago,** lake; **i laghi,** lakes
> **la bottega,** shop; **le botteghe,** shops

Otherwise these Nouns follow the rules stated, providing the stress is on the normal (penultimate) syllable. But if the stress is otherwise, as in **il medico,** *doctor*, or in **l'Austriaco,** *Austrian*, then the plural is formed in **-ci.** Thus: **i medici; gli Austriaci.**

(2) Most Nouns ending in **-cia** or **gia** drop the **i** in the plural unless it is stressed. Thus:

> **la pioggia,** rain; **le piogge,** rains
> **la provincia,** provence; **le province,** provences

but **la bugia,** meaning *lie* (or *candlestick*) has its plural in **-ie: le bugie.**

IRREGULAR PLURALS: Most Nouns come into the rules and categories stated, but there is a list of Nouns which are either irregular in the formation of their plurals or otherwise do not conform. They may for convenience be divided into two groups: (1) those which are in common use, and (2) those of less frequent occurrence. The first must be known, the second are given for reference—to be learnt on a second perusal of the course.

First Group—to be learnt

l'ala, wing	**le ali,** wings
l'amico, friend	**gli amici,** friends
il nemico, enemy	**i nemici,** enemies
il greco, Greek	**i greci,** Greeks

la forbice, earwig	**le forbici,** scissors
l'uomo, man	**gli uomini,** men
il bue, ox	**i buoi,** oxen
il Dio, God	**gli dei,** gods
la moglie, woman, wife	**le mogli,** women, wives
mille, thousand	**mila,** thousands
l'uovo, l'ovo, egg .	**le uova,** eggs (also **le ova**)
il centinaio, the hundred	**le centinaia,** hundreds
il migliaio, thousand	**le migliaia,** thousands
il miglio, mile	**le miglia,** miles
il paio, pair	**le paia,** pairs

MISCELLANEOUS: Some Nouns which may be masculine or feminine—gender being distinguished only by the article—(**il pianista, la pianista**) may have a masculine and a feminine form in the plural: **i pianisti, le pianiste.** Il fiorista, la fiorista, *florist*, plurals **i fioristi, le fioriste.** Il fratricida, la fratricida; i fratricidi, le fratricide. Similarly **parricida,** *parricide.*

SECOND GROUP: NOUNS WITH TWO PLURALS: FOR REFERENCE

The irregular (feminine form) plural of these words usually denotes the *literal*, the regular (masculine) usually the *figurative* meaning. Thus: " human arms " would be **le braccia,** " arms of the sea " would be **i bracci del mare.**

l'anello, ring, ringlet	**gli anelli,** rings	**le anella,** ringlets (of hair)
il braccio, arm	**i bracci,** arms	**le braccia,** arms
il calcagno, heel	**i calcagni,** heels	**le calcagna,** heels
il ciglio, brow, knoll	**i cigli,** brows, knolls	**le ciglia,** eyebrows
il corno, horn	**i corni,** horns (of the moon, instrument)	**le corna,** horns (of animals)
il dito, finger	**i diti,** fingers	**le dita,** fingers
il filo, thread	**i fili,** threads	**le fila,** threads, lint
il fondamento, foundation	**i fondamenti,** foundations	**le fondamenta,** foundations
il frutto, fruit	**i frutti,** fruits (of trees)	**le frutta,** fruits (dessert)
il gesto, exploit, gesture	**i gesti,** gestures	**le gesta,** exploits
il ginocchio, knee	**i ginocchi,** knees	**le ginocchia,** knees

il gomito, elbow	**i gomiti,** elbows	**le gomita,** elbows
il labbro, lip	**i labbri,** lips, edges (of a wound)	**le labbra,** lips
il legno, wood	**i legni,** timber	**le legna,** wood (fuel)
il lenzuolo, sheet	**i lenzuoli,** sheets	**le lenzuola,** the bed-clothes
il membro, limb	**i membri,** members	**le membra,** limbs
il muro, wall	**i muri,** walls (garden, house)	**le mura,** city walls
l'orecchio, ear	**gli orecchi,** ears	**le oreccha,** ears
l'osso, bone	**gli ossi,** bones (in general)	**le ossa,** bones (human)
il pugno, fist, blow	**i pugni,** blows	**le pugna,** fists
il riso, rice, laugh	**i risi,** rices	**le risa,** laughter

DEFECTIVE NOUNS: FOR REFERENCE

Singular Forms Only:

il brio, vivacity	**il fiele,** gall
l'uopo, need	

Plural Forms Only:

gli annali, annals	**i baffi,** moustache
le calende, kalends	**i calzoni,** trousers
le esequie, funeral honours	**le forbici,** scissors
le molle, tongs	**le nozze,** wedding
gli occhiali, spectacles, glasses	**i posteri,** descendants
le reni, loins	**le tenebre,** darkness
i viveri, provisions, foodstuffs	

Note: Wherever something is marked " For Reference ", you need not memorize it on first meeting it. But read it, and come back to it later, or on a second perusal of the book.

FORMATION OF PLURAL OF NOUNS: SUMMARY IN BRIEF

	Plural		Exceptions	
Singular Endings	*m.*	*f.*	*Singular*	*Plural*
-a	**-i**	**-e**		
-ca, -ga	**-chi, ghi**	**-che, ghe**	**Belga**	**Belgi**
-cia, -gia ⎰ i unstressed		**-ce, ge**	**audacia**	**audacie**
			camicia	**camicie**
			valigia	**valigie**
⎱ i stressed		**-cíe, gíe**		
-o	**-i**		**uovo**	**uova**
			lenzuolo	**lenzuola**
			riso	**risa**
			paio	**paia**
			miglio	**miglia**

	Plural		Exceptions	
Singular Endings	m.	f.	Singular	Plural
-io {i unstressed	-i		conio	conii
{i stressed	-ii		tempio	tempii, or
				templî
			dio	dei
-co, -go	-ci, -gi	-chi, -ghi		
-e	-i		mille	mila
			bue	buoi
-ie	-ie		moglie	mogli
			superficie	superfici

in accented vowel ⎫
in **i**   ⎬ invariable
in a consonant ⎭

Everyday Words and Phrases

il cameriere, the waiter   **c'è,** there is, there are
pronto, ready
Che cosa desidera?   What would you like?
Che c'è di pronto?   What's ready?
Ecco, here, is   **Ecco la carta,** Here's the bill of fare.
il vino, wine   **la birra,** beer
o, or (**od** before a vowel)
BEVE BIRRA O VINO?   Do you drink beer or wine?
Bevo acqua minerale.   I drink mineral water.
la pasta asciutta, the term for a great variety of Italian foodstuffs of which the base is fine flour made into a paste, and
   made up in many forms. **la pasta,** paste; **asciutta,** dry.
   See pages 249-250.
      Few Italian bills of fare will not have **pasta asciutta** in some
   form.   So one seldom asks:
C'è della pasta asciutta oggi?   Is there any p.a. to-day?
il formaggio, cheese   **dolce,** sweet; **dolci,** sweets
la prima colazione, (first, or light) breakfast
la colazione, lunch   **il pranzo,** dinner   **la cena,** supper
il pasto, meal   **la merenda,** snack   **il ristorante,**
                                                        the restaurant
la trattoria, small restaurant   **il gabinetto,** W.C.
   (French *bistro*)   **la frittata,** omelette
l'uovo, egg; **le uova,** eggs   **alla carta,** *à la carte*
MA, but   **PRANZARE,** to dine or
VOGLIO, I want, wish   lunch

Voglio pranzare. I wish to dine, lunch.
UNO, one
TRE, three
CINQUE, five

caro, dear
CON, with
DUE, two
QUATTRO, four
le lasagne, macaroni in strips

la tavola ⎱
il tavolo ⎰ table
una tavola libera
un tavolo libero

libero, free
per, for

C'è un tavolo per tre? Is there a table for three?
È libero il tavolo? Is the table free?
Mi dia, give me
subito, immediately
un bicchiere, a glass
la lista, bill of fare.

mi serva, serve me
Va bene, It's all right.
di, of

Andiamo a mangiare. Let's go and eat.
Ma dove? But where?
C'e una trattoria vicina che mi piace molto. There's a little restaurant near that I like very much.
E non è caro. And it's not dear.
Voglio una merenda. I want a snack.
Ed io voglio una buona colazione. And I want a good meal.
Mi serva della pasta asciutta. Che c'è oggi? What is there to-day?
C'è delle lasagne. E Lei vuole una frittata? Sì, una frittata con tre uova. Vuole un buon bicchiere di vino? No, grazie. Sì, per favore. Il pasto non costa caro.

Now continue to make up your own sentences.

LETTURA: Reading

In Tribunale

In court

Il presidente, *president, chairman, chief judge, magistrate.* **si china,** inclines himself, bows. **verso,** towards. **uno,** one. **dei,** of the. **giudici,** judges (sing. **giudice**). **e gli dice,** and says to him. **nell'** = **nelle,** in the. **orecchio,** ear. **il processo,** (the) case. **dovrebbe,** must.

tenersi, hold itself. **dovrebbe tenersi,** must be held. **a porte chiuse,** with, behind closed doors (**porta,** door. **chiusa,** closed). **perchè?** Why? **perchè,** because. (Note that the same word is used for *why* and *because*.) **da,** from, from the direction of. **quella,** that. **entra,** enters. **un'aria,** an air, draught. **maledetta,** cursed (masc. **maledetto,** but here it is feminine to agree with **aria.**

Il presidente si china verso uno dei giudici e gli dice

The presiding judge leans towards one of the (other) judges and

nell'orecchio:

says to him in the ear:

— Questo processo dovrebbe tenersi a porte chiuse.

" *This case must be held behind closed doors.*"

— Perchè?

" *Why?* "

— Perchè da quella porta entra un'aria maledetta.

" *Because from that door (there) enters a cursed draught.*"

avverto, I warn. **solennemente,** solemnly. **la manifestazione,** plural **le manifestazioni,** manifestation(s), demonstration(s). **qualsiasi,** whatever. **il senso,** sense. **sono proibite,** are prohibited. **chi,** who, **perciò,** therefore. **griderà,** will cry out. **Evviva,** "long live!" (exclamation). **Abbasso,** "Down with!" **sarà,** will be. **mandato,** sent. **fuori,** out, outside. **l'imputato,** the accused. **dalla sua,** from his. **la gabbia,** cage (i.e., from behind his bars). **incomincia,** begins. **a gridare,** to shout.

— Avverto — dice solennemente il presidente — che le manifestazioni in qualsiasi senso sono proibite; perciò chi griderà: Evviva o Abbasso sarà mandato fuori.

L'imputato dalla sua gabbia incomincia a gridare: — Evviva, Abbasso, Abbasso, Evviva!

TRANSLATION: " I warn (you)," says the presiding judge solemnly, " that demonstrations of any kind (in any sense) are prohibited; therefore whoever will shout 'Long live! (Hurrah!)' or 'Down with!' will be sent outside."

The accused from his cage (the dock) begins to shout: " Hurrah! Down with! Hurrah! Down with! "

In Società: In Society

molto bella, very beautiful. **Mi spiace (di),** forgive me (for). **non potere = non poter,** not being able. **dire,** to say. **altrettanto,** just as much. **di Lei,** for (about) you. **faccia,** do (from the verb **fare,** to do). **come me,** like me. **dica,** say, tell. **una bugia,** a lie.

IN SOCIETÀ

— Lei è molto bella, signorina.
— Mi spiace di non poter dire altrettanto di lei, signore.
— Faccia come me: dica una bugia.

In Society

TRANSLATION:

" You are very beautiful, Miss."
" Forgive me for not being able to say (just) as much about you, sir."
" Do like me: tell a lie."

LESSON II

§ 1. *Adjectives: Agreement—Plural of Adjectives—Position of Adjectives*—**BELLO, BUONO, GRANDE, SANTO**—*List of Countries and Nationalities—Towns—Other Geographical Names*—**AVERE** *and* **ESSERE**: *Past Participles —Compound Tenses—Situation Material: In the Street—***LETTURA**: *Texts, Vocabularies, and Translations*

AN Adjective describes the nature or quality of a Noun. In Italian there is agreement in gender and number with the Nouns or Pronouns to which the Adjectives relate, and they usually follow the Noun. Thus:

>**il fico fresco,** the fresh fig
>**le ragazze strane,** the strange girls

Most Adjectives end in **-o** in the masculine and change to **-a** in the feminine. Those ending in **-e** do not change in the feminine. These endings cover the majority of Adjectives.

PLURAL OF ADJECTIVES: Masculine Adjectives ending in **-o** in the singular change it to **-i** in the plural. Thus:

>**un bagno vasto,** a wide bath
>**i bagni vasti,** the wide baths

Feminine Adjectives ending in **-a** in the singular change it to **-e** in the plural. Thus:

>**la piccola chiesa,** the little church
>**le piccole chiese,** the little churches

It will be seen that, in these fundamental respects, Italian Adjectives follow similar rules to those for Nouns. The same applies to changes in spelling for euphony in Adjectives ending in **-co** and **-go**. Thus, **bianco,** *white,* changes to **bianchi** (masculine plural) and to **bianche** (feminine plural). Similarly:

39

lungo, *long,* to **lunghi** and **lunghe.** And: **tedesco,** *German,* to **tedeschi, tedesche.**

Adjectives ending in **-io** drop the **-o** in the masculine plural. Thus: **savio,** *wise,* plural **savi.** But feminine plural ends in **-ie—savie.**

POSITION OF ADJECTIVES: The qualifying Adjective is generally placed after the Noun, especially when it is closely descriptive, but there are some common Adjectives which usually come before. These must be known:

antico, ancient, antique	**grande,** big, great
bello, beautiful	**lungo,** long
breve, short	**nuovo,** new
brutto, ugly	**piccolo,** small
buono, good	**povero,** poor
cattivo, bad	**vecchio,** old
giovane, young	

But these can follow if used to distinguish one thing from another, or for emphasis, and sometimes with a slightly different meaning in English. Thus: **povero** before a Noun means *poor,* after a Noun it means *unfortunate.* These varying uses are best learnt by experience and practice, but, excepting for the Adjectives listed above, the learner should keep to the general rule of placing the Adjective after the Noun.

BELLO—BUONO—GRANDE—SANTO: These Adjectives require some special attention, because of certain modifications, as in:

(1) The masculine singular before a consonant, when they become: **BEL, BUON, GRAN** and **SAN.** Thus:

il bel prato, the beautiful meadow
un buon vino, a good wine
un gran castello, a great castle
San Giovanni, St. John
(**Il bel San Giovanni** is the name given to the Baptistery at Florence.)

(2) The masculine singular before a vowel, when they become **BELL', BUON, GRAND', SANT'.** Thus:

il bell'oggetto, the beautiful object
un buon'amico, a good friend
il grand'impero, the great empire
Sant'Antonio, Saint Anthony

Note: Before **S** or **Z** impure, or **ps** or **cs**, they do not change.

Plurals: The plural of **BEL is BEI,** the plural of **BELLO** and **BELL'** is **BELLI.** But it is **BEGLI** before a vowel, **s** or **z** impure, and **BEGL'** before an **i** in the plural. And the plural form **BELLI** is always used when this word does not accompany a Noun, as: **Questi quadri sono belli,** *these pictures are beautiful.*

Thus:

i bei fiori, the beautiful flowers
i begli animi, the beautiful souls
begli studii, beautiful studies

Feminines: All these Adjectives have regular feminine forms, except **GRANDE,** which becomes **GRAN** before a consonant: **la gran via,** *the large (main) street.* Before a vowel, elision is usual: **la buon' aria,** *the good air.*

List of Countries and Nationalities

*America, America	*un americano,	
*Gli Stati Uniti, The United States	an American	
Argentina, Argentina	un argentino	
Austria, Austria	un austriaco, pl.	austriaci
Belgio, Belgium	un belga	belgi
Brasile, Brazil	un brasiliano	
Canada, Canada	un canadese	canadesi
Cina, China	un cinese	cinesi
Cecoslovacchia, Czechoslovakia	un cecoslovacco	cecoslovacchi
Danimarca, Denmark	un danese	danesi
Egitto, Egypt	un egiziano	
*Inghilterra, England	*un inglese	inglesi
*La Gran Bretagna, Great Britain	*un britannico	
*Francia, France	*un francese	francesi

* Only those marked with an asterisk need be memorized on first perusal.

*Germania, Germany	*un tedesco	tedeschi
Grecia, Greece	un greco	greci
Olanda, Holland	un olandese	olandesi
I Paesi Bassi, The Netherlands		
Ungheria, Hungary	un ungherese	ungheresi
Irlanda, Ireland	un irlandese	irlandesi
*Italia, Italy	*un italiano	
Giappone, Japan	un giapponese	giapponesi
Jugoslavia, J(Y)ugoslavia	un jugoslavo	
Norvegia, Norway	un norvegese	norvegesi
Messico, Mexico	un messicano	
Polonia, Poland	un polacco	polacchi
Portogallo, Portugal	un portoghese	portoghesi
*Russia, Russia	*un russo	

*Unione delle Repubbliche Socialiste Sovietiche (URSS), Union of Socialist Soviet Republics (USSR)

Scozia, Scotland	uno scozzese	pl. scozzesi
Spagna, Spain	uno spagnolo	
Svezia, Sweden	uno svedese	svedesi
*Svizzera, Switzerland	*uno svizzero	
Africa	un africano	
Asia	un asiatico	asiatici
Australia	un australiano	
India	un indiano	
Europa	un europeo	

Towns

Basilea, Bâle	Colonia, Cologne	*Firenze, Florence
*Genova, Genoa	*Londra, London	Lione, Lyons
Livorno, Leghorn	Marsiglia, Marseilles	Milano, Milan
*Napoli, Naples	*Parigi, Paris	*Roma, Rome

* Only those marked with an asterisk need be memorized on first perusal.

Other Geographical Names in Italian

Adriatico, Adriatic	Sardegna, Sardinia
Ginevra, Geneva	Sicilia, Sicily
Losanna, Lausanne	Sempione, Simplon Pass
Lucerna, Lucerne	il Tamigi, Thames
la Manica, English Channel	il Tevere, the Tiber
Mantova, Mantua	il Tirreno, Tyrrhenian (Sea)
il Mare del Nord, North Sea	Torino, Turin
il Mediterraneo, the Mediterranean	Venezia, Venice
Mosca, Moscow	Vesuvio, Vesuvius
Padova, Padua	Zurigo, Zurich

Auxiliary Verbs AVERE, to have, ESSERE, to be

Past Participles

avuto, -a, had   stato, -a, been

Past participles are used to form Compound Tenses, which will be dealt with more fully later. But note now:

> **io ho avuto,** I have had
> **egli ha avuto,** he has had

and:

> **io sono stato,** I have been
> **egli è stato,** he has been

Note: **avere** is used to form the Compound Tenses of **avere**. **essere** is used to form the Compound Tenses of **essere**.

As these forms are in everyday use, they must be mastered now.

SITUATION MATERIAL

In the Street

Come si chiama questa strada? What's the name of this street?

Questa strada si chiama Via delle Quattro Fontane. This street is called Via delle Quattro Fontane.

Quale strada devo prendere per andare ala Piazza del Popolo? Which street must I take to go to the Piazza del Popolo?

Dov'è l'Ufficio Postale? Where is the Post Office?

Taxi, mi porti all'Ufficio Postale il più presto possibile. Taxi, take me to the Post Office as quickly as possible.

È questa la strada per . . .? Is this the street (way) to . . .?

Posso andare con l'autobus? Can I go by bus?

Con il tram, il metrò? By tram, underground (railway)?

Quanto tempo ci vuole? How much time, how long does it take?

Che cosa desidera? What do you want?

Capisco. I understand.

Non capisco. I don't understand.

Capisce (Lei)? Do you understand?

Ho fame. I'm hungry. **Ho,** I have.

Ho sete. I'm thirsty. **La fame,** hunger. **La sete,** thirst.

Sono stanco. I'm tired.

Ho perduto il mio passaporto. I have lost my passport. **Il mio,** my, mine.

Dov'è la questura? Where's the police station?

Sono pronto. I'm ready.

Parli lentamente. Speak slowly.

Vada diritto. Go straight on.

Vada a destra. Go to the right.

Vada a sinistra. Go to the left.

Abita qui il Signor Bianchi? Does Mr. Bianchi live here? (Lives here, etc.)

È in casa la Signora Bianchi? Is Mrs. Bianchi at home?

Non importa. It does not matter.

Prego. A useful word, literally " *I beg* ", can be used for " *Don't mention it* ", " *Please go ahead* " etc.

Non c'è altro? Is that all? Is there nothing else?

Come vuole. Just as you wish.

Scusi. Excuse me.

LETTURA : Reading

il significato, meaning. **illustrato,** illustrated. **papà,** papa, daddy. **la cosa,** thing. **vuol dire,** means. **Cosa vuol dire?** What (thing) does it mean? **cosmopolito, -a,** cosmopolitan. **Ecco,** here is, this is, this is (it). **te,** to you. **spiegherò,** I'll explain. **con,** with. **un esempio,** an example. **un ebreo russo,** a Russian Jew. **stabilito,** established, settled. **al Cairo,** in Cairo. **sposato,** married. **ad una,** to a. **spagnola,** Spanish (woman). **che,** who. **fuma,** smokes. **sigarette greche,** Greek cigarettes. **accendendole,** lighting them. **fiammiferi svedesi,** Swedish matches. **che gradisce,** who enjoys. **volontieri,** willingly. **una tazza,** a cup. (**di**) **caffè brasiliano,** (of) Brazilian coffee. **misto a,** mixed with. **la cicoria,** chicory. **olandese,** Dutch. **servito,** served. **in tazze giapponesi,** in Japanese cups. **che,** who. **quando,** when. **vede,** sees (she sees). **una baruffa,** a squabble, a row. **se la fila,** runs from it. **all'inglese,** English fashion. (**se la fila all'inglese** is an idiom meaning, she runs away for all she's worth.) **ha da pagare,** has to pay. **fa l'indiano,** pretends ignorance. (**far l'indiano,** also an idiom = to pretend ignorance, not to see a thing.) **quello,** that, that one.

SIGNIFICATO ILLUSTRATO

— Papà, cosa vuol dire " cosmopolita? "

— Cosmopolita?   Ecco: te lo spiegherò con un esempio.

Un ebreo russo, stabilito al Cairo, sposato ad una spagnola che fuma sigarette greche, accendendole con fiammiferi svedesi; che gradisce volentieri una tazza di caffè brasiliano, misto a cicoria olandese, servito in tazze giapponesi; che, quando vede una baruffa, se la fila all'inglese e che quando ha da pagare fa l'indiano . . . quello è un cosmopolita!

TRANSLATION:

Meaning Illustrated

" Papa, what does ' cosmopolitan ' mean? "

" Cosmopolitan? This is it: I'll explain to you with an example. A Russian Jew, established in Cairo, married to a Spanish woman who smokes Greek cigarettes, lighting them with Swedish matches; who gladly enjoys a cup of Brazilian coffee, mixed with Dutch chicory, served in Japanese cups; who, when she sees a squabble, flees from it and when she has to pay pretends not to see . . . that's a cosmopolitan! "

* * *

Che hai?—a colloquial way of saying **Che c'è mai?** = Whatever's the matter? **sei,** art thou (familiar) = are you. **così,** so. **accigliato,** from **accigliarsi,** to frown, knit the brows: here, to look worried. **figurati,** (just) imagine. **ho scritto,** I have written. **a mio padre,** to my father. **chiedendo,** asking for (from **chiedere,** to ask for). **il danaro,** money. **per comprare,** to buy. **dei libri,** of the books = some books. **Ebbene?** Well, well then? **Lui,** he. **mi,** to me. **ha mandato,** has sent. **i libri,** the books.

FRA STUDENTI

— Che hai? Perchè sei così accigliato?

— Figurati, ho scritto a mio padre chiedendo denaro per comprare dei libri.

— Ebbene?

— Lui mi ha mandato i libri.

TRANSLATION:

Among Students

" Whatever's the matter? Why are you so worried? "

" Just imagine, I've written to my father asking for money to buy some books."

" Well, then? "

" He has sent me the books."

§ 2. *Adjectives: Comparatives and Superlatives—Equality—The Superlative—Hotel and Boarding House—***LETTURA:** *Texts, Vocabularies, and Translations*

In English we have, for the comparative and superlative degrees of Adjectives, a simple working rule: add *-er* for the comparative, and *-est* for the superlative. Thus: *high, higher, highest.* This is for superiority. To express inferiority, we usually use *less* and *least*, as *less high, least high.*

In Italian, **più . . . di,** *more . . . than,* and **meno . . . di,** *less . . . than,* are used for both. Thus:

> **più alto di,** higher than
> **meno alto di,** less high than

Quest'albero è più alto di quella casa. This tree is higher than that house.
Questa casa è meno alta di quell'albero. This house is less high than that tree.

di is used for *than* before a Noun, Pronoun or a number.
But **che** is used for *than* before an Adjective, Verb or Adverb. Thus:

Il padre è più ricco del fratello. The father is richer than the brother.
Lo zio ha più di tre fratelli. The uncle has more than three brothers.

and:

Meglio tardi che mai. Better late than never.
Il tempo è più burrascoso che freddo. The weather is more stormy than cold.

EQUALITY: This is expressed by

così, as	**come,** as (*for manner*)
tanto, as	**quanto,** as (*for quantity*)
	(**tanto,** as much)

Thus: **così bello come,** *as beautiful as.* **così freddo come,** *as cold as.* Add: **tanto riso quanto,** *as much rice as.* **io ho tanti libri quanto Lei,** *I have as many books as you.*

The **così** or **tanto** is often omitted: **Io non sono alto quanto Lei.** *I am not as tall as you.*

THE SUPERLATIVE: This is usually expressed by **il più, il meno,** *the most, the least.* Thus:

> **il più alto,** the highest
> **il meno alto,** the least high, tall
> **Giovanni è il più stimabile dei fratelli.** John is the most estimable of the brothers.

These are the normal ways of expressing the superlative, but in speech one may often conveniently use the words **molto,** *very,* **assai,** *enough,* with an Adjective to express a superlative sense. Thus: **È molto ricco, è assai ricco,** with an expressive tone of voice can indicate that " *he* " is extremely rich. Another fairly common kind of superlative is made by repeating the Adjective expressively, as, for example: **Il cinese è una lingua difficile, difficile.** *Chinese is a very, very difficult language.* Note **piano, piano,** *very softly.*

Superlative Absolute: This can be formed by dropping the last vowel of an Adjective and adding the ending **-issimo,** of which the first **i** is always stressed. Thus:

> **bello,** beautiful; **bellissimo,** most beautiful
> **bravo,** brave; **bravissimo,** most brave
> **ricco,** rich; **ricchissimo,** most rich

This absolute superlative is much used in everyday speech, often as an explanation, to express enthusiasm, approval, or surprise. For instance, at a spectacle, game, or at the opera one often hears a player or an artist's performance approved by cries of:

Bellissimo! Bravissimo!

When used with a Noun, this superlative usually follows: **i metalli utilissimi agli uomini,** *the most useful metals for men.* *Other Comparatives and Superlatives:*

> **alto,** high; **superiore,** higher; **supremo,** highest
> **basso,** low; **inferiore,** lower; **infimo,** lowest
> **buono,** good; **migliore,** better; **ottimo,** best

cattivo, bad; **peggiore,** worse; **pessimo,** worst
esterno, external; **esteriore,** exterior; **estremo,** extreme
grande, big; **maggiore,** bitter; **massimo,** greatest
interno, inside; **interiore,** interior; **intimo,** innermost
piccolo, little; **minore,** lesser; **minimo,** least

And note also the following forms:

sommo, highest
acre, sharp, bitter; **acerrimo,** most pungent, sour
integro, honest; **integerrimo,** most honest, upright
misero, wretched; **miserrimo,** most wretched
salubre, healthy; **saluberrimo,** most healthy

These forms should be learnt as vocabulary so that the words are recognizable. Their use is best learnt by experience; those in the second list beginning with **sommo** are rarely required. Most of those in the first list have their common regular forms like **più alto, il più alto,** etc.

Many Adjectives acquire a strength similar to the superlative by prefixing the forms **stra-** (*extra*), **arci-** (like *arch-* in *archbishop*), and **sopra-** (*over-*). Thus:

stragrande, extra big
arcicontento, more than content, satisfied
sopraccarico, over-loaded, over-burdened

Useful words for comparisons generally are:

piuttosto, rather; **piuttosto grasso,** rather fat
oltremodo, extremely; **oltremodo grasso,** extremely fat

Hotel and Boarding House

l'albergo, hotel
una camera, room
i bagagli, luggage
la chiave, key
la seconda colazione, lunch
il pranzo, dinner
il ragazzo, boy
la pensione, boarding-house
il portiere, porter
il proprietario, proprietor
la prima colazione, breakfast
il bagno, bath
il cassiere, cashier

la cameriera, maid

il direttore, manager

suonare, to ring

il servizio, service

la partenza, departure

la pensione completa, full board and lodging

un letto, bed

a due letti, with two beds

acqua calda * e fredda, water h. & c.

compreso, including

il campanello, bell

riservare, to reserve

l'arrivo, arrival

la pensione, board

un piccolo albergo centrale, a small central hotel

un letto matrimoniale, double-bed

Desidero una camera.   I want a room.

Che prezzo è la camera?   What price is the room?

Tutto completo?   Including everything? (*or* **compreso**)

Prenderò } **la pensione completa.**   I'll take it } with full
Prenderemo }   We'll take it } board

Desidero una camera con bagno privato.   I want a room with private bath.

Mi mostri una camera più grande, per favore.   Show me a bigger room, please.

Non ha niente di meno caro?   Is there nothing cheaper?

La camera è troppo piccola.   The room is too small.

Per una sola notte.   Per una settimana.   Per quindici giorni.   For one night only.   For a week.   For a fortnight (fifteen days).

Vuol avere la bontà d'iscriversi sul registro.   Please sign the register.

Il cognome, surname; **Il nome,** Christian name.

Sposato o celibe?   Married or single?

La sua professione?   Your profession?

Il luogo di nascita.   Place of birth.

La data di nascita.   Date of birth.

La sua firma.   Your signature.

l'indirizzo abituale.   Permanent address.

La sua età?   Your age?

Qual'è il numero della mia camera?   What's the number of my room?

* Taps are marked **C** for **caldo**, *hot*, **F** for **freddo**, *cold*.

c

Dov'è la sala da pranzo?   Where's the dining room?
Parto stasera, domani.   I'm leaving this evening, to-morrow.
Il mio conto, per favore.   My bill, please.
Alto, high.
È troppo alto.   It's too much.
Vorrei vedere il direttore.   I'd like to see the manager.
Un conto saldato.   A receipted bill.
Di qua parto per . . .   I leave here for . . . (From here I leave for . . .)
Posso usare il telefono?   May I use the telephone?
Mi inoltri la correspondenza a . . .   Send on my mail to . . .
Mi svegli alle sette.   Wake me at seven o'clock.

LETTURA: READING

From now onwards, read over the Italian text and first do your best to get the gist of it, without looking at notes or translation. Then go over it with the notes, and make sure that you grasp the meaning of each word. If you have time, write out your own translation. Then compare your results with the translation. Finally, read over the Italian text several times until you are *thinking (it) in Italian*, without regard to English or the translation. In this way, you will gradually become accustomed to *thinking in Italian*.

A FIRENZE

Un ragazzino vede una signora di forme mastodontiche ferma davanti alla facciata di S. Maria del Fiore e dice forte ad un amico:
Ohè Gigi, vedi?   Quella deve essere la cupola che è venuta a vedere la facciata.

a Firenze, in Florence.   **un ragazzino,** a (nice) little boy.   **vede,** sees.   **la forma,** form, mould.   **di forme mastodontiche,** of mastodonic (= elephantine) proportions.   **ferma** (*from* **fermare**), to stop (*here* stopping, standing).   **davanti,** in front (of).   **alla,** at the.   **la facciata di S. Maria del Fiore,** the façade of Santa Maria del Fiore.   **il fiore,** flower.   **dice,** says.   **forte,** strong, strongly, loudly.   **ad un amico,** to a friend.   **Ohè,** Oh! Heavens!   **vedi?** do you see?   **Quella,** that (woman).   **deve essere,** must be.   **la cupola,** the dome, cupola.   **che è venuta,** that is (has) come.   **vedere,** to see.

TRANSLATION:

In Florence

A nice little boy sees a lady of mastodonic (vast, immense) proportions (who) stops in front of the façade of Santa Maria del Fiore and says loudly to a friend:

" Oh, Gigi, look! That one (woman) must be the dome that has come to see the façade."

IN CITTÀ

— Da voi, nella capitale, chi sa quante belle donne ci sono.

— Può darsi, ma io non le vedo mai. Il mio mestiere me lo impedisce.

— E dove lavorate?

— In un Istituto di Bellezza.

da voi, with you. **in città,** in (the) city, in town. **la capitale,** capital. **chi sa,** who knows. **quante,** how many (*f. plural of* **quanto,** how much). **belle donne,** beautiful ladies. **ci sono,** there are. **Può darsi,** *literally,* it can give itself (*meaning here* it can (well) be *or simply* maybe). **ma,** but. **io non le vedo,** I don't see them. **mai,** ever (*but with a negative* (**non** *herc*) *it means* never). **il mestiere,** trade, occupation. **me lo impedisce,** impedes, prevents me (from it) (**impedire,** to prevent). **dove,** where. **lavorate,** you work. **Istituto di Bellezza,** Institute of Beauty (Beauty Institute).

TRANSLATION:

In the City

" With you, in the capital, who knows how many beautiful ladies there are."

" There may be, but I don't ever see them. My occupation prevents me (from it, from doing so)."

" And where do you work? "

" In a Beauty Institute."

CAMPANILISMO ENOLOGICO

— Dite la verità, un vino come questo non lo bevete al vostro paese.

— È vero, lo mettiamo nell'insalata.

campanilismo, local-mindedness. **enologico,** the adjective from **enologia,** the science of wine growing. **campanilismo enologico,** wine-growing parochialism or local-mindedness. **dite,** say, tell. **la**

verità, the truth. **un vino,** a wine. **come questo,** like this (one). **non lo bevete,** you do not drink (it). **al vostro paese,** in your country, locality. **è vero,** it's true. **lo mettiamo,** we put it. **nell'insalata,** in the salad.

TRANSLATION:

Wine-growing Parochialism (Prejudice)

" Tell the truth, a wine like this you don't drink in your locality."
" It's true, we put it in the salad."

§ 3. *Cardinal Numbers:* 1–100—**CENTO, MILLE, UN MI-LIONE**—*Thinking in Numbers—The Time—Miscellaneous Words and Phrases—Money and Exchange—***LETTURA:** *Texts, Vocabularies, and Translations*

CARDINALS: The cardinal numbers are invariable except **UNO,** *one,* which changes to **UNA** in the feminine. It is the same when used to form a compound number as in **ventuno,** *twenty-one.* Note that the **i** of **venti** is dropped when a compound is formed, but the **i** is resumed in **ventidue, ventitre,** etc.

MILLE, *thousand,* changes to **MILA** in numbers above 1,000: **duemila,** 2,000, **tre mila,** 3,000, etc. **MILIONE,** *million,* changes to **MILIONI: un milione, due milioni.**

The words **CENTO,** *hundred,* and **MILLE,** *thousand,* do not require the article.

uno, a, one	**undici,** eleven	**ventuno, a,** twenty-one
due, two	**dodici,** twelve	**ventidue,** twenty-two
tre, three	**tredici,** thirteen	**trenta,** thirty
quattro, four	**quattordici,** fourteen	**quaranta,** forty
cinque, five	**quindici,** fifteen	**cinquanta,** fifty
sei, six	**sedici,** sixteen	**sessanta,** sixty
sette, seven	**diciassette,** seventeen	**settanta,** seventy
otto, eight	**diciotto,** eighteen	**ottanta,** eighty
nove, nine	**diciannove,** nineteen	**novanta,** ninety
dieci, ten	**venti,** twenty	**cento,** hundred

It is not difficult to learn the numbers by rote: **1, 2, 3, 4, 5,** etc., especially as you should by this time know many of them.

But there is a much better way in which you will learn to think in Italian, which is your ultimate goal.

THINKING IN NUMBERS: Instead of thinking of the English, always think of the Italian in relation to the written or printed number. Thus:

6	12	17	60	100
sei	**dodici**	**diciassette**	**sessanta**	**cento**

When you know all the cardinals in this way, you may go on to do little sums in addition:

$3 + 2 = 5$: **Tre più due fa cinque.** ⎧ **più,** here, *plus*
$6 + 3 = 9$: **Sei più tre fa nove.** ⎨ **fa,** makes

Continue this practice until you can think in terms of addition. Then you may go on to subtraction:

$3 - 2 = 1$: **Tre meno due fa uno.**   (**meno,** less)

Finally, you must try multiplication and division:

$5 \times 4 = 20$: **Cinque per quattro fa venti.**   (**per,** by)
$30 \div 5 = 6$: **Trenta diviso cinque fa sei.**   (**diviso,** divided (by)

You have already learnt how to memorize by visualization (page 16). Now you must carry this process further by *thinking as much as possible in Italian*, not only for names of things and numbers but, as far as possible, with all kinds of words and phrases. As regards numbers and some other words, you can have endless practice with dates, age, and time, for which a small vocabulary must be mastered. This will be given in the pages which follow.

The Time

Che ora è? Che ore sono? What time is it?
il mezzogiorno, midday   **la mezzanotte,** midnight
              (**è**) **il tocco** *or* **l'una,** one o'clock
(**sono**) **le due, le tre** (**ore**), etc., two o'clock, three o'clock, etc.
(**sono**) **le due e un quarto,** a quarter-past two
(**sono**) **le due e mezzo,** half-past two
(**sono**) **le due e tre quarti,** a quarter to three

Or:

(sono) le due e cinque minuti, five past two
          dieci minuti, ten past two
          quindici minuti, fifteen minutes past two, etc.

(sono) le due meno cinque minuti, five minutes to two
      le due meno un quarto, a quarter to two
      cinque minuti alle due, five to two
      dieci minuti alle due, ten to two, etc.

il giorno, day
il pomeriggio, afternoon
la notte, night
domani, to-morrow
la settimana scorsa, last week
stamane, this morning
stasera, this evening
di buon mattino, early in the morning

il mattino, morning
la sera, evening
oggi, to-day
ieri, yesterday
la prossima settimana, next week
tardi, late
presto, early for something

On time-tables and for announcements the twenty-four-hour clock is used. The twelve-hour clock is used in everyday conversation. For Time-table see page 73.

Suona l'una. One o'clock is striking.
Suonano le due. It's striking two.
Sono suonate le sei. It has struck six.
Qual'è l'ora esatta? What's the exact time?
Sono esattamente le diciotto e quindici. It's exactly 18.15.

MISCELLANEOUS WORDS AND PHRASES

un anno fa, a year ago
tutt' i due, tutt' i tre, tutt' i quattro, all two, three, four
ambedue, both
ogni, each

fra tre mesi, within three months
ai due, ai tre, on the 2nd, on the 3rd

For Reference

Need not be memorized on a first perusal.

zero, zero, nought
un paio, a pair, a brace
una coppia, a couple
una dozzina, a dozen
una ventina, a score
una trentina, thirty or so
il doppio, the double
il triplo, the triple
un trimestre, a term, quarter (three months)
un triennio, three years period

una quarantina, two score, 40
una cinquantina, half a hundred, 50
un centinaio, a hundred or so
un migliaio, a thousand or so
a centinaia, by hundreds
a migliaia, by thousands
uno ad uno, one by one
due a due, two by two
il quadruplo, the quadruple
un centuplo, a hundredfold

Money and Exchange

una lira, a lira (*plural* le lire)
i centesimi, cents
un soldo = 5 centesimi
i biglietti di banca, banknotes
la moneta, change
mille lire, 1,000 lire
la banca, bank
lo sportello, opening (window) at a counter
gli sportelli, openings
il cheque, cheque
la lettera di credito, letter of credit
il danaro, money
pagabile a vista, payable at sight
la lira sterlina, pound sterling

un centesimo, a cent
100 centesimi, 1 lire
il biglietto di banca, banknote
cento lire, 100 lire
un biglietto di cinque mille lire, a (bank)note of 5,000 lire
il cliente, customer
il contante, cash
la tratta, draft
l'assegno turistico, gli assegni turistici, travellers' cheque(s)
il cassiere, cashier
il dollaro, i dollari, dollar (-s)
la valuta straniera, foreign money

Dove posso cambiare? Where can I change (money)?
Mi può indicare la banca più vicina? Can you tell me where is the nearest bank?

Può cambiarmi alcune lire sterline? Can you change me some pounds sterling?

Alcuni dollari? Some dollars?

Che moneta desidera? What notes would you like?

A quanto è il cambio? What's the exchange?

Vuol darmi due cento lire in biglietti da dieci? Would you give me 200 lire in notes of 10?

Può cambiarmi alcuni assegni turistici? Can you change me some travellers' cheques?

Con molto piacere. With much pleasure.

Attenda un momento, per favore. Wait a moment, please.

Il mio nome è . . . My name is . . .

Ecco il mio passaporto per l'identificazione. Here's my passport for identification.

Perfettamente, signore. Right, sir.

Dovrò attendere molto? Have I long to wait?

Vuole i dati esatti? Would you like exact details?

Potrei parlare col direttore? Could I speak to the manager?

Potrebbero pagarmi questo cheque? Could you change me this cheque?

Vorrei ritirare del danaro. I want to draw some money.

Vorrei cambiare della valuta straniera. I want to change some foreign money.

Vuol firmare qui. Would you sign here.

Giri qui. Endorse here.

Vorrei comprare degli assegni turistici. I want to buy some travellers' cheques.

Vuol darmi il suo biglietto da visita? Would you let me have your visiting-card?

Vuol darmi un formulario? Would you give me a form?

Quanto sarebbero? What (how much) would that be?

LETTURA: Reading

TRA COLLEGHI

Due ubbriachi si farmano davanti a un monumento.

— È Galileo Galilei — dichiara il primo dopo aver faticosamente letto l'iscrizione.

— Galileo?   E che cosa ha fatto questo bel tipo?
— È lui che ha scoperto che la terra gira.
— Un collega, allora; — esclama il secondo ubbriaco,
togliendosi rispettosamente il cappello.

tra, among. **collega,** colleague; **colleghi,** colleagues. **ubbriaco,**
drunk. **due ubbriachi,** two drunk men. **si fermano,** stop. **un monumento,** a monument. **Galileo Galilei** (*known to us as* Galileo), famous
Italian physicist and astronomer. **dichiara,** declares. **il primo,** the
first. **dopo,** after. **aver faticosamente letto,** having laboriously read.
l'iscrizione, the inscription. **ha fatto,** has done. **bel tipo,** fine type,
fine fellow. **ha scoperto,** has discovered. **la terra,** the earth. **gira,**
turns round, spins. **allora,** now. **esclama,** exclaims. **il secondo,**
the second. **togliendosi,** from **togliere,** to take away, off, *here it means*
taking off. **rispettosamente,** respectfully. **il cappello,** the (his) hat.

TRANSLATION:

Between Colleagues

Two drunk men stop in front of a monument.
" It's Galileo Galilei," declared the first after having laboriously
read the inscription.
" Galileo?   And what (thing) has this fine fellow done? "
" It's he who (has) discovered that the earth spins."
" A colleague, then," exclaims the second drunk, taking off
respectfully his hat.

MEDICINA

— Come ha fatto il medico a guarire così rapidamente
tua moglie dai suoi disturbi nervosi?
— Le ha detto che erano indizio di vecchiaia.

la medicina, medicine. **il medico,** doctor. **guarire,** to cure.
così, so. **rapidamente,** rapidly, quickly. **la moglie,** woman, wife.
tua, your (Second Person Singular). **il disturbio,** trouble. **disturbi
nervosi,** nervous troubles. **detto,** said, told. **erano,** they were. **(un)
indizio,** (an) indication. **la vecchiaia,** old age.

TRANSLATION:

Medicine

" How (what) has the doctor done to cure so quickly your wife
of her nervous troubles? "
" He has told her that they were an indication (symptom) of
old age."

I RAGAZZI TERRIBILI

La maestra interroga Remo, un ragazzo dall'aria molto sveglia:
— Sentiamo, Remo!   Se ti dico: " io sono bella ", che tempo è?
— Passato remoto, signora maestra!

i ragazzi terribili, the terrible boys. **la maestra,** schoolmistress. **interroga,** interrogates, questions. **dall'aria,** with the look. **sveglio, -a,** wide-awake, alert. **sentiamo,** let's hear. **Se ti dico,** if I say to you. **che tempo è?**   What tense is it?   (**che ora è,** what time is it?   **il tempo** = *both* time *and* tense). **Passato,** past, **remoto,** remote—" remote past ", *as the Italians call our Pluperfect Tense.*

TRANSLATION:

The Terrible Boys

The schoolmistress questions Remo, a boy with a very alert look.

" Let's hear, Remo!   If I say to you, ' I am beautiful,' what tense is (it)? "

" Remote past, Signora maestra."

§ 4. *Ordinal Numbers: First to Twentieth—Fractions—Adjectives of Quantity—The Date—Days of the Week, Months— Festivals and Holidays—Seasons—Subject Personal Pronouns—Regular Verbs: in* **-ARE, -ERE, -IRE**—*Endings for the Present Tense of All Regular Verbs—Drinks, etc.: In the Café—*LETTURA: *Texts, Vocabularies, and Translations*

Ordinal numbers are treated as Adjectives and follow the general rules for Adjectives in regard to gender and number. Thus: **Il primo giorno di gennaio è una festa, la prima festa dell'anno.** *The first of January is a feast, the first feast of the year.*

The following should be known:

primo, a, first	**quarto, a,** fourth
secondo, a, second	**quinto, a,** fifth
terzo, a, third	**sesto, a,** sixth

settimo, a, seventh

ottavo, a, eighth

nono, a, ninth

decimo, a, tenth

undicesimo, a, eleventh

dodicesimo, a, twelfth

tredicesimo, a, thirteenth

quattordicesimo, a, fourteenth

quindicesimo, a, fifteenth

sedicesimo, a, sixteenth

diciassettesimo, a, seventeenth

diciottesimo, a, eighteenth

diciannovesimo, a, nineteenth

ventesimo, a, twentieth

and so forth **ventunesimo, a,** *twenty-first*, **ventiduesimo,** *twenty-second*, **ventitreesimo,** *twenty-third*, up to **millesimo,** *a thousandth,* after which the adjective is written separately **millesimo primo,** *thousand and first,* **millesimo secondo,** *thousand and second,* etc.

There is another form less common: **decimo primo,** instead of **undicesimo, decimo secondo, decimo terzo,** etc., and it is generally used to distinguish the order of *popes, kings, emperors, centuries,* and *volumes.* If it follows the name of a pope, king, or emperor the ordinal is used without the article.

> **Il papa Pio nono,** Pope Pius the Ninth
> **Leone decimo,** Leo the Tenth
> **Questo volume è il quarto,** this volume is the fourth
> **Il secolo decimoquarto,** the fourteenth century
> **Il re Franceso primo,** King Francis I

FRACTIONS:

una metà, $\frac{1}{2}$

un quarto, $\frac{1}{4}$

tre quarti, $\frac{3}{4}$

un terzo, $\frac{1}{3}$

un quinto, $\frac{1}{5}$

Una volta, one time

una volta, once

tre volte, three times

molte volte, many times

due volte, twice

quattro volte, four times, etc.

> **a uno per volta,** one at a time *or* **a uno a uno,** one by one
> **a due per volta,** two at a time *or* **a due a due,** two by two
> **ambedue i fratelli,** both brothers

Adjectives of Quantity:

tanto, -a, -i, -e, so much, so many
quanto, -a, -i, -e, how much, how many
molto, -a, -i, -e, much, many
nessuno, -a, -i, -e, not one, not any, no
parecchio, -a, -i, -ie, some, several
poco, -a, pochi, poche, little, few
punto, -a, -i, -e, not any, no
troppo, -a, -i, -e, too much, too many

and **tutto, -a, -i, -e,** *all*, which always has the Article after it.

THE DATE

Quanti ne abbiamo del mese? What's the date? **ne,** of it (the month)

Or:

Quanti ne abbiamo oggi? What's the date to-day?

Ne abbiamo uno, due tre. It's the first, second, third, etc.

Or: **È il primo,** followed by the name of the month: **è il primo gennaio.**

A letter is dated thus: **il 10 (di) marzo (di) 1958,** 10*th March,* 1958, the **(di)** may be omitted: **il 10 marzo 1958.**

Questa lettera non ha data. This letter has no date.

See Letter Writing, page 330.

Days of the Week

lunedì, Monday	**martedì,** Tuesday
mercoledì, Wednesday	**giovedì,** Thursday
venerdì, Friday	**sabato,** Saturday
domenica, Sunday	

Note: All are masculine except the last. No capital letters.

MONTHS OF THE YEAR

gennaio, January	**febbraio,** February
marzo, March	**aprile,** April
maggio, May	**giugno,** June

luglio, July	**agosto,** August
settembre, September	**ottobre,** October
novembre, November	**dicembre,** December

FESTIVALS AND HOLIDAYS

il capo d'anno, New Year's Day	**il Natale,** Christmas
la vigilia di Natale, Christmas Eve	**la Pasqua,** Easter
	la Pentecoste, Whitsuntide
il Venerdì Santo, Good Friday	**l'Epifania,** Epiphany
Mezz'estate, Midsummer	**la Candelora,** Candlemas
una festa nazionale, a national holiday	**le Ceneri,** Ash Wednesday
	il Ferragosto, August Festival

SEASONS

la stagione, season	**la primavera,** spring
l'estate, summer	**l'autunno,** autumn
l'inverno, winter	

Note that days of the week, months of the year, and all the seasons are written with small letters in Italian.

SUBJECT PERSONAL PRONOUNS: On page 17 you were introduced to these with the present tense of the auxiliary Verbs **avere,** *to have,* and **essere,** *to be.* Those of the third person singular and plural, with **Lei** and **Loro** (polite forms for *you,* singular and plural and for both genders) must be clear in the mind of the learner:

Singular:

he, **egli** *she,* **ella**

it { **esso** when referring to a masculine Noun.
{ **essa** when referring to a feminine Noun.

Plural:

they { **essi** when referring to a masculine Noun.
{ **esse** when referring to a feminine Noun.

Polite form for YOU:

> *Singular:* **Lei,** for both masculine and feminine singular.
> *Plural:* **Loro,** for both masculine and feminine plural.

Lei is followed by the Third Person Singular of the Verb.
Loro by the Third Person Plural.

Regular Verbs

As the endings of all regular Verbs in Italian indicate the person, the use of the personal pronouns with a Verb is optional. But the pronoun should always be used to avoid an ambiguity, and it is customary to use **Lei** and **Loro** for the polite *you.* This is because the form for the third person has to do for *he, she, it* (*m.* and *f.*) and *you* in the singular; and for *they* (*m.* and *f.*) and *you* in the plural. **PARLARE,** *to speak.* **-ARE** is Infinitive ending. **PARL-** is the root of the verb.

Present Tense	*Negative Form*
(io) **parl-o,** I speak, I do speak, I am speaking	**non parlo,** I do not speak, am not speaking, etc.
tu **parl- i,** thou speakest	**non parli**
(egli) (ella) (esso) } **parl-a,** he, she, it speaks, is speaking	**non parla**
(Lei) „ you speak	
(noi) **parl-iamo,** we speak } are speaking	**non parliamo**
(voi) **parl-ate,** you speak	**non parlate**
(essi) (esse) (Loro) } **parl-ano,** they speak, you speak } are speaking	**non parlano**

Interrogative form: This is usually expressed by an intonation of the voice with the tense. Thus:

> **Parlo?** Do I speak?
> **Parliamo?** Do we speak, are we speaking?
> **Parlate?** Do you speak, are you speaking?

But with the third person use **Lei** and **Loro**, for *you* in the interest of clarity. Thus:

> **Parla Lei?** Do you speak, are you speaking?
> **Parlano Loro?** Do they speak, are they speaking?

Note that the Italian present tense represents our simple, emphatic, and continuous present as in: *I speak, I do speak, I am speaking*, all represented in Italian by the one form **parlo.**

Non before the Verb is the negative for all Verbs.

Interrogation is shown by the tone of voice in most instances, and this also applies to the negative forms of Verbs: **Non parlo?** *Do I not speak? Am I not speaking?* But: **Non parla Lei? Non parlano Loro?** Interrogation is also expressed by putting the Subject Pronoun after the Verb:

> **Parlo io?** Do I speak?
> **Parliamo noi?** Do we speak? etc.

When the subject of a Verb is not a pronoun, in interrogative sentences it is placed at the end.
Thus:

> **I vostri amici parlano oggi.** Your friends are speaking to-day.

Interrogative:

> **Parlano oggi i vostri amici?** Do your friends speak to-day?

VERBS: The Infinitive of all Italian Verbs ends in either **-ARE, -ERE,** or **-IRE.** Thus **parlARE,** *to speak*; **temERE,** *to fear*; **dormIRE,** *to sleep.* Drop this ending and you get the root of the Verb: **parl-, tem-, dorm-.** It is to the root that the endings for tense are added, as in **parlO, parli, parlA, parliAMO, parlATE, parlANO** (with stress shifted to the first **a,** in all **-are** Verbs in the 3rd person plural).

The system of adding endings to show tense and person is called conjugation of Verbs.

Italian Verbs are classified in three conjugations in accordance with the ending of the Infinitive. Thus:

> Ending in **-ARE** are of first conjugation, as **parlare.**
>   ,,   **-ERE** are of second conjugation, as **temere.**
>   ,,   **-IRE** are of third conjugation, as **dormire.**

Endings for the Present Tense of all Regular Verbs:

I Infinitive **-ARE**	II Infinitive **-ERE**	III Infinitive **-IRE**
-o	-o	-o
-i	-i	-i
-a	-e	-e
-iamo	-iamo	-iamo
-ate	-ete	-ite
-ano	-ono	-ono

As in:

parlo, I speak, etc.	**temo,** I fear, etc.	**dormo,** I sleep, am sleeping, etc.
parli	temi	dormi
parla	teme	dorme
parliamo	temiamo	dormiamo
parlate	temete	dormite
parlano	temono	dormono

Note well that in the Third Person Plural the stress shifts from the penultimate to the antepenultimate syllable.

Similarly conjugated are:

cominciare, to begin   **godere,** to enjoy
fuggire, to flee, escape   **terminare,** to end
perdere, to lose   **partire,** to depart
occupare, to occupy   **ricevere,** to receive
seguire, to follow   **portare,** to carry
vendere, to sell   **sentire,** to feel
lavare, to wash   **credere,** to believe
servire, to serve

The majority of Italian Verbs end in **-ARE.** A peculiarity of **-ERE** Verbs is that the stressed vowel of the infinitive is not always the penultimate. As will be seen later, the number of **-IRE** Verbs like **dormire** is small, and there is another group of these Verbs conjugated slightly differently. But, for the moment, it is necessary to master only what has been given above.

Drinks, etc.: in the Café

il Caffè, the Café (place)
il caffè, coffee
una tazza di . . ., a cup of . . .
il caffè e latte, coffee with milk
il caffè nero, black coffee
la zuccheriera, coffee pot
un bicchiere, a glass
il caffè in ghiaccio, iced coffee
la limonata, lemonade, lemon squash
l'acqua, water
l'acqua di seltz, soda water
un bicchiere di . . ., a glass of . . .
una bottiglia di . . ., a bottle of . . .
l'acqua minerale, mineral water
l'acqua tonica, tonic water
l'aranciata, orangeade
il vino, wine
la birra, beer. **chiaro, -a,** light
scuro, -a, dark
il sidro, cider
la sciampagna, champagne
il whisky, whisky
il whisky al seltz, whisky and soda
il cognac, cognac, brandy
lo Sherry, Sherry

il tè, tea
una tazza di tè, a cup of tea
il bricco di tè, pot of tea
la zucchero, sugar
il latte, milk
la cioccolata, chocolate
il gelato, ice-cream
forte, strong. **debole,** weak
l'aperitivo, aperitive, appetiser
acqua ghiacciata, iced water
il gelato con sciroppo e seltz, ice-cream soda
la spremuta di . . ., squash (**di limone,** lemon squash, **d'arancia,** orange squash)
il vino secco, dry wine. **dolce,** sweet
il vino bianco, white wine
il vino rosso, nero, red wine
il vino fresco, fresh (draft) wine
il vino di botte, wine from the cask
il gin, gin
il liquore, liqueur
una bottiglia di Bordeaux, di Borgogna, a bottle of Bordeaux, Burgundy
il Vermouth, vermouth

See also pages 311, 317.

Vorrei qualche cosa da bere. I'd like something to drink.
Mi chiami un taxi. Call a taxi.
Ora mi porta a un buon Caffè. Now take me to a good Café.

Cameriere, desidero un bicchiere, una bottiglia di birra.
Waiter, I want a glass, bottle, of beer.

Ho sete e vorrei bere un aperitivo. I'm thirsty and would like an aperitive.

Vorrei un buon bicchiere di vino. I'd like a good glass of wine.

Vuole bere qualche cosa? Would you like a drink?

Mi può raccomandare un buon Caffè? Can you recommend me a good Café?

Cameriere, ha un tavolo per . . . persone? Waiter, have you a table for . . .?

Dove posso lavarmi le mani? Where can I wash my hands?

Vorremmo una bottiglia di vino e quattro bicchieri. We want a bottle of wine and four glasses.

Non è questo che desidero. This is not what I want.

Il conto, per favore. The bill please.

Tenga il resto per Lei. Keep the change.

C'è un errore nel conto. There's a mistake in the bill.

Non abbiamo preso . . . We didn't have . . .

Abbiamo avuto soltanto . . . We've had only . . .

Chiami il primo camariere. Call the head waiter.

Tutto va benone. Everything's quite all right.

Note that in many Cafés in Italy you can ask for:

un giornale, a newspaper
i dadi, dice
un orario dei treni, a railway time-table
delle carte da gioco, playing cards
una pianta della città, a plan of the city

LETTURA: READING

DIFESA

Un soldato si presenta al sergente che l'ha mandato a chiamare:

— Bene, bene — fa il sergente, — sei dunque tu che hai protestato perchè nella minestra c'era della sabbia?

— Signorsì.

Inviperito il sergente urla:

— Cosa credi, dunque, di essere venuto sotto le armi per
essere ben nutrito o per difendere il suolo della patria?
— Per difendere il suolo della patria, sergente, ma non
per mangiarlo!

un soldato, (private) soldier. **si presenta,** presents himself (*from*
presentare to present). **il sergente,** sergeant. **che l'ha mandato,**
who has sent (**mandare,** to send). **chiamare,** to call, call for. (**mandare
chiamare,** *lit.* to send to call for = to have called.) **Bene, bene,** well,
well = all right. **fa,** does, makes, *from* **fare,** to do, to make: *here used
for* **dice,** says. **sei tu,** art thou. **dunque,** then. **che,** who = the one
who. **hai protestato,** hast protested. **perchè,** because. **nella minestra,** in the soup. **c'era,** there was. **della sabbia,** some sand. **signorsì**
= **sì, signore.** **inviperire,** to grow very angry: **inviperito,** very angry.
urla, howls, *from* **urlare,** to howl. **cosa credi.** *lit.* thing believest = do
you believe. **essere venuto,** to have come. **sotto,** under. **le armi,**
arms. **per essere,** in order to be. **ben nutrito,** well nourished, fed.
per difendere, to defend. **il suolo,** the soil. **la patria,** the mother
country, fatherland. **ma,** but. **non per mangiarlo,** not (in order) to
eat it.

Translation:

Defence

A soldier presents himself (appears before) the sergeant who
has had him called.

" All right," says the sergeant, " it's you who have protested
because in the soup there was some sand? "

" Yes, sir."

Very angry, the sergeant shouted (at him):

" What do you think, then, that you've come under arms (come
into the army) to be well fed or to defend the soil of the fatherland? "

" To defend the soil of the fatherland, sergeant, but not to eat
it."

IN CAMPAGNA

— Cosa ti è successo?
— Mi hanno rubato sei polli e . . . il settimo . . .
— Che cosa?
— Me l'hanno lasciato con un cartello sul quale era
scritto: " Settimo non rubare ".

in campagna, in the country, countryside. **successo,** happened (*from*
succedere, to happen). **Cosa ti è successo?** = What has happened to
thee? **Mi hanno rubato,** they have robbed me. **il pollo, i polli,** fowl,
fowls. **il settimo,** the seventh. **Che cosa,** what thing (*here it means*

What about it? *or* Well, then?) **lasciato,** left (*from* **lasciare,** to leave). **me l'hanno lasciato,** they have left it to me (for me). **un cartello,** placard, bill, notice. **sul quale,** on which. **era scritto,** was written. **settimo non rubare,** seventh not to rob, to be robbed, stolen = The seventh (is) not to be stolen.

TRANSLATION:

In the Countryside

" What has happened to you? "

" They have robbed me (I have been robbed) of six fowls and . . . the seventh . . ."

" What about it? "

" They (have) left it for me with a notice on which was written : ' Seventh not to be stolen.' "

§ 5. *Adverbs: Definition and Kinds of—Position—Comparison— Adjectives Used as Adverbs—Adverbial Phrases—List of Adverbs: Affirmation and Negation; Time; Quantity; Choice and Doubt; Place; Miscellaneous Adverbial Expressions—At the Railway Station—***LETTURA:*** Texts, Vocabularies, and Translations*

An Adverb is a word which qualifies any part of speech except a Noun or Pronoun. It usually answers such questions as " *How?* ", " *When?* ", " *Where?* ". The Adverb does for other parts of speech what the Adjective does for the Noun or Pronoun. Thus: *I greatly admire his strength, he is much to be admired, he speaks remarkably well. greatly, much, remarkably* are Adverbs.

There are various kinds of Adverbs: for affirming, denying, asking questions, for manner, quantity, place, time, etc. But, of all these, those for manner—usually corresponding to Adverbs ending in -*ly* in English—are the commonest.

An Adverb of manner can usually be formed in Italian by adding the ending **-MENTE** to the feminine singular form of an Adjective. Thus:

Masculine	Feminine	Adverb
rapido	**rapida,** quick	**rapidamente,** quickly
vero	**vera,** true	**veramente,** truly
fortunato	**fortunata,** lucky	**fortunatamente,** luckily

When masculine and feminine forms are the same, and do not end in **-le** or **-re,** they simply add **-mente** to form their Adverbs:

> **felice,** happy; **felicemente,** happily
> **permanente,** permanent; **permanentemente,** permanently

But if they end in **-le** or **-re,** the final **-e** is dropped before adding the ending **-mente:**

> **generale,** general; **generalmente,** generally
> **reale,** royal; **realmente,** royally
> **particolare,** particular; **particolarmente,** particularly
> Except: **mediocre,** *mediocre,* which has **mediocremente.**

Position of Adverbs: The Adverb is usually placed immediately after the Verb, except **non,** which always comes before (see page 62).

> **Il giorno è passato piacevolmente.** The day (is) has passed peacefully.
> **Lei non parla bene.** You don't speak well.
> **Parlano spesso di Lei.** They often speak of you.

COMPARISON OF ADVERBS: They follow the same principles as those for Adjectives (see page 46):

> **più facilmente,** more easily
> **il più facilmente,** the most easily
> **meno facilmente,** less easily
> **il meno facilmente,** least easily

The superlative is sometimes formed by repeating the simple Adverb: **presto,** *soon;* **presto, presto,** *very soon;* **tardi, tardi,** *very late.*

ADJECTIVES USED AS ADVERBS:

chiaro, clear	**corto,** short
fisso, fixed	**lungo,** long
spesso, often, frequent	**alto,** high
basso, base, deep	**falso,** false
certo, certain	**sicuro,** sure
mezzo, half	**forte,** strong
piano, soft	

There are others, which will be met, but these must be learnt now.

ADVERBIAL PHRASES: Italian is rich in these phrases, which often take the place of a long or awkward Adverb, or when there is no Adverb to express the meaning.

LIST OF ADVERBS

This list is not exhaustive, nor it is intended that it should all be learnt at this stage. Those Adverbs or Adverbial Phrases marked with an asterisk should be memorized now. The list should be treated as useful vocabulary.

Affirmation and Negation

*sì, yes
*no, no
non, no, not
infatti, indeed
*certo
certamente } certainly
*sicuro
sicuramente } sure, surely
*davvero, truly, really
senza dubbio, without doubt
nè . . . nè, neither . . . nor
veramente, truly
non . . . che
oltanto } only
non . . . mai, never

non . . . punto, not at all
*non più, not any more, no longer
*neppure
neanche } not even
già, already
mica, not at all
*non ancora, not . . . yet
in nessun modo
in nessuna maniera } by no means
*proprio, exactly, positively
*nemmeno, not even
*niente, certainly not
mai, giammai, never
affatto, quite

Time

*ora, now
per ora, for the present
*poi, then, afterwards
*adesso, now
*oggi, to-day
ieri, yesterday
*domani, to-morrow
tosto, soon; . . . che, as soon as

piuttosto, rather
*subito, immediately
sempre, always
mai, never
*spesso, often, frequent
*presto, quick, favourable
*tardi, late
poscia, afterwards
già, already

*prima, before
quanto . . ., as soon as possible
*dopo, after, afterwards
*sovente, often

*stamane, stamattina, this morning
*stasera, this evening
*quando, when

Quantity

*molto, much, very much
*assai, enough
*troppo, too, too much
*tanto, so, so much
abbastanza, enough
di più, superfluous
più, more
eziandio, even
*pure, even, still, really
*non pure, not even
solamente, *solo} only
*soltanto

*poco, little
*meno, less
tanto . . . quanto, as much as
*quanto, how much
tanto più, meno, so much the more, less
affatto, quite
niente affatto, not at all
quasi, almost

Choice and Doubt

soprattutto, above all, especially
finalmente, finally
*perchè, because, why?
perciò, for that reason
*quasi, almost

*forse, perhaps
*circa, about
probabilmente, probably
piuttosto, rather
prima di tutto, first of all
eventualmente, eventually

Place

*dove, where, whither
onde, whence, wherefore
qui, here, hither
*là, there. (là là, so so)
di là da, the other side of
*lì, there. Lì! There!
sopra} on, upon, up
*su
lassù, up there
quassù, up here

quaggiù, down here
in su, upwards
di sopra, above, upstairs
*sotto, under, below
di sotto, below, downstairs
da parte, aside
giù, down
in giù, downwards
*abbasso, down, downstairs
*dentro, within, inside

*dietro, behind
*a destra } to the right
 a diritta
*a sinistra } to the left
 a manca
*avanti, forward
 davanti } before, in front of
 innanzi
*fuori, outside

dappertutto } everywhere
ognidove
qualche luogo, somewhere
altronde } elsewhere
altrove
ovunque, wherever
*ove, where
presso, near

Miscellaneous Adverbial Expressions

a bella posta, on purpose
*a buon mercato, cheap
*a cavallo, on horseback
*alla fine, at last, in fine
 alla lesta, quickly, nimbly
 alla muta, dumbly
 a maraviglia, marvellously
*a piedi, on foot
*a poco a poco, little by little
 a proposito, apropos, speaking of
 di buona voglia, with good will
 di mala voglia, with ill-will
*per di là, on that side of
*per di qua, on this side of
 in modo che, in order that
 invano, in vain
 a stento, hardly, with difficulty

di frequente, frequently
di solito, generally
*appena, scarcely
*a voce (ad alta voce), aloud
 apposta, on purpose
*a caso, by chance, accident
 adesso adesso, by and by
*fra breve, shortly, soon
 per lo più, mostly
 per bocca, by word of mouth
 tutt'al più, at the most
 dapprima, first(-ly)
*appunto, exactly
*dunque, therefore
 altrettanto, equally
 allorquando, at the time when
 senza dubbio, without doubt

Importance of Adverbs: The use of these words and expressions is, on the whole, straightforward. They are not difficult to memorize and, as they recur frequently, the most important (marked *) should be learnt as quickly as possible. In the Situation Material and Reading Matter they come up again and again, and in this way they can be consolidated in the memory with their use. See also later, page 135.

You will have noted that some of these adverbs come under

more than one classification. This is because of their nature. The above classification is not intended to be scientific, but merely for convenient listing, for reference, and for memorizing. Very often an Adverb or Adverbial phrase is most useful in conversation. For example: **senza dubbio,** *no doubt,* is often a useful reply to a question or speculation. And so also, **probabilmente; subito; in nessun modo; certamente; eventualmente; a proposito** and many others. This is another reason why these words (and especially those marked with *) should be memorized as quickly as possible. Many of them are among the most frequently used words in the language.

ORARIO   Time Table

FERROVIE DELLO STATO

145   (Trazione elettrica) **Milano-Lecco**

	Alt. s.m.	Dist. Km.	per Domodossola 54, Torino e Venezia 55, Chiasso e Genova 60, Bologna 65, Bergamo 148, Cremona 152	ET 522 accel I e2	ET 818 accel I e2	ET 802 I e2	ET 822 accel I e2	ET 824 accel I e2	340 diret I e2	1502 accel I e2	
1	130		▓ **Milano Centrale** .... p.	0 45	4 48	5 50	6 08	—	6 50	7 15	1
2	—	— ▓	▓ Milano P. Vittoria .... p.	—	—		—	...	—	—	2
3	125		▓ Milano Lambrate .... p.	—	—	I	—	...	—	—	3
4	131	4	▓ **Milano Greco** (Km. 1)	0 49	4 53		6 13	...	—	7 22	4
5	139	7 ▓	Sesto S. Giovanni	0 54	4 57		6 17	...	—	7 28	5
6	158	12	▓ **Monza** per Como e Chiasso 60 ⌠ a.	0 59	5 03	6 00	6 23	...	7 01	7 35	6
7			Molteno 333 .... ⌡ p.	1 00	5 04	6 02	6 25	...	7 03	7 38	7
8	190	19	▓ Arcore I	1 07	5 12		6 32	...		7 47	8
9	222	24	▓ **Carnate-Usmate** (Km. 1) ⌠ a.	1 12	5 18		6 38	...	7 15	7 54	9
10			per Seregno e Bergamo 153, 154 {	1 13	5 19		6 40	...	7 17	7 56	10
11	243	28 ▓	Osnago	1 17	5 24		6 44	...		8 02	11
12	258	29 ▓	Cernusco-Merate (Km. 1) ...	1 20	5 28		6 48	...	7 25	8 10	12
13	287	33	▓ Olgiate K. 1-Calco K. 1-Brivio	1 25	5 36		6 56	...	7 34	8 17	13
14	250	37	▓ Airuno I	1 29	5 44		7 00	...		8 23	14
15	210	43 ▓	Calolziocorte-Olginate (K. ⌠ a.	1 34	5 50		7 06	...	7 43	8 30	15
16			1) per Bergamo e Brescia 157 ⌡ p.	1 35	5 51		7 07	...	7 44	8 31	16
17	209	46 ▓	Vercurago-S. Girolamo	—	—		7 10	...			17
18	207	47 ▓	Lecco Maggiànico (Km. 1)	—	5 55		7 14	...			18
19			▓ **Lecco** ⌠ a.	1 42	6 00	6 36	7 18	...	7 53	8 40	19
20	214	50	per Brescia 157, Como 140, {	...	...	6 40	...	7 24	7 58	9 14	20
			762 Bellagio 442 ...... ⌡ p.								

Italian Time Tables use the twenty-four-hour clock

At the Railway Station

la stazione, station
il marciapiedi, platform
il facchino, porter
il treno, train

il treno diretto, express train
il treno omnibus, ordinary
   train
l'elettrotreno, electric train

il viaggiatore } traveller (*m.*
la viaggiatrice } & *f.*)
un accelerato, fast train
il vagone, carriage
(di) prima classe, 1st class
seconda classe, 2nd class
terza classe, 3rd class
il furgone, luggage van
il vagone letto, sleeper
il vagone ristorante, dining-car
il vagone bar, buffet car
il gabinetto, W.C.
la cuccetta, sleeping berth

superiore, inferiore, upper, lower
il biglietto, ticket
il biglietto d'andata, single ticket
il biglietto d'andata e ritorno, return ticket
il prezzo del biglietto, fare
la sala d'aspetto, waiting-room
in vettura! Take your seats!
l'orario } time-table
la guida }
il posto, seat, place

Quanto costa il biglietto per . . .? What is the fare to . . .?
Quanto costa il letto? How much does a sleeping berth cost?
Vorrei riservare un posto. I want to reserve a place, seat.
In uno scompartimento fumatori. Non fumatori. In a smoking compartment. Non-smoker.
È questo il treno giusto per . . . Is this the right train for . . .?
Questo treno si ferma a . . .? Does this train stop at . . .?
Si cambia durante il cammino? Is there any change on the way?
Questo è il mio posto. This is my seat.
Dov'è il chiosco dei giornale? Where is the newspaper kiosk?
Quando parte il treno per . . .? What time does the train for . . . leave?
Quanto tempo devo attendere? How long must I wait?
Dov'è lo sportello? Where's the booking-office?
Abbiamo perduto il treno. We've missed our train.
Ha collocato le mie valigie? Have you put my bags in?
Ho ancora tempo a prendere qualcosa? Have I still time to have something?
Dove si vendono giornali e libri? Where are newspapers and books sold?
Dove troverò un facchino? Where shall I find a porter?
Ho diritto di fermarmi a . . .? Have I the right to break my journey at . . .?

Controllore, a che ora arriveremo a . . . Conductor, when shall we arrive at . . .?

Fa troppo caldo qui. It's too hot here.

Posso aprire il finestrino? May I open the window?

Posso chiudere il finestrino? May I close the window?

Posso fumare, per favore? May I smoke, please?

Facchino, sorvegli il mio bagaglio, per favore. Porter, please look after my baggage.

Vorrei comprare sigarette. I want to buy some cigarettes.

Vorrei scendere a . . . I'd like to get off at . . .

Visitano i bagagli nel treno? Do they examine the luggage in the train?

Solo alla frontiera. Only at the frontier.

Grazie di tutto. Thanks for everything.

Buon viaggio. A good journey (to you).

LETTURA: READING

IN TRATTORIA

Il cliente: — Vi faccio le mie congratulazioni. È la prima volta che mi portate una bistecca mangiabile.

Il cameriere: — Davvero? Oh, che disgrazia! E ora come faccio?

— Ma che cosa dite?

— Ho sbagliato: vi ho portato quella del padrone.

---

la trattoria, restaurant, *usually a small one, where one can eat inexpensively and well, or bring one's food and eat it there—if one buys wine to accompany it!* **il cliente,** client, customer. **vi,** *object Pronoun of* **voi,** you. **vi faccio,** I make to you (**faccio** *from* **fare,** to make, *an irregular verb*). **le mie congratulazioni,** my congratulations. **la prima volta,** the first time. **che mi portate,** that you bring, carry me (from **portare,** to carry, fetch). **una bistecca,** a beefsteak. **mangiabile,** eatable, edible. **il cameriere,** the waiter. **Davvero?** Truly? Really? **Che disgrazia!** What a misfortune! **ora,** now. **come faccio?** (How) What do I do, am I doing? **Che cosa dite?** What thing art thou saying? = What's that you're saying? **ho sbagliato,** I've made a mistake. **vi ho portato,** I've brought you. **quella (bistecca),** that one. **del padrone,** of the master, owner, "boss".

TRANSLATION:

In (the) Restaurant

The customer: " I make (give) you my congratulations.   It's the first time that you bring me an edible beefsteak."

The waiter: " Really?   Oh, what a misfortune!   (And) now what am I doing? "

" What do you say? "

" I've made a mistake: I've brought you the one (of) for the owner."

DEBITO

La cuoca congedata, uscendo, getta 10 lire al cane.

— Che cosa fate? — domanda la padrona con aria di sorpresa.

— Sono in debito con quella povera bestia che ha sempre lavato i piatti.

il debito, debt, duty.   **il cuoco,** cook (male).   **la cuoca,** cook (female). **congedata,** discharged (*from* **congedare,** to discharge).   **uscendo,** going out (*from* **uscire,** to go out).   **getta,** throws (*from* **gettare,** to throw). **il cane,** dog.   **fate,** you do (*from* **fare**).   **domanda,** asks (*from* **domandare,** to ask).   **la padrona,** mistress.   **con aria di,** with an air (look) of.   **la sorpresa,** surprise.   **sono in debito con,** I'm in debt with (to). **povero, -a,** poor.   **la bestia,** beast, animal.   **sempre,** always.   **lavato,** washed (*from* **lavare,** to wash).   **il piatto, i piatti,** dish, dishes.

TRANSLATION:

Debt

The discharged (sacked) cook throws ten lire at (to) the dog.

" What are you doing? " asks the (her) mistress with a look of surprise.

" I'm in debt to that poor beast, which has always washed the dishes (plates)."

CONVERSAZIONE

— Quali sono i tuoi principii?

— Trovare i mezzi.

— Quali mezzi?

— I mezzi per raggiungere il fine.

— Quale fine?

— La fine del mese.

quali, *plural of* **quale,** what.   **il principio, -pii,** principle(s).   **trovare,** to find.   **il mezzo, -i,** means!   **raggiungere,** to overtake, to attain.   **la fine,** end.   **il mese,** month.

Translation:

Conversation

" What are your principles? "
" To find the means. "
" What means? "
" The means to attain the end. "
" What end? "
" The end of the month. "

LESSON III

§ 1. *Personal Pronouns Table—Subject and Object—Gender—Conjunctive and Disjunctive—Conjunctive Pronouns: Subject, Object, Elision,* **non** *before—In Compound Tenses—Model Sentence—***NE***—Polite* **Lei** *and* **Loro***—Pronouns joined to Verb—Use of* **sì** **(si)***—***ci***—***vi***—Note on* **se, sè** *—Object Pronouns with* **se***—Examples and Practice—Dealing with Baggage—***LETTURA***: Texts, Vocabularies, and Translations*

A PRONOUN is a word used to replace a Noun or a Noun equivalent. Thus: *John is a good man, but he is hasty*, here *he* replaces *man* and is a Pronoun. As will be seen, there are various kinds of Pronouns, all of which will be dealt with in this Lesson and elsewhere. Take this Section slowly and by parts.

I. First in importance are the Personal Pronouns, so called because they stand for the three persons singular and plural and have various forms for each. They are highly important, and must be learnt now. The *Table* given below is for reference and to help in memorizing. First learn the exact equivalents for the English Pronouns.

SUBJECT AND OBJECT: Subject Pronouns answer the question WHO or WHAT acted? Object Pronouns answer the question WHOM or TO WHOM? In the sentence *I gave it to him*, the word *I* is the Subject Pronoun, *it* is Direct Object Pronoun, (to) *him*, is Indirect Object Pronoun. The Direct Object is the primary or direct recipient of the action; the Indirect Object is the secondary or indirect recipient of the action.

GENDER: It is important always to remember that every Italian Noun is of either masculine or feminine gender, and that the Pronoun replacing a Noun must follow that gender. Thus English *it* and *they* will in Italian require a masculine or feminine form in accordance with the gender of the Italian Noun referred to.

78

TABLE OF PERSONAL PRONOUNS: FOR REFERENCE

Subject Pronouns	Direct Object	Conjunctive Object Pronouns: Indirect Object	Reflexive	Disjunctive or Emphatic
I **io** thou **tu**	**mi**, me **ti**, thee (you)	**mi**, to me **ti**, to thee	**mi**, myself **ti**, thyself	(a) **me** (a) **te**
he **egli** she **ella** it {**esso** (m.) {**essa** (f.)	**lo**, him, it **la**, her, it **lo**}it **la**}it	**gli**,† to him, it **le**, to her, it **gli**}to it **le**}to it	**si**, himself **si**, herself **si**, itself	(a) **lui**,‡ **sè** (a) **lei**, **sè** (a) **esso** (a) **essa**
YOU **LEI** (**Ella**)	**La**, you	**Le**, to you	**si**, yourself	(a) **Lei**, **sè**
we **noi** ye, you **voi** they {**essi** (m.) {**esse** (f.)	**ci**, us **vi**, ye, you **li**}them **le**}them	**ci**, to us **vi**, to ye, you **loro**}to them **loro**}to them	**ci**, ourselves **vi**, yourself(ves) **si**}themselves **si**}themselves	(a) **noi** (a) **voi** (a) **loro**, **sè** (a) **loro**, **sè**
YOU {**LORO**	**Li** (m.)}you **Le** (f.)}you	**LORO**, to you	**si**, yourselves	(a) **Loro**

NE, of it, of them, some, any, some of it, any of them

* **mi, ti, si, ci, vi** change to **me, te, se, ce, ve** before **lo, la, li, le, ne.**
† **gli** (or **le**) change with **lo, la, li, le** or **ne** to become **glielo, gliela, glieli, gliele** or **gliene.**
‡ **lui, lei,** and **loro** are used also as emphatic Subject Pronouns; for **sè** see page 87.

II. CONJUNCTIVE AND DISJUNCTIVE PRONOUNS: Conjunctive Pronouns are so called because they are "joined with" a verb, that is, *used with* it. Disjunctive are "disjoined from" or *used apart from* a verb. Thus: **io lo vendo,** *I sell it*, **io** is used with the verb, and is a Conjunctive Pronoun. **egli è il padre di Giovanni e non di Lei,** *He is John's father and not yours*—here **Lei** is a Disjunctive Pronoun.

REFLEXIVE AND EMPHATIC PRONOUNS: The Reflexive Pronouns are used with Reflexive verbs as when we say "I wash myself", **io mi lavo**—**mi** is a Reflexive Pronoun. Emphatic Pronouns are merely Disjunctives used with a Preposition to add emphasis. Thus: **Le parlo a Lei,** *I'm speaking to you* (or It's you I'm speaking to). The **Lei** is emphatic.

CONJUNCTIVE PRONOUNS—POSITION: I. *Subject Pronouns:* **io, tu, noi,** and **voi** are placed first or may be omitted, and often **egli** and **ella** also, when there is no ambiguity. But **Lei** and **Loro** (polite forms for *you*) and **esso, essa, essi, esse** should be used, **Lei** and **Loro** to make clear the politeness, and **esso, essa, essi, esse** because they make clear the implied gender in Italian which our English *it* and *they* do not:

Lei parla bene. You speak well.
Loro non parlano bene. You (*plural*) do not speak well.
Essi sono a Parigi. They (men) are in Paris.
Esse sono a Londra. They (women) are in London.
Vado a Londra. I'm going to London.
Siamo amici. We are friends.

III. *Object Pronouns:* (1) These usually precede the verb, except **loro,** which comes after it.

(2) The Indirect Object Pronoun precedes the Direct, except **loro.**

(io) lo vendo. I sell it.
Non lo vendo. I don't sell it.
Giovanni mi parla. John speaks to me.
Giovanni Le parla. John speaks to you (*polite*).
Giovanni parla loro. John speaks to them.
(io) ve lo mando per loro. I send it to you for them.

But:

> **Giovanni lo dice loro.** John tells it to them.
> **LORO,** in all its Object meanings, always comes after the Verb.
> **Egli lo dà loro.** He gives it to them.
> **Egli lo dà Loro.** He gives it to you (*plural*).

(3) **mi, ti, si, ci, vi** change to **me, te, se, ce, ve** before **lo, la, li, le,** and **ne.** **gli** (or **le**) change with **lo, la, li, le, ne** to become **glielo, gliela, glieli, gliele,** and **gliene.** Thus:

> **Giovanni glielo dice.** John tells it to him.
> **(io) glielo darò.** I'll give it to him.
> **Non gliela mostrerò.** I won't show it (*f.*) to her.
> **Non gliel' ho dato.** I haven't given it to him.

Note: Elision (see page 10): **mi, ti, vi, lo, la** become **m', t', v', l',** before any vowel or **h. ci** often becomes **c'** before **e** or **i. glielo, gliela** become **gliel'** before a vowel, as in the last example above.

mi, ti, ci, and **vi** are used for persons only, but the other Object Conjunctive Pronouns can be used for both persons and things.

(4) The negative is formed by placing **non** *before* any of the Object Pronouns which come before the verb. Thus:

> **(io) non ve lo mando.** I do not send it to you.
> **non glielo darò.** I won't give it to him.

(IV) In *Compound Tenses* (see page 43 and, later, 194): All Object Pronouns (except **loro**) precede the auxiliary in Compound Tenses:

> (*a*) **(Noi) vi siamo stati riconoscenti** (*masculine plural*).
>   We have been very grateful to you.
> (*b*) **(Noi) vi siamo state riconoscenti** (*feminine plural*).

In (*a*) a man is speaking for men; in (*b*) a woman is speaking for women.

Rule: (*a*) When **essere** is used to form Compound Tenses,

D

the Past Participle agrees in gender and number with the Subject
Pronoun, expressed or understood.

(*b*) But when **avere** is used the Past Participle agrees with the
Direct Object Pronoun that precedes the auxiliary:

> (**io**) **l'ho trovato.**   I have found *it* (**lo**) (*masculine singular*)
> (**io**) **l'ho trovata.**   I have found *it* (**la**) (*feminine singular*)
> (**io**) **li ho trovati.**   I have found *them* (**li**) (*masculine plural*)
> (**io**) **le ho trovate.**   I have found *them* (**le**) (*feminine plural*)

With **avere** the Past Participle does not agree with an Indirect
Object Pronoun: **Lei le ha parlato,** *you have spoken to her.*
To make the sense clear one should use the Emphatic **a lui** or
a lei. Thus: **Lei ha parlato a lui** (*to him*) or **a lei** (*to her*)
or **a loro** (*to them*).

Refer back to page 78 and make sure that you are clearly able
to distinguish between Direct and Indirect Object, and note
that when *to* is used it is nearly always an Indirect Object.

V. Here is a model sentence which is a general guide to the
position of the Conjunctive Pronouns:

(1)	(2)	(3)	(4)		(5)
EGLI	**ME**	**LO**	**DICE**	**PER**	**LEI.**
He	to me	it	tells	for	her.

He tells it to me for her.

(1) is Subject; (2) is Indirect Object; (3) is Direct Object;
(4) is the verb; (5) is a Disjunctive Pronoun with (in this case)
the Preposition **per.**

If this sentence and the rules are memorized, and understood,
it should prove a great help to the learner.

When we say **Giovanni mi parla,** *John speaks to me,* this is
the same as saying **Giovanni parla a me,** a form which is for
emphasis but is not much used, the first being the usual form.
And similarly:

> **Giovanni ti parla.**   John speaks to you (thee).
> **Giovanni gli parla.**   John speaks to him.
> **Giovanni le parla.**   John speaks to her.
> **Giovanni si parla.**   John speaks to himself.
> **Giovanni ci parla.**   John speaks to us.
> **Giovanni vi parla.**   John speaks to you (**a voi**).

And:

> **Giovanni parla loro.** John speaks to them.
> **Giovanni e Maria si parlano.** John and Mary speak to themselves (**a sè**).

When you have mastered these forms, you may go one step further by introducing a Direct Object (*it*, *them*) but then instead of **parla**, *speaks*, you must use **dice**, *says*, *tells* (from **dire**, *to say, to tell*). Thus:

> **Giovanni me lo dice.** John tells it to me.
> **Giovanni te lo dice.** John tells it to thee.
> **Giovanni glielo dice.** John tells it to him, to her.
> **Giovanni se lo dice.** John tells it to himself.
> **Giovanni ce lo dice.** John tells it to us.
> **Giovanni ve lo dice.** John tells it to you (**a voi**).

And:

> **Giovanni lo dice loro.** John tells it to them.
> **Giovanni e Maria se lo dicono.** John and Mary tell themselves.

Instead of **lo** (*m.*) or **la** (*f.*) both singular meaning *it*, you can use **li** (*m.*) or **le** (*f.*) both plural, meaning *them*, the Object Pronoun in English. Try using **li** and **le**.

Go over the **Giovanni ti parla** and **Giovanni me lo dice** drills a few times until you know them well before proceeding. By this time you will begin to realize that these Conjunctive Pronouns in Italian are not so difficult as they first seemed. Once you understand their use and placing, perfection and fluency in their use is a matter of practice. It pays not to hurry through them, and to review this whole subject from time to time, because the Personal Pronouns in Italian differ from English in their use and placing.

VI. **NE,** of it, of them, some, any, some of it, some of them, any of it, any of them

If you know the French word *en*, you will see that the Italian **ne** is its equivalent. **Ne** is a very useful Pronoun, but always remember that it must refer to something that goes before or is

implied. Thus: **Ha (Lei) del pane?** *Have you (any) bread?*
Ne ho molto. *I have much (plenty) of it.* Here one could very
well answer simply: **molto**, *plenty*, omitting the other words,
including **ne.** With a verb use **ne.**

Ne is *never* omitted when a number or an Adjective of quantity
comes after the verb and the noun is not repeated. Thus:
Quanti ne ha? *How many (of them) have you?* **Ne ho
cinque.** *I've five (of them).* This differs from English usage,
where we could say: *I've five.* It is usual to insert **ne** in Italian,
where we should very often omit *of it, of them, some, etc.,* in
English.

Ne covers all genders, singular and plural, and its can sometimes be used for a person. It usually comes before the verb,
but with an imperative it can come after, as in **parliamone,** *let
us speak of it,* and after an infinitive or Present Participle: **Non
voglio comprarne.** *I don't wish to buy any.* Thus: **Non
voglio crederne.** *I don't want to believe any of it.* **crederne
= credere ne,** *to believe (it).* For further examples, see page
88.

CI and VI used with ESSERE

When we wish to express existence, as in *there is, there are,*
the words **ci** and **vi** (from **ivi**) represent *there,* and can be
followed by any part of the verb **essere,** *to be.* Thus:

c'è, there is   **v'è,** there is
ci sono, there are   **vi sono,** there are

The interrogative forms are the same: **c'è? v'è? ci sono?
vi sono?**

  C'è una lettera per me? Is there a letter for me?
  Non ce n'è. There is not (any).
  Ve ne sono due. There are two of them.

Ci and **vi** have the same meaning (and correspond to the
French *y* in *il y a*). **C'è, ci sono** are perhaps more often used
in everyday conversation than **v'è, vi sono,** but they may be
regarded as interchangeable. When **ne** is used with them it
follows its own rules.

VII. *Polite Form for English YOU:* **Lei** and **Loro,** written with a capital letter, are almost universally used as a polite, everyday form for our *you,* and in Italian they take the Third Person of the verb. As these words are of great importance, their general use must be mastered now:

	Subject	Direct Object	Indirect Object	Reflexive Form
Singular:	**LEI** (m. and f.)	**La,** you	**Le,** to you	**si,** yourself (both genders)
Plural:	**LORO** (m. and f.)	**Li,** you (m.) **LE,** you (f.)	**LORO** (both genders)	**SI,** yourselves (both genders)

The singular form **LEI** is used when addressing one person of either gender, and similarly **LORO,** when addressing more than one person whether men or women. But note that **LORO** has **LI** in the plural for addressing more than one man, and **LE** for addressing more than one woman, when they are *direct objects.*

Thus:

Lei ha, you have (*singular, both genders*)
Loro hanno, you have (*plural, both genders*)
Lei non avrà tempo, you'll not have time (*singular*)
Loro non avranno tempo, you'll not have time (*plural*)
L'ha egli incontrato? Did he meet you? (*singular both genders*)

Li ha egli incontrati? Did he meet you? (*plural masculine*)
Le ha egli incontrate? Did he meet you? (*plural feminine*)

Note in the last two that the past participle is in the plural—masculine or feminine—to agree with the persons addressed.

Loro, *to you,* direct object, follows the verb:

io darò Loro la casa. I'll give you (*singular or plural both genders*) the house.

VIII. *Pronouns Joined to Verb:* Object pronouns, direct or indirect, excepting **loro,** are attached to the verb when this is an infinitive, a present participle, or a past participle used without an auxiliary, or an imperative affirmative:

Desidero conoscerla.   I'd like to know her.
Dagli un bicchiere di vino.   Give him a glass of wine.
Crediamolo.   Let us believe it.
Parliamone.   Let us speak of it.
Imparandolo.   (In) learning it.
Eccomi.   Here I am (see page 292).
Non avendolo finito.   Not having finished it.
Non posso trovarlo.   I can't find it.
Trovatoli (= found them); having found them

IX. *Uses of* **si:** The little words **sì** and **si** are often confusing to the learner, but their uses are not difficult.   First one must distinguish between their very different meanings:

(1) **sì,** *yes* (Adverb)

(2) **si,** *thus, as, so, so much, as much* (Adverb)

(3) **si,** *oneself* (Reflexive Pronoun, Third Person Singular and Plural).

(4) **si,** *one, we, they, people,* in such sentences as *One mustn't do it, people never see through him, they say that the train will be late.*   It is an Indefinite Personal Pronoun, like the French word *on,* and always has the Verb in the Third Person Singular or Plural.

(5) **si** is used as a Reflexive to form the equivalent of our passive when no agent is expressed.   Thus:

Si parla italiano.   Italian (is) spoken (= speaks itself).
Si dice.   It is said.
Come si pronunzia questa parola?   How is this word pronounced?

Note that it can be used with either the singular or plural forms of the Verb:

Si parlano italiano e francese.   Italian and French (are) spoken.

Examples:

(1) **Parla Lei italiano?** Do you speak Italian?
Sì, signore. Yes, sir.

(2) **Maria canta si dolcemente.** Maria sings so sweetly.

(3) **Egli si lava.** He washes himself.

(4) **Si deve lavorare bene.** One must work well.

(5) **Si mangia quando si ha fame.** One eats when one is hungry.

X. *Note on* **SE** *and* **SÈ:** **Se** has two meanings: (1) it is a Conjunction meaning *if*, and (2) it is used with an accent (**sè**) to mean *oneself, himself, herself, itself,* and *themselves.*

Note that **se stesso, se medesimo,** *himself,* etc., *even he, she,* etc., are written without the accent. **stesso, medesimo,** *self, same.*

Se si sa, non si dice. If it is known, it is not said.
Inghilterra farà da sè. England will act by itself, herself.
nel suo sè, in his self, his innermost self

XI. *Order of Object Pronouns with* **SE:** As we have seen on page 82, the normal order of Object Pronouns is for the Indirect to precede the Direct: **me lo dà; te lo dà; glielo dà.**

But in the Third Person with the impersonal construction listed as (5) under *Uses of* **si,** while this normal order still holds good, the Direct Object *may* precede the **si.** Thus:
Either:

lo si porta, it is carried   **lo si macina,** it is ground up

Or:

si lo porta   **si lo macina**

And when the Indirect Object Pronoun used with **si** is NOT Third Person, it *always precedes* **si.** Thus:

mi si dice, I'm told, they tell me
ci si mostra, they show us, we're shown

And: **NE** follows **si,** which becomes **se:**

se ne parla, it is spoken of

Examples and Practice with Pronouns

(io) devo parlare. I must speak.

Non devo parlare. I must not speak.

La ragazza non deve parlare. The girl must not speak.

Ella non deve parlare. She must not speak.

Il signore non può parlare. The gentleman cannot speak.

Egli non può parlare. He cannot speak.

(Noi) parliamo bene. We speak well.

Loro parlano inglese. They (or you) speak English.

(io) lo mando. I send it.

Egli non lo manda a lui. He does not send it to him.

(io) ve lo mando. I send it to you.

Mi dà un coltello. (**dà,** gives.) He gives me a knife.

Lei me lo manda. You send it to me.

Ella ci vede. (**vede,** sees.) She sees us.

(io) lo conosco. I know him.

Non la conosco. I don't know her.

Ecco l'amico e lo saluto. Here's the friend and I salute him.

Signor Bianchi, (io) La saluto. Signor Bianchi, I salute you.

Giovanni ce lo dice. John tells us.

Il fratello dice il fatto. The brother says (states) the fact.

Giovanni lo dice loro. John tells it to them.

Egli glielo dice. He says, tells it to him.

Maria racconta (tells) **la storia a Giovanni.** Mary tells the story to John.

Giovanni dà la rosa a Maria. John gives the rose to Mary.

Giovanni gliela dà. John gives it to her.

Ella gliela racconta. She tells it to him.

Parlo Loro. I speak to you (*plural*).

Parlo a Maria. I speak to Mary.

(io) le parlo. I speak to her.

Ella lo dice Loro. She tells it to you (*plural*).

Io regalo. I present, make a present of.

(io) lo regalo. I present it.

Glielo regalo. I present it to you (a man).

Lo regalo a Lei. I present it to you.

Lo regalo a Loro. I present it to you (*plural*).

L'inglese è insegnato. English is taught. (**insegnare,** to teach; **insegna,** teaches.)

S'insegna l'inglese e francese. English and French are taught.

Si parla l'italiano. Italian is spoken.

Si lo parla. It is spoken.

Si dice che . . . It is said that . . .

Lo si dice. They say so, one says so.

Se ne parla. They talk, one talks of it.

Ha del pane Lei? Have you (some) bread?

Ne ho molto. I have plenty (of it).

Non voglio comprarne. I don't want to buy (any of it).

Ne darò Loro. I'll give you (*plural*) (some of it).

Glielo mostro. I show it to you, to him, to her.

Desidera Lei conoscerla? Do you want to know her?

Si può. It is possible.

Si può vendere? Is it possible to sell (can you sell)?

Si può venderme? Can you sell me?

Si può venderne a me? Can you sell me some (of it, of them)?

Èccomi. Here I am.*

Èccolo.* Here he (it) is.

Lei deve andare con loro. You must go with them.

Ne parlo ora. I'm speaking of it now.

Se si sa, non se ne parla. If it's known, it's not spoken of.

Gli parla il cameriere? Is the waiter speaking to him?

Non gli parla. He's not speaking to him.

Ella ha trovato i cappelli? She has found the hats?

Non li ha trovati. She has not found them.

parlato, spoken **finito,** finished

mandato, sent **incontrato,** met

veduto, seen

(io) ho veduto. I have seen.

Non l'ho veduto. I haven't seen it.

Ha finito Lei? Have you finished?

L'ho finito. I've finished it.

Ce ne ha mandato il padre. The father has sent us some.

Che ci ha mandato? What has he sent us?

Egli non vuole venderlo. He doesn't want to sell it.

* See also page 292.

Ha veduto gli uomini?   Have you seen the men?
Essi non mi hanno parlato.   They haven't spoken to me.
Non me ne hanno parlato.   They haven't spoken to me of it.
Ne abbiamo veduti quattro.   We've seen four of them.
Ha incontrato l'amico?   Have you seen the (your) friend?
Non l'ho veduto.   I haven't seen him.
Egli ha veduto Lei e noi.   He has seen you and us.
Glielo dico.   I tell it to you.   (**dico,** I say, I tell).
Ho incontrato Lei e non il francese.   I've met you and not
the Frenchman.
Ho parlato con loro.   I've spoken with them.

il padre di lei, her father	**la madre di lui,** his mother
Sono io. It is I.	**È Lei.** It is you.
Siamo noi. It is we.	**Sono loro.** It is they.

È il cappello di lui e non di lei.   It's his hat and not hers.

FURTHER PRACTICE: You will find, onwards from the first
Situation Material given on page 12, and the first Reading
Matter given on page 22, that these Personal Pronouns are of
constant recurrence. As this material is natural Italian—words
are used as Italians would use them—it shows the use of these
Pronouns better, from a practical point of view, than isolated
examples or made-up sentences such as have been given in the
present Section. You will therefore find it advantageous to
pick out in the Situation and Reading Material sentences with
the Conjunctive and Disjunctive Pronouns, and observe closely
how they are used in everyday life. The same applies to this
material in the pages which follow.

Dealing with Baggage

i bagagli, baggage	**il baule,** trunk
un'eccedenza di peso, an excess in weight	**la valigetta,** small case
	la cesta, basket
direttamente a, direct to	**i necessari di toletta,** toilet set
il deposito dei bagagli, left luggage depot	**la cappelliera,** hat-box
la valigia, suit-case	**la macchina per scrivere,** typewriter
il portacarte, portfolio	

la sacca da golf, golf bag
il bagaglio pesante, heavy luggage
la visita doganale, customs examination
le mie cose, my things
lo scontrino dei bagagli, luggage receipt
il bagaglio registrato, registered luggage
spedire, to send

Quanto sarà da pagare? How much will there be to pay?

Porti i miei bagagli dalla vettura. Bring my baggage from the car.

Metta i bagagli nello scompartimento. Put the baggage into the compartment.

Mi dia lo scontrino. Give me the luggage receipt (voucher).

I bagagli devono essere spediti a . . . The baggage must be sent to . . .

Facchino, porti questi bagagli in un taxi. Porter, take this luggage to a taxi.

Vorrei lasciare le mie cose in deposito. I should like to leave my things in the cloak-room.

Posso prender meco * questo? Can I take this with me?

Eccovi lo scontrino. Here's the voucher (receipt).

Questo baule fu guastato. This trunk has been damaged.

Qualche cosa fu estratta. Something has been taken from it.

Dov'è il capostazione? Where's the stationmaster?

Faccia il possibile di ricuperarlo. Do your best to find it.

Vi sono due colli, tre colli. There are two, three packages.

Spediscalo all'albergo. Send it to the hotel.

Ho perduto i miei bagagli. I have lost my baggage.

Sorvegli le mie cose mentre chiamo un facchino. Look after my baggage while I call a porter.

Vorrei lasciare qui tutto. I want to leave it all here.

LETTURA

La gran risata

Sidney Chaplin, il figlio di Charlie, racconta:
— **Una volta entrai in un cinema di New York dove veniva proiettato un vecchio film di mio padre. Un**

* Meco = con me.

signore, dietro a me, rideva così forte che ebbi l'impressione lo facesse volutamente per disturbare lo spettacolo. Quando volli farlo cacciare dal locale, mi accorsi che . . . era mio padre!

racconta, relates (*from* raccontare, to relate, tell).   una volta, once. entrai, I entered (*from* entrare, to enter).   veniva proiettato, there was being projected, shown.   vecchio, old.   film, the common word now for a film shown in the cinema.   dietro, behind.   dietro a me, behind me.   rideva, was laughing (*from* ridere, to laugh).   così forte, so strongly.   ebbi, I had (*from* avere).   lo facesse, he was doing it.   disturbare, to disturb, upset.   lo spettacolo, the spectacle, show.   volli, I wished (*from* volere, to wish).   farlo cacciare, to get him thrown out. dal locale, of the locality, place.   mi accorsi, it came to me (*from* accorrere, to run up to, come together).

TRANSLATION:
(*The*) Great Laughter
Sidney Chaplin, (the) son of Charlie, relates:

" Once I went into a cinema in (of) New York where there was showing an old film of my father's.   A gentleman, behind me, was laughing so strongly (loudly) that I had the impression he was doing it wilfully in order to disturb (upset) the show.   When I wished to get him thrown out of the place, it came to me (I realized) that . . . he was my father."

* * *

Caso d'emergenza

Il nuovo inquilino guardava con aria insoddisfatta la camera che avrebbe dovuto prendere in affitto.

— La finestra è troppo piccola.   In caso d'emergenza, non si potrebbe nemmeno usarla!

— Non ci sarà nessun caso d'emergenza — scattò la signora con voce ferma — perchè lei mi pagherà sempre in anticipo!

l'inquilino, lodger.   guardava, was looking (*from* guardare, to look, look at).   con aria insoddisfatta, with (an) unsatisfied air, appearance. la camera, room.   avrebbe dovuto, he should have (had) to.   prendere, to take.   in affito, on lease.   la finestra, the window.   troppo, too, too much.   piccolo, -a, small, little.   in caso di, in case of.   emergenza, emergency.   non si potrebbe, one should not be able to.   nemmeno, not even.   usarla, to use it.   non ci sarà, there will not be.   nessun caso, not any case.   scattò, snapped (*from* scattare, to go off, of a gun). con voce ferma, with (in) a firm voice.   mi pagherà, will pay me. sempre, always.   in anticipo, in advance, anticipation.

TRANSLATION:

Case of Emergency

The new lodger was looking with an unsatisfied air at the room which he should have had to take on lease.

" The window is too small. In case of emergency one could not even use it."

" There will be no case of emergency," snapped (fired) the (land)lady in a firm voice, " because you will pay me always in advance."

EDUCAZIONE

— Devi perdere l'abitudine — disse la moglie al marito — di dire " i miei ". Sono stufa di sentirti " i miei libri ", " i miei mobili ", " i miei pasti " . . . Hai sentito quel che dico? . . . Si può sapere cosa stai cercando?
— Sto cercando i " nostri " pantaloni, cara!

devi, you must (Second Person Singular). **perdere,** to lose. **l'abitudine,** the habit. **disse,** said (*from* **dire,** to say). **la moglie,** the wife (woman). **il marito,** husband. **i miei,** my (*masculine plural*). **stufo, -a,** weary, " fed up with ". **sentire,** to hear. **ti,** you (*object pronoun of* **tu**). **i miei libri,** my books. **mobili,** personal property, furniture. **pasto, -i,** meal(s). **hai,** have (Second Person Singular) **sentito,** heard, understood. **quel che,** that which. **dico,** I say (*from* **dire**). **Si può?** Can one? **sapere,** (to) know. **cosa,** thing (what thing). **stai cercando,** you are looking for (*from* **stare,** *making with* **cercando** *the Continuous Present Tense*). **sto cercando,** I'm looking for. **i " nostri ",** " our ". **i pantaloni,** trousers. **caro, -a,** dear one, darling.

TRANSLATION:

Education

" You must lose the habit," said the wife to the husband, " of saying ' my '. I'm fed up with hearing you (say) ' my books ', ' my furniture ', ' my meals '. Have you heard what I say? . . . Can one know what you're looking for? "

" I'm looking for ' our ' trousers, my dear."

§ 2. *Relative Pronouns:* **CHE** *and* **CHI**—il quale—cui—quanto—*Interrogatives*—*At the Frontier*—**LETTURA:** *Texts, Vocabulary, and Translations*

RELATIVE PRONOUNS: are those which refer to some Noun which goes before, and join two sentences together. The house *which* I see is small. The man *who* spoke was ignorant. The man *whom* I saw. The woman *whose* sister is dead. The house *that* Jack built. In these sentences the words WHO, WHOM, WHOSE, WHICH, THAT are Relative Pronouns. WHO, WHOM, WHOSE are used in English for persons only, WHICH is used for inanimates and for animals, THAT is often used for WHO, WHOM, WHICH, but never for WHOSE. Relative Pronouns are often omitted in English but *never* in Italian. We are permitted to say *The house Jack built*, but in Italian one *must* say *The house that Jack built*.

The Relative Pronouns in Italian are:

CHE, *who, which, that* for both genders and numbers and for both persons and things.

CHI, *he who, she who, he whom, she whom; someone who, that; there is, are who.*

CHE and **CHI** are invariable. Thus:

l'uomo che parla, the man who speaks
la signorina che parla, the young lady who speaks
gli uomini che parlano, the men who speak
Le signorine che parlano, the young ladies who speak

Chi va piano va sano. He who goes slowly goes sensibly.
Chi va a sinistra, chi va a destra. Some (people) go to the right, some to the left.

CHE is much the commonest Relative and covers most instances in everyday life. But the following must also be known:
il quale, la quale, i quali, le quali, *who, whom, which,* and can be used for persons or things and should be so used when the relative clause demands either (*a*) *emphasis*, or *greater clarity*. Otherwise *che*, as in (*b*):

(*a*) **L'uomo, al quale ho dato tutto il danaro, è molto onesto.** The man, to whom I have given all the money, is very honest.

(*b*) **La lettera che vi ho scritta ieri, non è arrivata.** The letter, the one which I have written to you yesterday, has not arrived.

(b) **La lettera che Lei ha scritta è arrivata.** The letter which you have written has arrived.

Here (a) emphasizes and clarifies the relative clause and (b) make a simple statements without emphasis.

> **CUI**, *whom*, for both genders and numbers, persons or things, can be preceded by **di**, *of*, **a**, *to*, or **da**, *from*, *by*, and itself does not change:
>
> **l'uomo a cui** (or **al quale**) **ho parlato**, the man to whom I have spoken
>
> **la signora a cui** (or **alla quale**) **ho parlato**, the lady to whom I have spoken

WHOSE as a relative is expressed by either **il cui** or **del quale**, and then these relatives must each agree with the word to which *whose* refers. So we have: **il cui, la cui, i cui, le cui.**

> **l'amico il cui lavoro è finito**, the friend whose work is finished
>
> **la ragazza le cui sorelle ho vedute**, the girl whose sisters I have seen

Quanto, quanta, quanti, quante, *all that which*, *all those who*, are sometimes found as relatives, though their normal use is as interrogatives for *How much? How many?*

> **Quanti parlano devono tacere.** All those who are speaking must keep silent.
>
> **Quanto ha pagato?** How much have you paid?

Di chi è and **di chi sono** correspond to the English *whose is* and *whose are*, both as relatives and as interrogatives. As a Relative Pronoun, **di chi** is not greatly used. Thus:

> **l'uomo di cui questi sono i guanti**, the man whose gloves these are

But **di chi** is quite usual as an interrogative:

> **Di chi è questo coltello?** Whose is this knife?
>
> **Di chi sono questi cappelli?** Whose are these hats?

INTERROGATIVES: Most of the above Pronouns are used as interrogatives, **chi** for persons, **che,** for things:

chi? who?	**che?** what?
di chi? whose?	**di che?** of what?
a chi? to whom?	**a che?** to what?
da chi? from, by whom?	**da che?** from, by what?
quale? which one?	**quanto?** how much?
quali? which ones?	

Quale and **quali** are used instead of **che** for clarity, when the meaning to be expressed is *which one of two or more*, or *which particular ones:*

Quale è il suo cappello? Which one (of several) is your hat?

Quale is sometimes **qual** in everyday speech:

Qual è l'uscita dal museo? Which (of several) is the exit from the museum?

CHE often becomes **che cosa**, *what thing*, in everyday speech:

Che cosa fa? What are you doing?
Che cosa vende il negoziante? What does the shop-keeper sell?

and often just **cosa:**

Cosa vende? What does he sell?
Cosa vuole? What do you want?

Che, *what a!* in exclamations.

Che bella ragazza! What a beautiful girl!

At the frontier: Customs Examination

la frontiera, frontier	**la polizia,** police
il balcone, baggage counter	**i carabinieri,** armed guards,
la dogana, Customs	gensdarmes
il doganiere, Customs officer	**il segno,** Customs mark
la doganiera, Customs matron	**la chiave,** key

la **borsa,** hand-bag
il **bagaglio a mano,** hand-luggage
il **bagagliaio,** luggage van
la **macchina fotografica,** camera
la **moneta,** money
la **lira; le lire**
il **controllo,** inspection
ufficiale di dogana, Customs official
la **bottiglia di liquore,** bottle of liqueur
l'**articolo,** article

il **tabacco,** tobacco
per uso personale, for personal use
gli **effetti personali,** personal effects
le **cose usate,** things that have been worn
la **vacanza,** holiday
di passaggio, passing through
il **viaggio d'affari,** business trip
i **campioni commerciali,** commercial samples
la **valuta,** currency

Da questa parte alla dogana. This way to the Customs.
Questi sono i miei bagagli. These are my luggage.
Quanti sono i loro? How many (pieces) are yours?
Quanto si può passare? How much is allowed free?
Ha niente da dichiarare? Anything to declare?
Niente. Nothing.
Che è soggetto a dogana? What is dutiable?
Ho delle sigarette e del whisky, ma soltanto per uso personale. I have some cigarettes and whisky, but only for personal use.
Ha moneta italiana? Have you any Italian money?
Ho ventiduemila lire. I have 22,000 lire.
Allora va bene. That's all right.
Apra i colli, per favore. Open the packages, please.
Ho solo cose per uso personale. I've only things for personal use.
Paga dogana questo? Does this pay duty?
Quanto tempo resterà in Italia? How long will you stay in Italy?
Una settimana, due settimane, un mese—per una vacanza. A week, two weeks, a month—for a holiday.
Sono di passaggio. I'm just passing through.
Sono in viaggio d'affari. I'm on a business trip.

Vuol aprire il baule? Would you open the trunk?

Quanto danaro ha con sè? How much money have you with you?

Questo certificato dovrà mostrare lasciando il paese. This certificate must be shown on leaving the country.

È valido fino al . . . It is valid until . . .

Dov'è il controllo della valuta? Where is the currency control?

Da questa parte, signore. This way, sir.

Le signore devono andare con la doganiera. Ladies must go with the (examining) matron.

Subito. Immediately.

Facchino, mi porti i bagagli. Porter, take my luggage.

Quanti colli sono? How many pieces?

Ne abbiamo in tutto quattro. We have four altogether.

Deve attendere il suo turno. You must wait your turn.

Abbiamo finito qui? Have we finished here?

Si signore, andiamo. Yes, sir, let's go.

LETTURA

Un Accesso d'Ira

In un accesso d'ira, il signor Leon Seller sollevò la sua fidanzata e la lanciò fuori della finestra del suo appartamento situato al quarto piano dell'edificio. Fortunatamente la caduta della ragazza fu fermata dal tendone che sporgeva dal negozio sottostante. Illesa per miracolo, la ragazza risalì velocemente i quattro piani, entrò nella stanza del fidanzato, prese dal tavolo una bottiglia di vino e gliela spezzò in testa. Il Seller dovette essere ricoverato all'ospedale con prognosi riservata.

un accesso d'ira, a fit of anger. sollevò, lifted up (*from* sollevare, to lift). la fidanzata, betrothed, fiancée. lanciò, hurled, threw (*from* lanciare, to hurl, throw). fuori della finestra, out of the window. l'appartamento, apartment, flat. situato, situated. al quarto piano, on the fourth floor. dell' edificio, of the building. fortunatamente, fortunately. la caduta, the fall. la ragazza, the girl. fu fermata, was stopped (*from* fermare, to stop). il tendone, large curtain. spor-

geva, was protruding, sticking out (*from* **sporgere,** to protrude). **il negozio,** business, shop. **sottostante,** underneath (**sotto,** under, **stante,** standing below). **illeso, -a,** unharmed. **per miracolo,** by (a) miracle. **risalì,** re-ascended, went up again (*from* **risalire,** to re-ascend). **velocemente,** quickly. **i quattro piani,** the four storeys, floors. **entrò,** (she) entered (*from* **entrare,** to enter). **nella stanza,** into the room. **prese,** took (*from* **prendere,** to take). **dal tavolo,** from the table. **una bottiglia di vino,** a bottle of wine. **gliela,** to him it. **spezzò,** broke. **in testa,** on the head. (*Thus:* **gliela spezzò in testa,** broke it on his head. **spezzare,** to break in pieces.) **dovette essere,** had to be. **ricoverato,** given shelter, refuge (**ricoverare,** to give shelter, refuge). **all'ospedale,** in the hospital. **con prognosi,** with prognosis, forecast of probable course of the injury. **riservata,** reserved, withheld, not stated.

TRANSLATION:

A Fit of Anger

In a fit of anger Mr. Leon Seller lifted his fiancée and hurled her from the window of his apartment situated on the fourth floor of the building. Luckily the girl's fall was stopped by the large curtain which protruded from the shop below. Unharmed by a miracle, the girl went up again quickly the four floors, entered the room of (the) her fiancé, took from the table a bottle of wine and broke it (in pieces) on his head. (The) Seller had to be lodged in the hospital with outcome unstated.

LISTENING TO RADIO

From now onwards you can usefully listen to Radio broadcasts in Italian, though you must not expect to understand very much at this stage. Yet, if you listen carefully you will even now be able to pick out words and phrases, you will hear the sounds of the language, and in this way you can train your ear. For the self-taught this training is invaluable; it cannot fail to help all learners.

LISTEN TO BROADCAST ITALIAN AS OFTEN AS YOU CAN

Turn to page 141 and read through what is said about listening to Radio, and there you will find also a

☞ LIST OF ITALIAN BROADCASTING STATIONS

§ 3. *Demonstrative Adjectives and Demonstrative Pronouns*—**CI,
VI** *and* **NE**—(**ne** *and* **nè**)—*In the Port: Travel by Sea*—
LETTURA: *Texts, Vocabularies, and Translations*

Demonstrative Adjectives and Demonstrative Pronouns have
the same forms. The Demonstrative Adjective has a Noun
with it and qualifies that Noun, taking its number and gender.
The Demonstrative Pronoun is used alone and replaces a Noun.

DEMONSTRATIVE ADJECTIVES:

questo	**questa**	**questi**	**queste** = THIS THESE
			(near the speaker)
quello	**quella**	**quegli** *	**quelle** = THAT THOSE
			(away from speaker)
quel		**quei** †	
CODESTO	**codesta**	**codesti**	**codeste** = THAT THOSE
			(near the one who listens)

As Adjectives they agree with their Noun:

> **questo cavallo,** this horse; **questi cavalli,** these horses
> **quella ragazza,** that girl; **quelle ragazze,** those girls
> **codesto cavallo,** that horse *(over there near the listener)*
> **codesta grammatica,** that grammar *(near the listener)*

DEMONSTRATIVE PRONOUNS: The above are also Pronouns.
But, in addition, there are the following, which are used only as
Pronouns:

costui, this (man) **costei,** this (woman) **costoro,** these (*m.
& f.*)
colui, that (man) **colei,** that (woman) **coloro,** those (*m.
& f.*)

Costui and **colui,** with **costoro** and **coloro** for both genders,
are used only for persons. Some care is required in using these
words, because, depending on the intention of the speaker (as
shown by tone of voice and attitude), they can be used to indicate
either admiration or contempt. More often than not, in colloquial language they have a slight sense of contempt. Thus:

---

* Before vowel, impure **s** and **z**.
† Before a consonant.

Non mi parli di colui. *Don't speak to me about that fellow.*
Here the element of contempt, or indignation, is clear enough.

> **Che pensa Lei di Giacomo? Colui!** What do you
> think of James? Him!
> **Che cosa vuole?** What does he want?
> **Che cosa vuole costui?** What does this fellow want?

Note:

> **colui che,** he who; **coloro che,** those who (*when used in a
> general sense; persons only*)
> **ciò che,** that which (*also in a general sense;* **ciò** *is invariable*)
> **colui che parla,** he who speaks, whoever speaks
> **coloro che lavorono,** those who work
>
> **quegli,** the former; **questi,** the latter

These Pronouns, although plural in form, are singular in
meaning and refer only to males, in the sense of *the former one,
the latter one.* In all other instances use **quello,** *the former,* and
questo, *the latter.* These words agree with the Nouns to which
they relate.

Tale, *such a one,* has plural form **tali.**

Used with the definite article, **tale** denotes a person whose
name is unknown: **il tale vi cerca,** *So-and-so is looking for you.*
And note: **la signora Tal dei Tali,** *Mrs. So-and-so.*

Tale with the indefinite article also indicates an unknown
person but one to whom we do not wish to draw attention:

> **un tale,** someone (*but very vague*)
> **un tale racconta,** someone (or other) relates

Abbreviated forms: Demonstrative Adjectives drop the final
vowel for euphony where it can be dropped (**quell', quest'**).
But the same words as Demonstrative Pronouns are always written
in full.

CI, VI AND **NE**—FURTHER REMARKS: *Thither, to there* is
translated by

> **CI,** with a verb = here ⎱
> **VI,** „ „ = there *or* here⎰ French *y*

Thence, from there is translated by **NE,** = French *en.*

Lei va a casa? Are you going home, to your house?

No, ne vengo. No, I'm coming from there.

È stato Lei in Italia? Have you been in Italy?

No, ma vi andrò quest'anno. No, but I'm going there this year.

there is, **c'è** *or* **v'è**

there are, **ci sono** *or* **vi sono**

there was, **c'era** *or* **vi era**

there were, **c'erano** *or* **vi erano**

Pensa Lei a quella cosa? Are you thinking of that?

Ci penso. I am thinking of it. (Cf. French *j'y pense*)

In the Port: Travel by Sea

il molo, quay

la nave, ship

il piroscafo, steamer

il motoscafo, motor-launch

lo sportello, booking office

la sala da pranzo, dining-saloon

la salone, lounge

il bar, bar

il cameriere, steward

la cameriera, stewardess

il barista, barkeeper

il commissario, purser

il marinaio, sailor

il ponte, deck

il ponte di passeggiata, promenade deck

la stazione radio, wireless station

il deposito dei bagagli, baggage room

usati, worn (old, of clothes)

non usati, not worn (new, of clothes)

il comandante, captain

il macchinista, engineer

l'ufficiale, officer

il radiotelegrafista, wireless operator

la cabina, cabin

la passarella, gangway

la camera da letto, bedroom

l'appartamento, suite

il bagno, bath; **con bagno,** with bath

il passeggero, passenger

i passeggeri, passengers

la darsena, dock

il transatlantico, big liner

Vado in Sardegna. I'm going to Sardinia.

Che navi ci sono per . . .? What ships are there for . . .?

Quanto costa il biglietto? What does the ticket cost?

Dove si trova la cabina? Where's the cabin?

Non c'è una cabina libera? Isn't there a vacant cabin?

Vorrei prendere la mia automobile. I want to take my car.

A che ora parte la nave? What time does the ship leave?

A che ora ci si imbarca? At what time do we go on board?

Vorrei inscrivermi per la traversata. I should like to book for the trip.

Dov'è la sala da pranzo? Where's the dining-saloon?

Mi può mostrare la mia cabina? Can you show me my cabin?

Vorrei avere un bagno. I'd like to have a bath.

Mi chiuda il sabordo, per favore. Kindly shut the porthole.

Mi apra il sabordo, per favore. Kindly open the porthole.

Vorrei bere qualcosa. I'd like to have a drink.

Vorrei mangiare qualcosa. I'd like to have something to eat.

Dove si trova il medico? Where can the doctor be found?

Sono preso dal mal di mare. I'm feeling sea-sick.

Ora mi sento meglio. I feel better now.

Ho due bauli segnati " Non occorrenti " durante la traversata. I have two trunks marked " Not Wanted " on the voyage.

Andremo in una barca? Shall we go in a (row-)boat?

Andremo in questa canoa. We shall go in this motor-boat.

Dobbiamo salire a bordo. We must go (up) on board.

Dov'è la passerella? Where's the gangway?

Cercheremo di riservare una sedia. We'll try to reserve a deck-chair.

Stanno già per finire. They're nearly ready.

Ha il suo biglietto di sbarco? Have you your landing ticket?

Dov'è l'ufficio del commissario? Where's the purser's office?

È verso poppa. It's near the stern.

Cercheremo di favorirla. We'll try to arrange it.

LETTURA

Necrologio

" Winston," la più popolare delle quaranta bertucce che vivono sulla rupe di Gibilterra, è stata oggetto della seguente notizia necrologica nei libri ufficiali dell'amminis-

trazione inglese: " La scimmia Winston, dichiarata dis-
persa dal 9 Dicembre 1955, deve essere considerata morta.
Pertanto essa è da oggi radiata dai quadri degli effettivi
della fortezza."

il necrologio, obituary. la bertuccia, -e, ape(s). vivono, (they)
live. sulla, on the. la rupe, rocky cliff. la Gibilterra, Gibraltar.
è stato, -a, has been. l'oggetto, the object. seguente, following.
necrologico, -a, obituary (adj.). la notizia, notice. nei, in the. i libri
ufficiali, the official books. l'amministrazione, administration. la
scimmia, ape. dichiarato, -a, declared. disperso, dispersed, scat-
tered (from disperdere, to scatter, disperse). dal, from the. considerato, -a, considered (from considerare, to consider). morto, -a,
dead (from morire, to die). pertanto, on that account. essa, she (la
scimmia, the ape). da oggi, from to-day. radiato, -a, erased, struck
off. il quadro, cadre, skeleton military unit. l'effettivo, effective,
gli effettivi, military effectives or strength. la fortezza, fortress.

TRANSLATION :

Obituary

" Winston," the most popular of the forty apes which live on
the rock cliff of Gibraltar, has been the object to-day of the following obituary notice in the official books of the English administration : " The ape Winston, declared dispersed (strayed) from
9th December 1955, must be considered dead.　On that account
she (it) is from to-day struck off (from) the cadres of the strength
of the fortress."

*　　　*　　　*

Un Sondaggio dell'Opinione Pubblica

LA TELEVISIONE americana ha condotto uno dei
consueti sondaggi dell'opinione pubblica: questa volta,
per sapere che cosa nei diversi paesi si pensi degli americani. Il sondaggio è stato fatto in Francia, in Italia, in
Spagna, in Egitto, Israele, India, Giappone, Russia,
Inghilterra, Germania. Per la Francia, sono stati inter-
rogati gli abitanti di Le Vesinet, comune di quindicimila
abitanti. Hanno detto: gli americani sono simpatici negli
affari, pronti e tenaci nella realizzazione della propria
volontà, sicuro che la loro concezione della vita è la
migliore di tutte. Ama soprattutto gli interni francesi, e
preferisce lo stile Impero e il Luigi XIV: purchè, però,
provvisto di bagno e frigorifero.

un sondaggio, a sounding, test. **l'opinione pubblica,** public opinion. **un sondaggio dell'opinione pubblica** = a public opinion poll. **la televisione,** television. **condotto,** conducted (from **condurre,** to conduct, carry out). **consueto, -a,** accustomed, usual. **questa volta,** this time. **per sapere,** in order to know. **che cosa,** what thing, what. **diverso,** diverse, several, various. **il paese,** country (*plural* **i paesi**). **si pensi,** may be thought (*Present Subjunctive, see page* 174; *from* **pensare,** to think). **è stato fatto,** has been made. **interrogato, -a, -i, -e,** interrogated, questioned (*from* **interrogare,** to question). **l'abitante, gli abitanti,** inhabitant(s). **il comune,** commune (*smallest division for local government in France and some other European countries*). **hanno detto,** they have said (**detto** *from* **dire,** to say). **simpatico,** sympathetic, nice. **negli affari,** in business, everyday affairs. **pronto,** ready, prompt, quick. **tenace,** tenacious. **la realizzazione,** realization, achievement. **proprio, -a,** one's own. **la propria volontà,** (their) own will. **sicuro, -a,** sure, confident. **la concezione,** conception. **la vita,** life. **migliore di tutte,** best of all. **ama,** he loves. **soprattutto,** above all. **gli interni,** the interiors. **preferisce,** he prefers (*from* **preferire,** to prefer). **lo stile,** the style. **impero,** empire. **Luigi,** Louis. **purchè,** provided (that). **però,** however. **provvisto, -a, (di),** provided (with). **il bagno,** bath. **il frigorifero,** refrigerator.

TRANSLATION:

A Public Opinion Poll

American television has carried out one of the usual (common) polls of public opinion: this time in order to know what (thing) in the several (various) countries is thought of the Americans. The poll has been made (taken) in France, (in) Italy, (in) Spain, (in) Egypt, (in) Israel, (in) India, (in) Japan, (in) Russia, (in) England, (in) Germany. As regards France, (there) have been questioned the inhabitants of Le Vesinet, (a) commune of fifteen thousand inhabitants. They have said: the Americans are sympathetic (nice) in (everyday) affairs, prompt (quick) and tenacious in the achieving of their own will, confident that their conception of life is the best of all. He (the American) above all loves the French interiors, and prefers the Empire style and (that of) Louis XIV: provided, however, (that it is) supplied with bath and refrigerator.

§ 4. *Possessives: Adjectives and Pronouns—Avoiding Ambiguity— General Remarks on Possessives—Hiking: Walking—***LET- TURA:** *Newspaper Extracts, with Notes and Translations*

POSSESSIVES: Possessive Adjectives and Pronouns have the same forms in Italian. Possessive Pronouns are used alone, that is, without a Noun but to replace one. Thus: *That is my hat—*

my is a Possessive Adjective. *The hat is mine—mine* is a Possessive Pronoun.

These " Possessives " in Italian, unlike their counterparts in English, agree with the *thing possessed* and not with the possessor.

Masculine		Feminine		
Singular	*Plural*	*Singular*	*Plural*	
il mio	**i miei**	**la mia**	**le mie**	my, mine
il tuo	**i tuoi**	**la tua**	**le tue**	thy, thine
il suo	**i suoi**	**la sua**	**le sue**	{ his, her, hers; its; your, yours
il nostro	**i nostri**	**la nostra**	**le nostre**	our, ours
il vostro	**i vostri**	**la vostra**	**le vostre**	your, yours
il loro	**i loro**	**la loro**	**le loro**	{ their, theirs; your, yours

Note: As a general rule, the Possessives are preceded by the Definite Article. The forms **miei, tuoi** and **suoi** are slightly irregular. **loro** is invariable.

The Possessives of the polite forms **Lei** and **Loro** are **il suo** and **il loro**, written without a capital letter. **Il suo libro**, *your book*. But see below for avoiding ambiguity.

Examples:

> **il mio cappello,** my hat; **i miei cappelli,** my hats
> **la mia sorella,** my sister; **le mie sorelle,** my sisters

When speaking of a near relative in the *singular*, the Definite Article is omitted:

> **mio padre,** my father; **mia madre,** my mother

But the Article *must* be used when there is an Adjective qualifying the near relation in the singular, usually if that relation is in the plural, and if the Possessive is **loro**. Thus:

> **il mio caro fratello,** my dear brother
> **la mia cara madre,** my dear mother
> **i miei fratelli,** my brothers (*Plural* **i loro fratelli, la loro sorella**)

When a Possessive is preceded by the Verb **ESSERE**, the Article is usually omitted, though its use is optional. Thus:

> **Questa carta è sua**
> *or* **Questa carta è la sua** } This paper is his, hers, yours

AVOIDING AMBIGUITY: There can be ambiguity with **il suo** and **la sua,** because these can refer to *his*, *her*, *its* and polite form *your*. When there is any likelihood of ambiguity or misunderstanding, then one should use:

di lui for *his*   **di lei** for *her*

di Lei } for polite *your*   **di loro** for *their*
di Loro

Thus:

> **Questo libro è di lui e non di lei.** This book is his and not hers.

Note that these forms usually follow the Noun, as in:

> **Questo libro non è il mio ma di Lei.** This book is not mine but yours.

SOME GENERAL REMARKS ON POSSESSIVES: In everyday speech, when a Possessive Adjective before the Subject clearly indicates the possessor of the Object, there is no need to use a Possessive with the Object. Thus:

> **Mio padre fuma la pipa tutti i giorni.** My father smokes his pipe every day.

—**la sua** is unnecessary before **pipa,** and is replaced by the Definite Article (though it would not be incorrect to use **la sua**).

Unless the Article is required to make the meaning clear, it is omitted before a numeral or adjective of quantity:

> **quattro amici miei,** four friends of mine

but:

> **i quattro amici miei,** the four friends of mine

—the first means *any* four friends, the second means four definite friends.

Parts of the body are usually referred to with the Definite Article and not with a Possessive as in English, especially when a Reflexive Personal Pronoun makes clear the possessor:

> **Egli si lava le mani.** He is washing his hands.
> **Mi duole il capo.** *Literally* To me pains (aches) the head: My head aches. I have a headache.

Possessives may come after the Noun in such exclamatory phrases as:

Amico mio! My friend!   **Caríssima mia!** My darling!

And in a number of idiomatic phrases (see page 212) the Article is omitted:

a casa mia, in my house   **in nome mio,** in my name
da parte mia, on my part   **per conto mio,** on my account
per amor di Lei, for your sake   **è colpa mia,** it's my fault
il piacere è mio, the pleasure
is mine

Hiking: Walking

la scampagnata, country excursion

la passeggiata } walk
una camminata }

andare a piedi } to go on foot,
camminare } to walk

una camminata di tre ore, a three hours' walk

andare a spasso, to go for a walk

passeggiare, to stroll, walk

il campeggio, camping

il rifugio turistico, hostel

l'acqua potabile, drinking-water

il sacco, sack, haversack

il letto a sacco, sleeping-bag

il Thermos, Thermos flask

gli occhiali da sole, sunglasses

la carta, map

il portacarta, map case

indicare, to direct

all'aperto, in the open

il fornello da campo, camp stove

la latta, tin, can

il combustibile, fuel

la latta di combustibile, tin of fuel

il contadino, peasant

il fittaiuolo, tenant-farmer

la fittaiuola, farmer's wife

la raccolta, harvest

a grand'andare, with big strides

il bastone, stick

la campagna, countryside

la bussola, compass

Andiamo a passare la giornata in campagna. Let's spend the day in the country.

Andiamo a piedi. Let's go on foot, walk.

Sarà possibile avere da mangiare? Will it be possible to get something to eat?

Non so. Si può fare una merenda in campagna. I don't know. One could have a pic-nic in the country.

Posso comprare generi di drogheria, del pane e vino. I can buy some groceries, bread and wine.

Benone. Questo basta. Good. That'll be enough.

L'autobus Li porterà all'incrocio. The bus will take you to the cross-roads.

In un'ora faremo quattro chilometri. In a hour we'll walk four kilometres.

Vorrei trovare un rifugio turistico. I should like to find a hostel for tourists.

Si può comprare del latte in qualche fattoria? Can one buy milk at some farm?

Sì, è certissimo. E possibilmente panini imbottiti. Yes, certainly. And possibly sandwiches.

Dove posso avere dell'acqua potabile? Where can I get drinking-water?

Si può avere alloggio per la notte? Can one get lodging for the night?

Mi può indicare un luogo dove . . . Can you show me a place where . . .

Voglio accamparmi per la notte. I want to camp out for the night.

Mi sono fatto male. Mi duole il piede. I've hurt myself. My foot hurts.

Ho una cassetta di pronto soccorso. I have a first aid outfit.

Si porti soccorso—pronto! Bring help—quickly!

LETTURA : NEWSPAPER EXTRACT

UN LIBRO PREZIOSO

Cosenza, 30 luglio 1956

Egregio [1] Direttore,[2]

Le farò [3] una domanda [4] forse [5] un poco stupida, che mi sta a cuore,[6] siccome [7] sono a corto di [8] fantasia [9] le sarò [10] grato se vorrà [11] indicarmi [12] un libro che contenga [13] lettere d'amore,[14] dichiarazioni [15] ecc.[16]

G. M.

Ma come,[17] Lei non ha mai [18] sentito parlare [19] del " Segretario Galante "? [20] E' un aureo [21] libro, contiene dichiarazioni, lettere d'amore, di gelosia,[22] di passione, di rottura,[23] di sdegno,[24] per tutti i casi dell'amore.[25] Ne comperi [26] una copia, ne faccia comperare una anche all'oggetto delle sue premure [27] epistolari. Potrete [28] corrispondere senza fatica,[29] indicando [30] Lei semplicemente [31] il numero della pagina e della lettera che intenderebbe scrivere,[32] e rispondendole la sua bella [33] nella stessa maniera.[34]

NOTES

[1, 2] " Distinguished Director ", opening of a letter to an editor.
[3-4] " I shall make you a demand (request)."
[5] perhaps.
[6] that to me is at heart.
[7] inasmuch as.
[8] short of, lacking.
[9] fancy, imagination.
[10] I'd be grateful.
[11] if you will.
[12] indicate to me.
[13] which contains.
[14] love letters.
[15] declarations.
[16] **ecc. = eccetera,** et cetera, etc.
[17] but how.
[18] you have never.

[19] heard tell.
[20] gallant secretary.
[21] a golden book.
[22] jealousy.
[23] breaches, quarrels.
[24] scorn, indignation.
[25] for all cases of love.
[26] of it buy a copy, of it make buy one also.
[27] the object of your epistolary importance, eagerness.
[28] you will be able.
[29] without fatigue.
[30] (by) you indicating.
[31] simply.
[32] you would intend to write.
[33] your beautiful one (f.) replying.
[34] in the same manner.

TRANSLATION:

A Precious Book

Cosenza, 30th July 1956.

Distinguished Editor,
I shall make you a request, perhaps a little stupid, which is (much) in my heart, inasmuch as I am lacking in imagination, I shall be grateful to you if you will indicate to me a book that contains love letters, declarations, etc.

G. M.

But how (is it that), you have never heard tell of the " Gallant Secretary "? It is a golden book, contains declarations, love letters, (letters of) jealousy, of breaches (quarrels), of indignation, for all (the) cases of love. Buy yourself a copy of it, make buy one also the object of your epistolary importance (solicitude). You will be able to correspond without fatigue (tiring), (by) you indicating simply the number of the page and of the letter which you might intend to write, and your beautiful (girl) replying to you in the same manner.

*　　　*　　　*

Era una illusione ottica

NEW YORK, 4 — L'ispettore di polizia James Lehay non aveva visto bene. A questa conclusione è giunto [1] il giudice Milton Jacobs dopo un attento studio [2] dei fatti [3] che hanno condotto [4] in Tribunale la giovane attrice [5] Lynn York accusata di essersi presentata [6] nuda [7] sul palcoscenico [8] alla fine di una brillante commedia. La signorina si è difesa [8a] dicendo che indossava [9] vesti molto leggere [10] ma che non erano neppure [11] trasparenti. Il giudice ha ritenuto [12] che l'ispettore trovandosi [13] a dodici metri dal palcoscenico non poteva [14] vedere bene la scena che si svolgeva [15] a circa tre metri nell'interno dalle luci [16] della ribalta [17] e quindi [18] era rimasto vittima di una illusione ottica.[20] Il pubblico ha applaudito la sentenza con caloroso entusiasmo.[21]

NOTES

[1] reached, arrived.
[2] close, diligent, study.
[3] of the facts.
[4] which have conducted, led.
[5] the young actress.
[6] of having presented herself.
[7] nude.
[8] stage.
[8a] has defended herself.
[9] she put on.
[10] very light clothes.
[11] not even.

[12] has held, decided.
[13] finding himself.
[14] could not (see well).
[15] if she unwrapped.
[16] on the inside of the lights.
[17] **la ribalta,** the flap which may be turned up to screen off the footlights.
[18] and therefore (**quindi**).
[19] was caught as a victim.
[20] of an optical illusion.
[21] with heated enthusiasm.

TRANSLATION:

It was an Optical Illusion

NEW YORK, 4th—(The) inspector of police James Lehay had not seen well. To this conclusion has arrived (the) judge Milton Jacobs after a diligent study of the facts which led to court the young actress Lynn York accused of having presented herself nude on the stage at the end of a brilliant comedy. The young lady defended herself saying that she had put on very light clothes but which were not even transparent. The judge (has) held that the inspector find-

ing himself at twelve metres (yards) from the stage could not see well the scene (stage) if she unwrapped (stripped) at about three metres in the inside of the lights of the footlight flap and therefore he was caught a victim of an optical illusion. The public applauded the decision with warm enthusiasm.

N.B.—These translations are literal, not literary.

§ 5. *Indefinite Pronouns—List of Indefinite Pronouns—Words Used as Indefinite Pronouns—Eating and Drinking—Reading Test Without Notes:* **PADOVA,** *Text and Translation*

There is a number of very useful words which, for convenience, may be called Indefinite Pronouns, although sometimes their nature comes close to that of other parts of speech. Here is a first list, which must be known:

uno, one	**certuno,** a certain (man)
*****ogni,** each, every	**tutto,** the whole of
alcuno, some(one), anyone	**altro,** other, something else
un certo, a certain (one)	**taluno,** such a one
ognuno, each one, every one	*****nullo,** none, no one
qualcuno, somebody	*****qualunque,** any . . . whatever
*****qualche,** any, some	
un tale, such a one	*****nulla,** nothing
ciascuno, each one	*****niente,** nothing
qualcheduno, anybody, somebody	**nessuno,** no one
	*****chiunque,** whoever

Those marked * are invariable, the others are variable.

These " Indefinites " are generally used without the Article, except **altro, -a, -i, -e,** *other,* which may take the Article.

ognuno, -a; qualcuno, -a; nessuno, -a; ciascuno, -a; are used in the singular only.

When **nessuno** follows the Verb the negative **non** must precede the Verb.

The following quantitative words are often used as Indefinite Pronouns and may be included here, although they have already been met:

molto, -a, -i, -e, much, many
parecchio, -a, -i, -e, several, a great deal of
tutto, -a, -i, -e, all
poco, -a, -chi, -che, a few

troppo, -a, -i, -e, too much, too many (of)
un poco di or **un po' di,** a small quantity of

Nulla or, more commonly, **niente** takes a singular Verb.

Eating and Drinking

More will be given later on this subject. But the following essential words and phrases should be mastered now.

Dove c'è un buon ristorante? Where is there a good restaurant?

Il cameriere. The waiter.

È libera questa tavola? Is this table free?

La carta. The bill of fare, menu.

Va bene, grazie. It's all right, thank you.

Ne porti per me . . . Bring me some . . .

Antipasto. Hors d'oeuvres.

Pospasto. Dessert.

La sogliola alla molinera. Fried sole.

Cotoletta di vitello. Con salsa. Veal cutlet. With sauce.

Pollo arrosto. Roast chicken.

Dove posso lavarmi le maní? Where can I wash my hands?

Il pasto a prezzo fisso. *Table d'hôte.* Meal at fixed price.

Mi porti una porzione di . . . Bring me a portion of . . .

Una mezza porzione di . . . A half portion of . . .

La lista di vini, per favore. The wine list, please.

Una bottiglia di . . . A bottle of . . .

Il caffè. Nero. Con latte. Coffee. Black. With milk.

Pane e burro. Bread and butter.

Panini. Rolls.

Caffè con zucchero e panna. Coffee with sugar and cream.

Il Caffè. Café, coffee-house.

Il bar. The Bar.

La trattoria. Small eating-house-Café.

l'aperitivo. Aperitive, appetiser.

Una tazza di caffè. Espresso. A cup of coffee. Espresso.

E

Un bicchiere di vino. A glass of wine.

Il vino bianco. White wine.

Il vino rosso. Red wine.

Il bock di birra. Glass (large) of Beer.

Il tè. Tea.

Caffè in ghiaccio. Iced coffee.

La limonata. Lemonade.

Il gelato. Ice-cream.

La macedonia di frutta. Fruit Salad.

l'aranciata. Orangeade.

Acqua minerale. Mineral water.

Cameriere! Il conto. Waiter! The bill.

READING TEST: The following piece is given without notes so that you may make an extra effort at this stage to extract the meaning without their aid. You can always refer to the translation when you find it difficult. This extra effort helps you to begin to rely on your own ingenuity. Go over it several times and, if you find it still difficult, come back to it later.

PADOVA

Centro di cultura, Padova è famosa per la sua *Università*, fondata nel 1222 e oggi fra le più moderne per impianti scientifici. Il nome di Padova è legato a *S. Antonio*, di cui si venera la tomba nella grande Basilica, meta di pellegrinaggi da ogni parte del mondo. Padova custodisce il capolavoro di Giotto, nella *Cappella degli Scrovegni* all'Arena, affrescata con le storie di Maria e di Gesù.

Nei dintorni di Padova, le cui nobili e semplici architetture attestano una serena floridezza ed un vivere civile, sorgono castelli, ville, monasteri di alto interesse artistico e storico.

A 9 km. dalla città, ai piedi dei *Colli Euganei*, sorgono i grandi complessi alberghieri di *Abano Terme* e *Montegrotto*, attrezzati scientificamente per la cura dei fanghi, bagni, inalazioni (5000 letti, 500 camerini di cura). Tra gli ulivi ed i vigneti, nel piccolo borgo di *Arquà*, è sepolto Francesco Petrarca; la casa dove egli

sostare = s'arrêter

trascorse gli *u*ltimi anni e morì il 18 luglio 1374, è sosta di visita-
tori reverenti.

Padova è unita a Venezia dalla *Riviera del Brenta* e da una
moderna *Autostrada.*

ENTE.

TRANSLATION:

PADUA

An (ancient) centre of culture, Padua is famous for its University, founded in 1222 and to-day (ranked) among the most modern
for (its) scientific installations.   The name of Padua is linked to
that of St. Anthony, whose tomb is venerated in the great Basilica,*
the goal of pilgrims from every part of the world.   Padua keeps
custody of Giotto's masterpiece in the Chapel of Scrovegni in the
(Roman) Arena, (which is) frescoed (covered with frescoes) with
the stories of Mary and Jesus.

In the surroundings of Padua, whose noble and simple archi-
tectural (works) attest a serene abundance and a civilized way of
life (living), rise big castles, villas, (and) monasteries of great
artistic and historical interest.

At 9 kilometres from the town, at the foot of the Euganean Hills,
rise the big elaborate hotels of Albano and Montegrotto *Terme*
(thermal springs) scientifically equipped for cure with mud-baths,
baths, inhalations, etc. (5,000 beds—500 rooms for the cures).
Among the olive and vine groves of Arquà is buried Francesco
Petrarca: the house where he spent the last years of his life and
where he died is paused at by reverent visitors.

Padua is connected with Venice by the Riviera del Brenta and
by a modern motoring road.

* **Basilica,** a cathedral or large church, whatever its ground plan, but
not of Gothic architecture.   In Rome the term is applied to certain great
churches among which are: St. Peter's, St. John Lateran, St. Paul's
beyond the city walls, S. Maria Maggiore and S. Lorenzo.

LESSON IV

§ 1. *Conjunctions: List of Conjunctions in Common Use—Some Useful Conjunctive Phrases—The Post Office—***LETTURA: Soggiorni Estivi nelle Dolomiti**—*Text and Translation*

THOSE very common words which are used for connecting other words or statements are called Conjunctions, and they are invariable.

In Italian they are either simple words such as **e**, *and*, **o**, *or*, **però**, *however*, or compounds such as **eppure** (**e-pure**), *nevertheless*, or **perchè**, *because*; or they can be in the form of conjunctional phrases such as **di modo che**, *in order that*.

There is only one difficulty about their use in Italian, and this is that after certain conjunctions (introducing a subordinate clause) the Verb which follows must be in the Subjunctive. This will be more fully dealt with under the Subjunctive, for which see page 282.

For the rest, it is merely necessary to know the Conjunctions as vocabulary, and to make quite sure of their basic meanings.

LIST OF CONJUNCTIONS IN COMMON USE

Those marked * are less used and need not be learnt at this stage.

e }
ed } and

nemmeno, not even
neanche, not even

o }
od } or

anzi = au contraire même, de plus

anche, also
pure, still, really
***altresi,** likewise
ancora, again, yet, still
***inoltre,** besides
nè, neither, nor
neppure, not even

ma, but
anzi, rather, even
però, however, therefore
tuttavia, still, nevertheless
mentre, while

e . . . e, both . . . and
nè . . . nè, neither . . . nor

116

o . . . o, either . . . or
sia . . . sia, whether . . . or
ossia, or else

dunque, then, so
pertanto, in fact
perciò, for that reason
cioè, that is to say, that is
infatti, indeed

perchè, because, since, so
    that
poichè, since, as
*giacchè, inasmuch as
*ancorchè, even if
benchè, although
*quantunque, although
nonostante, notwithstanding
sebbene, though
senza che, without

se, if (see page 87)
*purchè, provided that
qualora, whenever, in case
eccettochè, except that

fuorchè, without, except
*altrochè, otherwise

affinchè, in order that
*acciocchè, in order that
che, that, than
che, much less

come, as, like
quasi, almost, as if
siccome, inasmuch as, as
    soon as
così . . . che, thus, so that
tanto . . . che, so much . . .
    as
allorchè, when, at the time
    when
finchè, until, as long as
quando, when
talmente . . . che, to such
    an extent that
qualunque, whatever
supposto che, supposing
    that

SOME USEFUL CONJUNCTIVAL PHRASES

di modo che, so that
allo stesso modo, in the same
    way
per conseguenza, as a result
per la qual cosa, wherefore
non pertanto, nevertheless

d'altra parte, on the other
    hand
caso mai che, if ever that
fino a tanto che, as long as
sennò, if not

These lists do not exhaust Conjunctions, especially the conjunctival phrases, which are many.

The Post Office

la posta, post, post office
l'ufficio postale, post office
il corriere, mail
ferma in posta, poste restante
la cartolina, post card
la lettera, letter
la buca, letter-box
la casetta delle lettere, pillar-box
raccomandata, registered

la busta, envelope
la distribuzione, delivery
l'indirizzo, address
il francobollo, postage stamp
la tassa, il porto, postage
il pacco, parcel
il mittente, sender
il destinatario, receiver
il telegramma, telegram

Qual'è l'affrancatura per queste lettere? What is the postage on these letters?

Aspetto una raccomandata. I'm expecting a registered (letter).

Dov'è la Posta Centrale? Where's the General Post Office?

Vorrei i seguenti francobolli . . . I want the following stamps . . .

Questo deve essere inviato. This must be sent:

per posta ordinaria, by ordinary post
raccomandato, registered
per aereo, air mail
come espresso, express
come stampa, as printed matter, or book post
come pacchetto postale, by parcel post

Riempia questo formulario. Fill up this form.

Inoltrare a . . . Forward to . . .

Desidero una vaglia postale per . . . I should like a postal order for . . .

Il postino, postman.

Il capo ufficio postale, postmaster.

Vorrei telefonare. I should like to use the telephone.

Vuole (Lei) chiamare questo numero. Would you kindly call this number.

Posso parlare con . . .? Can I speak to . . .?

Qui parla . . . This is . . . speaking.

La comunicazione interurbana. Trunk call.

Il mio numero di telefono è . . . My telephone number is . . .

Mi telefoni presto. Ring me soon.

La richiamerò stasera. I'll ring you this evening.

Ecco il suo numero. Here's your number.

Mi ha dato un numero sbagliato. You've given me a wrong number.

La linea è occupata. Line engaged.

Dove posso spedire un telegramma? Where can I send a telegram?

Un telegramma con risposta pagata. A reply paid telegram.

Un radiogramma, radiogram, wireless.

Col mezzo più rapido, the quickest way.

THE TELEPHONE—SOME USEFUL WORDS, ETC.: **la linea,** *line.* **la linea urbana,** *local line,* — **intercomunale,** *intercommunal or toll* —, **interurbana,** *trunk* —. When first you speak say: **Pronto!** and, when you hear the speaker, say **Pronto!** again and then: **Parla . . .** giving your name, and you may have to ask **Chi parla?** *Who's speaking?* The *operator* is **il** or **la telefonista,** and you speak into **il microfono.** **l'elenco telefonico,** *telephone directory.* **il servizio telefonico,** *telephone service.* **il posto telefonico pubblico,** *public telephone (booth).* **il ricevitore,** *receiver.* **l'attinenza,** *connection.* **attingere,** *to get through, make connexion with.* **la chiamata telefonica,** *'phone call.* **il telefono a commutazione automatica,** *automatic telephone.* **il disco combinatore,** *the dial (for automatic).*

See also page 190, Telephoning.

LETTURA:

SOGGIORNI ESTIVI nelle DOLOMITI

La provincia di Belluno è compresa [4] fra l'Alto Adige e l'Austria a nord, il Trentino a ovest, la Carnia e il Friuli a est, e la catena [5] prealpina che la separa [6] dalla Val Padana [7] a sud.

Una rete stradale [8] di prim'ordine adduce [9] a questa celebrata zona con itinerari tra i più vari e interessanti di tutto l'arco alpino,[10] alcuni superando [11] passi famosi come il Pordoi (m. 2.239), " tetto delle Dolomiti ".

Le DOLOMITI, appunto [12]—che sembrano squarciare [13] con le loro guglie [14] l'azzurro più bello d'Italia—e il fiume PIAVE [15] —che in massima parte [16] l'attraversa [17]—concorrono a caratterizzare [18] la provincia, la cui bellezza è tale da lasciare impressioni indelebili [19] in chi ne sappia comprendere [20] l'ineguagliabile fascino.[21]

Linee ferroviarie da Feltre, Belluno, Calalzo, Cortina, per tutte le destinazioni.

Accogliente e confortevole, in tutte le località di soggiorno, l'attrezzatura ricettiva.

Vi siete già chiesto [22] quale sarà la meta [23] della vostra villeggiatura [24] la prossima estate?   Il Cadore dalle ampie ridenti [25] vallate? la mirabile conca [26] ampezzana? le valli dell'Agordino, dove la grandiosità dell'architettura dolomitica ha del prodigioso? la idillica valle Zoldana? il verde Comelico? il giardino del' Alpago? il superbo anfiteatro [27] bellunese? il Feltrino, ospitale [28] e gentile?

Difficile dare un consiglio! [29] chè le Dolomiti in provincia di Belluno sono tutte meravigliose [30]: meritano [31] di essere " scoperte " [32] da ogni parte,[33] risalendo [34] di valle in valle, passando da rifugio a rifugio . . .

Veniteci [35] una volta, e vi resterà [36] vivo [37] il desiderio di tornarci sempre.

ENTE.

NOTES

[1] **il soggiorno,** stay, sojourn.

[2] **estivo,** of summer. **soggiorni estivi,** summer holidays.

[3] **Le Dolomiti,** the Dolomites (an Alpine range of mountains in N. Italy).

[4] is comprised = lies.

[5] chain.

[6] separates it from.

[7] valley of the (river) Po.

[8] net(work) of roads.

[9] leads to.

[10] Alpine arch.

[11] rising to.

[12] in fact.

[13] seem to pierce.

[14] with their peaks.

[15] the river Piave.

[16] for the most part.

[17] crosses it.

[18] concur, unite (to characterize).

[19] indelible, unforgettable.

[20] on who(ever) of it knows (how) to understand, appreciate.

Notes

[21] the unmatchable fascination.

[22] have you already asked yourself.

[23] aim, goal.

[24] country holiday.

[25] wide smiling valleys.

[26] hollow, valley. **ampezzana,** of Ampezzo.

[27] amphitheatre of Belluno.

[28] **ospitale,** hospitable (**ospedale** = hospital).

[29] counsel, advice.

[30] marvellous.

[31] they merit, deserve.

[32] discovered (*from* **scoprire,** to discover.

[33] **da ogni parte,** from every part, side.

[34] going up (*from* **risalire,** to go up).

[35] come to us (*from* **venire,** to come).

[36] to you will remain.

[37] alive, active.

Translation:

Summer Holidays in the Dolomites

The Province of Belluno lies between the Alto Adige and Austria to the North, the (Province of) Trento to the West, Carnia and Friuli to the East and the pre-Alpine chain (range), which separates it from the valley of the Po to the South. A network of first-class roads leads to this famous area, with itineraries (that are) among the most varied and interesting of the whole Alpine panorama, some (of these roads) rising to famous passes such as Pordoi (2,239 metres) " the roof of the Dolomites ".

The DOLOMITES, in fact, which seem to pierce with their peaks the most beautiful blue (sky) in (all) Italy—and the river PIAVE—which crosses it almost entirely—unite to form the characteristic features of this province whose beauty is such as to leave an indelible impression on (those) who can appreciate its matchless charm.

Railway lines from Feltre, Belluno, Calalzo, and Cortina for all destinations.

Welcoming and comfortable, in all (its) holiday resorts, (is the) equipment for receiving (visitors).

Have you already asked yourself what will be the goal of your holidays next summer? Cadore with its wide smiling valleys? The wonderful hollow of (Cortina d')Ampezzo? The vales of Agordino, where the grandeur of Dolomitic architecture has (something of) the prodigious. The idyllic valley of Zoldano? Green Comelico? The garden of Alpago? The superb amphitheatre of Belluno? Feltrino, hospitable and charming?

(It is) difficult to give advice! For the Dolomites in (the) Province of Belluno are all marvellous: they all deserve to be " discovered ", from every side, by going up from valley to valley, from (mountain) refuge to refuge.

Come to us once and the desire to come back will always remain active (alive) with you.

§ 2. *Prepositions—List: The most frequently Used Prepositions with Explanations—Travel by Car—*LETTURA: *Newspaper Extract, with Notes and Translation*

A Preposition is a word placed before a Noun or Pronoun to make clear its relation to another word in a sentence: *at, in, to* are Prepositions. *At* the theatre, *in* the house, *to* the station. Most Prepositions have to do with position or direction, and all Prepositions are invariable.

For Prepositions contracted with the Definite Article, see page 17.

It will be noted that some of the Prepositions given here have the same form as an Adverb. This is merely because the terms Adverb and Preposition are used in grammar to define the function of a word or words, and in one instance a word may be used as a Preposition and in another as an Adverb.

The most important thing for the learner to be sure of is the *meaning* of the words in the lists which follow. They are, most of them, in very common use—and should be known, first of all, as vocabulary.

Although Prepositions are among the most frequently used words in the language, their usage is often subtle, and then it is best learnt by experience: by hearing, reading, and practice in speaking and writing. It will be sufficient here to give a list of those which must be known, together with a statement of their everyday uses.

The most frequently used Prepositions with their English equivalents are:

> **A:** *at, to, in, by*, as in—
> > **a Londra,** in London
> > **vado a Londra,** I'm going to London
> > **vado a cavallo,** I'm going on horseback
> > **vado alle quattro.** I'm going at four o'clock
> > **sarò a casa alle due.** I'll be at home at two o'clock.
> > **una nave a vela,** a sailing-ship (description)

CON: *with,* in various connotations such as—

vado con lui, I'm going with him

con lui perderemo, with him we shall lose

colla sua dolcezza canterà con amore. With her sweetness, she will sing lovingly.

gli ho parlato con severità. I have spoken to him severely, with severity.

abbiamo mangiato pane col burro. We have eaten bread and butter.

Con questo bel tempo staremo di più in Italia. With this lovely weather we shall stay longer in Italy.

È un uomo colla barba nera. He's a man with a black beard.

con la posta aerea, by air mail

con la speranza che, in the hope that

con mia sorpresa, to my surprise

scusarsi con, to excuse oneself to (someone)

DA: *from, of, by, for,* as in—

Vengo da Firenze. I come from Florence.

il ragazzo fu punito dal maestro. The boy was punished by the master.

Non lo abbiamo veduto da anni. We haven't seen him for years. — **dall'anno scorso,** since last year.

la sala da pranzo, the dining-room

la carta da lettere, the writing-paper (for letters)

soffocato dal fumo, suffocated by smoke

è cieco da un occhio, he is blind of an eye

un bel cavallo da corsa, a fine race-horse

un ferro da calza, a knitting-needle

Lo cercai da mia zia. I looked for him at my aunt's (house).

Ho in tasca da cinquemila lire. I have about five thousand lire in my pocket.

DA: is used for *from* or to indicate *agency*, and for *for* as in *for many years*, **da molti anni,** and widely to denote *purpose* as in **la carta da scrivere**, writing-paper and **la sala da pranzo.**

These are regular usages, but it is also used in many idioms, which one must learn by experience.

DI: *of, by, at*, as in—

Sono arrivato di notte. I've arrived at (*or* by) night.

Mi alzo di buon mattino. I get up early.

La donna è vestita di bianco. The lady is dressed in white.

il libro di mia sorella, my sister's book (*one of the commonest uses—for the possessive*)

un vestito di lana, a woollen dress ⎫

una tomba di marmo, a marble tomb ⎬ *the material of which something is made*

un cappello di cotone, a cotton hat ⎭

Sono di Roma. I'm from Rome.

Sono più alto di lui. I'm taller than he.

Sono più alto di lui di due piedi. I'm taller than he by two feet.

Il piroscafo è uscito di porto. The mail-boat has gone out of (the) port.

Siamo contenti di loro. We're pleased with them.

un romanzo di Graham Green, a novel by Graham Greene

È morto di fame. He died of hunger.

d'inverno, di giorno, di notte, in winter, by day, by night

Vive di vegetali. He lives on vegetables.

DURANTE: *during* as in—

> **durante la settimana,** during the week
> **durante le vacanze,** during the holidays
> **durante la notte,** during the night

IN: *in, within, on, at,* as in—

> **Vivo in Londra.** I live in London.
> **Viaggio in Italia.** I'm travelling in Italy.
> **Lavoro in casa.** I work indoors (at home).
> **Vado in Italia.** I'm going to Italy.
> **i ragazzi sono in scuola.** The boys are at school.
> **in tavola,** at table
> **L'ho fatto in un mese, una settimana.** I have done it in a month, a week.
> **Siamo nel 1958.** We are in (the year) 1958.
> **È scritto in nero.** It is written in black.

Note that **in** is often used where another Preposition would be used in English:

in tavola
recato in dono, brought as a gift
una ragazza chiesta in sposa, a girl betrothed (as a wife)
cambiare in meglio, to change for the better

LUNGO: *along*—

> **lungo la parete,** along the wall (of a room)
> **lungo la spiaggia,** along the shore

PER: *for, through, by*—

> **Per quattro punti perdiamo il giuoco.** By four points we lose the game.
> **Ho preso l'uno per l'altro.** I've taken one for the other.
> **Combattiamo per la giustizia.** Let us fight for justice.
> **per istanza del tribunale,** by insistence of the court.

per tutta la vita, for (through) all one's life.

Lo spedirò per posta. I'll send it by post.

Bisogna partire per Roma. We must leave for Rome. (We = one, he, she, I.)

morire per la patria, to die for one's country.

Quelle penne non sono buone per Lei. Those pens are no good for you.

Egli correva giù per la scesa. He was running down the slope.

SU
(sur) : *up, upon, about, after*—

di su, off, from off

su di lì, somewhere up there

Lo trovò su per le scale. He found it up on the stairs.

su per giù (or **supergiù**), in a general way, more or less.

TRA
FRA : *among, between, within* (time)—

Fra mezz'ora ho finito. Within half an hour I've finished.

Fra le due case c'è un cortile. Between the two houses there is a courtyard.

Fra cane e gatto non c'è buon accordo. Between cat and dog there's not good agreement.

il migliore fra tutti, the best of (among) all.

Sia detto fra noi. Let it be said among ourselves

Verrò fra due ore. I'll see in (within) two hours.

TRA and **FRA** have the same meaning and either may be used, but careful writers observe euphony, so that, instead of **fra Francesi,** *among the French,* one usually sees or hears **tra Francesi.**

Travel by Car

la benzina, petrol, gasoline

il distributore di benzina, petrol station

il garage, garage

l'automobile
l'auto } car

la vettura aperta, open (touring) car

la strada, road

il meccanico, mechanic

il deposito, tank

la porta, door

il parabrezza, windscreen

il volante, steering-wheel

il faro, head-light

il pneumatico, tyre

la ruota, wheel

il motore, engine

il carburatore, carburettor

i sedili, seats

l'autista, driver

la targa, number plate

il portabagaglio, boot

un litro, litre

cinque litri, five litres

il chilometro, kilometer

i chilometri, kilometers

Dove posso lasciare l'auto? Where can I leave (park) the car?

Vuole mettermi benzina, per favore. Kindly put some petrol in.

Quanto vuole? How much do you want?

Vuole gonfiarmi questa ruota, e questa. Put some air into this tyre, and this one.

Vorrei una latta d'olio. I'd like a tin of oil.

Vuole ripassarmi . . . Would you look at . . . for me?

Potrà rimettermelo a punto? Can you put it right for me?

C'è una valvola rotta. There's a broken valve.

Ha messo l'acqua nel radiatore? Have you put water in the radiator?

È tutto a posto? Is everything all right?

Vorrei fare una gita in auto. I'd like to go for a drive.

Ci porti a . . . luoghi interessanti. Take us to . . . interesting places.

Vuole mostrarmi la strada su questa carta? Would you show me the road on this map?

Quanti chilometri ci sono per . . . How many kilometres (are there) to . . .

Conosce la strada? Do you know the road?

È buona? Is it a good one?

Taxi, ci porti in un buon ristorante. Taxi, take us to a good restaurant.

Posso fermarmi qui? May I stop (park) here?

Guidi adagio, in fretta. Drive slowly, quickly.

Attenzione! Look out!

Aspetti qui! Wait here!

Ferma! Stop!

Avanti! Go ahead!

Non importa. It doesn't matter.

Passaggio ostruito. Obstruction.

Passaggio a livello. Level crossing.

una svolta pericolosa. A dangerous corner.

Mi può indicare il garage più vicino, per favore? Can you please tell me where is the nearest garage?

Quanto tempo si ferma qui? How long do we stop here?

Mi porti alla stazione più presto possibile. Take me to the station as quickly as possible.

È questa la strada per . . .? Is this the road for . . .?

LETTURA: Newspaper Extract

Caprera, *agosto*

FRA pochi mesi Clelia Garibaldi compirà [1] i 90 anni. La vecchia signora, che è la sola superstite [2] dei figli che Garibaldi ebbe dalla terza moglie, Francesca Armosino, vive a Caprera, dove è nata, nella casa in cui l'eroe trascorse gli ultimi anni della sua avventurosa esistenza, in compagnia di una nipote [3] e di qualche persona di servizio.[4] Gli altri abitanti del nudo isolotto [5] sono un anziano maresciallo [6] di Marina e un piccolissimo reparto [7] di soldati preposti [8] ai servizi d'onore e di vigilanza. A Caprera, Garibaldi è sepolto [9] accanto [10] alla moglie Francesca e al figlio Manlio: nella medesima [11] tomba riposerà anche Clelia che per sè ha già dettato [12] e fatto incidere [13] l'epigrafe. La sua presenza intanto [14] fa sì che le memorie di Garibaldi, la casa che abitò, gli oggetti tra i quali visse,[15] le piante che coltivò, e alle quali la figlia ha dedicato tutte le sue cure, appaiano [16] al commosso [17] visitatore oggetti ancora caldi di vita. Alla memoria del padre, Clelia, che divise con lui le glorie e le amarezze [18] degli ultimi anni e che imparò [19] da lui il coraggio e lo spirito di sacrificio, ha dedicato l'intera vita. Nel 1947 Clelia Garibaldi ha raccolto in un libro, dettato alla nipote, i ricordi degli anni trascorsi accanto al padre.

A. d. M.

NOTES

[1] will complete.
[2] surviving.
[3] nephew.
[4] of service (to serve, look after him).
[5] naked island, isolated spot, place.
[6] officer of middle rank (a warrant officer).
[7] party, group.
[8] assigned, sent specially.
[9] buried.
[10] near to, beside.
[11] same.
[12] dedicated, solemnly written.
[13] to have cut, engraved.
[14] meanwhile.
[15] lived.
[16] seem, appear (*from* **apparire**).
[17] moved, impressed.
[18] bitternesses.
[19] learnt (*from* **imparare,** to learn).

Giuseppe Garibaldi (1807–82), Italian patriot and general.

TRANSLATION:

Caprera, August (1957).

Within a few months Clelia Garibaldi will complete the 90 years (will be ninety years of age). The old lady, who is the only surviving (one) of the children which Garibaldi had from the (his) third wife, Francesca Armosino, lives at Caprera, where she was born, in the house in which the hero spent the last years of his adventurous existence, in (the) company of a niece and (of) some persons of service (personal servants). The other inhabitants of the naked island (isolated spot) are an old naval warrant officer and a very small party of soldiers assigned to the service of honour and vigilance (security). At Caprera, Garibaldi is buried near the (his) wife Francesca and his son Manlio: in the same tomb will rest also Clelia who herself has (solemnly) written and had engraved the epitaph. Her presence meanwhile makes it as if the memories of Garibaldi, the house he inhabited, the objects among which he lived, the plants he cultivated, and to which (the) his daughter has dedicated all her care(s), appear to the impressed visitor (as) objects still warm with life. To the memory of her father, Clelia, who shared with him the glories and bitternesses of the last years and who learnt from him courage and the spirit of sacrifice, has dedicated her whole life. In 1947 Clelia Garibaldi has assembled (gathered) in a book, dictated to her niece, the recollections of the years passed near her father.

§ 3. *Other Prepositions—Prepositions not followed by* **A, DI,** *or*
DA—*Prepositions Usually Followed by* **A, DI,** *or* **DA**—*Main
Distinction between* **di** *and* **da**—*Music: General Vocabulary
—Musical Terms in Common Use: For Reference*

OTHER PREPOSITIONS: Although the Prepositions given in § 2
are the first which should be mastered, there are others, and, as
they are in fairly common use, they also will have to be learnt
sooner or later. They are given in groups for convenience:

PREPOSITIONS NOT FOLLOWED BY **A, DI,** OR **DA**

avanti, before, in front of,
  ahead
mediante, by means of
oltre, besides, beyond
contro, against, opposite to
eccetto⎱ except, save
salvo ⎰

verso, toward(s)
sopra, on, upon, over
dopo, after
giusta   ⎱ according to
secondo⎰
sotto, under
malgrado, notwithstanding

PREPOSITIONS USUALLY FOLLOWED BY **A, DI,** OR **DA**

By **A:**

fino, till, as far as
in faccia, opposite
circa   ⎱ about
incirca⎰
in mezzo, amidst
dentro, inside
innanzi⎫
dinanzi⎬ before
davanti⎭
attorno, around, all round

in rispetto⎱ concerning
inquanto ⎰
dietro   ⎱ behind
di dietro⎰
accanto, beside
intorno, about
vicino, near
conforme, as
rincontro, against, opposite

By **DI:**

fuori (di), out (of) outside
al di là, on the other side
al di quà, on this side
al di sopra, above
presso, near

alla volta di, in the direction
  of
a causa, by reason of
a ragione, on account of
per, by

a forza di, by dint of
prima, (of time) before
di sotto, underneath
di dentro, within
di fuori, outside
a seconda di, according to
a modo, in the manner

per mezzo, by means
in luogo }
invece } instead
a piè, at the foot
a dispetto, in spite of
in favore, in favour

By **DA:**

lontano da }
lungi da } far from

fin da, from
infuori da, except

The beginner is advised to learn these Prepositions as vocabulary to begin with. *Know the words and their meanings.* As in English, the use of Prepositions in Italian can be subtle and sometimes quite idiomatic. Once their basic meanings are known it is best to learn their use by experience and practice. In speaking or reading, when you come upon a sentence or phrase in which there is a Preposition, make a note of it and then learn it:

Come ha imparato Lei a parlare italiano? How have you learnt to speak Italian?

Ho imparato per mezzo di studio privato. I've learnt by (means of) private study.

Note well the main distinction between **di** and **da.** **Da** is used for *agency, cause, fitness, source:*

Il ragazzo fu punito dal maestro. The boy was punished BY the master.

Essa fu soffocata dal fumo. She was suffocated BY the smoke.

Discende da poveri cittadini. He is descended FROM poor citizens.

un uomo dabbene, an honest man

un uomo da poco, a good-for-nothing man

Tira da suo padre. He takes AFTER his father.

Egli combattè da eroe. He fought LIKE a hero.

Lo trattò da principe. He treated him LIKE a prince.

carta da disegno, drawing-paper

da uomo, like a man
è una cosa da sorprendere, it's a surprising thing
è una cosa da ridere, a thing to laugh at
è una cosa da deplorare, a deplorable thing
non è acqua da bere, it's not water (fit) to drink
un calzolaio da donna, a ladies' shoemaker
un parrucchiere da donna, a ladies' hairdresser

DI is commonly used for the English Preposition *to* before an Infinitive preceded by a part of another Verb, as in *I promise you to come.* **Vi prometto di venire.** Also:

Gli ha detto di non parlare. He told him not to speak.
Non ho paura di dirlo. I'm not afraid to say it.

But, when the first Verb is one of motion, *to* before the Infinitive is translated by **a:**

Vado a vedere Giovanni. I'm going to see John.

No Preposition is used after **potere,** *to be able;* **sapere,** *to know;* **dovere,** *to be obliged to, must,* and some other Verbs of less importance.

Music : General Vocabulary

la musica, music
l'orecchio musicale, musical ear
musicale, musical
il pezzo di musica, piece of music
la musica di strumenti a fiato, music of wind instruments
di strumenti a corda, of stringed instruments
strumenti di percussione, percussion instruments
la musica istrumentale, instrumental music

la musica vocale, vocal music
strumento, strumenti, instrument (-s)
il musicista, musician
il suono, sound
il direttore d'orchestra, conductor
il compositore, composer
il maestro, master, teacher, composer, and sometimes conductor
il musicante, inferior musician
il negozio di musica, music shop
lo spartito, score

FIRST PRINCIPLES **133**

l'accompagnamento, accompaniment
il duetto, il duo, duet
il terzetto, trio
il quartetto, quartet
il quintetto, quintet
il sestetto, sextet
il pianoforte, piano
il pianista, pianist
il violino, violin
il violinista, violinist
il mandolino, mandoline
il mandolinista, mandolinist
il canto, singing

la canzone, song
il bel canto, fine singing
l'aria, melody, air, tune
il coro, chorus, choir
il concerto, concert
il, la cantante, singer
l'opera, opera
l'opera seria, grand opera
l'opera buffa, comic opera
l'opera ballo, opera with ballet
il fischio, whistle, hissing (" the bird ")

Musical Terms in Common Use: For Reference

accelerando, gradually increasing speed
adagio, very slow
affettuoso, with affection, tenderness
agitato, troubled, agitated
allegro, lively, merrily
amoroso, lovingly
andante, moderately, almost slow
animato, with animation
appassionato, passionately
a tempo, in time
ben marcato, well emphasized
calmando, growing quieter and slower
cantabile, graceful singing style
cantando, singing
coda, end, tail, wind-up

con brio, with mettle, vigour
con fuoco, with fire
crescendo, growing, increasing in tone
decrescendo, growing softer
diminuendo, diminishing in tone
da capo, from the beginning (D.C.)
dolce, softly
espressivo, expressively
fine, end
forte, strong, loud
fortissimo, very loud
forzando, sudden force
giocoso, joyfully
giusto, steady, correct (time)
grave, slowest time
grazioso, gracious, graceful
largo, very slow

larghetto, slightly slow
legato, smoothly
leggiero, lightly
lento, slowly
liberamente, freely
ma non troppo, but not too much (as **allegro ma non troppo**)
mancando, fading away
marcato, emphasized, marked
meno forte, meno piano less strong, soft
mezzo, half (as **mezzoforte,** moderately loud)
moderato, moderately
molto, much
morendo, dying out
obbligato, compulsory (for a certain instrument)
pesante, heavily
piano, soft
pianissimo, (pp) very softly
pianississimo, as softly as possible
pizzicato, plucking the strings of the violin
poco adagio, poco forte, a little slow, strong
presto, very quick

rallentando, getting gradually slower
risoluto, vigorously
ritardando, holding back (time)
ritenuto, suddenly slowing time
sfogato, in singing, a light, easy style
sforzato, forcibly
sordina, an aid for muffling an instrument
sostenuto, sustained
spiritoso, spirited
sotto voce, in a soft voice
staccato, crisply
stretto, sharply
subito, suddenly
tempo, time
tenuto, held, sustained
tremolando, trembling, wavering
non troppo, not too much
tutta forza, with full power
vivace, vivo, lively
volta, turn over
tempo di marcia, march time **(di valzer, di minuetto,** etc.)

The words in this list are first-aid and do not represent more than a fraction of the Italian terms used in music. They are not intended for students of music, who should have recourse to a specialized work of reference.

Note: These terms are used internationally—in written western music. The values given are those used by Italian composers. See also page 205.

§ 4. *Other Words with Adverbial Meaning—Emphasis—Place after Past Participle—Cartoon—List of Adverbs: for Reference—Consulate: Passports—***LETTURA: LA TRIENNALE DI MILANO**

See pages 68 and 70.

Among the Italian terms used in music many end in **-ando, -endo** and others end in **-to,** especially **-ato.** The first are called Gerunds and are a part of the verb, the second are also a part of the verb: Past Participles. Many others, such as **con brio,** *with mettle, vigour*; **con amore,** *with love, lovingly*, are adverbial phrases; and others again are both adjectives and adverbs, for example, **piano,** *soft, softly.* The feature common to all those musical terms is that their meaning is always adverbial, even when an adverbial form is not used, as, for example, **adagio** (*very*) *slow*, which is intended to mean (*play* or *sing*) *very slowly.* You will realize later that **andante,** *moderately, almost slow*, is a Present Participle.

Attention is drawn to this to show how flexible Italian can be in making use of other forms to convey an adverbial meaning.

You have already been given some of the commonest adverbs and adverbial phrases and, as these are *always invariable* and of great utility in conversation and reading, some further aspects of adverbs and adverbial phrases are dealt with now. All these words and phrases should first be learnt as vocabulary, as their use is straightforward.

Primieramente, *first(ly)*, and **secondariamente,** *second(ly)*, are the only ordinal numbers which take the adverbial ending **-mente.** But **primo** and **secondo** can be used as adverbs, and for all other ordinal numbers one can usually use the forms given on page 58, or, better, **in terzo luogo,** *in the third place* (*thirdly*); **in quarto luogo,** *in the fourth place* (*fourthly*), and so on.

EMPHASIS: This can be expressed by placing the adverb at the beginning of a sentence or clause: **Felicemente arrivo a tempo,** *happily I arrive in time.* Otherwise, you will remember (page 69) that the adverb is normally placed after the verb:

non parlo bene, *I don't speak well*; **in Parigi si parla molto italiano,** *in Paris much Italian is spoken* (*Italian is spoken very much*).

PLACE AFTER PAST PARTICIPLE: In compound Tenses the adverb usually comes after the Past Participle. Thus:

> **Quel politico ha parlato molto male.** That politician has spoken very badly.
>
> **Abbiamo parlato spesso di Lei.** We have often spoken of you.

In Italian it is preferable to keep the auxiliary and the Past Participle together, whereas in English the adverb often comes between them, as in the last example.

The adverb **bene,** *well,* changes to **benino,** *pretty well, fairly well,* and to **benone,** *very well, fine.* Thus:

> **Come sta Lei?** How are you?
>
> *Answer:* **Benino** *or* **Benone** *as the case may be.*

—Mani in basso!

LIST OF ADVERBS: FOR REFERENCE

Continued from pages 70–72.

Affirmation and Negation

*appunto, exactly

*soprattutto, above all, especially

non . . . già, not yet, not even

*finalmente, finally

*non . . . ancora, not yet

primo, -a di tutto, first of all

*non . . . mica, not at all, certainly not

Doubt

pressochè, almost

Manner

Some adverbs with the ending -oni:

ruzzoloni, rolling

tentoni, gropingly

bocconi, face downwards

tastoni, by feeling

carponi, on all fours

cavalcioni, astride

penzoloni, dangling

ginocchioni, kneeling

And note:

*così, thus

talmente, to such an extent

*come, as, how

comunque, in whatever manner

Quantitative

in più, more, above

eziandio, even

alquanto, some, a little

pure anco, even yet

*moltissimo, very much

nonchè, also, as well as

*pochissimo, very little

Place

*qua, here

quindi, here, therefore

di qua, on this side of

quivi, there

di qui, hence

colà, there

costì, there (near person spoken to)
*__lontano,__ far, distant
*__ivi, vi,__ there

*__vicino,__ neighbouring
entro, within
*__ci,__ there
ognidove, everywhere

Time

*__allora,__ then, now
adesso, now

testè, lately
*__tardi,__ late, slowly

Miscellaneous

a mente
a memoria } by heart
*__di rado,__ seldom
*__d'ordinario,__ usually, as a rule
*__adesso adesso,__ by and by
alla muta, dumbly
*__di fuori,__ outside
ad alta voce, loudly
del tutto, at all
*__a buon mercato,__ cheaply
*__in fretta,__ in haste

*__a caso,__ by chance
in furia, in a great hurry
*__a stento,__ with difficulty
per fortuna, fortunately
*__appena,__ hardly, scarcely
tutt'al più, at the most
apposta, on purpose
con prudenza, prudently
con comodo, leisurely
di sbieco, crookedly
*__di cuore,__ heartily

Those marked * should be memorized first.

Consulate: Passports

il consolato italiano
il consolato inglese
il turista, tourist
il segretario, -a, secretary
il portiere, doorkeeper
il passaporto, passport
il visa
il visto } visa
il documento
i documenti } document(s)
l'imposta
la tassa } tax (stamp)

il banco, desk
i dati, data
il nome, name
l'indirizzo, address
la nazionalità, nationality
la data di partenza, date of leaving
la nascita, birth
il luogo, place
la durata, duration
la permanenza, stay, sojourn

la destinazione, destination
l'ingresso, entrance
l'uscita, exit
aperto, open
chiuso, closed
chiuso dalle . . . alle . . .,
  closed from . . . to . . .

il giorno festivo, public holiday
la festa nazionale, national
  holiday
la sala d'aspetto, waiting-
  room
l'ascensore, lift, elevator

Avrei intenzione di fare un viaggio in Italia. I intend to go
  on a trip to Italy.
Ho un passaporto americano, inglese. I have an American,
  English passport.
Vorrei viaggiare in Italia. I want to go to Italy.
Vorrei fare una vacanza. I wish to have a holiday.
Dov'è il consolato inglese? Where is the English (British)
  Consulate?
Mi bisogna* un visto per Italia? Do I require a visa for Italy?
A che ora si apre il consolato? At what time does the
  Consulate open?
A che ora si chiude? At what time does it close?
Esiste qualche dificoltà per viaggiare? Is there any
  difficulty about travelling?
Voglio dire difficoltà di documenti. I mean difficulties
  about documents.
Assolutamente nessuna. None at all.
Si bisogna* una fede di nascita? Is a birth certificate neces-
  sary?
No, Signore, solamente il passaporto. No sir, only the
  passport.
Eccolo! Here it is.
Quando pensa partire? When are you thinking of leaving?
La prossima settimana. Next week.
Fra tre settimane. Within three weeks.
Devo riempire questo modulo? Must I fill in this form?
Sì, Signore, con tutt'i dati. Yes, sir, with all the information.
Quanto tempo si fermerà in Italia? How long will you
  remain in Italy?

* Or : **Mi abbisogna . . .**

Conto stare tre settimane. I reckon to stay three weeks.

A che luogo si dirige? What part are you making for?

Andiamo a Roma. We are going to Rome?

Solamente a Roma? Only to Rome?

Vorrei andare a Napoli. I should like to go to Naples.

I suoi documenti sono in regola. Your documents are in order.

Mille grazie, signor console. Very many thanks, Mr. Consul.

Prego, Signore. Not at all, sir.

LETTURA

LA TRIENNALE DI MILANO

Esposizione internazionale delle arti decorative ed
International exhibition of modern decorative and
industriali moderne e dell'architettura moderna
industrial arts and of modern architecture

La Triennale di Milano è la più grande esposizione del
The Milan Triennial is the biggest exhibition in the
mondo delle arti decorative ed industriali moderne e
world of modern decorative and industrial art and modern
dell'architettura moderna. La Triennale invita i citta-
architecture. *The Triennial invites (the) citi-*
dini di ogni paese alla sua manifestazione che, dopo un
zens of every country to its exhibition (show) which, after a
felice esperimento più che trentennale, intende portare
happy experience (of) more than thirty years, intends to carry
il suo contributo allo studio e alla soluzione dei problemi
its contribution to the study and solution of artistic
artistici in intimo nesso con quelli tecnici ed economici.
problems intimately linked with those (that are) technical and eco-
La Triennale che ha posto a base del suo programma i
nomic. The Triennial (which) has placed at the base of its pro-
seguenti temi: relazione fra le arti, architettura con-
gramme the following themes: relation between the arts, con-

temporanea, abitazione, produzioni d'arte e «Industrial
temporary architecture, dwelling-house(s), art production and Indus-
Design», presenterà le proprie mostre nel Palazzo dell'-
trial Design, (and) will present the relevant show in the
Arte e nel suo splendido parco.
Palace of Art and in its splendid park.

la mostra, display, show
l'architettura contemporanea, contemporary architecture
la mostra delle sculture all'-aperto, display of sculpture in the open
le mostre dei concorsi per tes-

suti stampati, merletti, ala-bastro, shows of competitions for printed fabrics, lace, alabaster
La Triennale = L'Esposizione triennale, The Triennial Exhibition (of Milan).

§ 5. *Learning from Radio—Italian and Other Programmes: Wave-lengths—The Arts: Vocabulary*—**LA NUOVA RADIO VATICANA**

On page 99 emphasis was placed on the importance of radio broadcasts for practice in listening to spoken Italian, not only in the interests of the self-taught but of all students of the language. It is not difficult to see why. In these broadcasts, which include TV (**la televisione,** not always receivable outside Italy), the listener has a choice of programmes and can hear a great variety of voices. He or she will probably be content to begin with by listening to the News (**le notizie,** also called **Giornale radio**) or Weather Bulletins (**Previsioni del tempo**) until he becomes accustomed to the sounds and rhythms of native speakers from different parts of Italy. Gradually confidence is gained until one can begin to listen to a play, usually found in a programme with the title **Teatro.** Besides, there are many Talks on diverse subjects of interest, each with its own title (as **Oggi in Vetrina,** *To-day in Vetrina,* **Novità librarie,** *News about books,* etc.). These are all useful for the student of the language. It need hardly be said that the Italians do not neglect entertainment, and here is relief in interludes which embrace everything from Grand Opera to the latest jazz.

There is in Italy a three-network system for sound-broadcasting, the object being to cater for the requirements of all types of listeners. And then there is **Radio Vaticana,** Vatican Radio, which is quite separate. The three-network system broadcasts the following programmes:

PROGRAMMA NAZIONALE: from 6.40 a.m. until midnight, a very varied general programme with News, Weather Bulletins, Talks, Music, Occasional Plays, Cabaret, etc.

SECONDO PROGRAMMA: from 9,00 to 23,30 (all programmes use the 24-hour clock), Italian Time (**Ora Europa Centrale**), with News and **Ultime Notizie** at 21,00 o.

TERZO PROGRAMMA: from 19,00 to 23,05 with **il Giornale del Terzo** described as **Note e corrispondenze sui fatti del giorno,** which embraces news plus a commentary, and **Ultime Notizie** at 21,00.

RADIO VATICANO stands in a class by itself, broadcasting in Italian at 14,30 (**Radiogiornale**), **Trasmissione estere** at 15,00 and **Orizzonti cristiani** at 21,15. This station also broadcasts Talks on subjects of interest: on Christian and other philosophy, thoughts, selections from suitable music, films, etc., all of special interest to Roman Catholic listeners. **Radio Vaticana** is highly efficient, and it broadcasts in many languages. See page 145 for wavelengths and kilocycles.

Italian time is normally one hour later than English time. See the *Table of Comparison of Times for European Countries* on page 146.

The British Broadcasting Corporation and Voice of America also broadcast in Italian. Information and wavelengths can be obtained from the B.B.C. or the nearest American Consulate; or from the nearest British Council or the American Information Service.

STAZIONI ITALIANE

Regione	MODULAZIONE DI FREQUENZA				ONDE MEDIE			
	Località	Progr. Nazionale	Secondo Progr.	Terzo Progr.	Località	Progr. Nazionale	Secondo Progr.	Terzo Progr.
		Mc/s	Mc/s	Mc/s		kc/s	kc/s	kc/s
Piemonte	Aosta	93,5	97,6	99,7				
	Candoglia	91,1	93,2	96,7	Aosta		1115	
	Courmayeur	89,3	91,3	93,2	Alessandria		1578	
	Plateau Rosa	94,9	96,9	99,1	Biella		1578	
	Premeno	91,7	96,1	99,1	Cuneo		1578	
	Torino	98,2	92,1	95,6	Torino	656	1448	1367
	Sestriere	93,5	97,6	99,7				
	Villar Perosa	92,9	94,9	96,9				
Lombardia	Bellagio	91,1	93,2	96,7	Como		1578	
	Como	92,3	95,3	98,5	Milano	899	1034	1367
	Milano	90,6	93,7	99,4	Sondrio		1578	
	Monte Creò	87,9	90,1	92,9				
	Monte Penice	94,2	97,4	99,9				
	Sondrio	88,3	90,6	95,2				
	S. Pellegrino	92,5	95,9	99,1				
	Stazzona	89,7	91,9	94,7				
Trentino Alto Adige	Bolzano	95,1	97,1	99,5	Bolzano	656	1484	1367
	Maranza		91,1		Bressanone		1578	
	Paganella	88,6	90,7	92,7	Brunico		1578	
	Plose	90,3	93,5	98,1	Merano		1578	
	Rovereto	91,5	93,7	95,9	Trento	1331	1578	
Veneto	Asiago	92,3	94,5	96,5	Belluno		1578	
	Col Visentin	91,1	93,1	95,5	Cortina		1578	
	Cortina	92,5	94,7	96,7	Venezia	656	1034	1367
	Monte Venda	88,1	89,9	89	Verona	1484	1578	1367
	Pieve di Cadore	93,9	97,7	99,7	Vicenza		1578	
Venezia Giulia e Friuli	Gorizia	89,5	92,3	98,1	Gorizia		1484	
	Tolmezzo	94,4	96,5	99,1	Trieste	818	1115	1578
	Trieste	91,3	93,5	96,3	Udine	1331	1448	
	Udine	95,1	97,1	99,7	Trieste A (autonoma in sloveno)	980		
Liguria	Bordighera	89	91,1	95,9				
	Genova	89,5	94,9	91,9	Genova	1331	1034	1367
	La Spezia	89	93,2	99,4	La Spezia	1484		
	Monte Beigua	94,5	91,5	98,9	Savona		1578	
	Monte Bignone	90,7	93,2	97,5	S. Remo		1448	
	Polcevera	89	91,1	95,9				
Emilia e Romagna	Bologna	90,9	93,9	96,1	Bologna	1331	1115	1367
Toscana	Carrara	91,3	93,5	96,1	Arezzo		1578	
	Garfagnana	89,7	91,7	93,7	Carrara	1578		
	Lunigiana	94,3	96,9	99,1	Firenze	656	1448	1367
	M. Argentario	90,1	92,1	94,3	Livorno			1578
	Monte Serra	88,5	90,5	92,9	Pisa		1115	1578
	S. Cerbone	95,3	97,3	99,3	Siena		1578	
	S. Marcello Pistoiese	94,3	96,9	98,9				
Umbria	Monte Peglia	95,7	97,7	99,7	Perugia	1578		
	Spoleto	88,3	90,3	92,3	Terni	1578		
	Terni	94,9	96,9	98,9				

Regione	MODULAZIONE DI FREQUENZA				ONDE MEDIE			
	Località	Progr. Nazionale	Secondo Progr.	Terzo Progr.	Località	Progr. Nazionale	Secondo Progr.	Terzo Progr.
		Mc/s	Mc/s	Mc/s		kc/s	kc/s	kc/s
Marche	Ascoli Piceno	89,1	91,1	93,1	Ancona	1578	1448	
	Monte Conero	88,3	90,3	92,3	Ascoli P.		1578	
	Monte Nerone	94,7	96,7	98,7				
Lazio	Campo Catino	95,5	97,3	99,5	Roma	1331	845	1367
	Monte Favone	88,9	90,9	92,9				
	Roma	89,7	91,7	93,7				
	Terminillo	90,7	94,5	98,1				
Abruzzi e Molise	C. Imperatore	97,1	95,1	99,1	Aquila	1484	1578	
	Pescara	94,3	96,3	98,3	Campo-basso		1578	
	Sulmona	89,1	91,1	93,1				
	Teramo	87,9	89,9	91,9	Pescara	1331	1034	
					Teramo		1578	
Campania	Golfo Salerno	95,1	97,1	99,1	Avellino		1484	
	Monte Faito	94,1	96,1	98,1	Benevento		1578	
	Monte Vergine	87,9	90,1	92,1	Napoli	656	1034	1367
	Napoli	89,3	91,3	93,3	Salerno		1578	
Puglia	Martina Franca	89,1	91,1	93,1	Bari	1331	1115	1367
	M. Caccia	94,7	96,7	98,7	Brindisi	1578		
	M. Sambuco	89,5	91,5	93,5	Foggia		1578	
	M. S. Angelo	88,3	91,9	93,9	Lecce	1578	1448	
					Taranto	1578		
Basilicata	Lagonegro	89,7	91,7	94,9	Potenza	1484	1578	
	Pomarico	88,7	90,7	92,7				
Calabria	Catanzaro	94,3	96,3	98,3	Catanzaro	1578	1484	
	Crotone	95,9	97,9	99,9	Cosenza	1578	1484	
	Gambarie	95,3	97,3	99,3	Reggio C.	1331		
	Monte Scuro	88,5	90,5	92,5				
	Roseto Capo Spulico	94,5	96,5	98,5				
Sicilia	Alcamo	90,1	92,1	94,3	Agrigento		1578	
	M. Cammarata	95,9	97,9	99,9	Catania	1331	1448	1367
	M. Lauro	94,7	96,7	98,7	Caltanis-setta	566	1448	
	M. Soro	89,9	91,9	93,9				
	Noto	88,5	90,5	92,5	Messina		1115	1367
	Palermo	94,9	96,9	98,9	Palermo	1331	1448	1367
	Trapani	88,5	90,5	92,5				
Sardegna	M. Limbara	88,9	95,3	99,3	Cagliari	1061	1448	
	M. Serpeddì	90,7	92,7	96,3	Sassari		1448	
	P. Badde Ur.	91,3	93,3	97,3				
	Sassari	90,3	92,3	94,5				

la radio, radio in general or radio set.
l'altoparlante, loud speaker.
il programma, programme.
la presa di terra, earth.
la selettività, selectivity.
l'interferenze, interference.
l'evanescenza, fading.
la riproduzione, reproduction.

l'apparecchio (radio), radio set.
l'ascoltatore, listener.
l'antenna, or **l'aereo,** aerial.
la stazione (trasmittente), station.
i disturbi, disturbances, atmospherics.
l'annunciatore, announcer.
la fedeltà, fidelity.
Il segnale orario, time signal.

TELEVISIONE ITALIANA

CANALI

A (0)	-	Mc/s 52,5–59,5
B (1)	-	Mc/s 61–68
C (2)	-	Mc/s 81–88
D (3)	-	Mc/s 174–181
E (3a)	-	Mc/s 182,5189,5
F (3b)	-	Mc/s 191–198
G (4)	-	Mc/s 200–207
H (5)	-	Mc/s 209–216

RADIO VATICANA

(Kc/s. 1529 - m. 196; Kc/s. 6190 - m. 48,47; Kc/s. 9646 - m. 31,10) 14,30 Radiogiornale - 15 Trasmissioni estere - 21,15 Orizzonti cristiani: Notiziario - «Mondo femminile» settimanale della donna - Pensiero della sera.

Nocturne from Italy

23.35–06.40	Daily	Varied Musical Programme; News at 1; 2; 3; 4; 5; 6.	Me 355

Possible changes in times and wavelengths will be notified during transmissions.

13.91 meters = 21.56 Mc/s	31.15 meters = 9.63 Mc/s
16.85 „ = 17.80 „	31.33 „ = 9.57 „
16.88 „ = 17.77 „	41.15 „ = 7.29 „
16.91 „ = 17.74 „	41.24 „ = 7.27 „
19.48 „ = 15.40 „	49.50 „ = 6.06 „
19.58 „ = 15.32 „	49.92 „ = 6.01 „
19.84 „ = 15.12 „	50.34 „ = 5.96 „
25.20 „ = 11.90 „	355 „ = 845 Kc/s
30.90 „ = 9,71 „	

The three National Programmes of the RAI are broadcast on short waves as well as on medium waves—See pages 143–144.

Hours of transmission and the wavelengths.

	Daily	Hour	Wavelength			
1st Programme	Holidays	6.40–11; 12–24.10	approx. 49.50 meters	= 6.06	Mc/sec.
	Weekdays	6.40–9; 11–14.30; 16.20–24.10	31.53 „	= 9.515	„
2nd Programme	Holidays	8.30–12; 13–23.30	41.81 „	= 7.175	„
	Weekdays	9–11; 13–23.30			
3rd Programme	Holidays	16–18.30; 19–24 approx.	75.09 „	= 3.995	„
	Weekdays	19–24 approx.			

F

TABELLA DI COMPARAZIONE DELLE ORE PER I PAESI EUROPEI

		ORA NORMALE	ORA LEGALE
2° FUSO ORARIO	**ORA EUROPA OCCIDENTALE** (H. E. OCC.)	PORTOGALLO INGHILTERRA dal 6-X-1957	
2° FUSO ORARIO	**ORA EUROPA CENTRALE** (H. E. C.)	AUSTRIA - ● BELGIO CECOSLOVACCHIA DANIMARCA - ● FRANCIA GERMANIA - ITALIA ● LUSSEMBURGO NORVEGIA ● PAESI BASSI - POLONIA ● SPAGNA-SVEZIA-SVIZZERA JUGOSLAVIA	INGHILTERRA fino al 5-X-1957

Change of Wavelengths, etc.: Wavelengths and Hours of Transmission are liable to change. The nearest Italian Consulate, or **Radio Italiana, Via del Babuino 9, Roma,** will supply information. A weekly **RADIOCORRIERE,** published by Radio Italiano, gives full details of all programmes. It corresponds to the *Radio Times,* published by the B.B.C.

The Arts: Vocabulary

l'arte (*f.*), art
le arti, the arts
la pittura, painting, paint
il pittore, la pittrice, painter (*m.* & *f.*)
il quadro, picture
l'acquarello, water-colour
a olio, in oil(s)
l'acquaforte (*f.*), etching
l'incisione (*f.*), engraving
lo schizzo, sketch
il disegno, drawing, design
il disegnatore, draughtsman
la scultura, sculpture, (*also* piece of sculpture)
lo scultore, sculptor (*also* carver)

il colore, colour
chiaro, light
oscuro, dark
chiaroscuro, monochrome (*also* light and shade)
il rilievo, relief
il bassorilievo, bas-relief
l'altorilievo, haut-relief
il dilettante, dilettante
il busto, bust
la statua, statue
il gruppo, group
la colonna, column
la torre, tower
il campanile, bell-tower
l'architettura, architecture
l'architetto, architect

Colours: **il colore (-i)**

*verde, green
grigio, grey
*marrone, brown
nero, black
turchino, azzuro, blue
rosso, red

*rosa, rose
bianco, white
giallo, yellow
paonazzo, purple, violet
cupo, sombre, dark
castagno, brown

Churches

la chiesa, church
la cura, priest's house
la basilica, basilica
il duomo, cathedral
la cattedrale, cathedral
la cappella, chapel
l'oratorio, oratory
la pieve, principal parish church
la certosa, Carthusian monastery

il sacrario, sacristy
la chiesuola, small country church
il santuario, sanctuary
il tempio, temple
la collegiata, collegiate church
il monastero, monastery
il convento, convent (or monastery)
la Messa, Mass

What is given above is intended only as first aid for tourist or traveller. Each of the arts has a rich vocabulary of its own. For Music see pages 132–133.

* These adjectives are invariable.

LA NUOVA RADIO VATICANA

La nuova stazione radio vaticana è entrata in funzione domenica mattina (3 Novembre 1957) alle 10,30, con una breve cerimonia che è stata ripresa dalle radio di tutto il continente e dalla TV italiana. Voluto da Pio XII, che fin dall'inizio del suo pontificato ha sempre avuto particolarmente a cuore il problema della radiodiffusione e realizzato in gran parte con le offerte dei fedeli di tutto il mondo, il nuovo centro trasmittente è stato inaugurato dallo stesso Pontefice. Dopo aver pronunciato le brevi parole di una benedizione da Lui composta appositamente per la circostanza, Pio XII si è accostato al tavolo di commutazione situato al centro della sala e, premendo uno dopo l'atro tre pulsanti, ha dato il via ai tre trasmettitori: uno a onde medie della potenza di 120 kW, che irradierà le trasmissioni vaticane in Italia, per un raggio di circa 200 chilometri intorno a Roma; uno a onde corte di 100 kW (offerto dai fedeli di Olanda) e un altro, ancora a onde corte composto di due piccoli trasmettitori di 10 kW l'uno, che serviranno per le emissioni dirette alle altre regioni d'Italia e all'estero.

La singolarità del nuovo complesso, che sorge a Ponte Galeria, sulla via braccianese, a una ventina di chilometri da Roma, in un'area già di proprietà del Collegio germanico e ora dichiarata extraterritoriale, sta nella efficienza e nella funzionalità perfetta delle sue attrezzature; le ha studiate una grande impresa tedesca, che si è valsa dei più moderni risultati della scienza radiofonica per creare un complesso assolutamente inedito. Dall'edificio centrale partono infatti in tre direzioni diverse, tre file di torri a traliccio, di altezza variabile fra i 34 e i 54 metri; e nello spazio intercorrente fra le singole torri si stendono le antenne: ventuno antenne, esattamente (sette per ogni fila) a cortine di dipoli orizzontali, per lunghezze d'onda di m. 49, 41, 31, 25, 19, 17, 13 e 11.

Tale sistema permette di regolare perfettamente la direzione delle emissioni che la radio vaticana prepara in tante lingue diverse per tutti i paesi del mondo, in modo da far giungere a ciascuno la voce del Papa, e della Chiesa.

RADIOCORRIERE

The new Vatican radio station (has) entered into activity on Sunday morning (3rd November 1957) at 10.30 with a brief ceremony which has been taken up by the ratio (stations) of the whole continent and by Italian TV. Desired by Pius XII, who even from the beginning of his pontificate has always had particularly at heart the problem of radiodiffusion and achieved in great part by the offerings of the faithful of the whole world, the new transmitting centre has been inaugurated by the same Pontiff. After having pronounced the brief words of a benediction composed by himself appositely for the circumstance(s), Pius XII sat (down) at the broadcasting table situated in the centre of the hall and, pressing one after another three buttons (switches), has given the way to three transmitters: one of medium wave with (the) power (of) 120 kilowatts, which will send out the Vatican transmissions in Italy on a radius of about 200 kilometres around Rome; one of short wave of 100 kilowatts (offered by the faithful of Holland) and another, also on short wave, consisting of two small transmitters of 10 kilowatts each, which will serve for the direct emissions to the other regions of Italy and abroad.

The singular feature of the new whole (radio station), which rises at Ponte Galeria, on the Via Bracciano, at (some) twenty kilometres from Rome, in an area already property of the German College and now declared extraterritorial, is (lies) in the efficiency and perfect functioning (qualities) of its equipment(s); they have been studied (worked out) by a great German enterprise, which has used the most modern results in radiophonic science to create a whole absolutely new. From the central building indeed (in fact) spread out in three different directions, three rows of network towers of variable heights between 34 and 54 metres; and in the intermediate space between the single towers the antennæ extend: twenty-one antennæ, exactly (seven for each row) with a curtain of horizontal posts, for wavelengths of 49, 41, 31, 25, 19, 17, 13 and 11 metres.

Such a system permits perfect regulation of the direction of the emissions which Vatican radio prepares in so many diverse languages for all the countries of the world, so as to make the Pope's voice and that of the Church reach each one.

RADIOCORRIERE

3–9 November 1957.

BEFORE PROCEEDING TO PART II YOU SHOULD FEEL
FAIRLY CONFIDENT THAT YOU KNOW PART I.

PART II

THE FRAMEWORK OF THE LANGUAGE

> Language is nothing but a set of human habits, the purpose of which is to give expression to thoughts and feelings . . . linguistic intercourse takes place not in isolated words as we see them in dictionaries, but by connected communications, chiefly in the form of sentences.
>
> *Jespersen*

HOW TO STUDY PART II

1. In general, follow the advice given on page 2 for Part I. This applies especially to self-taught learners.

2. Pay particular attention to all Reading Matter. Always read the Italian over once or twice *before looking at the translation* and do you best to make sense of it. Then read the translation *to make sure of the sense*. Next, go over it once very carefully, comparing text and translation, until you know every meaning. Make a list of new words. Finally, read over the Italian text without thinking of the English, so that you are thinking in Italian.

MAKE A POINT OF GOING BACK OVER ALL READING MATTER UNTIL YOU ARE QUITE CONFIDENT THAT YOU CAN READ AND UNDERSTAND IT ALL WITHOUT DIFFICULTY.

3. Take the grammar easily. Do not proceed until you understand. Revise constantly. Memorize all new words and all examples.

4. Never forget that language does not consist of grammar or of isolated words, but of connected communications, chiefly in the form of sentences. These sentences represent *habits of speech*. Reading Matter exemplifies them in a form you can study at your leisure. By listening to Radio, you hear them in rapid action. Speak Italian as often as you can.

GRAMMAR IS THEORY—READING AND RADIO LISTENING PROVIDE THIS THEORY IN PRACTICE.

21-11-64

LESSON V

§ 1. *The Verb—Forms of the Verb—Parts of the Verb Which Must Be Known—Full Conjugation of* **ESSERE**—*Gender of Past Participle—Change of Stressed Syllables in* **ESSERE**—*Laundry: List and Phrases—Radio Broadcasts in Italian—Continuous Reading—Your First Italian Author*—**I PROMESSI SPOSI** **1**

A VERB is a word which tells what *is* or *is done:* the part of speech which expresses a *state* or an *action.* The Italian Verb varies in form for persons, number, and tense. These forms are grouped for convenience in " moods " which indicate the nature of the state or action. Thus:

I. **The Infinitive Mood,** which indicates the action without reference to person or number, as when we say *to be, to have, to sing.* Italian Infinitives end in **-are, -ere,** or **-ire: parlare,** *to speak;* **credere,** *to believe;* **finire,** *to finish.*

II. **The Indicative,** which is the mood of *certainty,* of statement of fact, as when we say *I go, he spoke, she sat down,* etc.

III. **The Subjunctive,** which is the mood of *doubt,* uncertainty, wish: as in, *I may go,* he said *that he might come,* it was not certain *that he would come,* etc.

IV. **The Conditional,** which expresses *an action of a subordinate nature* depending on one of certainty, as when we say: You will progress *if you would study well.*

V. **The Imperative,** which gives a *command. Do that. Stop talking.*

VI. **The Participles,** Present and Past. These might be called " verbal adjectives " because they can have the nature of both Verb and Adjective, as in the English words *loving* (Present Participle) and *loved* (Past Participle). The Italian Present Participle is less frequently employed than

151

is its English equivalent, except when it is used as a real Adjective. Instead, in Italian the Gerund is used.

VII. **The Gerund,** which in intransitive verbs has the function of a Noun, as in " fond of *sleeping* ", and in transitive Verbs retains the functions of a Verb, as in " fond of *playing* games ". Italian Gerunds end in **-ando** for **-are** verbs, **-endo** for **-ere** and **-ire** verbs.

Note: an intransitive Verb is one in which the action stops with the doer, a transitive Verb passes the action from the doer on to some other person or thing. *I sleep* is intransitive. *I play chess*, *play* is transitive.

In addition to this general classification, the Indicative has Tenses (Present, Past, Future, etc.), and so also has the Subjunctive. The uses of the latter will be dealt with more fully on page 282. The learner need not ever attempt to use the Subjunctive at this stage, but he ought to be able to recognize a Subjunctive when he sees one.

PARTS OF THE VERB WHICH MUST BE KNOWN: It is desirable to know the parts of the two Auxiliary Verbs *ESSERE* and **AVERE,** though they need not all be mastered at once. As will be seen, they are used in forming the compound tenses of all Verbs. But the learner *must* know certain parts of *all* Italian Verbs. He must know:

(1) The **Infinitive: COMPRARE,** *to buy*.

(2) The **Present Tense,** Indicative, which has three equivalents in English. Take the verb **COMPRARE,** *to buy*. The Present Tense is given in full on page 173, but in the First Person Singular **compro** means *I buy*, *I am buying*, and *I do buy*; and so on throughout the tense. This must never be forgotten.

(3) The **Imperfect Tense,** Indicative, which is used for a continuous or habitually repeated action in the past. It has also three equivalents in English. For example, the Italian **compravo** can mean *I bought*, *I was buying*, *I used to buy*. This also is important to remember.

(4) The **Past Definite,** Indicative, which represents a past, " definite " action, one that has been completed.

Thus: **comprai** means *I bought, I did buy* (on such and such an occasion).

(5) The **Simple Future Tense,** Indicative, which corresponds to both the English *I shall* or *I will* forms. Thus: **comprerò** = *I shall* or *will buy.*

(6) The **Past Participle,** which in meaning usually corresponds to the English Past Participle ending in *-ed* or *-t.* Thus: **comprato,** *bought.* This is a most useful form in Italian, because, with the aid of an auxiliary Verb, it is used to form compound tenses. For example: **io ho comprato,** *I have bought.*

(7) The *Gerund:* The difference between the Italian Gerund and Past Participle will be more fully explained on page 272. It should meanwhile be noted that in the Verb **AVERE** there is a form **avendo** for the Gerund and one **avente** for our Present Participle. But otherwise the same form is used for both. The Italian Gerund is usually equivalent to the English Present Participle, but the Italian Present Participle is an adjectival form, like the English Present Participle used as an Adjective, as in " *the singing kettle* ". **Essere** has only the Gerund form.

Italian verbs are mostly regular: that is, they form their tenses in accordance with certain fixed rules which can be learnt. There are also " irregular " Verbs which do not follow these rules; they will be dealt with fully later. But there are the two auxiliaries **avere** and *essere* which are irregular and must be mastered as soon as possible, because they are in themselves in common use, and they are used to make compound tenses of other verbs.

Note that in the conjugations of the auxiliary Verbs which follow, the parts to be mastered first are those stated above, with the Gerund, which is nearly always regular. Some of the tenses are already known, and are given again to complete the picture.

IT IS DESIRABLE TO GO OVER ALL THIS PART ABOUT VERBS SEVERAL TIMES UNTIL THE PRINCIPLES ARE KNOWN, AND TO KNOW THE AUXILIARIES THOROUGHLY BEFORE PROCEEDING TO THE GENERAL TREATMENT OF REGULAR VERBS.

The full conjugation of the auxiliary Verbs *ESSERE* and **AVERE** will be given first, because these are the two commonest Verbs in the language, and are used not only in their basic sense but to form compound tenses of all verbs, and secondly, because it is desirable for the learner to have a picture of this full conjugation in his mind, even although some of the tenses given here are hardly ever used in speech and not often met in reading. Only those parts of these verbs that are marked with an asterisk * need be memorized at this stage. First read the conjugation and then glance at page 277, §2.

Infinitive: **ESSERE,** to be
Past Infinitive: **essere stato,** to have been

Participles

Present: **ente,** being (*very seldom used, and then as noun*)
Past: **stato,** been

Gerunds

Present: **essendo,** being
Past: **essendo stato,** having been

Indicative

* Present

SING.

1. **io sono,** I am
2. **tu sei,** thou art
3. **egli è,** he is †

PLUR.

1. **noi siamo,** we are
2. **voi siete,** you are
3. **essi sono,** they are †

* Imperfect

1. **io ero,** I was, used to be
2. **tu eri,** thou wert
3. **egli era,** he was

1. **noi eravamo,** we were
2. **voi eravate,** you were
3. **essi erano,**† they were

* Past Definite

1. **io fui,** I was
2. **tu fosti,** thou wert
3. **egli fu,** he was

1. **noi fummo,** we were
2. **voi foste,** you were
3. **essi furono,**† they were

* Simple Future

1. **io sarò,** I shall, will be
2. **tu sarai,** thou shalt, wilt be
3. **egli sarà,** he will be

1. **noi saremo,** we shall, will be
2. **voi sarete,** you will, shall be
3. **essi saranno,** they will, shall be

* Perfect

1. **io sono stato (a),** I have been
2. **tu sei stato (a),** thou hast been
3. **egli è stato (a),** he has been

1. **noi siamo stati (e),** we have been
2. **voi siete stati (e),** you have been
3. **essi sono stati (e),** they have been

† Do not forget that the Third Person Singular and plural of all tenses are used for *YOU*, with **LEI** and **LORO.**

Pluperfect (1)

1. **io ero stato (a)**, I had been
2. **tu eri stato (a)**, thou hadst been
3. **egli era stato (a)**, he had been

1. **noi eravamo stati (e)**, we had been
2. **voi eravate stati (e)**, you had been
3. **essi *e*rano stati (e)**, they had been

Pluperfect (2)

1. **io fui stato (a)**
2. **tu fosti stato (a)**
3. **egli fu stato (a)**
1. **noi fummo stati (e)**
2. **voi foste stati (e)**
3. **essi *fu*rono stati (e)**

} I had been, etc., as pluperfect (1)

Future Anterior

1. **io sarò stato (a)**
2. **tu sarai stato (a)**
3. **egli sarà stato (a)**
1. **noi saremo stati (e)**
2. **voi sarete stati (e)**
3. **essi saranno stati (e)**

} I shall, will have been, etc.

Subjunctive

Present

1. **Che io s*i*a**
2. „ **tu s*i*a**
3. „ **egli s*i*a**
1. **Che noi siamo**
2. „ **voi siate**
3. „ **essi s*i*ano**

} that I be, may be, etc.

Perfect

1. **Che io s*i*a stato (a)**
2. „ **tu s*i*a stato (a)**
3. „ **egli s*i*a stato (a)**
1. **Che noi siamo stati (e)**
2. „ **voi siate stati (e)**
3. „ **essi s*i*ano stati (e)**

} That I have been, etc.

Imperfect

1. **Che io fossi**
2. „ **tu fossi**
3. „ **egli fosse**
1. **Che noi fossimo**
2. „ **voi foste**
3. „ **essi fossero**

} that I were, might be, etc.

Pluperfect

1. **Che io fossi stato (a)**
2. „ **tu fossi stato (a)**
3. „ **egli fosse stato (a)**
1. **Che noi fossimo stati (e)**
2. „ **voi foste stati (e)**
3. „ **essi fossero stati (e)**

} That I had been etc.,

Note that in places one vowel is printed in contrasting type to indicate the change of stress to that syllable.

Conditional

	Present			Past	
1.	io sarei	⎫	1.	io sarei stato (a)	⎫
2.	tu saresti	⎬ that I should, would be, etc.	2.	tu saresti stato (a)	
3.	egli sarebbe	⎪	3.	egli sarebbe stato (a)	That I
					should
1.	noi saremmo	⎪	1.	noi saremmo stati (e)	⎬ have
2.	voi sareste	⎪	2.	voi sareste stati (e)	been,
3.	essi sarebbero *	⎭	3.	essi sarebbero stati (e)	etc.

Imperative

	* Present			Future †	
1.	none	⎫	1.	none	⎫
2.	sii tu,* be thou		2.	sarai tu, be thou	
3.	sia colui, let him be		3.	sarà colui, let him be	
		⎬ now			⎬ in the future
1.	siamo noi, let us be		1.	saremo noi, let us be	
2.	siate voi, be (ye, you)		2.	sarete voi, be (ye, you)	
3.	siano essi, let them be	⎭	3.	saranno essi, let them be	⎭

The Subjunctive need not be memorized now, but should be recognizable. Excepting those tenses marked with the asterisk, the table of **essere** is given for reference. The tenses marked with the asterisk must be known—now.

GENDER OF PAST PARTICIPLE: It will be seen that the masculine and feminine forms of the Past Participle are given with **essere**. In this verb the Past Participle agrees in gender and number with the subject.

CHANGE OF STRESSED SYLLABLES in **ESSERE:** You have noted that one vowel in certain parts of the verb **essere** is printed in contrasting type. This is to indicate that the stress is moved to that syllable, and does not follow the general rules given on page 4 for stress. Note that the stress is usually changed in the following important parts:

* Note that in places one vowel is printed in contrasting type to indicate the stress.

† This form is seldom used.

Third Person Plural of the Imperfect: **erano**

   ,,   ,,   ,,   Past Definite: **furono**

   ,,   ,,   ,,   Present Subjunctive: **siano**

   ,,   ,,   ,,   Conditional: **sarebbero** ·

The Third Person Plural of Present Subjunctive: **siano**.

The Imperative is similar to the Present Subjunctive, but has no First Person.

Laundry: List and Phrases

la lista del bucato, laundry list

il bucato, washing, bleaching

la biancheria, washing, laundry

signori, gentlemen

donne, ladies

la biancheria da donne, da signori, ladies' laundry

la camicia (-ie), shirt (-s)

i colletti, collars

i calzini da uomo, socks

i fazzoletti, handkerchiefs

le mutande, pants

i calzoni corti, short pants

le calze da donna, lady's stockings

la maglia (-ie), underwear

la camicia da notte, night-dress

i pigiami, pyjamas

un pigiama, (one) pair of pyjamas

l'abito (-i), dress (-es)

la camicetta (-e), shirt-blouse

la sottana, petticoat

la biancheria da bambino, babies' washing

il lavandaio (la -a), laundry-man, -woman

in ordine, in order, ready for wear

la pulitura, cleaning

a secco, dry

la nota, note

la roba, clothes, things

gli asciugamani, towels

pronto per . . ., ready (in time) for . . .

staccato, detached (of a button)

Facciamo la lista del bucato. Let's make the laundry list.

Viene oggi il lavandaio? Does the laundryman come to-day?

È il suo giorno. It's his day.

Lei non ha delle liste del bucato? You haven't any printed (laundry) lists?

Ecco una lista della mia biancheria sudicia. Here's a list of my soiled linen.

Esamini la lista subito.   Check the list immediately.

Voglio sapere che non ci sono sbagli.   I want to know that there are no mistakes.

Tutto va bene.   Non va bene.   It's all right.   It's not right.

Vorrei far lavare questa roba.   I want these things (clothes) washed.

Voglio far stirare tutto.   I want everything ironed.

Vorrei far pulire a secco . . .   I want . . . dry cleaned.

Ne ho bisogno il più presto possibile.   I need it as quickly as possible.

Quando l'avrò di ritorno?   When shall I have it back?

Attaccatemi questi bottoni, per piacere.   Would you kindly sew on these buttons.

Questi bottoni si sono staccati.   These buttons have come loose.

Questo non è mio.   This isn't mine.

Mancano . . .   There are missing . . .

Vorrei verificare la lista.   I want to check the list.

Mi rammendi queste calze, per favore.   Would you please mend these stockings.

Questa roba va in bucato.   These things are going to be washed.

RADIO BROADCASTS IN ITALIAN: You have already begun to listen to Radio Broadcasts in Italian, and should by now be quite accustomed to the sounds of the language. The more you listen, the more you concentrate, the more you should understand. From now onwards you should not let a day pass without listening for at least a quarter of an hour. On pages 142–145 you will find a list of Radio Stations. Every station broadcasts News (**le notizie**) and a weather bulletin. Always listen to News. When you have gained confidence, try listening to a play. At first you may not catch very much. It will come with practice.

CONTINUOUS READING: Experience shows that continuous reading of a suitable work by a good writer is one of the best forms of practice for learners of a foreign language. But learners require considerable help, especially in the first stage, and no help can be better than an interlinear literal translation, which explains each word as you go along. The particular advantage of continuous reading is that not only does the learner become accustomed to a good, pure style in the language he is learning, and takes in innumerable new words and turns of phrase, but he is also held by the story, which, if good enough, never loses interest. The self-taught student is advised to proceed as follows:

Method: First read the Italian text aloud slowly, disregarding the translation, and make the best you can of the general sense.

Then read over the Italian more quickly—at least twice.

Now read over the translation to get as much understanding as possible from it. Do this once, and then go over the whole piece word for word, comparing the Italian original with the literal translation, until every word and sentence is understood.

Finally, read the Italian aloud again, *thinking in the* language. If necessary, do this a few times, referring, wherever you may be doubtful of meaning, to the translation. You should in the end feel that you can follow the author almost as well as if he were writing in your own language.

FROM NOW ONWARDS THIS MUST BE, WITH SITUATION MATERIAL AND RADIO, YOUR PRACTICE IN THE LANGUAGE.

YOUR FIRST ITALIAN AUTHOR: For this highly important purpose an important Italian novel has been chosen: **I PROMESSI SPOSI,** by Alessandro Manzoni. (**Sposo** is *bride* or *betrothed*, **promesso** is *promised*, hence the title can be translated as THE BETROTHED.) The finally corrected Italian edition was published 1840–42. You should know that, before the appearance of this great novel, the various dialects spoken in Italy were much stronger than they now are, and Manzoni, in writing **I Promessi Sposi,** set himself the task of writing a pure style which would be accepted all over Italy. In this he succeeded. Every generation of Italians reads this book, which is a model of how such a book should be written. You will not find it nearly so difficult as you may have imagined, but take it slowly and carefully in the way recommended above. An excellent free translation by Archibald Colquhoun—easily the best in English —is published in Everyman's Library. It is always good to compare such a translation with the literal version necessary here. And, when you have finished the extracts given in these Lessons, you can use the Colquhoun translation to help you to finish reading the Italian in the edition published by Le Monnier, Florence, with notes. This is the text used here. Chapter I is omitted as much too difficult. The story begins with Chapter II.

I **I PROMESSI SPOSI**

Si racconta che il Principe di Condé dormì profonda-
It is related that the Prince of Condé slept deeply
mente la notte avanti la giornata di Rocroi;[1] **ma, in**
(*on*) *the night before the morning of Rocroi: but, in*
primo luogo, era molto affaticato; secondariamente aveva
(*the*) *first place, he was very fatigued; secondly he had already*
già date tutte le disposizioni necessarie, e stabilito ciò
given (*made*) *all the arrangements necessary, and settled that*
che dovesse fare, la mattina. Don[2] **Abbondio in vece**
which must be done (*next*) *morning. Don Abbondio instead did*
non sapeva altro ancora se non che l'indomani sarebbe
not yet know otherwise but that the next day would be
giorno di battaglia; quindi una gran parte della notte fu
(*the*) *day of battle; hence a great part of the night was*
spesa in consulte angosciose. Non far caso dell'intima-
spent in anxious consultations. Not to heed the rascally intima-
zione ribalda, nè delle minacce, e fare il matrimonio, era
tion, or the menaces, and go through with
un partito, che non volle neppur mettere in deliberazione.
the marriage, was a course he would not even wish to consider.
Confidare a Renzo l'occurrente, e cercar con lui qualche
To confide in Renzo what happened, and to seek with him some
mezzo . . . Dio liberi! " Non si lasci scappar parola . . .
means . . . God free us! " Do not let a word escape . . .
altrimenti . . . ehm!" aveva detto un di que' bravi; e,
otherwise . . . h'm!" had said one of those bravos, and,
al sentirsi rimbombar quell' . . . ehm! nella mente, don
on hearing resound that h'm! in his mind, Don
Abbondio, non che pensare a trasgredire una tal legge, si
Abbondio, not that he would think of disobeying such a law,

pentiva anche dell'aver ciarlato con Perpetua. Fuggire?
regretted also having chatted with Perpetua. To flee?
Dove? E poi! Quant'impicci, e quanti conti da rendere!
Where? And then? How many embarrassments, and how many
A ogni partito che rifutava, il pover'uomo si rivoltava nel
accounts to render! At every step that he rejected, the poor man
letto. Quello che, per ogni verso, gli parve il meglio o
turned in the (his) bed. That which, at every step, seemed to him
il men male, fu di guadagnar tempo, menando Renzo per
best or the least bad, was to gain time, leading Renzo (away) by
le lunghe. Si ramentò a proposito, che mancavan pochi
the reins. He remembered apropos, that there lacked few days to
giorni al tempo proibito per le nozze; — e, se posso tenere,
the time forbidden for marriages; — and, if it were possible to hold,
a bada, per questi pochi giorni, quel ragazzone, ho poi due
waiting, for those few days, that big boy, I have then two
mesi di respiro; e, in due mesi, può nascer di gran cose.
months' respite; and, in two months, great things can be born.
— Ruminò pretesti da metter in campo; e, benchè gli
— He turned over pretexts to put in action; and, although they
paressero un po' leggieri, pur s'andava rassicurando col
might seem a little flimsy, still he went on reassuring himself with
pensiero che la sua autorità gli avrebbe fatti parer di
the thought that his authority would have made up the
giusto peso, e che la sua antica esperienza gli darebbe
just weight, and that his old (long) experience would give him
gran vantaggio sur un giovanetto ignorante. — Vedremo,
a great advantage over an ignorant youth. — We'll see,
— diceva tra sè: — egli pensa alla morosa; ma io penso
— he said to himself, — he's thinking of his loved one; but I'm
alla pelle: il più interessato son io, lasciando stare che
thinking of my skin: the most interested am I, allowing it to be that
sono il più accorto. Figliuol caro, se tu ti senti il bruciore
I'm the shrewder. (My) dear son, if you feel the burning
addosso, non so che dire; ma io non voglio andare di
on the back, I don't know what to say; but I don't want to walk
mezzo.[3]
in the middle (of it).

NOTES

[1] The battle of Rocroi, at which the Prince of Condé defeated the Spaniards in the Ardennes on 19th May 1643.

[2] Don, a title given to priests in Tuscany and to men of good family in Rome, Milan, and elsewhere in Italy.

[3] The last sentence might be freely translated: *My dear son, if you feel all hot about it, I can't say anything, but I don't want to be mixed up in it.* The Italian is rather racy, as is the Italian in much of the dialogue in this novel.

FREE TRANSLATION: In the above the translation is kept as closely as possible to the words of the original Italian. Naturally, such a literal translation cannot be expected to pass as literary English, which necessarily must be much freer. Here is the same passage rendered freely, so that you may see what can be legitimately made of the literal rending:

It is related that the Prince of Condé slept deeply on the night before the morning of the battle of Rocroi: but, in the first place he was very tired; secondly, he had already made all the necessary arrangements and settled what must be done next morning. All Don Abbondio knew, on the other hand, was that next day would be the day of battle; hence a great part of the night was spent in agonizing consultations. Not to pay attention to the rascally intimation or the menaces, and go through with the marriage, was a course he did not want even to contemplate. To confide in Renzo what happened, and to seek with him some way out . . . God forbid! " Don't let a word get out . . . otherwise . . . h'm," one of those roughs had said, and, on hearing that h'm resound in his mind, Don Abbondio, not that he would think of disobeying such a law, also regretted having chatted with Perpetua. To flee? Where to? And then what? How many difficulties, and how many accounts to clear up? At every solution that he rejected, the poor man turned over in his bed. What at each step seemed best to him, or the least evil, was to gain time, putting Renzo off the track. Apropos he remembered that in a few days would come the time when marriages were forbidden; and, if it were possible, to hold back that big boy for those few days, I then have two months' respite; and in two months great things can happen.— He turned over pretexts that could be put in action; and, although they might seem a little flimsy, still he went on reassuring himself with the thought that his authority would make up the balance and that his long experience would give him a great advantage over an ignorant youth. We'll see, he said to himself: he's thinking of his lady love, but I'm thinking of my skin. I'm the most interested party, admitting that I'm the shrewder. My dear son, if you feel all hot about it, I can't say anything, but I don't want to get mixed up in it.

Note: All the interlinear translations in this book are literal and not literary or free. You will make your own free translations.

§ 2. *Full Conjugation of* **AVERE**—*Change of Stressed Syllables in* **avere**—*Weights and Measures: For Reference—Sight Seeing* —**I Promessi Sposi 2**

FULL CONJUGATION OF THE AUXILIARY VERB **AVERE**

Infinitive: **AVERE,** to have
Past Infinitive: **avere avuto,** to have had

Participles

Present: **avente,** having (*seldom used*)
Past: **avuto,** had

Gerunds

Present: **avendo,** having
Past: **avendo avuto,** having had

Indicative

* Present

io **ho,** I have
tu **hai,** thou hast
egli **ha,** he has

noi **abbiamo,** we have
voi **avete,** you have
essi **hanno,** they have

* Perfect

io **ho avuto**
tu **hai avuto**
egli **ha avuto** ⎫
noi **abbiamo avuto** ⎬ I have had, etc.
voi **avete avuto**
essi **hanno avuto** ⎭

* Imperfect

io **avevo**
tu **avevi**
egli **aveva** ⎫ I had, was having,
noi **avevamo** ⎬ used to have,
voi **avevate** ⎭ etc.
essi **avevano**

Pluperfect (1)

io **avevo avuto**
tu **avevi avuto**
egli **aveva avuto** ⎫ I had had,
noi **avevamo avuto** ⎬ etc.
voi **avevate avuto**
essi **avevano avuto** ⎭

* Past Definite

io **ebbi**
tu **avesti**
egli **ebbe** ⎬ I had, etc.
noi **avemmo**
voi **aveste**
essi **ebbero**

Pluperfect (2)

io **ebbi avuto**
tu **avesti avuto**
egli **ebbe avuto** ⎫ I had had,
noi **avemmo avuto** ⎬ etc.
voi **aveste avuto**
essi **ebbero avuto** ⎭

* Simple Future

io **avrò**
tu **avrai**
egli **avrà** ⎫ I shall, will have,
noi **avremo** ⎬ etc.
voi **avrete**
essi **avranno** ⎭

Future Anterior

io **avrò avuto**
tu **avrai avuto**
egli **avrà avuto** ⎫ I shall, will
noi **avremo avuto** ⎬ have had,
voi **avrete avuto** ⎭ etc.
essi **avranno avuto**

Subjunctive

Present
Che io *a*bbia ⎤
„ tu *a*bbia ⎥
„ egli *a*bbia ⎥ that I may
Che noi abbiamo ⎱ have, etc.
„ voi abbiate ⎥
„ essi *a*bbiano ⎦

Perfect
Che io *a*bbia avuto ⎤
„ tu *a*bbia avuto ⎥ that I
„ egli *a*bbia avuto ⎥ may
Che noi abbiamo avuto ⎱ have
„ voi abbiate avuto ⎥ had,
„ essi *a*bbiano avuto ⎦ etc.

Imperfect
Che io av*e*ssi ⎤
„ tu av*e*ssi ⎥ that I had,
„ egli av*e*sse ⎥ was hav-
Che noi av*e*ssimo ⎱ ing, used
„ voi av*e*ste ⎥ to have,
„ essi av*e*ssero ⎦ etc.

Pluperfect
Che io av*e*ssi avuto ⎤
„ tu av*e*ssi avuto ⎥ that I
„ egli av*e*sse avuto ⎥ might
Che noi av*e*ssimo ⎱ have
avuto ⎥ had,
„ voi av*e*ste avuto ⎥ etc.
„ essi av*e*ssero
avuto ⎦

Conditional

Present
io avr*e*i ⎤
tu avr*e*sti ⎥
egli avr*e*bbe ⎥ that I should,
noi avr*e*mmo ⎱ would have,
voi avr*e*ste ⎥ etc.
essi avr*e*bbero ⎦

Past
io avr*e*i avuto ⎤
tu avr*e*sti avuto ⎥ that I
egli avr*e*bbe avuto ⎥ should,
noi avr*e*mmo avuto ⎱ would
voi avr*e*ste avuto ⎥ have
essi avr*e*bbero ⎥ had,
avuto ⎦ etc.

Imperative

Present
ňone ⎤
abbi tu ⎥ have, have thou,
abbia colui ⎱ let him have,
abbiamo noi ⎥ etc.
abbiate voi ⎥
abbiano essi ⎦

Future †
none ⎤
avrai tu ⎥
avrà colui ⎱ have, etc. (in the
avremo noi ⎥ future)
avrete voi ⎥
avranno essi ⎦

CHANGE OF STRESSED SYLLABLES IN **AVERE:** The stress changes in syllables of the same parts as those of **essere,** for which see page 154.

WEIGHTS AND MEASURES: FOR REFERENCE: The decimal system is used throughout Italy (for money see page 55), but

Italic indicates the stressed syllable.
† This form is rarely used.

in many places **la libbra,** an old measure for a pound of 12 ounces, is still used.

Weights

il grammo⎫
il gramma⎭ (= 0·03527 oz.), the gram = 0·001 kilogram

l'ettogrammo (= 3½ oz. approx.), the hectogram = 0·1 kilogram

il chilogrammo (= 2·204 lb. approx.), the kilogram = 1,000 grams

la tonnellata (= 2,204 lb.), the ton = 1,000 kilograms

Approximate Italian Equivalents for English Weights

1 oz. = 28 grams
2 „ = 56   „
3 „ = 85   „
4 „ = 113   „
1 lb. = 454 grams or nearly ½ kilogram

The Italian quintal (**un quintale**) = 100 kilograms = 1 cwt. 3 qrs. 20 lb.

Note that **il grammo** and **il gramma** are used.

Length

1 metro = 1 metre = 39·09361 inches
1,000 metri = 1 **chilometro** = 0·6 of a mile = just over ½ or ⅝
1 English yard = **0·91 metro**

Liquid

		Equivalent to:
un litro = 1 litre		= 1¾ pints
5 litri = 5 litres		= 1 gallon and 0·80 of a pint
10 litri = 1 decalitro		= 2 gallons and 1½ pints
20 litri = 2 decalitri		= 4 gallons and 3·2 pints
30 litri = 3 decalitri		= 6 gallons and 4·79 pints
40 litri = 4 decalitri		= 8 gallons and 6·3 pints
50 litri = 5 decalitri or ½ ettolitro		= 10 gallons + 7·99 pints

Area

Unit is **il metro quadrato,** *the square metre.*

10,000 square metres = **unettaro,** one hectare = 2·471 acres.

Sight Seeing

la gita, trip, excursion
il museo, museum
la galleria d'arte, art gallery
la cattedrale }
il duomo } cathedral
la chiesa, church
la guida, guide, guide book
Attenzione ai borsaiuoli!
    Beware of pickpockets!
la entrata, l'ingresso, en-
    trance
l'uscita, exit
l'università, university
il museo di belle arti, mu-
    seum of fine arts
il museo storico, museum of
    history
il museo di storia naturale,
    natural history
l'orto botanico, botanical gar-
    den

il giardino zoologico, zoo
il municipio, Town Hall
la Città del Vaticano, Vatican
    City
libero, free
l'obelisco, obelisk
la fontana, fountain
l'arco, arch
il mosaico, mosaic
il portico, portico
la scultura, sculpture
la statua, statue
il tempio, temple
la facciata, façade
l'opera di, the work of . . .
la piazza, place, square, circus
lo stile, style
stile di . . ., style of . . .
la cupola, cupola
la porta, door

    Great Periods: **il Trecento,** the fourteenth century
    il Quattrocento, the fifteenth century
    il Cinquecento, the sixteenth century

The word **mille** is omitted. **Mille trecento, quattrocento, cinquecento** would be 1300 (A.D.), 1400, 1500. In these centuries Italian art flourished. Note the capital letters. The adjectival ending is **-esco,** so **trecentesco (-eschi),** *of the fourteenth century,* etc.

Desiderei una guida che parla inglese. I should like a guide who speaks English.

Quanto costa al giorno una guida? How much does a guide cost per day?

Vorrei vedere . . . I'd like to see . . .

Desiderei una guida di questo luogo. I'd like a guide (guide book) for this place.

Vorrei vedere le cose notevoli, di maggiore interesse.
I want to see noteworthy things, of major interest.

Che c'è ancora di interessante? Is there anything more of interest?

Si fermi qui un poco. Stop here for a little.

Desidero fare qualche fotografia. I want to take some photographs.

Dove si può mangiare? Where can we eat?

Si può trovare da bere? Can we find something to drink?

Non voglio vedere più, sono stanco. I don't want to see any more, I'm tired.

Prenderò un taxi ad ora per vedere la città. I'll take a taxi by the hour to see the city.

Quanto all'ora? How much (is it) an hour?

Desidero vedere il corso e le vie. I want to see the main street and the avenues.

il migliori negozi. il fiume. The best shops. The river.

Chi ha costruito questa basilica? Who built this basilica?

È opera di . . . It's the work of . . .

Dov'è il punto d'ingresso a . . . Where's the entrance to . . .

Di che stile è il duomo? What style is the cathedral?

È di stile rinascimento, trecentesco. It's renaissance style, fourteenth century.

Che sono quelle statue? What are those statues?

Si può entrare? Can one go in?

La entrata è libera. Entrance is free.

Questo si chiama la Porta Santa. This is called the Porta Santa (Holy Door).

Si può entrare tutti i giorni tranne le domeniche. One can go in every day except on Sundays.

2   **I PROMESSI SPOSI**

— **Fermato così un poco l'animo a una deliberazione,**
— *Stopped thus a little his mind at a resolution,*[1]
potè finalmente chiuder occhio: ma che sonno! che sogni!
he was able finally to close eye: but what sleep! what dreams!

Bravi, don Rodrigo, Renzo, viottole, rupi, fughe,
Bravos, Don Rodrigo, Renzo, narrow paths, cliffs, flights,
inseguimenti, grida, schioppettate.
pursuits, shouts, gun-shots.

    Il primo svegliarsi, dopo una sciagura, e in un im-
(On) first waking, after a setback, and in an em-
piccio, è un momento molto amaro. La mente, appena
barrassment, is a moment of great bitterness. The mind, hardly
risentita, ricorre all'idee abituali della vita tranquilla
feeling again, returns to habitual ideas of (the) previous
antecedente; ma il pensiero del nuovo stato di cose le si
quiet life; but the thought of the new state of affairs
affaccia subito sgarbatamente; e il dispiacere ne è più
breaks in at once rudely; and the displeasure of it is more
vivo in quel paragone istantaneo. Assaporato dolorosa-
alive in that sudden comparison. (Having) tasted pain-
mente questo momento, don Abbondio ricapitolò subito i
fully that moment, Don Abbondio quickly went over
suoi disegni della notte, si confermò in essi, li ordinò
his intentions of the night, confirmed (himself) (in) them, ordered
meglio, s'alzò, e stette aspettando Renzo con timore e, ad
them better, got up, and was waiting for Renzo with fear and,
un tempo, con impazienza.
at the same time, with impatience.

    Lorenzo o, come dicevan tutti, Renzo non si fece molto
Lorenzo or, as all said, Renzo did not make him wait
aspettare. Appena gli parve ora di poter, senza indis-
(for) long. Hardly (to him) it appeared now to be able, without
crezione, presentarsi al curato, v'andò, con la lieta furia
imprudence, to present himself to the priest, he went,
d'un uomo di vent'anni, che deve in quel giorno sposare
with the happy haste of a man of twenty years, who must that
quella che ama. Era, fin dall'adolescenza, rimasto privo
day marry whom he loves. He was, at the end of (his) youth, left
de' parenti, ed esercitava la professione di filatore di seta,
without parents, and practised the profession of weaver of silk,
ereditaria, per dir così, nella sua famiglia; professione,
hereditary, so to say, in his family; (a) profession (trade)

negli anni indietro, assai lucrosa; allora già in decadenza,
in years gone by, quite lucrative; now already in decline,
ma non però a segno che un abile operaio non potesse
but not however so far that a clever worker could not
cavarne di che vivere onestamente. Il lavoro andava di
extract wherewithal to live honestly. The work went from
giorno in giorno scemando; ma l'emigrazione continua
day to day dwindling; but continual emigration of workers, attracted
de' lavoranti, attirati negli stati vicini da promesse, da
in(to) neighbouring states by promises, by privileges
privilegi e da grosse paghe, faceva sì che non ne mancasse
and high payments, made it that there did not then lack
ancora a quelli che rimanevono in paesi. Oltre di questo,
for those who remained in (the) locality. Apart from this,
possedeva Renzo un poderetto che faceva lavorare e
Renzo owned a patch of land which he got worked and
lavorava egli stesso, quando il filatoio stava fermo; di
worked himself, when the weaving was stopped; so
modo che, per la sua condizione, poteva dirsi agiato. E
that, for his condition (in life), he could call himself comfortably off.
quantunque quell'annata fosse ancor più scarsa delle
And although that year was still leaner than the
antecedenti, e già si cominciasse a provare una vera
ones before, and already (one) began to feel a real
carestia, pure il nostro giovine, che, da quando aveva
dearth, anyhow our young man, who, from when he had
messi gli occhi addosso a Lucia, era divenuto massaio, si
put (set) his eyes on Lucia, had become (a) householder, (and) found
trovava provvisto bastantemente, e non aveva a contrastar
himself well enough provided (for), and did not have to fight
con la fame.
against hunger.

NOTE
[1] His mind more or less made up on a decision.

§ 3. *Regular Verbs: Some General Principles—Table of Inflections of Regular Verbs—Verbs in* **-are**—*Model Verb:* **comprare,** *to buy—Orthographic Changes in* **-are** *Verbs—Changes in Stressed Syllable in Verbs—Travel by Air—***I Promessi Sposi 3**

Before proceeding to learn the forms for Regular Verbs, as set out in " Models " for memorizing, there are certain principles worth noting, if only because they are of considerable help in mastering the important parts of all verbs that are not irregular. We begin with the Infinitive, which always ends in **-ARE, -ERE,** or **-IRE.** When these endings are dropped from a Verb the part which remains is called the stem. Thus:

I. **COMPR-** is the stem of **COMPRARE,** *to buy*
   VEND- is the stem of **VENDERE,** *to sell*
   FIN- is the stem of **FINIRE,** *to finish*

It is to this stem that endings are added to form *all* parts of regular and irregular Verbs. For example, the Present Tense Indicative is formed by adding the following endings to the stem:

II.   *In the Singular*

Verbs in	First Person	Second Person	Third Person
-ARE	**-O**	**-I**	**-A**
-ERE	**-O**	**-I**	**-E**
-IRE * (*a*)	**-O**	**-I**	**-E**
-IRE * (*b*)	**-iscO**	**-iscI**	**-iscE**

In the Plural

Verbs in	First Person	Second Person	Third Person
-ARE	**-IAMO**	**-ATE**	**-ANO**
-ERE	**-IAMO**	**-ETE**	**-ONO**
-IRE * (*a*)	**-IAMO**	**-ITE**	**-ONO**
-IRE * (*b*)	**-IAMO**	**-ITE**	**-iscONO**

* Note that **-IRE** verbs have either one or the other of two forms, one of which introduces **-isc-** before the ending.

Now turn to page 173 and you will see the forms in full for the Present Tense of **COMPRARE: compro, compri, compra, compriamo, comprate, comprano.**

III. In the same way the Imperfect Tense Indicative of *all* Regular Verbs is made by adding to the stem:

-VO First Person Singular **-VAMO** First Person Plural
-VI Second Person Singular **-VATE** Second Person Plural
-VA Third Person Singular **-VANO** Third Person Plural

IV. The Past Definitive Indicative is formed by adding to the stem:

-ARE verbs:

-AI -ASTI Ò- -AMMO -ASTE -*A*RONO, stressed **a**

-ERE verbs:

-EI -ESTI -È -EMMO -ESTI -*E*RONO, ,,   **e**

-IRE verbs:

-*II* -ISTI -Ì -IMMO -ISTE -*I*RONO, ,,   **i**

V. The Simple Future is formed by adding to the stem:
-ARE verbs:

-ERÒ -ERAI -ERÀ -EREMO -ERETE -ERANNO

Note that the ending is **-erò,** etc., and not **-arò,** etc.

-ERE verbs: the same endings as for **-ARE** verbs.

-IRE verbs:

-IRÒ -IRAI -IRÀ -IRAMO -IRATE -IRANNO

VI. The Conditional is formed similarly with the endings **-erEI** for **-ARE** and **-ERE** verbs, and **irEI** for **-IRE** verbs. In the latter **-erEI** changes to **-irEI,** etc. Otherwise the Conditional endings are:

-EI   -ESTI -EBBE -EMMO -ESTE -*E*BBERO

Thus: **comprerei,** etc.; **capire,** *to understand*; **capirò,** *I shall understand*; **capirei,** *I should, would understand*, etc.

VII. The polite form of the Imperative—the one that is most useful for the learner—always has the same ending as the Third

TABLE OF INFLECTIONS OF VERBS

Verbs in -ARE (stem compr-)

Present	Imperfect	Past Definite	Future	Conditional	Imperative	Present Subjunctive	Imperfect Subjunctive
-o	-Avo, -Ava	-Ai	-erò	-erEi	—	-i	-Assi
-i	-Avi	-Asti	-erAi	-erEsti	-a	-i	-Assi
-a	-Ava	-ò	-erà	-erEbbe	-i	-i	-Asse
-iAmo	-avAmo	-Ammo	-erEmo	-erEmmo	-iAmo	-iAmo	-Assimo
-Ate	-avAte	-Aste	-erEte	-erEste	-Ate	-iAte	-Aste
-ano	-Avano	-Arono	-erAnno	-erEbbero	-ino	-ino	-Assero

Verbs in -ERE (stem vend-)

Present	Imperfect	Past Definite	Future	Conditional	Imperative	Present Subjunctive	Imperfect Subjunctive
-o	-evo, -Eva	-Ei	-erò	-erEi	—	-a	-Essi
-i	-Evi	-Esti	-erAi	-erEsti	-i	-a	-Essi
-e	-Eva	-è	-erà	-erEbbe	-a	-a	-Esse
-iAmo	-evAmo	-emmo	-erEmo	-erEmmo	-iAmo	-iAmo	-Essimo
-Ete	-evAte	-Este	-erEte	-erEste	-Ete	-iAte	-Este
-ono	-Evano	-Erono	-erAnno	-erEbbero	-ano	-ano	-Essero

Verbs in -IRE (stem sent-)

Present	Imperfect	Past Definite	Future	Conditional	Imperative	Present Subjunctive	Imperfect Subjunctive
-o	-Ivo, -Iva	-ii	-irò	-irEi	—	-a	-issi
-i	-Ivi	-isti	-irAi	-irEsti	-i	-a	-issi
-e	-Iva	-ì	-irà	-irEbbe	-a	-a	-isse
-iAmo	-viAmo	-immo	-irEmo	-irEmmo	-iAmo	-iAmo	-Issimo
-Ite	-ivAte	-iste	-irEte	-irEste	-Ite	-iAte	-iste
-ono	-Ivano	-Irono	-irAnno	-irEbbero	-ano	-ano	-Issero

Gerunds: -ando; -endo; -endo   Present Participles: -ante; -ente; -ente   Past Participles: -ato; -uto; -ito

Stressed Syllables: A capital letter indicates that this vowel is stressed, as are the accented vowels ò, è, and the i of the Past Definite of -ire Verbs, and the à of the Futures.

Person, Singular and Plural, of the Present Tense Subjunctive. Thus:

	Verbs in -ARE:	-i	(singular)	-ino	(plural)
	-ERE:	-a	,,	-ano	,,
(a)	-IRE	-a	,,	-ano	,,
(b)	-IRE	iscA	,,	-iscANO	,,

A Table of the Inflections of Regular Verbs is given on page 172, and it should be referred to from time to time until the learner becomes quite familiar with these endings. At first it is advisable to be content to recognize them and their meanings, but sooner or later they should be known so that they can be *used* with confidence. Experience will show that those parts of each regular verb which in these pages are marked with an asterisk * recur again and again, others less frequently, and the remainder rarely except in reading matter.

Verbs ending in **-are** are by far the most numerous, and are called verbs of the First Conjugation. All new verbs that are added to the language are given this ending: as **telefonare**, *to telephone*; **telegrafare**, *to telegraph*. Furthermore, all but three (**andare**, *to go, walk*; **dare**, *to give*; and **stare**, *to stay, to be at, to live*) are regular. The importance of this conjugation needs no emphasis, and the forms of the typical verb **comprare**, *to buy*, must be mastered before proceeding further.

You are already acquainted with the endings of **-are** verbs. They will be given again with the various forms of **comprare** to drive them home.

COMPRARE, to buy

Gerund: -ando: *comprando, buying
Past Participle: -ato: *comprato, bought

*Present Tense

-O	1. compro	
-I	2. compri	
-A	3. compra	I buy, am buying, do
-IAMO	1. compriamo	buy, etc.
-ATE	2. comprate	
-ANO	3. comprano †	

*Imperfect Tense

-AVO	1. compravo	
-AVI	2. compravi	
-AVA	3. comprava	I bought, was buying,
-AVANO	1. compravamo	used to buy, etc.
-AVATE	2. compravate	
-*A*VANO	3. compr*a*vano †	

*Past Definite

-AI	comprai	
-ASTI	comprasti	
-Ò	comprò	I bought, etc.
-AMMO	comprammo	
-ASTE	compraste	
-*A*RONO	compr*a*rono †	

Present Subjunctive ‡

-I	compri	
-I	compri	
-I	compri	
-IAMO	compriamo	(that I may) buy, etc.
-IATE	compriate	
-INO	comprino †	

*Future

-ERÒ	comprerò	
-ERAI	comprerai	
-ERÀ	comprerà	I shall, am going to buy,
-EREMO	compreremo	etc.
-ERETE	comprerete	
-ERANNO	compreranno	

† Stress moves to antipenultimate vowel.
‡ The Imperative is the same as the Present Subjunctive, except that the Second Person Singular is **compra,** seldom used by foreigners.

Past Subjunctive

-ASSI	comprassi	
-ASSI	comprassi	
-ASSE	comprasse	} (that) I might buy
-ASSIMO	comprassimo	
-ASTE	compraste	
-ASSERO	comprassero	

Conditional

-EREI	comprererei	
-ERESTI	compreresti	
-EREBBE	comprerebbe	} I should buy, etc.
-EREMMO	compreremmo	
-ERESTE	comprereste	
-EREBBERO	comprerebbero	

Compound Past Tense

ho comprato, I have bought

Made with **AVERE** and the Past Participle.

For other compound tenses see pages 195–196.

You will have noticed, in the treatment of *essere* and **avere** given on pages 154 and 163, that there are other tenses, but they are not immediately essential and need not be memorized now. The same applies to compound tenses, excepting the Past Tense, given above: this must be memorized, as it is in common use.

ORTHOGRAPHIC CHANGES: (1) Verbs ending in **-care** (such as **mancare,** *to lack, to be in fault*) and **-gare** (**pregare,** *to pray, beg*) retain the hard **c** or **g** sound throughout, and, to do so, an **h** is added after the **c** or **g** when either comes before the vowels **e** and **i**. This is merely a change in spelling. Thus: **manchi, manchiamo, mancherò,** etc., and **paghi, paghiamo, pagherò,** etc. (*thou lackest, we lack, I shall or will lack; thou payest, we pay, I shall, will pay*).

(2) Similarly, verbs ending in **-ciare** (**cominciare,** *to begin*) and **-giare** (**mangiare,** *to eat*) retain the soft **c** and **g** throughout and so, when the ending is **-erò,** the **i** is unnecessary and is

dropped. Thus: **comincerò; mangerò** (*I shall, will begin;
I shall, will eat*).

(3) Verbs in **-iare,** which have an unstressed **i** in the first
person Present Indicative, drop this **i** in endings which begin
with an **i**. Thus: **studiare,** *to study*, drops the **i** of the Second
Person Singular, which becomes **studi** (and not **studii**). And
-iare verbs, which in the Present Indicative have a stressed **i,**
lose it only before the ending **-iamo** and **-iate**. Thus: **avviare,**
to give a start to, has these endings in the Present Indicative: **avvio, avvii, avvia, avviamo, avviate, avviano.**

There are very few of these verbs, so **studiare** and **avviare**
should be memorized.

(4) Verbs ending in **-gnare** drop the **i** in the ending **-iamo,**
where it is not necessary. Thus: **segnare,** *to indicate, point
out*; **segnamo,** *we point out*. Again, this is to preserve the
sound of **segnare.**

CHANGES IN STRESSED SYLLABLE IN VERBS: The rules for
stressed syllable (tonic accent) have been given on page 4, but
it will be noticed that in some forms of all verbs the stress
usually moves, from the syllable before the last, back to the one
before it. This happens in both regular and irregular verbs
throughout the language, and the learner will find that, if he
pays attention from the beginning, he will quickly develop the
habit of stressing correctly until it becomes quite natural. Here
are some hints which will help:

> *ESSERE* and **AVERE** have been dealt with on pages 154 and
> 163.

In all other verbs similar principles are followed in the tenses
to be known, which may conveniently be repeated here:

> Imperfect, Past Definite and Future of the Indicative,
> Present Subjunctive and Conditional:

In all Third Persons Plural the stress moves back one syllable:

> **compr*a*vono—compr*a*rono—c*o*mprino—comprereb-
> bero**

The Imperative follows the same rules as the Present Subjunctive, the only change being in the Second Person Singular, rarely used.

When you come to deal with regular verbs in **-ere** and **-ire** you will find that similar principles apply.

The Imperfect Subjunctive, which the learner will seldom meet, moves the stress back also in the First Person Plural, which becomes **comprassimo, compraste,** and **comprassero.** In **-ere** verbs: **vendessimo, vendessero.** In **-ire** verbs: **sentissimo, sentissero.**

You should refer to these hints from time to time while learning verbs, whether regular or irregular, noting any exceptions.

Travel by Air

l'areoporto, airport
il volo, flight
un volo diretto, a direct flight
l'aeroplano, aeroplane
il pilota, pilot
il passeggero, passenger
arrivare, to arrive
arriva, arrives
partire, to leave
parte, leaves
in partenza il, leaving on
a che ora? at what time?
il chilo, kilo; **i chili,** kilos
la scala, stopping-place
l'altoparlante, loud-speaker
il mal d'aria, air-sickness

un rimedio (contro), a remedy (against)
il tragitto, flight
la poltrona, seat
la cuccetta, berth
il servizio di ristorante, restaurant service
i cibi leggeri, light refreshments
la velocità, speed
l'altezza, height
superiore, upper
inferiore, lower
libero, free
il peso, weight
fino a, up to

Desidero fissare un posto, posti. I want to reserve a seat, seats.

Quanto peso libero di bagaglio permettono? How much free baggage is allowed?

Fino a diciotto chili. Up to eighteen kilos.

Quanto costa l'eccedenza? How much does the excess cost?

Si servono bibite durante il volo? Are drinks served during the flight?

la bevanda
la bibita

G

Desidero un rimedio contra il mal d'aria. I want a remedy
against air-sickness.

Quanti passeggeri porta quest'aeroplano? How many
passengers does this plane carry?

A che ora parte? At what time does it leave?

A che ora arriva? At what time does it arrive?

Partiremo all'ora fissata? Shall we leave on time?

Partiremo a mezzogiorno in punto. We shall leave at noon
sharp.

Quando parte l'aeroplano per Napoli? When does the plane
for Naples leave?

Lo avverte l'altoparlante. The loud-speaker announces it.

Passeggeri per Roma, prepararsi! Passengers for Rome, get
ready!

Dove presento il passaporto? Where do I show my passport?

All'agente di polizia. To the policeman.

S'accomodi qui per la pesatura. Sit here please, to be
weighed.

Dov'è il controllo di biglietti? Where are tickets examined?

Mi seguano all'ufficio. Follow me to the office.

3 **I PROMESSI SPOSI**

Comparve davanti a don Abbondio, in gran gala, con
He appeared before Don Abbondio, in (his) best clothes,
penne di vario colore al cappello, col suo pugnale del
with feathers of various colours in his hat, with his
manico bello, nel taschino dei calzoni, con una cert'aria
dagger of ornate handle, in the pocket of his trousers, with a certain
di festa e nello stesso tempo di braveria, comune allora
festive air and at the same time (one of) swagger, common now
anche agli uomini più quieti. L'accoglimento incerto e
even among the quiestest men. The uncertain and
misterioso di don Abbondio fece un contrapposto singolare
mysterious reception of him by Don Abbondio made a singular con-
ai modi gioviali e risoluti del giovinotto.
trast to the jovial and resolute manner of the young man.

— Che abbia qualche pensiero per la testa, — argomentò
— He might have some (deep) thought in his head,
Renzo tra sè; poi disse: «son venuto, signor curato, per
Renzo argued to himself; then he said: " I have come, signor priest,[1]
sapere a che ora le comoda che ci troviamo in chiesa.»
to know at what time it suits you for us to be in church."

— Di che giorno volete parlare?
" Of what day do you wish to speak? (mean)."

«Come, di che giorno? non si ricorda che s'è fissato per
" How so, what day? don't you remember that it was fixed for
oggi?»
to-day? "

«Oggi?» replicò don Abbondio, come se ne sentisse
" To-day," replied Don Abbondio, as if he heard
parlare per la prima volta. «Oggi, oggi . . . abbiate
speak of it for the first time. " To-day, to-day . . . have
pazienza, ma oggi non posso.»
patience, but to-day I cannot."

«Oggi non può! Cos'è nato?»
" To-day you can't! What's happened? "

«Prima di tutto, non mi sento bene, vedete.»
" First of all, I don't feel well, you see."

«Mi dispiace; ma quello che ha da fare è cosa di così
" I'm sorry; but what has to be done is a matter of so
poco tempo, e di così poca fatica . . .»
little time and of so little effect (fatigue)."

«E poi, e poi, e poi . . .»
" And then, and then, and then . . ."

«E poi che cosa?»
" And then what? "

«E poi c'è degli imbrogli.»
" And then there are complications (tangles)."

«Degl'imbrogli? Che imbrogli ci può essere?»
" Complications? What complications can there be? "

«Bisognerebbe trovarsi nei nostri piedi, per conoscer
" You would need to find yourselves in our shoes,[2] to know
quanti impicci nascono in queste materie, quanti conti
how many difficulties arise in these matters, how many accounts

s'ha da rendere.   Io sono troppo dolce di cuore, non penso
must be rendered.   I'm too soft (sweet) at heart, I only
che a levar di mezzo gli ostacoli, a facilitar tutto, a far le
think of clearing away the obstacles, to facilitate everything, to do
cose secondo il piacere altrui, e trascuro il mio dovere;
things according to the wishes of others, and I neglect my duty;
e poi mi toccan de' rimproveri, e peggio.»
and then they reprimand me, and worse."

   «Ma, col nome del cielo, non mi tenga così sulla corda,
*   " But in heaven's name, don't hold me thus on the rope suspended,*
e mi dica chiaro e netto cosa c'è.»
and tell me clear and short, what it's (all) about."

NOTES

   [1] **signor curato,** *literally* Mr. Parish Priest *but we say* Your Reverence.
   [2] **nei nostri piedi,** *literally* in our feet = in our shoes.

§ 4. *Regular Verbs: Second Conjugation ending* **-ERE**—*Model*
    Verb: **vendere,** to sell—*Short List of Verbs like* **vendere**—
    The Hairdresser—**I Promessi Sposi 4**

SECOND CONJUGATION VERBS IN **-ERE**

*VENDERE, to sell.   Root: **VEND-**

Gerund:* **-ENDO.   VENDENDO
Past Participle:* **-UTO.   VENDUTO, sold

*Present Tense

-O	**vendo**	
-I	**vendi**	
-E	**vende**	I sell, am selling, do sell,
-IAMO	**vendiamo**	etc.
-ETE	**vendete**	
-ONO	**vendono**	

* These parts of the verb must be memorized now.

*Imperfect Tense

-EVO	vendevo	
-EVI	vendevi	
-EVA	vendeva	I was selling, used to sell, etc.
-EVAMO	vendevamo	
-EVATE	vendevate	
-EVANO	vendevano	

*Past Definite

-EI	vendei (-etti) †	
-ESTI	vendesti	
-È	vendè (-ette) †	
-EMMO	vendemmo	I sold, did sell, etc.
-ESTE	vendeste	
-ERONO	venderono (-ettero †)	

Present Subjunctive

-A	venda	
-A	venda	
-A	venda	
-IAMO	vendiamo	(that) I may sell, etc.
-IATE	vendiate	
-ANO	vendano	

*Future

-ERÒ	venderò	
-ERAI	venderai	
-ERÀ	venderà	
-EREMO	venderemo	I shall, will sell, etc.
-ETE	venderete	
-ERANNO	venderanno	

† The second form is sometimes seen, but need not be memorized now.

Past Subjunctive

-ESSI	vendessi	
-ESSI	vendessi	
-ESSE	vendesse	(that) I might sell, etc.
-ESSIMO	vendessimo	
-ESTE	vendeste	
-ESSERO	vendessero	

Conditional

-EREI	venderei	
-ERESTI	venderesti	
-EREBBE	venderebbe	I should, would sell
-EREMMO	venderemmo	
-ERESTE	vendereste	
-EREBBERO	venderebbero	

*Compound Past Tense

io ho venduto, I have sold

Made with **AVERE** and the Past Participle.

Imperative

vendi—venda—vendiamo—vendete—vendano

The number of regular verbs in this conjugation is small, so small that the learner is advised to memorize them now. When they are known it may be taken that all *other* verbs in **-ere** are irregular in some way. These irregular **-ERE** verbs will be dealt with later (pages 218 *et seq.*).

The following are regular, like **vendere:**

abbattere, to knock down	**precedere,** to precede
BATTERE, to beat, strike	**premere,** to press
cedere, to yield	**prescindere,** to put aside
COMBATTERE, to fight	**PROCEDERE,** to proceed
competere, to compete	**RICEVERE,** to receive
CREDERE, to believe	**riflettere,** to reflect
dibattere, to debate	**ripetere,** to repeat
DIPENDERE, to depend	**scernere,** to discern

fremere, to rage, fume, fret
gemere, to groan
mescere, to mix
mietere, to reap
pascere, to feed, graze
pendere, to hang
PERDERE, to lose

SOLVERE, to solve
soccombere, to succumb
splendere, to shine
stridere, to shriek, creak
tessere, to weave
tondere, to shear

Note that in all the above verbs the stress is on the syllable before the ending **-ere.** Two common regular verbs have the stress on the **e** of the ending **-ere:**

GODERE, to enjoy   **TEMERE,** to fear

The Hairdresser

il parrucchiere, hairdresser
il barbiere, barber
il taglio dei capelli, haircut
il ragazzino, boy apprentice
la ragazzina, girl apprentice
il cliente ⎫
la cliente ⎭ customer
corto, short
normale, medium
il seggiolone, chair
le forbici, scissors
il camiciotto, cloth
il pettine, comb
il rasoio, razor

la spazzola, brush
shampooing, shampoo
la bruciatura delle punte, singe
il massaggio facciale, face massage
radere, far la barba, shave
il massaggio a vibrazione, vibro-massage
un asciugamano caldo, hot towel
lo spruzzatore, spray
i capelli, hair

Vorrei farmi—spuntare, I want a trim
ondulare, I want a wave
pettinare, I want my hair dressed
ombreggiare, I want my hair tinted
tingere, I want my hair dyed
lavare (all'henné), I want my hair (henna) washed
una frizione, I want a friction

Mi spunti i capelli sulla nuca ed attorno agli orecchi. I want a trim at the back of the neck and around the ears.

Ho fissato un appuntamento alle . . . I've fixed an appointment for . . .

Me li ritocchi solamente. Non troppo corti. Just a trim. Not too short.

Corti dietro e più lunghi davanti. Short at the back, longer in front.

Me li tagli lo stretto possibile. Cut it as little as possible.

Vorrei farmi ondulare i capelli. I want my hair waved.

Farmi lavare e pettinare i capelli. Wash and set my hair.

Farmi ombreggiare i capelli, per favore. Please tint my hair.

Mi aggiusti i capelli. Put my hair in order.

Me li accorci di più dietro. Più alle basette. Cut it more at the back. More at the temples.

Le basette più corte. Shorter at the temples.

Vorrei farmi radere, *or* **farmi la barba.** I want a shave.

Il rasoio fa male. The razor hurts.

Desidero lavarmi la testa. I want my head washed.

Desidero una lozione, buona. I want a hair tonic, a good one.

Desidero un poco di brillantina. Pochissima. I want a little brilliantine. Very little.

Quanto le debbo? How much do I owe?

Così va meglio. That's better.

Desidero la frizione. I'd like a dry shampoo.

Dove pago? Where do I pay?

Paghi alla cassa. Pay at the desk.

Mi faccia la riga in mezzo, da una parte. Part my hair in the middle, at the side.

4　　　　　　I PROMESSI SPOSI

«**Sapete voi quante e quante formalità ci vogliono per**
"*Do you know how very many formalities are required to*
fare un matrimonio in regola?»
carry out a marriage in (accordance with) rule(s)?" [1]

«**Bisogna ben ch'io ne sappia qualche cosa,**» **disse Renzo,**
"*It is very necessary (that) I knew something (about it)," said Renzo,*

cominciando ad alterarsi, «poichè me ne ha già rotta
beginning to get angry, " because you have already sufficiently
bastantamente la testa, questi giorni addietro. Ma ora
broken my head about it, these last days.[2] *But now*
non s'è sbrigato ogni cosa? non s'è fatto tutto ciò che
hasn't everything been settled: hasn't everything been done that
s'aveva a fare?»
had to be done?"

sbrigarsi = se dépêcher

«Tutto, tutto, pare a voi: perchè, abbiate pazienza, la
" Everything, everything, it seems to you: for, have patience,
bestia son io, che trascuro il mio dovere, per non far
the beast (ass) am I, who pass by my duty, so as not to make
penare la gente. Ma ora . . . basta, so quel che dico.
people suffer. But now . . . enough, I know what I'm saying.
Noi poveri curati siamo tra l'ancudine e il martello: voi
We poor priests are between the anvil and the hammer: you (are)
impaziente; vi compatisco, povero giovane; ed i su-
impatient; I sympathise with you, poor young man, and the (my) su-
periori . . . basta, non si può dir tutto. E noi siamo quelli
periors . . . enough, all can't be said. And we are the ones who
che ne andiamo di mezzo.
are in the middle." [3]

«Ma mi spieghi una volta cos'è quest'altra formalità che
" But explain to me once what is this other formality which
s'ha a fare, come dice; e sarà subito fatta.»
has to be done, as you say; and it will at once be done."

«Sapete voi quanti siano gl'impedimenti dirimenti?»
" Do you know how many are the annulling impediments?"

«Che vuol ch'io sappia d'impedimenti?» — e comin-
" What do you wish that I should know of impediments?" — and
ciava don Abbondio, contando sulla punta delle dita.
Don Abbondio, (began) counting on the tips of his fingers.
«Dunque se non sapete le cose, abbiate pazienza, e rimet-
" Then if you don't know the things, have patience, and leave
tetevi a chi le sa.»
yourself to him who knows them."

«Orsù!»
" Now then!"

«Via, caro Renzo, non andate in collera, che son pronto
" *Come now, dear Renzo, don't get in anger, as I'm ready*
a fare . . . tutto quello che dipende da me. Io, io vorrei
to do . . . all that depends on me. I, I should like
vedervi contento; vi voglio bene io. Eh! . . . quando
to see you happy; I wish you well. Eh! . . . when
penso che stavate così bene; cosa vi mancava? v'è
I think that you were so well (off); what (thing) was lacking to you?
saltato il grillo di maritarvi . . .»
you are jumping (like) the cricket to get married."

«Che discorsi sono questi, signor mio?» proruppe Renzo,
" *What speeches are these, my (dear) sir? " burst out Renzo,*
con un volto tra l'attonito e l'adirato.
with a countenance between astonishment and rage.

«Dico per dire, abbiate pazienza, dico per dire. Vorrei
" *I am saying (this) to say (mean), have patience, that's what I*
vedervi contento.»
mean. I'd like to see you happy."

«In somma . . .»
" *In fact . . ." (to sum up).*

NOTES

[1] = a legitimate, proper marriage.
[2] = you've worried my head off about it.
[3] I.e., between hammer and anvil = bearing the brunt of something.

§ 5. *Regular Verbs: Third Conjugation Ending* -IRE—*Two Forms:*
(1) *Like* sentire, to feel, perceive, hear; (2) *Like* capire, to
understand—*Model Verb:* (1) sentire—*Short List of Verbs
Conjugated Like* sentire—*Model Verb* (2) capire, to understand—*Telephoning*—I Promessi Sposi 5

THIRD CONJUGATION VERBS IN -IRE—TWO FORMS: This
conjugation comprises a limited number of verbs like SENTIRE,
to feel, *perceive*, *hear*, and a considerable number of verbs that
are conjugated like FINIRE, *to finish*. The SENTIRE and
FINIRE Verbs both have the same terminal inflections, but the
FINIRE Verbs take -ISC- between the root and the ending in
parts of the Present Tense, the Present Subjunctive and the

Imperative. In all other inflections, they follow the model
SENTIRE, which is best learnt first. Thus:

I. *SENTIRE, to feel, perceive, hear

Gerund: **sentendo**
Past Participle: **SENTITO**

*Present Tense

-O	**sento**	
-I	**senti**	
-E	**sente**	I feel, etc.
-IAMO	**sentiamo**	
-ITE	**sentite**	
-ONO	**sentono**	

*Imperfect Tense

-IVO	**sentivo**	
-IVI	**sentivi**	
-IVA	**sentiva**	I was feeling, etc.
-IVAMO	**sentivamo**	
-IVATE	**sentivate**	
-IVANO	**sentivano**	

*Past Definite

-II	**sentii**	
-ISTI	**sentisti**	
-Ì	**sentí**	I felt, etc.
-IMMO	**sentimmo**	
-ISTE	**sentiste**	
IRONO	**sentirono**	

Present Subjunctive

-A	**senta**	
-A	**senta**	
-A	**senta**	(that) I may feel, etc.
-IAMO	**sentiamo**	
-IATE	**sentiate**	
-ANO	**sentano**	

*Future

-IRÒ	sentirò	
-IRAI	senterai	
-IRÀ	sentirà	
-IREMO	sentiremo	I shall, will feel, etc.
-IRETE	sentirete	
-IRANNO	sentiranno	

Past Subjunctive

-ISSI	sentissi	
-ISSI	sentissi	
-ISSE	sentisse	
-ISSIMO	sentissimo	(that) I might feel, etc.
-ISTE	sentiste	
-ISSERO	sentissero	

Conditional

-IREI	sentirei	
-IRESTI	sentiresti	
-IREBBE	sentirebbe	
-IREMMO	sentiremmo	I should, would feel, etc.
-IRESTE	sentireste	
-IREBBERO	sentirebbero	

Compound Past Tense

io ho sentito, I have felt, etc.

Made with **AVERE** and the Past Participle.

Imperative: senti, senta, sentiamo, sentite, sentano

It is important to know the Verb **SENTIRE** as a " basic " Model for inflections, and also the short list of Verbs conjugated like it. These are:

AVVERTIRE, to warn	**CUCIRE,** to sew
BOLLIRE, to boil	**DIVERTIRE,** to amuse
CONSEGUIRE, to obtain	**DORMIRE,** to sleep
consentire, to consent	**FUGGIRE,** to flee
CONVERTIRE, to convert	**PARTIRE,** to start, leave

PENTIR (SI), to repent   ***SENTIRSI,** to feel
PERVERTIRE, to pervert   **TOSSIRE,** to cough
PROSEGUIRE, to follow   **VESTIRE,** to dress
SEGUIRE, to follow   **TRAVESTIRE,** to disguise

* See page 200, Reflexive Verbs. **SENTIRSI** is more common than **SENTIRE** for *to feel*. **SENTIRE** usually means *to perceive* by the senses and includes hearing.

THIRD CONJUGATION VERBS IN **-IRE**—SECOND FORM WITH **-ISC-:** In this category come the majority of **-IRE** Verbs, and it may be taken as a working rule that all **-IRE** Verbs not given in the above list (which follow the Model of **SENTIRE**) follow the rule for conjugation of the second form:

> *Rule:* All Verbs in **-IRE,** not conjugated like **SENTIRE,** insert **-ISC-** between the stem and the inflections of all Persons of the Singular and in the Third Person Plural of both Present Tense Indicative and Subjunctive, and in the Imperative.

Example:

*CAPIRE, to understand.   Stem: **CAP-**

*Gerund: **capendo**
*Past Participle: **CAPITO**

Present Case (Indicative)	*Present Tense Subjunctive*
cap**ISC**o ⎫	cap**ISC**a ⎫
cap**ISC**i	cap**ISC**a
cap**ISC**e ⎬ I understand, etc.	cap**ISC**a ⎬ (that) I may understand, etc.
CAPIAMO	**CAPIAMO**
CAPITE	**CAPIATE**
cap*IS*Cono ⎭	cap*IS*Cano ⎭

Imperative

cap**ISC**i, understand (thou)   cap**ISC**a, let him, her under-
CAPIAMO, let us understand   stand
cap*IS*Cano, let them under-   **CAPITE,** understand (you)
stand

ALL other forms of **CAPIRE** are conjugated like **SENTIRE**.

The important thing to remember is that pronunciation changes when -ISC- comes before **-i** and **-e.** Thus: **Lei capisce?** *Do you understand?*

Imperfect: **capivo, capivi, capiva, capivamo, capivate, capivano**

Perfect: **capii, capisti, capì, capimmo, capiste, capirono**

Future: **capirò, capirai, capirà, capiremo, capirete, capiranno**

Conditional: **capirei, capiresti, capirebbe, capiremmo, capireste, capirebbero**

Telephoning

il telefono, telephone

chiamare, to call

il numero, number

richiamare, to ring again

la linea, line

telefonare, to telephone

domandare, to ask for

la comunicazione interurbana, long distance call

la cabina telefonica, telephone box

Vorrei telefonare, per favore. I'd like to telephone, please.

La linea non è libera. The line's not free.

Quando è libera, vuole chiamare questo numero? When it's free, would you kindly call this number?

Qui è . . . Qui parla . . . This is . . . This is . . . speaking.

Con chi parlo? Who am I speaking to?

Vorrei parlare personalmente con . . . I want to speak to . . . personally.

Suo numero di telefono è? Your telephone number is?

Il mio numero è . . . My number is . . .

Vuole chiamarmi questo numero, per favore? Would you please call this number?

Lo (la) chiami ancora una volta. Call him (her) again.

La richiamerò stasera. I'll call you again this evening.

La linea è occupata. Occupata. The line's engaged (or simply " Engaged ").

Signorina, mi ha dato un numero sbagliato. Miss, you've
given me a wrong number.
Ha una comunicazione telefonica per . . . There's a call
for . . .
Ecco il suo numero . . . Here's your number.
La posso raggiungere domani? Can I get you (on the phone)
to-morrow?
Mi può telefonare stasera. You can phone me this evening.
A rivederci, e mi telefoni presto. Au revoir, and phone me
soon.
Dove posso trovare un telefono pubblico? Where can I find
a public telephone?
Mi metta in comunicazione col numero . . . Put me
through to number . . .
Quanto debbo pagare per il telefono? How much have I to
pay for the telephone?
La tariffa è . . . The charge is . . .

See also under Post Office, page 118, and The Telephone—Some
Useful Words, etc.

5 **I PROMESSI SPOSI**

«In somma, figliuolo caro, io non ci ho colpa; la legge
" *In short, my dear son, I'm not the one who's to blame; the law*
non l'ho fatta io. E, prima di conchiudere un matrimonio,
I have not made. And, before concluding a marriage,
noi siamo propio obbligati a fare molte e molte ricerche,
we are simply obliged to make very many inquiries,
per assicurarci che non ci siano impedimenti.»
to make sure that there are not any impediments."
«Ma via, mi dica una volta che impedimento è soprav-
" *But come now, tell me once (and for all) what impediment has*
venuto?»
arisen? "
«Abbiate pazienza, non sono cose da potersi decifrare
" *Have patience, they are not things (that) can be deciphered*
così su due piedi. Non ci sarà niente, così spero; ma, non
on two feet.[1] There will not be anything, so I hope; but, nevertheless,

ostante, queste ricerche noi le dobbiamo fare. Il testo è
these   inquiries   we   must   make.   The   text   is
chiaro e lampante.»
clear and shining."

«Le ho detto che non voglio latino.»
" *I have told you that I don't wish for Latin.*" [2]

«Ma bisogna pure che vi spieghi . . .»
" *But it is just necessary that I explain to you.*"

«Ma non le ha già fatte queste ricerche?»
" *But haven't you already made these inquiries into it?* "

«Non le ho fatte tutte, come avrei dovuto, vi dico.»
" *I haven't made all (of them), as I ought to have (done), I tell you.*"

«Perchè non le ha fatte a tempo? perchè dirmi che tutto
" *Why did you not make them in time?   Why tell me that all*
era finito? perchè aspettare . . .»
was finished, why wait . . ."

«Ecco! mi rimproverate la mia troppa bontà. Ho
" *See! you reproach me for my over-kindness.   I have*
facilitato ogni cosa per servirvi più presto: ma . . . ora
made easy everything to serve you more quickly; but . . . now
mi sono venute . . . basta, so io.»
have come to me . . . enough of this, I know."

«E che vorrebbe ch'io facessi?»
" *And what would you wish me to do?* "

«Che aveste pazienza per qualche giorno. Figliuolo
" *That you have patience for a few days.   My dear*
caro, qualche giorno non è poi l'eternità: abbiate pazi-
son, a few days don't make (is not then) eternity: have pati-
enza.»
ence."

«Per quanto?»
" *For how long?* "

— Siamo a buon porto, — pensò fra sè don Abbondio; e,
" *We're at a good port,*" [3] *thought Don Abbondio to himself; and*
con un fare più manieroso che mai, «via,» disse: «in
with a manner more polite than ever, " Come now," he said, " in
quindici giorni cercherò . . . procurerò . . .»
a fortnight I'll try . . . I'll obtain . . ."

«Quindici giorni! oh questa sì ch'è nuova! S'è fatto
" *A fortnight! oh this indeed is (something) new! Everything you*
tutto ciò che ha voluto Lei; s'è fissato il giorno; il giorno
wished has been done; the day was fixed; the day
arriva; e ora Lei mi viene a dire che aspetti quindici
arrives; and now you are telling me to wait for a
giorni! Quindici . . .»
fortnight! A fortnight! . . ."

NOTES

[1] = These are not things to be sorted out in a straightforward manner.
[2] Meaning that he did not want Don Abbondio to quote church law
(in Latin) to him.
[3] At a good port = getting along nicely.

LESSON VI

§ 1. *Compound Tenses of All Verbs—Infinitives, Gerunda and Compound Tenses Explained*—TABLE OF COMPOUND TENSES (*For Reference*): **aver amato**—*Photography*—**I Promessi Sposi 6**

COMPOUND tenses of all verbs are made with the Past Participle of the main verb preceded by the necessary parts of **AVERE,** but, as you have seen on page 154, *ESSERE* is used to form its own compound tenses (**io sono stato,** *I have been,* etc.) and also to form the compound tenses of a limited number of verbs which have to be memorized as you go along. Let us take as examples **amare,** *to love,* **temere,** *to fear* and **sentire,** *to feel.*

> **Present Infinitives:* **amare,** to love; **temere,** to fear; **sentire,** to feel, hear.

> **Past Infinitives:* **aver amato,** to have loved; **aver temuto,** to have feared; **aver sentito,** to have felt. Note that the final **e** of **avere** is dropped.

> **Past Gerunds:* **avendo amato,** having loved; **avendo temuto,** having feared; **avendo sentito,** having felt.

> INDICATIVE: *Perfect Tense:* **ho amato,** I have loved; **ho temuto,** I have feared; **ho sentito,** I have felt.

This indicates a recent action or state in the past, and this form of the Perfect Tense is the commonest of all compound tenses, as well as the easiest. As will be seen from the tables given below, all other compound tenses are formed in the same way with the required part of **avere** (or in some verbs with the required part of *essere*). These other compound tenses are not greatly used in speech, but are constantly coming up in reading matter. It is therefore necessary to know their meaning and to be able to recognize their use. Briefly, it is as follows:

Pluperfect Tense (1): This first form of the Pluperfect corresponds to the English *I had . . .* or *I was . . .*, and is used to indicate an action already completed by the time another action *started*. Thus: **io avevo passeggiato quando l'amico venne ad invitarmi** = *I had walked* (or *been walking*) *when the friend came to invite me.*

Pluperfect (2): indicates an action in every way completed in a remote time before another action or state that was also completed in a remote time. Thus: **dopo che ebbi passeggiato andai a trovare l'amico** = *after I had walked* (*finished walking*) *I went to find the friend.*

Future Anterior: indicates a future action which must be completed before another action, also in the future, begins. Thus: **avrò già fatto il mio passeggio quando Lei verrà da me** = *I shall already have made* (*completed*) *my walk when you* (*shall*) *come to me.*

The Subjunctive Tenses will be required only in reading, and are given in the tables which follow:

TABLE OF COMPOUND TENSES: *For Reference*

INDICATIVE
Perfect Tense

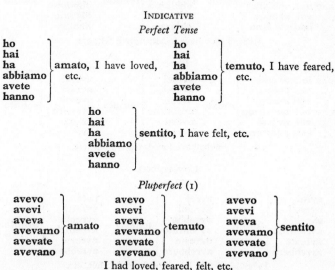

ho		
hai		
ha	amato, I have loved,	
abbiamo	etc.	
avete		
hanno		

ho		
hai		
ha	temuto, I have feared,	
abbiamo	etc.	
avete		
hanno		

ho		
hai		
ha	sentito, I have felt, etc.	
abbiamo		
avete		
hanno		

Pluperfect (1)

avevo		avevo		avevo	
avevi		avevi		avevi	
aveva	amato	aveva	temuto	aveva	sentito
avevamo		avevamo		avevamo	
avevate		avevate		avevate	
avevano		avevano		avevano	

I had loved, feared, felt, etc.

Pluperfect (2)

ebbi		ebbi		ebbi	
avesti		avesti		avesti	
ebbe	amato	ebbe	temuto	ebbe	sentito
avemmo		avemmo		avemmo	
aveste		aveste		aveste	
ebbero		ebbero		ebbero	

I had loved, feared, felt, etc.

Future Anterior

avrò		avrò		avrò	
avrai		avrai		avrai	
avrà	amato	avrà	temuto	avrà	sentito
avremo		avremo		avremo	
avrete		avrete		avrete	
avranno		avranno		avranno	

I shall, will love, fear, feel, etc.

SUBJUNCTIVE
Perfect

che io	abbia		abbia		abbia	
„ tu	abbia		abbia		abbia	
„ egli	abbia	amato	abbia	temuto	abbia	sentito
che noi	abbiamo		abbiamo		abbiamo	
„ voi	abbiate		abbiate		abbiate	
„ essi	abbiano		abbiano		abbiano	

(that) I may have loved, feared, felt, etc.

Pluperfect

che io	avessi		avessi		avessi	
„ tu	avessi		avessi		avessi	
„ egli	avesse	amato	avesse	temuto	avesse	sentito
che noi	avessimo		avessimo		avessimo	
„ voi	aveste		aveste		aveste	
„ essi	avessero		avessero		avessero	

(that) I might have loved, feared, felt, etc.

CONDITIONAL
Perfect

avrei		avrei		avrei	
avresti		avresti		avresti	
avrebbe	amato	avrebbe	temuto	avrebbe	sentito
avremmo		avremmo		avremmo	
avreste		avreste		avreste	
avrebbero		avrebbero		avrebbero	

I should, would have loved, feared, felt, etc.

Photography

la **fotografia**, photography
l'**apparecchio fotografico,** or
l'**apparecchio,** the camera
l'**apparecchio cinemato-
grafico,** cine-camera
il **mirino,** view-finder
lo **scatto,** shutter
la **chiave,** winding key
il **filtro,** filter
il **telemetro,** range finder
l'**esposimetro,** exposure meter
il **rotolo,** roll film
la **fotografia,** photo, snapshot
la **busta,** camera case

lo **sviluppo,** development
il **positivo,** positive
il **negativo,** negative
l'**ingrandimento,** enlargement
il **filtro per i colori,** colour-
filter
pronto, ready
una **pellicola,** film
la **stampa, i stampi,** print (-s)
la **copia,** copy, print
il **rullo,** roll
il **millimetro,** millimetre
i **millimetri,** millimetres

Sviluppi questi negativi, per favore. Please develop these
negatives.

**Mi può mettere questa macchina (quest'apparecchio) in
ordine?** Can you put this camera in order?

Vorrei un rullo per film a colore. I want a colour-film roll.

Stampi una copia di ciascuna. Make one copy of each.

Desidero un ingrandimento di ciascuna. I'd like one enlargement of each.

Quando saranno pronte? When will they be ready?

Vuol dirmi il prezzo di questo? Will you tell me the price of
this?

È per pellicola di sedici millimetri? Is it for a film of
sixteen millimetres?

Costa sessanta mila lire. It costs sixty thousand lire.

Voglio dei rotoli di pellicola. I want some roll films.

I dimensioni? Dimensions? Size?

Voglio una pancromatica. I want a panchromatic (film).

Sarà meglio. It would be better.

Questa è buona? This is a good one?

È la migliore. It's the best.

Mi può caricare quest'apparecchio? Can you load this
camera for me?

Voglio un rotolo di piccolo formato. I want a miniature-sized roll.

Come debbo usarlo? How must I use it?

Che esposizione devo dargli? What exposure must I give it?

Vuol'istruirmi sul modo di usarlo, per favore? Would you kindly show me the way to use it?

Per istantanea, scatti a duecento. For a snapshot, release at 200.

Desidero che mi sviluppino due rotoli. I'd like you to develop two films for me.

Quante copie di ciascun negativo? How many copies of each negative?

Due copie ed un ingrandimento di ciascuno. Two copies and an enlargement of each.

E l'ingrandimento, di che dimensioni? And what sized enlargement?

Di cartolina postale. Post card (size).

Molto bene. Domani saranno pronte. Very well. They'll be ready to-morrow.

Vuol darmi uno scontrino, per favore? Will you give me a receipt, please?

Sì, signore. Eccolo. Yes, sir. Here it is.

L'apparecchio non funziona bene. The camera doesn't work well.

Potrà mettermelo a posto? Can you put it right?

6 I PROMESSI SPOSI

«Quindici . . .» riprese poi, con voce più alta e stizzosa,
" A fortnight . . ." he resumed then, with a louder, more angry
stendendo il braccio, e battendo il pugno nel l'aria; e chi
voice, stretching out his arm and beating his fist in the air; and who
sa qual diavoleria avrebbe attaccata a quel numero, se
knows what devilment he might have added to that word,[1] if
don Abbondio non l'avesse interrotto, prendendogli l'altra
Don Abbondio had not interrupted him, taking hold of his other
mano, con un'amorevolezza timida e premurosa: «via,
hand, with a timid eager friendliness: " Come,

via, non v'alterate, per amor del cielo. Vedrò, cercherò
come, don't get angry, for love of heaven. I'll see, I'll try
se, in una settimana . . .»
if, in a week . . ."

«E a Lucia che devo dire?»
" And to Lucia what must I say? "

«Ch'è stato un mio sbaglio.»
" That it has been my mistake (a mistake of mine)."

«E i discorsi del mondo?»
" And the speeches (talk, gossip) of people? "

«Dite pure a tutti, che ho sbagliato io, per troppa furia,
" Say simply to all that I have made a mistake,
per troppo buon cuore: gettate tutta la colpa addosso a me.
through too great haste, too good heart: throw all the blame on my
Posso parlare meglio? via, per una settimana.»
back. Can I speak better (say more)? Off (with you), for a week."

«E poi, non ci sarà più altri impedimenti?»
" And then, there won't be any other impediments? "

«Quando vi dico . . .»
" When I tell you . . ."

«Ebbene: avrò pazienza per una settimana; ma ritenga
" All right: I'll have patience for a week: but remember
bene che, passata questa, non m'appagherò più di chiac-
well that (when) passed this (week), I'll not be satisfied with
chere. Intanto la riverisco.» E così detto, se n'andò,
chatter. Meantime I pay my respects." And so said, he went off,
facendo a don Abbondio un inchino meno profondo del
giving to Don Abbondio a bow less deep than usual, and
solito, e dandogli un'occhiata più espressiva che riverente.
giving him a look more expressive than (it was) reverent.

Uscito poi, e camminando di mala voglia, per la prima
Gone out then, and walking with ill will, for the first
volta, verso la casa della sua promessa, in mezzo alla
time, towards the house of his promised (girl), in the midst of his
stizza, tornava con la mente su quel colloquio; e sempre
anger, he turned his mind on that conversation, and always
più lo trovava strano. L'accoglienza fredda e impicciata
found it stranger.[2] The cold and embarrassed reception

di don Abbondio, quel suo parlare stentato insieme e
of   Don   Abbondio;   that   hesitating   and   also
impaziente, que'due occhi grigi che, mentre parlava,
impatient talking of his, those two grey eyes, which, while he
eran sempre andati scappando qua e là, come se avesser
was speaking, were always shifting here and there, as if he might have
avuto paura d'incontrarsi con le parole che gli uscivan di
had   fear   of   meeting   with   the   words   which   went   out   of
bocca, quel farsi quasi nuovo del matrimonio così espressa-
his mouth, that almost starting afresh about the marriage so defi-
mente concertato, e sopra tutto quell'accennar sempre
nitely arranged, and above all that pointing (hinting) always
qualche gran cosa, non dicendo mai nulla di chiaro.
at something important, never saying anything that was clear.

NOTES

[1] **a quel numero,** to that number (**quindici (giorni)**). As the
Italians use **quindici giorni** for our " fortnight ", we must here translate " that number " by " that word ".

[2] = the more he turned it over in his mind, the stranger he found it.

§ 2. *Reflexive Verbs—Model Verb:* **LAVARSI,** *to wash oneself—
The Passive of Verbs—Model Passive:* **essere creduto,** *to
be believed—Recapitulation of Active, Reflexive and Passive:
Principal Tenses of* **lavare,** *to wash,* **lavarsi,** *to wash one-
self,* **essere lavato,** *to be washed—Theatre: Opera—*I
Promessi Sposi 7

Turn to the Table of Pronouns on page 79 and distinguish
between the Reflexive and Emphatic forms in Italian, and note
also the Adjective **stesso, -a,** meaning *self* when used with a
Noun or Pronoun: **io stesso,** *I myself;* **essa stessa,** *she herself.*
Here **stesso, -a** is emphatic. It is not reflexive.

When we say *I wash myself, I* is the subject and *myself* is the
object of the Verb *wash.* When the action is performed and
suffered by the same person or thing, as in *I wash myself,* the
Verb is called " reflexive ". The Italian for *to wash oneself* is
LAVARSI, the Verb **lavare** + **si** with **e** eliminated.

Italian Reflexive Verbs are conjugated in exactly the same way as simple verbs, but the Reflexive Pronoun is placed before the Verb, being the object, except in the Infinitive, and the Participles, when it is joined after them. Thus:

LAVARSI, to wash oneself
lavandosi, washing oneself

and (though seldom used)

lavatosi, washed oneself

Present Tense (*Indicative*)
  (io) **mi lavo,** I wash myself
  (tu) **ti lavi**
  egli ⎱
  essa ⎰ **si lava**
  Lei ⎰
  (noi) **ci laviamo**
  (voi) **vi lavate**
  essi ⎱
  esse ⎰ **si lavano**
  Loro ⎰

Present Subjunctive: **io mi lavi,** etc.

Imperfect (*Indicative*): **io mi lavavo**

Past Definite: **io mi lavai,** etc.

Future: **io mi laverò,** etc.

Conditional: **io mi laverei,** etc.

Imperfect (*Subjunctive*): **io mi lavassi**

Note: (1) Compound Tenses of all Reflexive Verbs are made with **ESSERE: io mi sono lavato,** *I have washed myself.*

(2) When the Infinitive is used, the Reflexive Pronoun must be changed to agree in person with the antecedent subject. Thus:

io devo lavarmi
Lei deve lavarsi
noi dobbiamo lavarci
Loro devono lavarsi

Otherwise Reflexive Verbs in Italian follow the general rules for inflections in the Tables of Verbs on pages 170–196, and the irregularities of the irregular Verbs.

The above statement covers the straightforward or " true " Reflexive Verbs. But there are " reciprocal " Verbs with exactly the same form as the reflexives, but sometimes require another word or phrase to clarify the meaning. Thus: **noi ci**

odiamo, *we hate ourselves*, and **noi ci odiamo l'un l'altro,** *we hate one another*, have quite different meanings. As well as the pronominal phrase **l'un l'altro,** *one another*, adverbs can be used to strengthen or clarify meaning: **Le due squadre si batterano accanitamente.** *The two squadrons fought bitterly.* Here **si batterano** is clearly *fought one another*, and the adverb strengthens it. **Vicendevolmente,** *reciprocally, mutually*, is a useful word. And **a vicenda,** *in turns*.

> *Rule:* ALL REFLEXIVE VERBS ARE CONJUGATED WITH **ESSERE** IN THEIR COMPOUND TENSES.

> Thus: **mi sono lavato,** *I have washed myself*—and so on.

See Recapitulation on pages 203–205.

THE PASSIVE OF VERBS: A Verb is said to be in the passive (or passive voice) when the subject suffers the action implied in the Verb. Thus: *I am believed, I am knocked down, I am struck.* These are passive forms of *to believe, to knock down, to strike.*

As in English, the Italian passives are made with the relevant parts of the verb *to be*. Thus: **io sono creduto,** *I am believed*; **io fui creduto,** *I was believed*. But the Italian Past Participle with **essere** agrees in number and gender with the subject. Thus, when a woman speaks she says: **Io sono creduta.** When two women speak, or one speaks for two, the form is: **noi siamo credute,** *we are believed*. In this the Past Participle resembles an adjective.

With the verb **essere,** *to be* and its forms, all forms of the passive can be made. Take the simple verb **credere,** *to believe*. The conjugation of the principle tenses is as follows:

> *Infinitive:* **essere creduto, -a, -i, -e,** to be believed
> *Gerund:* **essendo creduto, -a, -i, -e,** being believed
> *Past Participle:* **stato creduto, -a, -i, -e,** been believed

Present Tense Indicative

sono creduto, -a,* I am believed
sei creduto, -a, thou art believed

* Note that the Past Participle changes to agree in number and gender with the speaker or person who suffers the action.

è creduto, -a, he is believed
siamo creduti, -e, we are believed
siete creduti, -e, you (ye) are believed
sono creduti, -e, they are believed
Lei è creduto, -a, you are believed (*singular*)
Loro sono creduti, -e, you are believed (*plural*)

Imperfect

ero creduto, -a, I was believed
eravamo creduti, -e, we were believed

Past Definite: **fui creduto,** I was believed
Future: **sarò creduto,** I shall, will be believed
Conditional: **sarei creduto,** I should be believed
Present Subjunctive: **che (io) sia creduto,** that I may be believed

Polite Imperative

sia creduto, be believed
siano creduti, -e, be believed (*plural*)

Compound Tenses: When we use the compound past (*I have been believed*) the Italian form is: **sono stato creduto** or **sono stata creduta** and plural **siamo stati creduti** or **siamo state credute,** in accordance with number and gender.

RECAPITULATION TABLE OF THE REGULAR VERB **LAVARE** IN ACTIVE, REFLEXIVE, AND PASSIVE FORMS OF PRINCIPAL TENSES

Active	Reflexive	Passive
lavare, to wash	**lavarsi,** to wash one-self	**essere lavato, -a,** to be washed
lavando, washing	**lavandosi,** washing oneself	**essendo lavato, -a,** being washed

INDICATIVE

Present

lavo	mi lavo	sono lavato, -a
lavi	ti lavi	sei lavato, -a
lava	si lava	è lavato, -a
laviamo	ci laviamo	siamo lavati, -e
lavate	vi lavate	siete lavati, -e
lavano	si lavano	sono lavati, -e

Perfect

Active	Reflexive	Passive
ho ⎫	mi sono ⎫	sono stato, -a ⎫
hai ⎪	ti sei ⎬ lavato, -a	sei stato, -a ⎬ lavato, -a
ha ⎬ lavato	si è ⎭	è stato, -a ⎭
abbiamo ⎪	ci siamo ⎫	siamo stati, -e ⎫
avete ⎪	vi siete ⎬ lavati, -e	siete stati, -e ⎬ lavati, -e
hanno ⎭	si sono ⎭	sono stati, -e ⎭

Imperfect

lavavo	mi lavavo	ero lavato, -a
lavavi	ti lavavi	eri lavato, -a
lavava	si lavava	era lavato, -a
lavavamo	ci lavavamo	eravamo lavati, -e
lavavate	vi lavavate	eravate lavati, -e
lavavano	si lavavano	erano lavati, -e

Pluperfect

avevo ⎫	mi ero ⎫	ero stato, -a ⎫
avevi ⎪	ti eri ⎬ lavato, -a	eri stato, -a ⎬ lavato, -a
aveva ⎬ lavato	si era ⎭	era stato, -a ⎭
avevamo ⎪	ci eravamo ⎫	eravamo stati, -e ⎫
avevate ⎪	vi eravate ⎬ lavati, -e	eravate stati, -e ⎬ lavati, -e
avevano ⎭	si erano ⎭	erano stati, -e ⎭

Past Definite

lavai	mi lavai	fui lavato, -a
lavasti	ti lavasti	fosti lavato, -a
lavò	si lavò	fu lavato, -a
lavammo	ci lavammo	fummo lavati, -e
lavaste	vi lavaste	foste lavati, -e
lavarono	si lavarono	furono lavati, -e

Simple Future

laverò	mi laverò	sarò lavato, -a
laverai	ti laverai	sarai lavato, -a
laverà	si laverà	sarà lavato, -a
laveremo	ci laverete	saremo lavati, -e
laverete	vi laveremo	sarete lavati, -e
laveranno	si laveranno	saranno lavati, -e

Conditional

laverei	mi laverei	sarei lavato, -a
laveresti	ti laveresti	saresti lavato, -a
laverebbe	si laverebbe	sarebbe lavato, -a
laveremmo	ci laveremmo	saremmo lavati, -e
lavereste	vi lavereste	sareste lavati, -e
laverebbero	si laverebbero	sarebbero lavati, -e

Present Subjunctive

Active	Reflexive		Passive	
lavi	mi	lavi	sia	
lavi	ti	lavi	sia	}lavato, -a
lavi	si	lavi	sia	
laviamo	ci	laviamo	siamo	
laviate	vi	laviate	siate	}lavati, -e
lavino	si	lavino	siano	

The Imperative is like the Present Subjunctive, except Second Person Singular **lava.**

Note: The recapitulation of these forms of **lavare** is important for reasons which the learner will already have appreciated. **Lavare** is a verb of the first conjugation, and is therefore a model for thousands of verbs ending in **-are.** The reflexive form is a model for all reflexive forms, the only change being due to the conjugation: **-ere** verbs follow **vendere;** and **-ire** verbs follow **sentire** or **capire.** And similarly the passive form of all verbs follows **lavare, vendere, capire,** or **finire,** with the relevant parts of **essere.**

ESSERE is used to form all reflexives and passives.

Theatre: Opera

il teatro, theatre

la cassa } **del teatro,** box office
il botteghino }

il programma, programme

il ridotto, foyer

il biglietto, ticket

la contromarca, cloakroom ticket

un'opera, opera

un'operetta, light opera

un'opera buffa, musical comedy

il dramma, play

la commedia, comedy

la tragedia, tragedy

l'orchestra, orchestra

il direttore d'orchestra, conductor

il teatro d'opera, opera house

il posto, seat; **i posti,** seats

un'agenzia dei teatri, a booking agency

la poltroncina, seat in the stalls

la prima fila, first row

la prima galleria, balcony

la piccionaia, gallery, gods

il palco, box

la scena, stage

l'attore, l'attrice, actor, actress

la maschera, attendant

il suggeritore, prompter	**la rappresentazione,** the show
gli spettatori, audience	
le quinte, wings	**la guardaroba,** cloak-room
l'atto, act	**l'intervallo,** interval
il sipario, curtain	**la platea,** pit
il cannocchiale, opera glass	

Vorrei alcuni posti per . . . I'd like seats for . . .

Per la rappresentazione di stasera, di domani sera. For this evening's, to-morrow evening's show.

Lasciamo i cappelli e le cose in guardaroba. Let's leave our hats and things in the cloakroom.

Potrei avere un programma? Could I have a programme?

Suona il campanello e questo indica il cominciare della rappresentazione. The bell is sounding and that indicates the beginning of the show.

Si alza il sipario. Attenzione! The curtain's going up. Pay attention!

A che ora comincia? At what time does it begin?

A che ora è l'intervallo? At what time is the interval?

Quanto dura l'intervallo? How long does the interval last?

Vuol indicarmi il bar? Would you show me where the bar is?

Vuol indicarmi la toletta? Where is the W.C.?

Che bravi attori sono! What good actors they are!

Bisogna dare una mancia alla maschera. One has to tip the attendant.

A che ora finisce lo spettacolo? At what time does the show end?

All'una della mattina. At one o'clock in the morning.

Per Bacco! Andiamo a vedere il ridotto. Good gracious! Let's go and see the foyer.

Saremo un poco in ritardo. We shall be a little late.

Questo non importa in Italia. That doesn't matter in Italy.

L'azione del dramma avviene in Palermo. The action of the play is in Palermo.

Il terzo atto è finito. Andiamo! The third act is finished. Let's go!

Portiere, dov'è il guardaroba? Porter (commissionaire),
where's the cloakroom?
Volgiamo andare ad un cinema domani? Shall we go to a
cinema to-morrow?
Sì, vorrei vedere un film inglese. Yes, I'd like to see an
English film.
Questo non sarà difficile. That will not be difficult.
Non ci sono più biglietti. There are no more tickets.

7   I PROMESSI SPOSI

Tutte queste circostanze messe insieme facevano
All these circumstances put together made
pensare a Renzo che si fosse sotto un mistero diverso da
Renzo think that he was under (dealing with) some
quello che don Abbondio aveva voluto fare credere.
kind of a mystery different from what Don Abbondio had wished to
Stette il giovine in forse un momento di tornare indietro,
make him think. The young man was a moment in doubt about turn-
per metterlo alle strette, e farlo parlare più chiaro; ma,
ing back, to squeeze him, and make him speak more clearly; but,
alzando gli occhi, vide Perpetua che camminava dinanzi
raising his eyes, he saw Perpetua who was walking ahead
a lui, ed entrava in un orticello pochi passi distante della
of him, and going into a little garden (a) few steps distant from the
casa. Le diede una voce, mentre essa apriva l'uscito;
house. He gave her a call, as she opened the door (gate);
studiò il passo, la raggiunse, la ritenne sulla soglia, e, col
he quickened (his) pace, caught her up, kept her on the threshold, and,
disegno di scovare qualche cosa di più positivo, si fermò
with the design of discovering something more positive, stopped
ad attaccare discorso con essa.
to open (a) conversation with her.

    «Buon giorno, Perpetua: io sperava che oggi si sarebbe
" Good morning, Perpetua: I was hoping that to-day one (we)
stati allegri insieme.»
would have been merry together."
    «Ma! quel che Dio vuole, il mio povero Renzo.»
" Oh, well! What God wills, my poor Renzo."

«Fatemi un piacere: quel benedett'uomo del signor
"*Do me a favour: that blessed man the priest*
curato m'ha impastocchiate certe ragioni che non ho
has plastered me (with) certain reasons which I have not
potuto ben capire: spiegatemi voi meglio perchè non può
been able to understand: (do) explain to me better why he can't
o non vuole maritarci oggi.»
or doesn't want to marry us to-day."

«Oh! vi par egli ch'io sappia i segreti del mio padrone?»
"*Oh! does it seem to you that I may know my master's secrets?*"

— L'ho detto io, che c'era mistero sotto, — pensò Renzo;
I've said it myself that there was (a) mystery behind (it), — *thought*
e, per tirarlo in luce, continuò: «via, Perpetua; siamo
Renzo; and, to bring it into light, he continued: "Come, Perpetua;
amici: ditemi quel che sapete, aiutate un povero
we're friends: tell me what you know, help a poor
figliuolo.»
fellow."

«Mala cosa nascere povero, il mio caro Renzo.»
"*It's a bad thing to be born poor, my dear Renzo.*"

«È vero,» riprese questo, sempre più confermandosi
"*That's true,*" *resumed the latter, always more confirming*
ne'suoi sospetti; e, cercando d'accostarsi più alla ques-
himself in his suspicions; and, trying to approach nearer to the
tione, «è vero,» soggiunse, «ma tocca ai preti a trattare
matter, "*it's true,*" *he added,* "*but it ill behoves priests to deal*
male co' poveri.»
badly with the poor."

«Sentite, Renzo; io non posso dire niente, perchè . . .
"*(Just) think, Renzo; I can't say anything, because . . .*
non so niente; ma quello che vi posso assicurare è che il
I don't know anything; but what I can assure you of is that
mio padrone non vuole fare torto, nè a voi nè a nessuno;
my master doesn't wish to do harm, neither to you nor to anybody;
e lui non ci ha colpa.»
and he's not in fault."

§ 3. *Using the Principal Parts of Regular Verbs to Form Other Tenses—Irregular Verbs—Most Irregular Verbs are Regular in their Terminations—Parts of Irregular Verbs Most Likely to Be Irregular—Derivative and Compound Verbs—Irregular Verbs Ending* **-ARE**—*Idioms with* **andare, dare, stare**—*Semi-irregular Verbs in* **-are**—*Accidents: Emergencies*—**I Promessi Sposi 8**

I. The majority of Italian verbs follow the " Models " given for **COMPRARE, VENDERE, SENTIRE,** and **CAPIRE,** for which reason alone it is important to know those Models well, and especially the following parts:

II. (1) Infinitive; (2) Present Tense Indicative; (3) Simple Future; (4) Past Definite Indicative; (5) Past Participle.

The learner will soon realize from his own experience that, if these parts of a verb are known, all other parts can be formed from them.

III. Verbs which do not follow the Models for **comprare, vendere, sentire,** or **capire** are called " irregular ", but they also (with few exceptions) follow certain principles, one of which is that, if the five " principal parts " stated above are known, all other parts of that irregular verb can be formed from them.

IV. The next general principle in regard to irregular verbs is this: *irregular verbs are regular in their terminations.*

You can always refer to the Table of Inflections on page 172 for the termination or terminations required for a particular part of any verb, regular or irregular. These terminations are not difficult to master, and you should now make sure that you are familiar with them before proceeding any further.

V. In the irregular verbs the part most likely to be irregular is the Present Tense Indicative, to which particular attention must be paid while studying the irregular verbs.

VI. In the irregular verbs: (1) The Gerund is always regular. (2) The stem of the Imperfect is regular, that is, it does not change. Thus:

-ARE:	andavo	davo	stavo	*Gerund:*	andando
-ERE:	discutevo	dovevo	mettevo	„	discutendo
-IRE:	aprivo	salivo	venivo	„	aprendo

H

—and, as the terminations also do not change, the Imperfect of irregular verbs may be regarded as consistently regular.

VII. The Imperfect Subjunctive of irregular verbs always follows the regular forms.

VIII. The Imperative polite form (the most important for the learner) is the same as the Third Person Singular or Plural of the Present Subjunctive. You will remember that in **-are** verbs, the final vowel of the Third Person Present Subjunctive becomes **-i**, the final of **-ere** and **-ire** verbs, **-a** (see page 173).

IX. The Past Definitive Indicative, when irregular, usually has these terminations:

First Person Singular: **-i**
Third Person Singular: **-e, ì**
Third Person Plural: **-rono** or **-ero**

X. Derivative and compound Verbs follow the irregularities of their simple Verbs: **disfare,** *to undo*, is conjugated like **fare.** One must be careful to distinguish between a real compound or derivative Verb and one which is not so by its nature. For example, **costare,** *to cost*, is not related to **stare,** *to stay*, *stand*. But **sottostare,** *to stand beneath*, is obviously a compound of **sotto** and **stare,** and therefore follows **stare.**

It is not necessary to learn all the Irregular or Defective Verbs at this stage, but only those which recur again and again, although it is advisable to have access to some work such as a dictionary which notes all the irregularities: *A Short Italian Dictionary*, Italian–English part, by Alfred Hoare (Cambridge University Press) can be recommended.

In the lists which follow, the regular parts of Verbs are stated only when it is inconvenient to dissociate them from the irregular.

TENSES WHICH ARE NOT GIVEN IN THE FOLLOWING LISTS MAY BE ASSUMED TO FOLLOW THE REGULAR CONJUGATION.

In text-books for English learners the irregular Verb **fare** is usually given under the first conjugation (verbs ending in **-are**). Here it will be given under Verbs ending in **-ere,** because **fare** is merely a contraction of **facere,** and this accounts for such forms as **io faccio.** The Infinitive **facere** is no longer used.

With these general principles in mind, you may approach the closer study of the irregular verbs without too many fears or misgivings. Little by little, as you master the parts of each irregular verb given in the following pages, your confidence will increase until, in time, even the irregular verbs will " go with a swing ". They are really not difficult.

IRREGULAR VERBS ENDING IN **-ARE:** There are only three irregular Verbs in this conjugation, but as they are in everyday use they must be known thoroughly.

ANDARE, to go

Gerund: **andante**
Past Participle: **andato**
Gerund: **andando**
Present Indicative: **vado, (or vo), vai, va, andiamo, andate, vanno**
Future: **andrò (or anderò), andrai, andrà, andremo, andrete, andranno.**
Conditional: **andrei,** etc.
Imperative: **va' or vai, andiamo, andate, vadano.** *Polite Forms:* **vada, vadano.**

All other forms are regular.

Like **andare: riandare,** to go again.

This Verb and **riandare** are conjugated in the compound tenses with **essere: sono andato,** I have gone, etc.

DARE, to give

Gerund: **dando**
Past Participle: **dato**
Present Indicative: **do, dài, dà, diamo, date, dànno**
Future: **darò,** etc.
Conditional: **darei,** etc.
Present Subjunctive: **dia, dia, dia, diamo, diate, diano (or dieno)**

Imperfect Subjunctive: **dessi, dessi, desse, dessimo, deste, dessero**

Past Definite: **diedi** (or **detti**), **desti, diede** (or **dette**), **demmo, deste, diedero** (or **dettero**)

Imperative: **da'** (or **dai**), **diamo, date.** *Polite Forms:* **dia, diano**

All other forms are regular.

Like **dare: addarsi,*** *to perceive*; **ridare,** *to give again.*

STARE, to stay, to stand

Gerund: **stando**
Past Participle: **stato**
Present Indicative: **sto, stài, stà, stiamo, state, stanno**
Future: **starò,** etc.
Conditional: **starei,** etc.
Present Subjunctive: **stia, stia, stia, stiamo, stiate, stiano**
Imperative Subjunctive: **stessi**
Past Definite: **stetti, stesti, stette, stemmo, steste, stettero**

(Like **dare** except in the Past Definite.)

All other forms are regular.

Like **stare:**

> **ristare,** to go on staying (*conjugated with* **essere**)
> **soprastare,** to be situated above (*conjugated with* **avere**)
> **sottostare,** to stand at the foot of (*conjugated with* **essere**)

STARE is very much used with a Gerund for *continuous action*, as an equivalent for the English *to be* with that Participle for our " Continuous " Present and other tenses: *I am waiting, I was waiting, I shall be waiting*, etc.: **sto aspettando, stavo** or **stetti aspettando, starò aspettando.**

The importance of **andare, dare,** and **stare** is not limited to their ordinary uses to convey their straightforward meanings. They are also used to form many common idiomatic phrases.

IDIOMS WITH **ANDARE, DARE, STARE:** *Definition:* An idiom is a combination of words which requires a different com-

---

* Conjugated with **essere**.

bination or use of words to translate it into another language. For example: **fa freddo,** *it makes cold*, becomes *it is cold* in English. Idioms are often difficult, and are best learnt by experience. But there are many, and especially with these Verbs, which occur frequently and should be known. Here is a short list:

ANDARE, to go

andare a cavallo, to ride on a horse
andare in automobile, to drive in a car
andare a piedi, to go on foot
andare (a) male, to decay, to decline in health
andare di bene in meglio, to get better and better
andare di male in peggio, to get worse and worse
andare in collera, to get angry
andare superbo, to be proud

Andare may be used in the sense of *it, he, she, must.*

Non va fatto così, It must not be done thus
Non va svegliato, He must not be awakened
Non va lasciata sola, She must not be left alone

DARE, to give (*often used in the form* **dar**)

dar ad intendere, to make believe
dar fuoco, to set on fire
dar a bere, to make one believe
dar del Lei, del voi, etc., to address one in the Third Person Singular—in the Second Person Plural (polite and familiar forms)
dar in préstito, to lend
dar luogo, to occasion, to give rise to
dar parola, to give one's word
darsi bel tempo, to seek one's leisure, ease
darsi pensiero, to take to heart, worry
dare disturbo, to give trouble
dare nel naso, to make one suspicious

STARE (*often* star)

To be well, ill, or *badly,* either in health or personal appearance, is rendered by the verb **stare** in Italian instead of **essere.**

Non sta bene. He is unwell
Sta scomoda. She is uncomfortable
Egli sta meglio. He is better
star di casa, to live, to inhabit
lasciare stare, to let a person or a thing alone
star allegro, be happy
star di buon *a*nimo, to be of good courage
star quieto, to be quiet
star in forse, to be doubtful, in doubt
star in piedi, to stand (be on foot)
star zitto, to be silent

SEMI-IRREGULAR VERBS IN **-are:** In addition to the above " true " irregulars in **-are,** there are some like **sonare,** *to sound, ring, play (music),* which take the diphthong **uo** instead of **o** in inflections when the stress is on it, or **o** if the tonic accent is on another syllable:

Present Indicative: **suono, suoni, suona, soniamo, sonate, suonano**
Present Subjunctive: **suoni, suoni, suoni, soniamo, soniate, suonino**
Imperative: **suona, soniamo, soniate.** *Polite Forms:* **suoni, suonino**

Similarly:

accorare, to grieve	**rinnovare,** to renew
arrotare, to sharpen	**risonare,** to resound
consonare, to suit	**rotare,** to wheel
giocare, to play	**sonare,** to sound, to ring
infocare, to inflame	**tuonare,** to thunder
nuotare, to swim	**vuotare,** to empty

Accidents: Emergencies

la guardia, policeman
un accidente, an accident
un'ambulanza, ambulance
la benda, bandage
un patereccio, whitlow
svenuto, fainted
gonfiato, swollen
la ferita, wound
un accesso, an attack
l'avvelenamento, poisoning
il veleno, poison
velenoso, poisonous
una storta, sprain
travolto, knocked down (by a car, etc.)
morsicato, bitten (by a dog)

ustionato, scorched, burnt
un'infermiera, nurse
l'ospedale, hospital
la frattura, fracture
la stecca, splint
la respirazione artificiale, artificial respiration
annegare (si), to drown, get drowned
una collisione, collision
scottato, scalded
congelato, frostbitten
la cassetta di pronto soccorso, first-aid outfit
gravissimo, very serious

Si porti soccorso—subito! Bring help—immediately!

È accaduto un grave accidente. There's been a serious accident.

Un uomo è ferito. A man has been hurt (wounded).

Una persona è caduta nell'acqua e si annega. Somebody has fallen into the water and is drowning.

Il mio amico si è fatto male. My friend has hurt himself.

Che cosa è? What's the matter?

Chiami una guardia. Call a policeman.

Chiami un medico. Call a doctor.

Chiami un'ambulanza. Call an ambulance.

Mi fa male qui. It hurts (pains) me here.

Ho male al petto. I have pain in my chest.

Sento oppressione al respirare. I feel a weight when I breathe.

Un pedone è stato travolto da un auto. A pedestrian has been knocked over by an automobile.

Egli è stato morsicato da un cane. He has been bitten by a dog.

(Mi) porti dell'acqua fredda, calda. Bring (me) some cold, hot water.

Mi sono tagliato la mano. I have cut my hand.

Mi sono slogato il ginocchio. I have dislocated by knee.

Mi sono rotto la caviglia. I have broken my ankle.

La donna è svenuta. The lady has fainted, swooned.

La testa sanguina. His (her) head is bleeding.

Mi aiuti a . . . Help me to . . .

Mi aiuti a trasportarlo (-la) all' automobile. Help me to carry him (her) to the car.

La ferita è velenosa. The wound is poisoned.

Ella non può muovere. She cannot move.

C'è un farmacista qui vicino? Is there a chemist's near?

Vorrei telefonare al medico. I want to telephone the doctor.

Sa il numero di telefono di un dottore? Do you know the telephone number of a doctor?

Si può telefonare alla polizia? Can one telephone to the police?

Qual' è il numero? What's the number?

8 **I PROMESSI SPOSI**

«**Chi è dunque che ha colpa?**» domandò Renzo, con un
" *Who is it, then, who has fault?* " [1] *asked Renzo, with a*
cert'atto trascurato, ma col cuore sospeso, e con l'orec-
kind of disregard, but with his heart suspended, and with
chio all'erta.
ears on the alert.

«**Quando vi dico che non so niente . . . In difesa del**
" *When I tell you I don't know anything . . . In defence of*
mio padrone, posso parlare; perchè mi fa male sentire
my master, I can speak; because it hurts me to hear
che gli si dia carico di volere fare dispiacere a qual-
that he is charged with wishing to do harm to any-
cheduno. Pover'uomo! se pecca, è per troppa bontà.
body. Poor man! If he sins, it's from too much goodness.

C'è bene a questo mondo de' birboni, de' prepotenti, degli
There are really in this world some rascals, some tyrants,[2] some
uomini senza timor di Dio . . .»
men without fear of God . . ."

— Prepotenti! birboni! — pensò Renzo: — questi non
" Tyrants! Rascals!" thought Renzo: " these are not
sono i superiori. «Via,» disse poi, nascondendo a stento
his superiors." " Come now," he said then, hiding with
l'agitazione crescente, «via, ditemi chi è.»
difficulty (his) increasing agitation, " Come now, tell me who it is."

«Ah! voi vorreste farmi parlare; e io non posso parlare,
" Ah! You would wish to make me talk; and I cannot talk,
perchè . . . non so niente: quando non so niente, è come
because . . . I don't know anything: when I don't know anything,
se avessi giurato di tacere. Potreste darmi la corda, che
it's as if I'd sworn to keep silent. You could give me the rope, and
non mi cavereste nulla di bocca. Addio; è tempo per-
not extract anything from my mouth. Good-bye; it's wasted time
duto per tutt'e due.» Così dicendo, entrò in fretta nell'orto,
for us both." So saying, she started in a hurry
e chiuse l'uscio. Renzo, rispostole con un saluto, tornò
into the garden and shut the gate. Renzo replied with a salutation,
in dietro pian piano, per non farla accorgere del cammino
turned back very quietly, so as not to let her know the road
che prendeva; ma, quando fu fuor del tiro dell'orecchio
he was taking; but, when he was out of earshot
della buona donna, allungò il passo; in un momento fu
of the good woman, he lengthened his step; in a moment he was
all'uscio di don Abbondio; entrò, andò diviato al salotto
at Don Abbondio's door; he entered, went straight to the parlour
dove l'aveva lasciato, ve lo trovò, e corse verso lui, con
where he had left him, found him, and ran towards him, with
un fare ardito, e con gli occhi stralunati.
a bold air and with eyes staring (out of his head).

«Eh! eh! che novità è questa?» disse don Abbondio.
" Hey! Hey! what novelty [3] is this?" said Don Abbondio.

«Chi è quel prepotente,» disse Renzo, con la voce d'un
" Who's that tyrant," said Renzo, with the voice of a

uomo ch'è risoluto d'ottenere una riposta precisa, «chi è
man who is resolved to obtain a precise reply, " who is
quel prepotente che non vuol ch'io sposi Lucia?»
that tyrant who does not wish that I marry Lucia? "

«Che? che? che?» balbettò il povero sorpreso, con un
" What? What? What? " stammered the poor, surprised, man,
volto fatto in un instante bianco e floscio, come un cencio
with a face in an instant white and flabby, like a rag
che esca del bucato.
that comes out of the wash.

NOTES

[1] Whose fault is it, then?
[2] **prepotente,** usually *tyrant,* here *a bully, overbearing person.*
[3] **Che novità è questa?** What's this about? What's the matter now?

§ 4. *Irregular Verbs in* -ERE—*First Group in* -RE *and* -RRE— *Some Idioms with* FARE—*Sports*—I Promessi Sposi 9

The irregular verbs ending in **-ERE** are the most numerous and, because this conjugation includes a few ending in **-RRE,** as well as **FARE** (from the old form **facere**) and **DIRE** (from Latin *dicere*), these verbs can be troublesome. It is necessary to divide them into groups for study. The verbs ending in **-RRE** have merely dropped the **-e-** before the ending **-re.** Bearing these factors in mind, all the irregular **-ere** verbs can be divided into three groups for study, as follows:

I. The **-RE** group, with **BERE** (which is also **bevere**), **FARE,** and **DIRE.**

II. A group in which the stress is normal, falling on the syllable before the last: **cadere,** *to fall.*

III. A much larger group of **-ere** verbs in which the stress falls on a syllable before the last but one: **evadere,** *to evade;* **perdere,** *to lose.*

If each group is mastered separately the irregular verbs in this broad category do not present many difficulties. As in the

-are and **-ire** categories, derivative verbs are conjugated like the model given here. The most useful derivatives will be noted with each verb given in these pages.

-ERE IRREGULAR VERBS: *Group 1 ending in* -RE, -RRE

BERE *or* BEVERE, to drink

Gerund: **bevendo**

Past Participle: **bevuto**

Present Indicative: has two forms, regular and irregular, the latter (not much used) is as follows: **beo, bei, bee, beviamo, bevete, beono**

Regular Present Indicative: **bevo, bevi, beve, beviamo, bevete, bevono**

Future: **berrò** (or **beverò**, etc.)

Conditional: **berrei** (or **beverrei**, etc.)

Past Definite: **bevvi, bevesti, bevve, bevemmo, beveste, bevvero**

   Note: Regular forms are based on **bevere** (stress on first **-e-**).

DIRE, to say

Gerund: **dicendo**

Past Participle: **detto**

Present Indicative: **dico, dici, dice, diciamo, dite, dicono**

Present Subjunctive: **dica, dica, dica, diciamo, diciate, dicano**

Imperfect: **dicevo**, etc.

Past Definite: **dissi, dicesti, disse, dicemmo, diceste, dissero**

   Like **dire** are:

benedire, to bless	**interdire,** to interdict, prohibit
contraddire, to contradict	
disdire, to give notice	**maledire,** to curse
indire, to announce	**predire,** to predict
	ridire, to find fault

Note that these derivatives make **benedici, contraddici,** etc. in the Second Person of the Imperative. **benedire** and

maledire sometimes make an irregular *Imperfect:* **benedivo,
maledivo.** And *Past Definite:* **benedii, maledii,** etc.

FARE, to do, make

Gerund: **facendo**
Past Participle: **fatto**
Present Indicative: **fo** (*or* **faccio**), **fai, fa, facciamo, fate,
    fanno**
Imperfect: **facevo,** etc.
Future: **farò,** etc.
Conditional: **farei**
Past Definite: **feci, facesti, fece** (*or* **fè**), **facemmo, faceste,
    fecero**
Present Subjunctive: **faccia, —, —,* facciamo, fate, facciano**
Imperative: **fa'** (or **fai**), **faccia, facciamo, fate, facciano**

Note that the Verb **fare** comes from the obsolete form **facere,**
and that some of the inflections spring from the old form. **Fare**
is sometimes (wrongly) classified with **-are** Verbs.

Like **fare** are:

assuefare, to accustom	**disfare,** to undo
confare, to suit	**liquefare,** to liquefy
confarsi, to be suitable	**mansuefare,** to soften
contraffare, to counterfeit	**soddisfare,** to satisfy

* The — means that Second and Third Person Singular are the same
as First.

SOME IDIOMS WITH FARE:

fare il sarto, il calzolaio, to be a tailor, a shoemaker
fare un bagno—una passeggiata, to take a bath, a walk
fare un brindisi, to drink a toast
fare una visita, to pay a call, a visit
far le veci di, to replace, to represent
far naufragio, to be shipwrecked
far vela, to set sail
far vista (di), to pretend
far animo, to give courage

farsi *a*nimo, to take courage
farsi beffe (di), to ridicule, to make fun (*of*)
far il sordo, to turn a deaf ear
far mostra, to make a show

See also under Impersonal Verbs (page 267) for the use of **fare** in terms for the weather.

PORRE, to put

Gerund: **ponendo**
Past Participle: **posto**
Present Indicative: **pongo, poni, pone, poniamo, ponete, pongono**
Future: **porrò, porrai, porrà, porremo, porrete, porranno**
Past Definite: **posi, ponesti, pose, ponemmo, poneste, posero**
Imperfect: **ponevo,** etc.
Present Subjunctive: **ponga, ponga, ponga, poniamo, poniate, pongano**
Imperfect Subjunctive: **ponessi, ponessi, ponesse, ponessimo, poneste, ponessero**
Imperative: **poni, ponga, poniamo, ponete, pongano**
Like **porre** are **suporre,** *to suppose,* and the following:

comporre, to compose
opporre, to oppose
decomporre, to decompose
deporre, to put down, depose
predisporre, to predispose
disporre, to dispose
presupporre, to presuppose

esporre, to expose
proporre, to propose
frapporre, to interpose
scomporre, to decompose
imporre, to impose
sottoporre, to put under

TRADURRE, to translate

Gerund: **traducendo**
Past Participle: **tradotto**
Present Indicative: **traduco, traduci, traduce, traduciamo, traducete, traducono**
Imperfect: **traducevo,** etc.
Future: **tradurrò,** etc.

Conditional: **tradurrei,** etc.

Past Definite: **tradussi, traducesti, tradusse, traducemmo, traduceste, tradussero**

Present Subjunctive: **traduca, —, —, traduciamo, -ucete, -ucano**

Imperative: like *Present Subjunctive*

Like **tradurre** are:

condurre, to lead	**riprodurre,** to reproduce
ricondurre, to bring back	**introdurre,** to introduce
dedurre, to deduce, to infer	**ritradurre,** to retranslate
ridurre, to reduce	**produrre,** to produce
indurre, to induce	**sedurre,** to seduce

TRARRE, to draw, drag

Gerund: **traendo**

Past Participle: **tratto**

Present Indicative: **traggo, trai, trae, traiamo** (or **traggiamo**), **traete, traggono**

Future: **trarrò,** etc.

Conditional: **trarrei,** etc.

Present Subjunctive: **tragga, —, —, traiamo, traiate, traggano**

Imperative Subjunctive: **traessi**

Past Definite: **trassi, traesti, trasse, traemmo, traeste, trassero**

Imperative: like *Present Subjunctive*

Conjugated like **trarre** are:

attrarre, to attract	**detrarre,** to detract
estrarre, to extract	**ritrarre,** to draw, to pull again
contrarre, to contract	**distrarre,** to distract, to divert
protrarre, to protract	**sottrarre,** to subtract

Sports

lo sport, gli sports, sport, sports	**il golf,** golf
il (giuoco del) calcio, football (game of)	**il campo di golf,** golf links
	il tennis, tennis
lo stadio, stadium	**il campo da tennis,** tennis court

doppio, doubles
singolare, singles
doppio misto, mixed doubles
il campo sportivo, sports field
la corsa, racing
il terreno delle corse, race-course
il nuoto, swimming
lo sciare, skiing

le corse, races
lo sciatore, skier
gli sci, skis
il canottaggio, rowing
la partita, game, match
la gara, competition
la racchetta, racket
il ballo, dancing
l'alpinismo, mountaineering

Le piace il calcio? Do you like football?

Sono sempre stato amante del calcio. I've always loved football.

Dov'è lo stadio, il campo del calcio? Where's the stadium, football ground?

Vorrei assistere ad una partita. I'd like to see a game, match.

Facciamo una partita a tennis? Shall we have a game of tennis?

Facciamo un singolare (single). Let's play a single.

Vuol servire il primo? Will you serve first?

È un bello sport. It's a fine sport.

Io non pratico molto. I don't practise very much.

A che punto è il gioco? How's the game?

Desidero vedere la finale. I'd like to see the final.

Vorrei assistere alla finale del calcio. I'd like to be at the football final.

Gioca Lei a golf? Do you play golf?

Ogni tanto, ma non bene. Sometimes, but not well.

È pronto a cominciare? Are you ready to begin?

Le piace la corsa? Do you like horse racing?

Mi piace molto. I like it very much.

Dove si può comprare una racchetta? Where can one buy a tennis racket?

Mi piacerebbe vedere una partita di tennis. I should like to see a tennis match.

C'è un ' tennis court ' nella città? Is there a tennis court in the city?

Mi può dire dov'è il campo del calcio? Can you tell me where the football ground is?

Le piace il nuoto? Do you like swimming?

Lo praticai in giuventù, ma ora sono troppo vecchio. I practised it when young, but now I'm too old.

Preferisco i bagni di mare. I prefer sea-bathing.

Non sono mai stato amante dell'acqua. I've never been a great lover of the water.

Non mi piace vivere pericolosamente! I don't like to live dangerously!

Sono i miei ultimi giorni qui, e vorrei vedere il mare. It's my last days here, and I'd like to see the sea.

Mi piace la pesca, e a Lei? I like fishing, and you?

La trovo noiosa. I find it boring.

Che facciamo, allora? What shall we do then?

Andiamo a vedere il Mediterraneo. Let's go and see the Mediterranean.

Sì, l'Italia è un paese meraviglioso. Yes, Italy's a wonderful country.

9 ## I PROMESSI SPOSI

E, pure brontolando, spiccò un salto dal suo seggiolone,
And, still muttering, he took a jump (jumped) from his armchair,
per lanciarsi all'uscio. Ma Renzo, che doveva aspettarsi
to dash for the door. But Renzo, who must have been expecting
quella mossa, e stava all'erta, vi balzò prima di lui, girò
that move, and was on the alert, bounded before him, turned
la chiave, e se la mise in tasca.
the key, and put it in his pocket.

   «Ah! ah! parlerà ora, signor curato? Tutti sanno i fatti
   " So! So! Will you speak now, reverend priest? All know my
miei, fuori di me. Voglio saperli, per bacco, anch'io.
affairs except myself. I want to know them, by Baccus, I also.
Come si chiama colui?»
What's his name? "

«Renzo! Renzo! per carità, badate a quel che fate;
" *Renzo! Renzo! for charity's sake, take care what you do;*
pensate all'*a*nima vostra.»
think of your soul."

«Penso che lo voglio sapere s*u*bito, sul momento.» E,
" *I'm thinking that I want to know now, this very moment."*
così dicendo, mise, forse senza avvedersene, la mano sul
And so saying, he put, perhaps without realizing it, his
m*a*nico del coltello che gli usciva dal taschino.
hand on the handle of the knife which stuck out from his pocket.

«Misericordia!» esclamò con voce fioca don Abbondio.
" *Mercy!" exclaimed in a weak voice Don Abbondio.*

«Lo voglio sapere.»
" *I want to know it."*

«Chi v'ha detto . . .»
" *Who has told you . . ."*

«No, no; non più fandonie. Parli chiaro e s*u*bito.»
" *No, no; no more fibs. Speak clearly and at once."*

«Mi volete morto?»
" *Do you wish me dead?"*

«Voglio sapere ciò che ho ragione di sapere.»
" *I want to know what I have reason to know."*

«Ma se parlo sono morto. Non m'ha da pr*e*mere la mia
" *But if I speak I'm dead. Am I not to consider my*
vita?»
life?"

«Dunque parli.»
" *Then speak."*

Quel «dunque» fu proferito con una tale energia, l'aspetto
That ' then' was uttered with such (an) energy, the appearance
di Renzo divenne così minaccioso, che don Abbondio non
of Renzo became so threatening, that Don Abbondio could
potè più nemmen supporre la possibilità di disubbidire.
not (any) more even suppose the possibility of disobeying.

«Mi promettete, mi giurate,» disse «di non parlarne con
" *You promise me, swear to me," he said, " not to speak with*
nessuno, di non dire mai . . .?»
anybody, never to say . . .?"

«Le prometto che fo uno sproposito, se Lei non mi dice
"*I promise that I('ll) do an absurdity,*[1] *if you don't tell me*
subito subito il nome di colui.»
very quickly the name of that fellow."

A quel nuovo scongiuro, don Abbondio, col volto, e con
At that new entreaty, Don Abbondio, with the countenance, with
lo sguardo di chi ha in bocca le tanaglie del cavadenti,
the look of one who has in his mouth the pincers of the dentist,
proferì: «don . . .»
uttered: " Don . . ."

NOTES

[1] **fo uno sproposito. fo,** another form for **faccio.** I do an absurdity
= I'll be doing something absurd.

§ 5. *Irregular Verbs in* **-ERE:** *Second Group: Stress on Penultimate* **-e**—*Doctor and Dentist*—**I Promessi Sposi 10**

CONJUGATION OF IRREGULAR VERBS ENDING **-ERE**—*contd.*

Second Group: those with stress on penultimate **-E-**

CAD*E*RE, to fall

Gerund: **cadendo**
Past Participle: **caduto**
Present Indicative: Regular—**cado, cadi, cade,** etc.
Future: **cadrò, cadrai, cadrà, cadremo, cadrete, cadranno**
Conditional: **cadrei**
Past Definite: **caddi, cadesti, cadde, cademmo, cadeste, caddero**
Present Subjunctive: **cada, cada, cada, cadiamo, cadiate, cadano**
Imperative: **cadi, cada,** etc., *like Present Subjunctive*

Compound Tenses are formed with *essere:* **sono caduto,** *I have fallen.* Like **cadere** are conjugated with *essere:*

accadere, to happen   **decadere,** to decay
ricadere, to fall again

DOLERE, to ache, to pain

Gerund: **dolendo**
Past Participle: **doluto**
Present Indicative: **dolgo, duoli, duole, dogliamo, dolete, dolgono**
Future: **dorrò,** etc.
Conditional: **dorrei,** etc.
Past Definite: **dolsi, dolesti, dolse, dolemmo, doleste, dolsero**
Present Subjunctive: **dolga, —, —, dogliamo, dogliate, dolgano**

This Verb is more commonly used in the reflexive form:
DOLERSI, meaning *to regret.* **Mi dolgo che,** *I regret that* . . .
The Third Person Singular of **dolere** is used with a pronoun and
the part of the body to indicate *pain in:* **mi duole il capo,** *I
have a pain in the head, a headache.*

Like **dolere** are **condolersi (di),** *to condole* (with) and
ridolere, *to ache again.*

DOVERE, to be obliged to, (must), to owe

Gerund: **dovendo**
Past Participle: **dovuto**
Present Indicative: **devo** (or **debbo**)**, devi, deve, dobbiamo, dovete, devono** (or **debbono**)
Future: **dovrò,** etc.
Conditional: **dovrei,** etc.
Past Definite: **dovei** (or **dovetti**)**, dovesti, dovè** (or **dovette**) **dovemmo, doveste, doverono** (or **dovettero**)
Present Subjunctive: **debba, —, —, dobbiamo, dobbiate, debbano**

DOVERE is much used as an auxiliary meaning *must:* **devo
apprendere la lezione,** *I must learn the lesson.* In the Imperative it is mostly used for *owe:* **Non dobbiamo danaro.**
Let us not owe money.

GODERE, to enjoy

Future: **godrò, godrai, godrà, godremo, godrete, godranno**
Conditional: **godrei**
Past Definite: **godei** (or **godetti**), **godesti**, **godè** (or **godette**),
 godemmo, **godeste**, **goderono** (or **godettero**)
Imperative: **godi, goda, godiamo, godete, godano**
 Otherwise regular: **godo,** *I enjoy.*
Present Subjunctive: **goda,** etc.

PARERE, to seem, to appear

Gerund: **parendo**
Past Participle: **parso**
Present Indicative: **paio, pari, pare, paiamo, parete, paiono**
Future: **parrò,** etc.
Conditional: **parrei,** etc.
Past Definite: **parvi, paresti, parve, paremmo, pareste,
 parvero**
No Imperative. Auxiliary: **essere**

PERSUADERE, to persuade

Gerund: **persuadendo**
Past Participle: **persuaso**
Past Definite: **persuasi, persuadesti, persuase, persuadem-
 mo, persuadeste, persuasero**
 All other parts are regular.

 Like **persuadere** are:
 radere, to shave   **dissuadere,** to dissuade
 evadere, to evade   **invadere,** to invade

PIACERE, to please

Gerund: **piacendo**
Past Participle: **piaciuto**
Present Indicative: **piaccio, piaci, piace, piacciamo, piacete,
 piacciono**

Past Definite: **piacqui, piacesti, piacque, piacemmo, piacesti, piacquero**
Future: **piacerò,** etc.
Conditional: **piacerei,** etc.
Present Subjunctive: **piaccia, piaccia, piaccia, piacciamo, piacciate, piacciano**
Imperative like *Present Subjunctive,* except Second Person Singular: **piaci**

Like **piacere** are:

compiacere, to please (**avere**)	**spiacere,** to displease (**essere**)
dispiacere, to displease (**essere**)	**soggiacere,** to lie under (**essere**)
giacere, to lie down (**essere**)	**tacere,** to be silent (**avere**)

Note: **Mi piace,** *it pleases me.* *Auxiliary:* **essere.**

POTERE, to be able

Gerund: **potendo**
Past Participle: **potuto**
Present Indicative: **posso, puoi, può, possiamo, potete, possono**
Future: **potrò,** etc.
Conditional: **potrei,** etc.
Present Subjunctive: **possa, possa, possa, possiamo, possiate, possono**

RIMANERE, to remain

Gerund: **rimanendo**
Past Participle: **rimasto** (or **rimaso**)
Present Indicative: **rimango, rimani, rimane, rimaniamo, rimanete, rimangono**
Past Definite: **rimasi, rimanesti, rimase, rimanemmo, rimaneste, rimasero**
Future: **rimarrò,** etc.
Conditional: **rimarrei,** etc.

Present Subjunctive: **rimanga, —, —, rimaniamo, rimaniate, rimangano**

Imperative: **rimani, rimanga, rimaniamo, rimanete, rimangano**

SAPERE, to know

Gerund: **sapendo**
Past Participle: **saputo**
Present Indicative: **so, sai, sa, sappiamo, sapete, sanno**
Past Definite: **seppi, sapesti, seppe, sapemmo, sapeste, seppero**
Future: **saprò,** etc.
Conditional: **saprei,** etc.
Present Subjunctive: **sappia, —, sappiamo, sappiate, sappiano**
Imperative: **sappi, sappia, sappiamo, sappiate, sappiano**

Like **sapere: risapere,** *to know again.*

SEDERE, to sit

Gerund: **sedendo**
Past Participle: **seduto**
Present Indicative: **siedo** (or **seggo**), **siedi, siede, sediamo, sedete, siedono** (or **seggono**)
Past Definite: **sedei** (or **sedetti**), **sedesti, sedè** (or **sedette**), **sedemmo, sedeste, sederono** (or **sedettero**)
Future: **sederò** (or **sedrò**), etc.
Conditional: **sederei** (or **sedrei**)
Present Subjunctive { **sieda, sieda, sieda / segga, segga, segga** } **sediamo, sediate, siedano** (or **seggano**)
Imperative: **siedi, sieda (segga), sediamo, sediate, siedano** (or **seggano**)

TENERE, to hold, keep

Gerund: **tenendo**
Past Participle: **tenuto**
Present Indicative: **tengo, tieni, tiene, teniamo, tenete, tengono**

Past Definite: **tenni, tenesti, tenne, tenemmo, teneste, tennero**
Future: **terrò,** etc.
Conditional: **terrei,** etc.
Present Subjunctive: **tenga, —, —, teniamo, teniate, tengano**
Imperative: **tieni, tenga,** etc. like *Present Subjunctive*

   Like **tenere** are:

appartenere, to belong	**ritenere,** to retain
ottenere, to obtain	**intrattenere,** to entertain
attenersi, to keep to (**essere**)	**sostenere,** to sustain
rattenere, to detain	**mantenere,** to maintain
contenere, to contain	**trattenere,** to keep waiting

VALERE, to be worth

Gerund: **valendo**
Past Participle: **valso**
Present Indicative: **valgo, vali, vale, valiamo, valete, valgono**
Past Definite: **valsi, valesti, valse, valemmo, valeste, valsero**
Future: **varrò,** etc.
Conditional: **varrei,** etc.
Present Subjunctive: **valga, valga, valga, valiamo, valiate, valgano**

   Similarly: **equivalere,** to be equivalent to
              prevalere, to prevail

VEDERE, to see

Gerund: **vedendo**
Past Participle: **veduto** (or **visto**)
Present Indicative: **vedo** (or **veggo**), **vedi, vede, vediamo, vedete, vedono**
Past Definite. **vidi, vedesti, vide, vedemmo, vedeste, videro**
Future: **vedrò,** etc.
Conditional: **vedrei,** etc.

Present Subjunctive: $\left\{ \begin{array}{l} \textbf{veda, veda, veda} \\ \textbf{vegga, vegga, vegga} \end{array} \right\}$ $\left. \begin{array}{l} \textbf{vediamo, vedi-} \\ \textbf{ate, vedano}(\text{or} \\ \textbf{veggano}) \end{array} \right.$

Similarly:

antivedere, to foresee   **provvedere,** to provide
avvedersi, to perceive   **ravvedere,** to reform
divedere, to evince   **rivedere,** to see again
prevedere, to foresee   **travedere,** to see indistinctly

The Future and Present Conditional of **provvedere** are regular: **provvederò,** etc., **provvederei,** etc.

VOLERE, to wish, to want, be willing to

Gerund: **volendo**
Past Participle: **voluto**
Present Indicative: **voglio, vuoi, vuole, vogliamo, volete, vogliono**
Past Definite: **volli, volesti, volle, volemmo, voleste, vollero**
Future: **vorrò,** etc.
Conditional: **vorrei,** etc.
Present Subjunctive: **voglia, voglia, voglia, vogliamo, vogliate, vogliano**
Imperative: **vogli, voglia,** etc.

Note: The conditional **vorrei** is used politely for *I should like to:* **vorrei parlare con Lei.**

Similarly conjugated are: **disvolere,** to decline, refuse
                                 rivolere, to want again

Doctor and Dentist

il medico, il dottore, doctor   **lo svenimento,** fainting
il dentista, dentist   **l'insolazione,** sunstroke
lo specialista, specialist $\left. \begin{array}{l} \textbf{l'influenza} \\ \textbf{la grippe} \end{array} \right\}$ influenza
la clinica, clinic
il dolore, pain, ache   **l'infezione,** infection
la tosse, cough   **l'indigestione,** indigestion
la febbre, fever   **la diarrea,** diarrhoea

la cura, cure
la malattia, malady, illness
l'oculista, oculist
la ricetta, prescription
la temperatura, temperature
l'ammalato, sick person
il lassativo, laxative
l'aspirina, aspirin
l'iniezione, injection
la testa, head
il dente, tooth
i denti, teeth
l'occhio, eye
il petto, chest

lo stomaco, stomach
mal di denti, toothache
male all'orecchio, earache
mal di testa, headache
male allo stomaco, stomach-
  ache
male, sick, ill
debole, faint, weak
febbricitante, feverish
in disordine, out of order
essere raffreddato, to have a
  cold
la costipazione, constipation
l'onorario, fee

Ho mal di testa, di denti, etc.   I have a headache, toothache,
  etc.
Ho male qui.   I have a pain here.
Ho mal di gola.   I have a sore throat.
Mi sono fatto un taglio molto brutto.   I've cut myself very
  badly.
Mi può indicare una clinica?   Can you tell me where there's
  a clinic?
Vuole chiamarmi un medico?   Would you call a doctor for
  me?
Mi dà qualche cosa contro . . .   Give me something for . . .
Mi sento febbricitante.   I feel feverish.
Che cosa posso mangiare?   What may I eat?
Vorrei un calmante.   I would like a tranquillizer.
Desidero un sonnifero.   I'd like a soporific.
Vorrei un rimedio contro le bruciature di sole.   I'd like
  something for sunburn.
Ho un dente da togliere.   I have a tooth to be extracted.
Vorrei una nuova otturazione in questo dente.   I'd like a
  new filling in this tooth.
La dentiera ha bisogno di essere riparata.   The denture
  needs repairing.
Si può riparare questo?   Can this be repaired?

Può raccomandare un buon dentista? Can you recommend
a good dentist?

Mi può procurare . . .? Can you get . . . for me?

Credo che sono molto raffreddato. I think I have a very bad
cold.

Non posso tenere alcun cibo. I can't retain any food.

Temo di avere una malattia contagiosa. I fear I have a
contagious ailment.

Mi bisogna una ricetta per . . . I need a prescription for . . .

Mi duole quest'orecchio. I have a pain in this ear.

Noto qualche cosa qui al respirare. I feel something here
when I breathe.

Si prenda questo medicamento. Take this medicine.

Quant'è il suo onorario? What is your fee?

10   I PROMESSI SPOSI

«**Don?**» **ripetè Renzo, come per aiutare il paziente a**
" *Don?* " *repeated Renzo, as if to help the patient to*
buttar fuori il resto; e stava curvo, con l'orecchio chino
throw (*get*) *out the rest; and he was bent, with his ear close*
sulla bocca di lui, con le braccia tese, e i pugni stretti
to the mouth of him (*the other*), *with* (*his*) *arms tense, and his fists*
all'indietro.
clenched behind him.

«**Don Rodrigo!**» **pronunziò in fretta il forzato, precipi-**
" *Don Rodrigo!* " *spoke out hastily the forced man, rush-*
tando quelle poche sillabe, e strisciando le consonanti,
ing (*together*) *those few syllables, and slurring the consonants,*
parte per il turbamento, parte perchè, rivolgendo pure
partly through agitation, partly because, turning also
quella poca attenzione che gli rimaneva libera, a fare una
that little awareness that remained to him, to make a
transazione tra le due paure, pareva che volesse sottrare
compromise between the two [1] fears, it seemed that he wished to with-
e fare scomparir la parola, nel punto stesso ch'era costretto
draw (*the word*) *and make it disappear, at the very moment that he*
a metterla fuori.
was forced to put it out (*utter it*).

«Ah cane!» urlò Renzo. «E come ha fatto? Cosa le ha
" *Ah (the) dog!* " *howled Renzo.* " *And how has he*
detto per . . .?»
done (it)? What did he tell you . . .? "

«Come eh? Come?» rispose, con voce quasi sdegnosa,
" *How so? How?* " *replied, in a tone almost indignant,*
don Abbondio, il quale, dopo un così gran sagrifizio, si
Don Abbondio, who, after so great a sacrifice, felt
sentiva in certo modo divenuto creditore. «Come eh?
himself in a certain way become (a) creditor. " *How so?*
Vorrei che la fosse toccata a voi, come è toccata a me,
I wish that it had touched (happened to) you, as it happened to me,
che non c'entro per nulla; che certamente non vi sarebber
who do not enter it in any way; certainly you would not have
rimasti tanti grilli in capo.» E qui si fece a dipingere con
so many crickets left in (your) head." [2] *And here he started to paint*
colori terribili il brutto incontro; e, nel discorrere, accor-
with terrible colours the brutal encounter; and in the discourse, he
gendosi sempre più d'una gran collera che aveva in corpo,
felt more and more [3] *of a great anger that he had within him,*
e che fin allora era stata nascosta e involta nella paura, e
and which till now had been hidden and involved in (his) fear, and
vedendo nello stesso tempo che Renzo, tra la rabbia e la
seeing at the same time that Renzo, between rage and
confusione, stava immobile, col capo basso, continuò
confusion, stood motionless, with head down, he went on
allegramente: «avete fatta una bella azione! M'avete
merrily [4]: " *You've done a nice thing! You've*
reso un bel servizio! Un tiro di questa sorte a un galant-
rendered me a nice service! A trick of this kind on a man of honour,
uomo, al vostro curato! in casa sua! in luogo sacro!
on your priest! in his (own) house! in a sacred place!
Avete fatta una bella prodezza! Per cavarmi di bocca il
You've done a brave act! To draw from my mouth my misfortune,
mio malanno, il vostro malanno! ciò ch'io vi nascondevo
your misfortune! What I was hiding from you
per prudenza, per vostro bene! E ora che lo sapete?
out of prudence, for your good! And now that you know?

Vorrei vedere che mi faceste . . .!   Per amor del cielo!
I'd like to see what you do to me . . .!   For heaven's sake!
Non si scherza.   Non si tratta di torto o di ragione; si
We're not joking.   It's not a matter of wrong or right; it's a
tratta di forza.   E quando questa mattina, vi davo un buon
matter of might.   And when this morning, I gave you (a) good
parere . . . eh! subito nelle furie.   Io avevo giudizio per
advice . . . eh! suddenly in (a) fury.   I had judged for
me e per voi; ma come si fa?   Aprite almeno; datemi
me and for you; but how is it done?   Open at least; give me
la mia chiave.»
my key."

NOTES

[1] to compromise between two fears, to strike a balance between two dangers.

[2] = so many bees in your bonnet.

[3] **accorgendosi sempre più,** feeling himself more and more, etc.

[4] **allegramente,** *literally merrily, happily,* but here probably ironical (as Don Abbondio would hardly be feeling merry or happy).

LESSON VII

§ 1. *Irregular Verbs in* **-ERE:** Third Group, with Stress on the Syllable before the Penultimate—Bill of Fare: Menu— Shops and Stores—**I Promessi Sposi 11**

INTO the third group of irregular verbs ending in **-ERE** come all irregulars of this conjugation which have not been dealt with already. The full list is a long one, but many of the verbs are seldom met and can be learned later, one at a time as they are met. The list given here is selective and practical, and should be mastered little by little. The learner will notice that most of these verbs are only slightly irregular, so he need not be dismayed by the length of the list. The parts given are essential, because from them all other parts can be made with the Table of Inflections (always regular) on page 172.

LIST OF IRREGULAR VERBS IN **-ERE**

Third Group: verbs with stress before the penultimate syllable.

Infinitive	Present Indicative	Past Definite	Past Participle
AFFIGGERE, *to affix*	**affiggo**	**affissi**	**affisso**

Similarly: **crocifiggere,** to crucify; **figgere,** to fix; **prefiggere,** to prefix.

AFFLIGGERE, *to afflict*	**affliggo**	**afflissi**	**afflitto**

Similarly: **configgere,** to fix tightly; **friggere,** to fry; **infliggere,** to inflict; **sconfiggere,** to discomfit; **trafiggere,** to transfix.

ANNETTERE, to annex	**annetto**	**annettei**	**annesso**

Similarly: **connettere,** to connect; **sconettere,** to disconnect; **deflettere,** to deflect; **flettere,** to bend; **riflettere,** to reflect.

ARDERE, *to burn*	**ardo**	**arsi**	**arso**

Infinitive	Present Indicative	Past Definite	Past Participle
ASSISTERE, to assist	assisto	assistei (-etti)	assistito

Similarly: **coesistere**, to coexist (**essere**); **consistere**, to consist (**essere**); **desistere**, to desist (**avere**); **esistere**, to exist (**essere**); **insistere**, to insist (**avere**); **persistere**, to persist (**avere**); **resistere**, to resist (**avere**); **sussistere**, to subsist (**essere** and **avere**).

ASSOLVERE, to absolve	assolve	assolsi	assolto (-oluto)

Similarly: **dissolvere**, to dissolve; **evolversi**, to evolve (*Past Participle:* **evoluto**); **risolvere**, to resolve, solve (*Past Participle:* **risolto** = solved, settled. **risoluto** = determined, resolved, resolute (*adj.*).

ASSUMERE, to assume	assumo	assunsi	assunto

Similarly: **desumere**, to deduce; **presumere**, to presume, estimate.

CHIEDERE, to ask	chiedo } chieggo }	chiesi	chiesto

CHIUDERE, to shut	chiudo	chiusi	chiuso

CINGERE, to gird	cingo	cinsi	cinto

Similarly: **accingersi**, to get ready; **attingere**, to attain; **dipingere**, to depict; **fingere**, to feign; **infingersi**, to pretend; **intingere**, to dip (*a pen in ink*); **pingere**, to paint, depict; **respingere**, to send back; **ritingere**, to redye; **sospingere**, to stimulate; **spingere**, to impel, push; **stingere**, to change, fade; **tingere**, to dye.

COGLIERE, to gather also **corre**	colgo	colsi	colto

Similarly: **accogliere**, to welcome; **distogliere**, to dissuade; **incogliere** (or **incorre**), to catch *and* to happen unawares; **prosciogliere**, to release; **raccogliere**, to gather, collect; **togliere** (*or* **torre**), to seize, prevent.

COMPIERE, to accomplish	compio	compii (-iei)	compiuto (-ito)

Similarly: **adempiere** (or **adempire**), to fulfill; **empiere** (or **empire**), to fill.

Infinitive	Present Indicative	Past Definite	Past Participle
CONCEDERE, to concede	**concedo**	**concessi** (-edei)	**concesso** (-eduto)

>   Similarly: **retrocedere** (**essere**, **avere**), to give back; **succedere**, to succeed; **cedere**, to yield.

CONOSCERE, to know	**conosco**	**conobbi**	**conosciuto**

>   Similarly: **disconoscere,** to refuse recognition; **misconoscere,** to refuse recognition; **riconoscere,** to recognize

CORRERE, to run	**corro**	**corsi**	**corso**

>   Similarly: **accorrere,** to hasten to; **concorrere,** to concur; **decorrere,** to pass; **discorrere,** to discourse; **incorrere,** to fall into; **intercorrere,** run between; **occorrere,** to be necessary; **percorrere,** to run through; **ricorrere,** to run again; **scorrere,** to run through; **soccorrere,** to succour, help; **trascorrere,** to run over, out (of time).

CRESCERE, to grow	**cresco**	**crebbi**	**cresciuto**

>   Similarly: **accrescere,** to augment; **decrescere,** to decrease (**essere**); **increscere,** to be sorry (**essere**); **rincrescere,** to regret (**essere**). **Mi rincresce,** I'm sorry.

CUOCERE, to cook	**cuocio**	**cossi**	**cotto** (**cociuto**)

DEPRIMERE, to depress	**deprimo**	**depressi**	**depresso**

>   Similarly: **comprimere,** to compress; **esprimere,** to express; **imprimere,** to impress (**impresso**, printed); **opprimere,** to oppress; **reprimere,** to repress; **sopprimere,** to suppress.

Bill of Fare: Menu

Vocabulary

LA LISTA DELLE VIVANDE,
  the Menu
antipasti, hors d'œuvres
acciughe, anchovies
ostriche, oysters
olive, olives

sardine, sardines
prosciutto, ham
salame, spiced sausage
il pane, bread
il burro, butter

MINESTRE: ZUPPE, soup

consumè, consommé, clear soup

brodo di pollo, chicken soup

minestrone, a mixed soup, with vegetables, spaghetti, etc.

zuppa di pesce, fish soup

crema, thick soup

minestrina, often used for clear soup

zuppa di pomodoro, tomato soup

minestra di verdura, vegetable soup

tagliatelle in brodo, soup with vermicelli

zuppa di sedano, celery soup

PESCE, fish

caviale, caviar

salmone, salmon

tonno, tunny

baccalà, dried cod (salt)

trota, trout

pesce passera, plaice

pesce passerina, halibut

calamari, squid, octopus

rombo, brill

merluzzo, cod

gamberi, shrimps

aragosta, lobster

scampi, prawns

sogliola, sole

grancchio, crab

telline, mussels (clams)

UOVA, eggs

frittata, omelette

semplice, plain

alla coque, boiled (soft)

sode, boiled (hard)

fritte, fried

uova al prosciutto, ham and eggs

frittata al rognone, kidney omelette

frittata al prosciutto, ham omelette

frittata con funghi, mushroom omelette

frittata con aragosta, lobster omelette

uovo affogato, poached egg

uova al piatto, fried eggs

LA PASTA, general term for the foodstuffs known under their special names. **la pasta asciutta** is what one asks for, adding the word to indicate the special form, for which see pages 249–250.

CARNE, meat

vitello, veal

agnello, lamb

carne di manzo, beef

maiale, pork

bistecca, beefsteak

porchetta, young pig
rosbiffe, roast beef
cotoletta, cutlet
zampone, leg
rognoni, kidneys
trippa, tripe
fegato, liver

cervella, brains
lingua, tongue
rotoli di manzo, rolled fillets
scaloppa di vitello, escallope of veal
arrosto, roast meat

ai ferri, grilled
bollito, boiled
fritto, fried
arrostito, roasted
affumicato, smoked
in fricassea, fricassee
in umido, stewed

farcito, stuffed
ben cotto, well done
al sangue, underdone
alla italiana, francese, in Italian, French style
tritato, minced

For *Drinks* see page 65, SOFT DRINKS; and page 317, ALCO-
HOLIC DRINKS. For PASTA ASCIUTTA see page 249. For WINES
see pages 311–312.

UCCELLI, poultry
cacciagione, game
pollo, chicken
pernice, partridge
tacchino, turkey
anitra, duck
coniglio, rabbit
lepre, hare
beccaccino, snipe

gallo cedrone, grouse
galletto, spring chicken
anitrotto, duckling
anatra arrosto, roast duck
oca, goose
pollo con riso e salsa di curry, curried chicken with rice

VERDURA, legumi, greens, vegetables
patate, potatoes
fagioli, beans
piselli, peas
funghi, mushrooms
cipolle, onions
patatine fritte, fried potatoes
pomodoro, tomato
sedano, celery
asparagi, asparagus

carciofi, artichokes
cipollette, leeks
cocomero, cucumber
cavolo, cabbage
carote, carrots
navone, turnips
prezzemolo, parsley
cavolo acido, sauerkraut
spinaci, spinach
riso, rice
risotto, savoury rice

I

INSALATA, salad
insalata di patate, potato salad
—di uova, egg salad
insalata di pomodoro, tomato salad

insalata di asparagi, asparagus salad
insalata di barbabietole, beetroot salad

SALSA, sauce, gravy
salsa inglese, Worcester, H.P. or other English bottled sauce
salsa mayonaise, mayonnaise dressing
salsa di limone, lemon sauce

burro fuso, melted butter
salsa di rafano, horse-radish sauce
salsa tartara, Tartar sauce
olio d'oliva, olive oil
aceto, vinegar

POSPASTI, dessert
crostata, pie
crostata di mele, apple pie
macedonia di frutta, fruit cocktail
gelato, ice-cream

frutta, fruit
mista, mixed
dolci, sweets
formaggio, cheese
formaggio tenero, cream cheese

Shops and Stores

la libreria, bookstore
la farmacia, chemist
i grandi magazzini, departmental stores
il negozio di antichità, antique shop
il negoziante di . . ., the dealer in . . .
i mobili, furniture
le stoffe, dry goods, drapery
il negozio di stoffe, draper, dry goods business
la cappelleria, hat shop
il gioielliere, jeweller
l'ottico, optician
il profumiere, perfumier
la calzoleria, shoe shop

la libreria d'occasione, secondhand bookshop
il cartolaio, stationer
la valigeria, bag and trunk shop
la tabaccheria, tobacconist
la rivendita di vino, wine shop, store
il fornaio, baker
il sarto, tailor
la modista, milliner
la sarta, dressmaker
l'orologiaio, watchmaker
il mercato, market
il macellaio, butcher
il salumaio, pork butcher
il droghiere, grocer

Vorrei comprare un impermeabile. I want to buy a raincoat.

Dove posso comprare . . .? Where can I buy . . .?

Dove posso trovare un assortimento di . . .? Where can I find an assortment of?

A che serve questo? What is this for?

Mi bisogna diverse cose. I want several things.

Sarà possibile? Will it be possible?

Mi può raccomandare questo? Can you recommend this?

Mi faccia vedere . . . Let me see . . .

Mi dia pure . . . Give me also . . .

Non posso aspettare. I can't wait.

Mi piace assai. I rather like it.

Dov'è la sezione calzature? Where's the shoe department?

Al primo, secondo, terzo, quarto piano. On the first, second, third, fourth floor.

Che numero porta il Signore, la Signora, la Signorina? What size do you take?

Che numero calza? What size fits you?

Il numero . . . Size . . .

Desidero anche un paio di calzerotti. I also need a pair of socks; **calze,** stockings.

Quanto in totale? How much altogether?

Mi faccia vedere dei campioni. Let me see some samples.

Può farmi un vestito da estate? Can you make me a summer dress?

Quando posso venire per la prova? When can I come for a try on?

Quanto costa questa qualità? How much does this quality cost?

Vorrei un paio di scarpe. I want a pair of shoes.

Potrebbe mostrarmi dei guanti? Could you show me some gloves?

Li voglio in colore. I want them coloured.

Vorrei vedere la sfilata dei modelli. I'd like to see the show of models.

Potrei vedere i figurini? Can I see the fashion plates?

Questo non mi piace. I don't like this one.

È troppo eccentrico quello.   That one's too showy.
Mille grazie.   Very many thanks.
Si paga alla cassa.   Pay at the cash desk.

II   I PROMESSI SPOSI

«Posso aver fallato,» rispose Renzo, con voce raddolcita
" I can have made a mistake," replied Renzo, in a tone softened
verso don Abbondio, ma nella quale si sentiva il furore
towards Don Abbondio, but in which was felt the fury
contra il nemico scoperto: «posso aver fallato; ma si
towards the enemy discovered: " I can have erred; but put
metta la mano al petto, e pensi se nel mio caso . . .»
your hand on your breast, and think if in my case (place) . . ."

Così dicendo, s'era levata la chiave di tasca, e andava
So saying, he took the key from (his) pocket, and went
ad aprire. Don Abbondio gli andò dietro, e, mentre
to open.   Don Abbondio went after him, and, while
quegli girava la chiave nalla toppa, se gli accostò, e, con
the former turned the key in the lock, came near him, and, with
volto serio e ansioso, alzandogli davanti agli occhi le tre
serious and anxious face, raised before his eyes the three
prime dita della destra, come per aiutarlo anche lui dal
fingers of his right (hand), as if to help him also
canto suo, «giurate almeno . . .» gli disse.
in return, " Swear at least . . ." he said to him.

«Posso aver fallato; e mi scusi,» rispose Renzo, aprendo,
" I may have erred; and forgive me," replied Renzo, opening
e disponendosi ad uscire.
the door, and getting ready to go out.

«Giurate . . .» replicò don Abbondio, afferrandogli il
" Swear . . ." replied Don Abbondio, grasping his
braccio con la mano tremante.
arm with (his) trembling hand.

«Posso aver fallato,» ripetè Renzo, sprigionandosi da
" I can have erred," repeated Renzo, releasing himself from
lui; e parte in furia, troncando così la questione, che, al
him; and left in a rage, cutting (short) thus the question, which, like

pari d'una questione di letteratura o di filosofia o d'altro,
a   matter   of   literature   or   of   philosophy   or   suchlike,
avrebbe potuto durar dei secoli, giachè ognuna delle parti
could have lasted for some centuries, inasmuch as each one of the
non faceva che replicare il suo proprio argomento.
parties did nothing but repeat his own argument.

«Perpetua!   Perpetua!» gridò don Abbondio, dopo avere
" Perpetua!   Perpetua! " cried Don Abbondio, after having
invano richiamato il fuggitivo.   Perpetua non risponde:
in vain recalled the fugutive.   Perpetua did not reply:
don Abbondio non sapeva più in che mondo si fosse.
Don Abbondio did not know in what world he was.[1]

È accaduto più d'una volta a personaggi di ben più alto
It has happened more than once to personages of far higher
affare che don Abbondio, di trovarsi in frangenti così
business[2]   than   Don   Abbondio,   to   find   themselves
fastidiosi, in tanta incertezza di partiti, che parve loro un
in breakers[3] so difficult, in such uncertainty of action, that it seemed
ottimo ripiego mettersi a letto con la febbre.   Questo
to them a best recourse to go to bed with fever.   This
ripiego, egli non lo dovette andare a cercare, perchè gli
recourse,   he   did   not   have   to   go   to   seek,   because   it
offerse da sè. La paura del giorno avanti, la veglia
came   of   itself.   The   fright   of   the   day   before,   the
angosciosa della notte, la paura avuta in quel momento,
agonizing vigil of last night, the fright (he had) had in that (last)
l'ansietà dell'avvenire, fecero l'effetto.
moment, the anxiety for the future, made (brought about) the effect.

NOTES

[1] whether he was on his head or his heels.
[2] of much greater importance.
[3] **il frangente,** the difficulty.   Plural **i frangenti,** the breakers.   *So, here it could be* in heavy seas.

§ 2. *Irregular Verbs in* -ERE: *Third Group*—contd.—LA PASTA *illustrated*—I Promessi Sposi 12

Infinitive	Present Indicative	Past Definite	Past Participle
DIR*I*GERE, *to* direct	dirigo	diressi	diretto

Similarly: eri*g*ere, to erect; predil*i*gere, to prefer.

| DISC*U*TERE, *to* discuss | discuto | discussi (-tei) | discusso |

Similarly: esc*u*tere, to interrogate; inc*u*tere, to inspire (awe).

| DIST*I*NGUERE, to distinguish | distinguo | distinsi | distinto |

Similarly: contraddist*i*nguere, to contradistinguish (*distinguish by contrast*); est*i*nguere, to extinguish.

| DIVELLERE, *to* uproot | divello | divelsi | divelto |

Similarly: ecc*e*llere. *Past Participle:* eccelso, to excel; sv*e*llere, to uproot, pluck up.

| EM*E*RGERE, *to* emerge | emergo | emersi | emerso |

Similarly: asp*e*rgere, to sprinkle; cosp*a*rgere, to strew; det*e*rgere, to cleanse; imm*e*rgere, to immerse; somm*e*rgere, to submere; t*e*rgere, to wipe.

| *E*RGERE, *to* stand erect | ergo | ersi | erto |

Similarly: ad*e*rgersi, to rise.

| ES*I*GERE, *to* exact | esigo | esigei (-etti) | esatto |

Similarly: trans*i*gere, to make a compromise.

| ESP*E*LLERE, *to* expel | espello | espulsi | espulso |

| FONDERE, *to* melt, cast | fondo | fusi | fuso |

Similarly: conf*o*ndere, to confound; diff*o*ndere, to diffuse; eff*o*ndere, to pour out; inf*o*ndere, to infuse; prof*o*ndere, to lavish; rif*o*ndere, to recast; trasf*o*ndere, to infuse, transfuse.

Infinitive	Present Indicative	Past Definite	Past Participle
LEDERE, *to offend*	**ledo**	**lesi**	**leso**
LEGGERE, *to read*	**leggo**	**lessi**	**letto**

Similarly: **correggere,** to correct; **eleggere,** to elect; **proteggere,** to protect; **reggere,** to rule, govern; **scorreggere,** to mark down; **sorreggere,** to sustain, hold up.

METTERE, *to put*	**metto**	**misi**	**messo**

Similarly: **commettere,** to put together; **compromettere,** to risk; **dimettere,** to dismiss; **emettere,** to send out; **framettere,** to interpose; **omettere,** to omit; **permettere,** to permit; **premettere, promettere,** to promise; **rimettere,** to replace; **scommettere,** to bet; **sottomettere,** to subdue, subject; **trasmettere,** transmit to.

MORDERE, *to bite*	**mordo**	**morsi**	**morso**
MUOVERE, *to move*	**muovo**	**mossi**	**mosso**

Similarly: **commuovere,** to excite; **rimuovere,** to remove; **smuovere,** to move with effort; **sommuovere,** to incite.

NASCERE, *to be born:*

Present Indicative: **nasco, nasci, nasce, nasciamo, nascete, nascono.**
Past Definite: **nacqui, nascesti, nacque, nascemmo, nasceste, nacquero.**
Present Subjunctive: **nasca—nasciamo, nasciate, nascano.**
Past Participle: **nato.**

Similarly: **rinascere,** to be born again, relive.

NUOCERE, *to injure*	**noccio** (**nuoco**)	**nocqui**	**nociuto**
PERDERE, *to lose*	**perdo**	**persi (-dei, -detti)**	**perso** (**perduto**)

Similarly: **disperdere,** to waste; **sperdere,** to nullify, lose.

PIANGERE, *to weep*	**piango**	**piansi**	**pianto**

Similarly: **compiangere,** to pity; **frangere,** to smash; **infrangere,** to infringe, break into; **rimpiangere,** to lament over; **rifrangere,** to refract.

Infinitive	Present Indicative	Past Definite	Past Participle
PORGERE, *to offer, tender*	**porgo**	**porsi**	**porto**

Similarly: **accorgersi,** to perceive; **insorgere,** to rebel; **scorgere,** to perceive; **sporgere,** to protrude.

| **PRENDERE,** *to take* | **prendo** | **presi** | **preso** |

Similarly: **accendere,** to kindle; **appendere,** to hang (*up*); **apprendere,** to learn; **arrendere,** to give up; **ascendere,** to ascend; **attendere,** to attend; **comprendere,** to comprise; **condiscendere,** to condescend; **contendere,** to contend; **difendere,** to defend; **dipendere,** to depend; **discendere,** to descend; **distendere,** to distend, stretch; **estendere,** to extend; **imprendere,** to undertake; **intendere,** to understand; **offendere,** to offend; **pretendere,** to pretend; **rapprendere,** to congeal; **rendere,** to give back; **riprendere,** to retake; **scendere,** to descend; **sorprendere,** to surprise; **sospendere,** to suspend; **spendere,** to spend; **stendere,** to extend, spread out; **tendere,** to tend; **trascendere,** to transcend.

| **PUNGERE,** *to prick* | **pungo** | **punsi** | **punto** |

Similarly: **aggiungere,** to add; **compungere,** to sting; **congiungere,** to unite; **disgiungere,** to disjoin; **disungere,** to remove grease; **espungere,** to expunge; **giungere,** to arrive; **mungere,** to milk; **raggiungere,** to overtake; **trapungere,** to sting, prick through; **ungere,** to grease.

| **RADERE,** *to shave* | **rado** | **rasi** | **raso** |

Similarly: **dissuadere,** to dissuade; **evadere** (**essere**), to escape; **invadere,** to invade; **persuadere,** to persuade(es).

| **REDIGERE,** *to edit, draw up* | **redigo** | **redassi** (**-igei**) | **redatto** |

LA PASTA, *paste* (also *dough, pulp, pastry*) is the generic name given to the multiform varieties of " pastes " made from flour and water, and representing a staple in the food of the Italian people. **Past'asciutta** (*dry paste*) is the general term given to those forms of it which, in themselves, with sauce or other additions such as cheese, constitute dishes. When added to soups it is usually referred to as *pasta* only. In the English-speaking world we seldom find **past'asciutta** other than as **vermicelli, spaghetti,** or **maccheroni,** but in Italy the varieties are almost without number, and each province has its own specialities of the food. On page 250 will be found illus-

trations of some twenty-five forms of **pasta,** culled from a manu-
facturer's catalogue which illustrates eighty-seven different
varieties! Those illustrated here on page 250 are perhaps the
commonest in everyday use. A few words of explanation may
be helpful. Take them by the numbers which go with the
illustrations on page 250:

(1) **sopracapellini** = a thin form of what we call
   vermicelli.
(2) **spaghettini** = thin strings of **maccheroni.**
(3) **spaghetti mezzani** = middle-sized spaghetti.
(4) **spaghetti** = the everyday form in solid strings.
(5) **spaghettoni** = slightly thicker than (4).
(6) **spaghetti bucati** = about the same thickness as (4),
   but tubular.
(7) **foratini** = a tubular form of **pasta** used in soup.
(8) **mezzi-zita** = similar to (7) but larger.
(9) **zita** = a still larger size of (7).
(10) **fettucce, fettuccine** = strips of solid **pasta.**
(11) **francesine** = similar to (10), broader, wavy edge.
(12) **mezza lasagne** = ribbon **maccheroni,** smaller than
   (13) and with ornamental edges.
(13) **lasagne** = broad, ribbon **pasta.**
(14) **tagliatelle** = narrow, ribbon **pasta,** in flat strips
   shaped like noodles.
(15) **rigatoni** = large tubular **pasta** with striped pattern.
(16) **penne rigate** = tubular, patterned **pasta,** used in soup.
(17) **sedani elicoidali** = resemble (16), often flavoured.
(18) **creste di gallo** = a **pasta** in the shape of a cockscomb.
(19) **farfalloni** = " big butterfly " shape.
(20) **gnocchetti** = " little dumplings ", often with stuffing.
(21) **fusilli** = shaped like a little spindle.
(22) **ruote** = " wheels ".
(23) **lumache di mare** = **pasta** the shape of sea-snail.
(24) **stellette** = " asterisks ", much used in clear soups.
(25) **primiera** = the word means a card game, and in some
   of the little shapes of **pasta** one can recognize cards
   (diamonds, hearts, clubs, spades).

Note: The names given above are taken as printed in the **Catalogo delle Paste** of the Pastificio A. Bonaca, Perugia. Many of these words will not be found in dictionaries available to the foreign student, who must not be surprised when he meets them or others on a menu. Such words are often used by imaginative manufacturers to describe their products.

PASTA

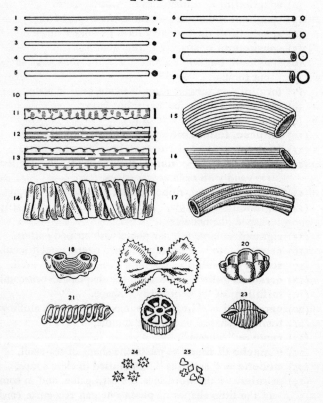

HORNE SHEPHERD

Affannato e balordo, si ripose sul suo seggiolone, com-
Panting and stupefied, he sat (back) on his armchair, (and) be-
minciò a sentirsi qualche brivido nell'ossa, si guardava
gan to feel some shiver in his bones, (and) he looked
le unghie sospirando, e chiamava di tempo in tempo, con
at his nails sighing, and called from time to time, with
voce tremolante e stizzosa: «Perpetua!» La¹ venne
a trembling and petulant voice: "Perpetua!" She came
finalmente, con un gran cavolo sotto il braccio, e con la
at last, with a big cabbage under her arm, and with her
faccia tosta, come se nulla fosse stato. Risparmio al
face impassive, as if nothing had happened. I spare the reader the
lettore i lamenti, le condoglianze, le accuse, le difese,
laments, the condolences, the accusations, the defences,
i «voi sola potete aver parlato», e i «non ho parlato», tutti
the " only you could have spoken ", and the " I haven't spoken ", all
i pasticci in somma di quel colloquio. Basti dire che don
the scramblings in fine of that conversation. Enough to say that Don
Abbondio ordinò a Perpetua di metter la stanga all'uscio,
Abbondio ordered Perpetua to put the bar on the door,
di non aprir più per nessuna cagione, e, se alcun bussasse,
(and) not to open for any cause, and, if anyone should knock,
risponder dalla finestra che il curato era andato a letto
to reply from the window, (and) that the priest had gone to
con la febbre. Salì poi lentamente le scale, dicendo, ogni
bed with fever. He then slowly went up the stairs, saying, every
tre scalini, «son servito»; e si mise davvero a letto, dove
three steps " I've been served "²; and he really went to bed, where
lo lasceremo.
we'll leave him.

Renzo intanto camminava a passi infuriati verso casa,
Renzo meantime was walking at (a) furious pace towards home,
senza aver determinato quel che dovesse fare, ma con
without having determined what he ought to do, but with
una smania addosso di far qualcosa di strano e di terribile.
a longing on him to do something strange and terrible.

I provocatori, i soverchiatori, tutti coloro che, in qual-
Provocators, overbearing people, all those who, in any
unque modo, fanno torto altrui, sono rei, non solo del
way, do injury to others, are guilty, not only of the
male che commettono, ma del pervertimento ancora a
evils that they commit, but also of the perversion (caused) to
cui portano gli animi degli offesi. Renzo era un giovine
those who have the minds of the offended.[3] Renzo was a
pacifico e alieno dal sangue, un giovine schietto e nemico
peaceful young man and averse from bloodshed, a frank young man
d'ogni insidia; ma, in quei momenti, il suo cuore non
and an enemy of every deceit, but in those moments, his heart beat
batteva che per l'omicidio, la sua mente non era occupata
only for murder, his mind was occupied only in
che a fantasticare un tradimento. Avrebbe voluto cor-
indulging in fancies of treachery. He would have liked to run
rere alla casa di don Rodrigo, afferrarlo per il collo, e . . .
to the house of Don Rodrigo, seize him by the neck, and . . .
ma gli veniva in mente ch'era come una fortezza, guar-
but then it came to mind that it was like a fortress, garri-
nita di bravi al di dentro e guardata al difuori; che i soli
soned with bravos inside and guarded outside; so that only
amici e servitori ben conosciuti v'entravan liberamente,
friends and well-known servants entered it freely,
senza essere squadrati da capo a piedi; che un artigianello
without being scrutinized from head to feet; that an unknown
sconosciuto non vi potrebb'entrare senza un esame, e
little artisan could not enter without an examination, and
ch'egli sopra tutto . . . egli vi sarebbe forse troppo conosciuto.
that he above all . . . he would be perhaps too well known.

NOTES

[1] **La venne.** Here **la** is used for **ella,** and is called " pleonastic **la** ",
common in Milanese usage. Manzoni tends to employ such variations
in his style.

[2] **sono servito,** a rather colloquial expression which corresponds to
our slang, " I've had it! " or, " It's all up with me."

[3] Not too clear in the original. The meaning is that those who harm
others are guilty not only of the direct harm but on account of the twists
cause by the harm in the minds of the injured parties.

§ 3. *Irregular Verbs in* -ERE: *Third Group* contd.—
Chemist's: Drug Store—I Promessi Sposi 13

Infinitive	Present Indicative	Past Definite	Past Participle
RED*I*MERE, *to* redeem	redimo	redensi	redento
R*I*DERE, *to laugh*	rido	risi	riso

> *Similarly:* **arridere**, to smile; **assidersi**, to seat oneself; **coincidere**, to coincide; **collidere**, to collide; **decidere**, to decide; **deridere**, to deride; **dividere**, to divide; **elidere**, to elide; **incidere**, to incise; **irridere**, to deride; **sorridere**, to smile; **uccidere**, to kill.

RIF*U*LGERE, *to* shine	rifulgo	rifulsi	rifulso
RISP*O*NDERE, *to reply*	rispondo	risposi	risposto

> *Similarly:* **corrispondere**, to correspond; **nascondere**, to hide.

RODERE, *to gnaw*	rodo	rosi	roso

> *Similarly:* **corrodere**, to corrode; **esplodere**, to explode.

ROMPERE, *to* break	rompo	ruppi	rotto

> *Similarly:* **corrompere**, to corrupt; **dirompere**, to make supple, break in; **erompere**, to erupt (*no Past Participle*); **interrompere**, to interrupt. **irrompere**, to burst in; **prorompere**, to burst out.

SCEGLIERE, *to* choose	scelgo	scelsi	scelto

> *Similarly:* **prescegliere**, to select (from many).

SC*I*NDERE, *to* separate	scindo	scissi	scisso

> *Similarly:* **prescindere**, to set aside; **rescindere**, to rescind.

SCR*I*VERE, *to* write	scrivo	scrissi	scritto

> *Similarly:* **ascrivere**, to ascribe; **descrivere**, to describe; **inscrivere, iscrivere**, to inscribe; **prescrivere**, to prescribe *and other derivatives of* **scrivere**.

| | Present | Past | Past |
Infinitive	Indicative	Definite	Participle
SCUOTERE, to shake	scuoto	scossi	scosso

Similarly: **percuotere,** to strike, smite; *and other derivatives.*

| SPARGERE, to scatter | spargo | sparsi | sparso (-to) |

Similarly: **cospargere,** to sprinkle.

| SPEGNERE ⎱ to ex-
spengere ⎰ tinguish | spengo | spensi | spento |

| STRINGERE, to fade | stringo | strinsi | stretto |

| STRUGGERE, to melt | struggo | strussi | strutto |

Similarly: **distruggere,** to destroy.

| TORCERE, to twist | torco | torsi | torto |

Similarly: **attorcere,** to twist up; **contorcere,** to contort; **estorcere,** to extort; **ritorcere,** to twist back; **storcere,** to untwist

| VINCERE, to vanquish | vinco | vinsi | vinto |

Similarly: **avvincere,** to bind; **convincere,** to convince; **rivincere,** to win back; **stravincere,** to conquer completely.

| VIVERE, to live | vivo | vissi | vissuto |

Similarly: **convivere,** to live together; **rivivere,** to relive, revive; **sopravvivere,** to survive.

| VOLGERE, to turn round | volgo | volsi | volto |

Similarly: **avvolgere,** to wrap; **capovolgere,** to turn upside down; **coinvolgere,** to involve; **involgere,** to wrap up; **rivolgere,** to turn round; **sconvolgere,** to throw into confusion; **svolgere,** to writhe; **travolgere,** to upset.

Chemist's: Drug Store

la ricetta, prescription
il medicamento, medicine
la garza gommata, adhesive tape

il termometro, thermometer
lo scaldapiedi, hot-water bottle
gli occhiali neri, dark glasses

il **sapone,** soap
le **pillole,** tablets, pills
la **capsula,** capsule
l'**ovatta,** cotton wool
il **mantile,** sanitary towel
il **dentifricio,** tooth paste
la **benda,** bandage
il **talco,** talc powder
le **lame di rasoio,** razor blades
il **pennello da barba,** shaving-brush
il **sapone da barba,** shaving-soap

lo **spazzolino da denti,** tooth-brush
il **piumino,** puff
il **portacipria,** compact
la **matita,** lipstick; *also* pencil
la **crema per il viso,** face cream
la **spazzola per capelli,** hair-brush
la **lozione capillare,** hair-lotion
il **gargarismo,** gargle
l'**aspirina,** aspirin

Vorrei comprare . . . I want to buy . . .
Vorrei vedere . . . I want to see . . .
Questo non è ciò che voglio. This is not what I want.
È troppo caro. It is too dear.
Voglio qualche cosa meno caro. I want something cheaper.
È questo il più a buon mercato? Is this the cheapest?
Non ha del, della . . .? Haven't you any . . .?
Qualche cosa di meglio? Anything better?
Un poco più caro? A little dearer?
Lo prendo. I'll have it.
Quanto costa? How much does it cost?
Datemi anche del, della . . . Give me also (some) . . .
Posso pagare in valuta straniera? Can I pay in foreign currency?
Ritornerò più tardi. I'll come back later.
Mi dà per piacere . . . Kindly give me . . .
Mi dà della tintura di iodio. Give me some tincture of iodine.
Uso esterno. Scuotere la bottiglia. External use. Shake the bottle.
Tre pillole al giorno. Three pills a day.
Ogni quattro ore. Every four hours.
Vorrei delle spille di sicurezza. I want some safety pins.

Mi prepari questa ricetta, per favore. Kindly make up this prescription for me.

Desidero un sedativo. I want a sedative.

Vorrei della polvere di riso. I want some rice powder.

Quando sarà pronto? When will it be ready?

13 I PROMESSI SPOSI

Si figurava allora di prendere il suo schioppo, d'ap-
He now imagined himself taking his shot-gun, hiding
piattarsi dietro una siepe, aspettando se mai, se mai colui
behind a bush, awaiting if ever, if ever, that fellow
venisse a passar solo; e, internandosi, con feroce com-
happened to pass by alone; and identifying himself, with fierce satis-
piacenza, in quell'immaginazione, si figurava di sentire
faction, with such imaginings, he thought he heard
una pedata, quella pedata, d'alzar chetamente la testa;
a footstep, that footstep, to raise his head quietly,
riconosceva lo scellerato, spianava lo schioppo, prendeva
(and he) recognized the villain, raised his shot-gun, took
la mira, sparava, lo vedeva cadere e dare i tratti, gli
aim, fired, saw him fall at the point of death, flung
lanciava una maledizione, e correva sulla strada del
him a curse, and ran (away) on the road to the
confine a mettersi in salvo.—E Lucia?—Appena questa
border to put himself in safety.—And Lucia?—Hardly was this word
parola si fu gettata a traverso di quelle bieche fantasie,
thrown across these knavish fantasies, the better
i migliori pensieri a cui era avvezza la mente di Renzo,
thoughts to which Renzo's mind was accustomed,
v'entrarono in folla. Si rammentò degli ultimi ricordi
entered it in a crowd. He remembered the last memories
de'suoi parenti, si rammentò di Dio, della Madonna e
of his parents, he remembered God, the Madonna and
de'santi, pensò alla consolazione che aveva tante volte
the saints, he thought of the consolation he had
provata di trovarsi senza delitti, all'orrore che aveva
so many times experienced to find himself without misdeeds, of the

tante volte provato al racconto d'un omicidio; e si
horror he so often felt at the account of a murder; and he
risvegliò da quel sogno di sangue, con ispavento, con
awoke from that bloody dream, with terror, with
rimorso, e insieme con una specie di gioia di non aver
remorse, and also with a kind of joy at not having
fatto altro che immaginare. Ma il pensiero di Lucia,
done otherwise than imagine (it all). But the thought of Lucia,
quanti pensieri tirava seco! Tante speranze, tante
how many thoughts it drew with it! So many hopes, so many
promesse, un avvenire così vagheggiato, e così tenuto
promises, a future so delightful, and so held for
sicuro, e quel giorno così sospirato! E come, con che
certain, and that day so longed for! And how, with what
parole annunziarle una tal nuova? E poi, che partito
words to announce to her such news? And then, what course to
prendere? Come farla sua, a dispetto della forza di
take? How to make her his, despite the power of
quell'iniquo potente? E insieme a tutto questo, non un
that iniquitous potentate? And together with all this, not a
sospetto formato, ma un'ombra tormentosa gli passava
suspicion formed, but a tormenting shadow passed
per la mente. Quella soverchieria di don Rodrigo non
across his mind. That outrage of Don Rodrigo could
poteva esser mossa che da una brutale passione per Lucia.
only be started by a brutal passion for Lucia.
E Lucia? Che avesse data a colui la più piccola occasione,
And Lucia? That she had given him the very smallest occasion,
la più leggiera lusinga, non era un pensiero che potesse
the very slightest encouragement, was not a thought that could
fermarsi un momento nella testa di Renzo. Ma n'era
remain a moment in Renzo's head. But was she
informata? Poteva colui aver concepita quell'infame
informed of it? Could that man have conceived that infamous
passione, senza che lei se n'avvedesse? Avrebbe spinte
passion, without her being aware of it? Would he have
le cose tanto in là, prima d'averla tentata in qualche modo?
pushed things to that point, before having tempted her in some way?

E Lucia non ne aveva mai detta una parola a lui! al suo
And Lucia had never said a word to him! to her
promesso!
promised (man)!

§ 4. *Irregular Verbs in* **-IRE**: *Eight Models—Motoring: Vocabulary and Phrases*—**I Promessi Sposi 14**

The irregular Verbs ending in **-IRE** are not many, and follow the models of the following eight Verbs:

APPARIRE, to appear	**SALIRE,** to climb, mount
APRIRE, to open	**UDIRE,** to hear
CUCIRE, to sew	**USCIRE,** to go, out
MORIRE, to die	**VENIRE,** to come

The derivative and compound Verbs, springing from these, are conjugated in the same way as the originals.

CONJUGATION OF IRREGULAR VERBS ENDING **-IRE**

APPARIRE, to appear

Gerund: **apparendo**
Past Participle: **apparso** (or **apparito**)
Present Indicative:

appaio	or apparisco
appari	apparisci
appare	apparisce
appariamo	
apparite	
appaiono	appariscono

Past Definite:

apparii	or apparsi (or -arvi)
apparisti	apparisti
apparì	apparse (or -arve)
apparimmo	
appariste	
apparirono	apparsero (or apparvero)

Future: **apparirò**
Conditional: **apparirei**
Present Subjunctive: **appaia** or **apparisca**, —, —, **appariamo**,
 appariate, **app*a*iano** (or **appar*i*scano**)
Imperative: **appari, appaia,** etc., *like Present Subjunctive.*
 Apparire and the following derivatives are conjugated with
essere in the compound tenses:

 comparire, to show up well **disparire,** to disappear
 scomparire, to disappear *and* to cut a poor figure

APRIRE, to open

Gerund: **aprendo**
Past Participle: **aperto**
Present Indicative: **apro, apri, apre, apriamo, aprite, *a*prono**
Past Definite: **aprii** (or **apersi**), **apristi, aprì** (**-erse**), **aprim-**
 mo, apriste, apr*i*rono (**-ersono**)
Future: **aprirò**
Conditional: **aprirei**
Present Subjunctive: **apra,** —, —, **apriamo, apriate, *a*prano.**
 Similarly the Imperative, except **apri** (Second Person Singular)
 and **aprite** (Second Person Plural).

 Like **aprire** are:

 coprire, to cover   **scoprire,** to uncover, unveil
 offrire, to offer   **scovrire,** to discover
 riaprire, to reopen   **soffrire,** to suffer

CUCIRE, to sew

Gerund: **cucendo**
Past Participle: **cucito**
Present Indicative: **cucio, cuci, cuce, cuciamo, cucite,**
 c*u*ciono
Past Definite: **cucii, cucisti, cucì, cucimmo, cuciste,**
 cuc*i*rono
Future: **cucirò**
Conditional: **cucirei**
Present Subjunctive: **cucia,** —, —, **cuciamo, cuciate, c*u*ciano**

 Like **cucire: scucire** *and* **sdrucire,** *both* to unstitch

MORIRE, to die

Gerund: **morendo**
Past Participle: **morto**
Present Indicative: **muoio, muori, muore, moriamo, morite, muoiono**
Past Definite: **morii, moristi, morì, morimmo, moriste, morirono**
Future: **morirò** or **morrò**
Conditional: **morirei** or **morrei**
Present Subjunctive: **muoia, —, —, moriamo, moriate, muoiano**
Imperative: **muori, muoia,** etc.

Similarly: **premorire,** to predecease

Morire and **premorire** are conjugated with *essere.*

SALIRE, to climb, mount

Gerund: **salendo**
Past Participle: **salito**
Present Indicative: **salgo, sali, sale, saliamo, salite, salgono**
Past Definite: **salii, salisti, salì, salimmo, saliste, salirono**
Present Subjunctive: **salga, —, —, saliamo, saliate, salgano**
Imperative: **sali, salga, —, salite, —**

Similarly: **assalire,** to assail; **risalire,** to climb again.

Although verbs of motion, **salire, assalire,** and **risalire** are conjugated with **avere.**

UDIRE, to hear

Gerund: **udendo**
Past Participle: **udito**
Present Indicative: **odo, odi, ode, udiamo, udite, odono**
Past Definite: **udii, udisti, udì, udimmo, udiste, udirono**
Present Subjunctive: **oda, —, —, udiamo, udiate, odano**
Future: **udirò** or **udrò**
Conditional: **udirei** or **udrei**
Imperative: **odi, oda,** etc. *like Present Subjunctive.*

In the Present Indicative and Subjunctive, this Verb also has the forms with **-isco-** and **isca-.**

USCIRE, to go out

Gerund: **uscendo**
Past Participle: **uscito**
Present Indicative: **esco, esci, esce, usciamo, uscite, escono**
Past Definite: **uscii, uscisti, uscì, uscimmo, usciste, uscirono**
Future: **uscirò**
Conditional: **uscirei**
Present Subjunctive: **esca, —, —, usciamo, usciate, escano.**
  Similarly, the Imperative, except Second Person Plural **uscite**.
  This and the following similar verbs are conjugated with **essere**:

escire, to go out   **riescire,** to go out again
riuscire, to succeed

VENIRE, to come

Gerund: **venendo**
Past Participle: **venuto**
Present Indicative: **vengo, vieni, viene, veniamo, venite, vengono**
Past Definite: **venni, venisti, venne, venimmo, veniste, vennero**
Future: **verrò**
Conditional: **verrei**
Present Subjunctive: **venga, —, —, veniamo, veniate, vengano**
Imperative: **vieni, venga, veniamo, venite, vengano**
  Venire is conjugated with **essere** in compound tenses.
  All of the following similar Verbs are conjugated with **essere** except those marked **(av)** which take **avere**:

addivenire, to occur   **contravvenire (av),** to con-
provenire, to arise   travene
avvenire, to happen   **rinvenire (av),** to rediscover
riconvenire (av), to agree   **convenire,** to come together,
  afresh   agree

rivenire, to come again
sconvenire, to be unbecoming
divenire, to become
sopravvenire, to supervene
intervenire, to intervene

sovvenire (av), to assist
pervenire, to arrive at
svenire,* to faint
prevenire (av.), to arrive before, anticipate

* Future and Conditional: **svenirò, svenerei.**

Motoring: Vocabulary and Phrases

la manutenzione, maintenance
il distributore di benzina, petrol, gasoline station
esaminare, to examine
lavare, to wash
il parabrezza, windscreen
pulire, to clean
il meccanico, mechanic
l'automobile, l'auto, automobile
il cofano, bonnet
il volante, steering-wheel
il radiatore, radiator
il faro, headlight
la ruota, wheel
il pneumatico, tyre
cambiare, to change
il motore, engine
i fili (elettrici), wiring
la candela, sparking plug
il cilindro, cylinder
l'olio, lubricating oil
la vettura, the car
accomodare, to adjust
mettere in ordine, to put in order
ingrassare, to grease
il garage, garage

funzionare, to function
la riparazione, repair
la foratura, puncture
il carburatore, carburetter
gonfiare, to inflate (a tire)
la gonfiatura, blowing up a tire
fermarsi, to stop (at)
il freno, brake
andare adagio, presto, to go slowly, fast
il passeggiero, passenger
prendere all'ora, a giornata, to take (hire) by the hour, the day
il posto, place (in a car)
stare seduto comodo, to be comfortably seated
anteriore, posteriore, front, back
la direzione, direction
posto davanti, dietro, front, back seat
l'utensile, tool
la chiave inglese, monkey wrench
la panna, breakdown
forare una gomma, to have a punctured tyre

Dove c'è un garage? Where is there a garage?

Voglio mettere la vettura in garage. I want to garage the car.

Vuole lavare, pulire l'auto? Will you wash, clean the car?

Vorrei . . . litri di benzina. I want . . . litres of petrol, gasoline.

Riempia il serbatoio. Fill the tank.

Vuole esaminare . . . Have a look at, examine . . .

Riempia il radiatore d'acqua. Fill the radiator with water.

Accomodi il carburatore. Adjust, fix the carburetter.

Ripari il pneumatico, la foratura. Repair the tyre, puncture.

Metta in ordine il parabrezza. Put the windscreen in order.

Questo non funziona bene. This does not work well.

Cambi questo, per favore. Change this, please.

Può mandare qualcuno per riparare il motore? Can you send somebody to repair the engine?

Abbiamo avuto una panna. We've had a breakdown.

Quando sarà pronto? When will it be ready?

Può essere pronto per le sei? Can it be ready by six o'clock?

Vuole gonfiarmi questa ruota? Will you blow up this tyre?

Vuole ripassarmi il carburatore? Will you look over the carburetter for me?

Non ho trovato la causa. I haven't found the cause.

Potrà rimettermelo a punto? Will you be able to put it right?

Vuole fare un ripasso generale? Will you give it a general look over?

Ha riparato l'auto? Have you repaired the car?

Allora, tutto è a posto? Is everything all right now?

Quanto costa tutto? How much does it all cost?

14   I PROMESSI SPOSI

Dominato da questi pensieri, passò davanti a casa sua,
Dominated by these thoughts, he passed in front of his
ch'era nel mezzo del villaggio, e, attraversatolo, s'avviò
house, which was in the middle of the village, and,

a quella di Lucia, ch'era in fondo, anzi un po'fuori.[1] Aveva
having gone through it, went on to Lucia's, which was at the end, also
quella casetta un piccolo cortile dinanzi, che la separava
a little beyond.   That cottage had a little (court)yard in front,
della strada, ed era cinto da un murettino. Renzo entrò
separating it from the road, and it was surrounded by a small wall.
nel cortile, e sentì un misto e continuo ronzio [2] che veniva
Renzo entered the yard, and heard a mixed and continuous hum (of
da una stanza di sopra. S'immaginò che sarebbero
talk) which came from an upstairs room.   He imagined it might be
amiche e comari, venute a far corteggio a Lucia; e non
friends and neighbours, come to be in attendance on Lucia; and he
si volle mostrare a quel mercato,[3] con quella nuova in
did not wish to show himself to that group, with that news in (his)
corpo e sul volto. Una fanciulletta che si trovava nel
body and on (his) face.   A (nice) little girl who was in the
cortile, gli corse incontro gridando: «lo sposo! lo sposo!»
yard, ran to him crying out: " The bridegroom! the bridegroom!"

    «Zitta, Bettina, zitta!» disse Renzo. «Vien' qua; va su
    " Hush, Bettina, hush!" said Renzo. "Come here: go up
da Lucia, tirala in disparte, e dille all'orecchio . . . ma
to Lucia, take her aside, and tell her in her ear . . . but
che nessun senta, nè sospetti di nulla, ve' . . . dille che
(so) that no one hears, or suspects anything, (you) see . . . tell her
ho da parlarle, che l'aspetto nella stanza terrena, e che
that I must talk to her, that I'm waiting for her in the
venga subito.» La fanciulletta salì in fretta le scale, lieta
downstairs room, and to come at once.   The little girl went hastily up
e superba d'avere una commissione segreta da eseguire.
the stairs, glad and proud to have a secret commission to carry out.

    Lucia usciva in quel momento tutta attillata dalle mani
    Lucia was coming out at that moment all dressed up
della madre. Le amiche si rubavano la sposa, e le
from her mother's hands.   The friends bustled around the bride, and
facevan forza perchè si lasciasse vedere; e lei s'andava
made her let herself be seen;   and she was warding
schermendo, con quella modestia un po' guerriera delle
(them) off,   with   that   modesty   a   little   aggressive   of

contadine, facendosi scudo alla faccia col gomito, chinan-
peasant women, making a shield for her face with her elbow, dropping
dola sul busto, e aggrottando i lunghi e neri sopraccigli,
it on her bosom, and banking down her long black eyebrows,
mentre però la bocca s'apriva al sorriso.   I neri e giovanile
yet her mouth opened in a smile.   Her black, youthful
capelli, spartiti sopra la fronte, con una bianca e sottile
hair, divided over her forehead, with a white, cunning
dirizzatura, si ravvolgevan, dietro il capo, in cerchi
parting, was wound round, behind her head, in multiple
moltiplici di trecce, trapassate da lunghi spilli d'argento,
(circled) plaits, pierced with long hairpins of silver,
che si dividevano all' intorno, quasi a guisa de' raggi d'un'
which were spread out all round, as if in the manner of a
aureola, come ancora usano le contadini nel Milanese.
halo, as still used by the peasants in the Milanese.[4]
Intorno al collo aveva un vezzo di granati con bottoni
Around her neck she had a necklace of (red) granite
d'oro filigrana.
with links of filigree gold.

NOTES

[1] **fuori,** outside (the village).
[2] **ronzio,** buzzing (as of bees).
[3] **il mercato,** literally *market* but here a busy group of people.
[4] **nel Milanese,** of (the province of) Milan.

§ 5. *Defective Verbs—List of Common Defective Verbs—Impersonal Verbs—List of Impersonal Verbs—Road Signs—Public Notices: General—I Promessi Sposi 15*

DEFECTIVE VERBS: There are some Italian Verbs which are used only in certain tenses, and most of them in the Third Person Singular only. They are " defective ". One meets them in reading, some of them only in poetry. It is unnecessary to know all these defective verbs at this stage: the majority are best learnt as they are met in reading. But it is advisable to memorize certain parts of the commonest, which are listed on page 266.

LIST OF COMMON DEFECTIVE VERBS

addirsi, to be suitable: **si addice,** it is suitable; **si addiceva,** it was suitable

aggradare, to please: **v'aggrada,** (as) it pleases you

***calere,** to matter: **cale,** it matters; **mi cale,** it matters to me; **carrà** or **calerà,** it will matter

capire, to fit, to go into: **cape,** it fits, there's room (for it)

constare, to consist of, to result from, to be proved: **consta,** (it) is proved; **non consta,** not proven

fallare, to lack, be short of: **falla,** (it) is short of

fervere, to be fervent, to boil, seethe: **ferve,** (he, she, it) is fervent, seething

molcere, to sooth, to be soothing: **molce,** it sooths, is soothing; **molceva,** was soothing

prudere, to itch: **prude,** it itches

solere, to be wont, to be accustomed to: **suole,** (he, she, it) is wont, accustomed (followed by an infinitive)

vigere, to be in force (legal term): **vige, vigono,** it is, they are in force. **vigeva,** it was in force; **vigerà,** it will be in force

---

* **CALERE** is the most likely of these verbs to be met in its various parts. It is irregular, employed only in the Third Person, and takes the Indirect Object (Dative) pronoun (see Table on page 79). The following parts are given for reference, to be memorized later:

Imperfect: **caleva,** it mattered; **mi caleva,** it mattered to me
Future: **mi carrà** or **calerà,** it will matter to me
Conditional: **gli carebbe** or **calerebbe,** it should matter to him
Present Subjunctive: **calga** or **caglia,** it may matter
Gerund: **calendo,** mattering
Past Participle: **caluto**

It forms compound tenses with *essere:* **è caluto,** *it has mattered.*

IMPERSONAL VERBS: Are so called because they do not refer to any definite person or thing, as when we say " *it is necessary* " or " *it's raining* ". They are found only in the Third Person Singular, and in Italian the English *it* is included in the verb. Thus: **fa freddo,** *it's cold*; **tuona,** *it thunders* (*there's thunder*).

The following list includes most of the impersonal verbs:

LIST OF IMPERSONAL VERBS

(1) From **fare,*** *to make, to do:*
  fa freddo, it's cold
  fa caldo, it's hot
  fa fresco, it's cool
  fa bel tempo, it's fine (weather)
  fa cattivo tempo, it's bad (weather)

(2) Other impersonal verbs relating to weather: †
tirare vento: tira vento, it's windy (wind blows)
piovere: piove, it's raining
diluviare: diluvia, it's pouring rain
lampeggiare: lampeggia, it lightens (there's lightning)
tonare: tuona, it thunders
gelare: gela, it's freezing
sgelare: sgela, it's thawing
grandinare: grandina, it's hailing
nevicare: nevica, it's snowing

(3) Miscellaneous impersonal verbs: ‡
bastare: basta, it's enough. **Basta!** Enough!
bisognare: bisogna, it's necessary
accadere: accade, it happens; **accadde,** it happened
convenire: conviene, it suits, it is convenient
importare: importa, it matters. **non importa,** it doesn't matter
occorrere: occorre, it's needful, it happens
dovere essere: dovrebb' essere, it ought to be
parere: pare, it appears, seems
sembrare: sembra, it seems
avvenire: è avvenuto (che), it happened (that)
piacere: piace, it pleases; **mi piace,** it pleases me, I like
and essere, as in **c'è** *or* **v'è,** there is *or* there are; **ci, vi sono;**
  c'erano *or* **ci furono,** there were; **ci sarà,** etc.

* **Fare** used impersonally is conjugated with **avere: ha fatto freddo,** *it was, has been cold.*
† These verbs are conjugated with **essere: è tonato,** *it has thundered.*
‡ These verbs are not often met except in the forms given, which must be memorized.

Road Signs

PERICOLO, Danger

LENTAMENTE, Slowly

RALLENTARE, Go slow

ALT! Stop!

STRADA SBARRATA, Road Closed

PARCHEGGIO, Parking

VIETATO IL PARCHEG-GIO, Parking forbidden

PASSAGGIO A LIVELLO, Level Crossing

SCUOLA, School

INCROCIO, Cross-roads

INCROCIO PERICOLOSO, Dangerous Cross-roads

CURVA ⎱ PERICOLOSA,
SVOLTA ⎰ Dangerous Bend

LAVORI STRADALI, Work on the Road

SENSO UNICO, One Way

GRANDE VIA, Main Thoroughfare

PROCEDERE, Go ahead. Keep moving

VELOCITÀ ⎱ Maximum
MASSIMA ⎬ Speed
10 Km. ⎰ 10 Km.

PROIBITO IL PASSAGGIO, No Thoroughfare

LOCALITÀ POPOLATA, (Thickly) Populated Area

Road Signs and Other Notices

i segnali luminosi, light signals

rosso (red) = **Alt!** = Stop!

giallo (yellow) = **Cambiamento di Segnale** = Change of Signal

verde (green) = **Via Libera** = Road clear: Go!

la strada privata, private road

la strada di grande comuni-cazione, main road, thoroughfare

passaggio per pedoni, crossing for pedestrians

linea d'arresto, stopping line before lights or a crossing

traffico circolare, roundabout traffic

strada nazionale, national road

autostrada, (good) motoring road

posto di pronto soccorso, first aid station

il distributore di benzina, petrol, gasoline station

il posto di polizia, police station

l'autorimessa, il garage, garage

veicoli ad andatura modera-ta, drive slowly

vietato il transito, no thoroughfare

chiuso al transito, closed to traffic

Public Notices: General

Attenzione! Attention!

Appartamento(-i) d'affittare, flat, apartment (-s) to let

Attenti al cane! Beware of dog!

Cambiare per . . ., Change for . . .

Pericolo, Danger

Vietato . . . It is forbidden . . .

Vietato fumare, Smoking forbidden

Non sporgersi, Do not lean out

Entrata libera, Entrance free

Entrata, Entrance

Uscita, Exit

Prezzi fissi, Fixed prices

SIGNORI or **UOMINI:** Gentlemen, Men

SIGNORE or **DONNE,** Ladies

Vietato andare sull'erba, Keep off the grass

Tenere la destra, sinistra, Keep to the right, left

Vietato sputare, Spitting forbidden

Si paga qui, Pay here

Si paga alla cassa, Pay at the cash desk

CESSO } W.C., Public
LATRINA } Lavatory

SUONATE, Ring

Spingere, Push, press the bell

Pedoni, Pedestrians

Chiudere la porta, Shut the door

SI LOCA or **Appigionasi,** To Let

Occupato, Engaged, Occupied

FERMATA, Stopping-place

FERMATA OBBLIGATORIA, Stopping-place, all trams and buses

FERMATA FACOLTATIVA, Request Stop

Avanti senza bussare, Come in without knocking

Non toccare, Do not touch

Ascensore, lift, elevator

Orario dei Treni, Time-table

UFFICIO INFORMAZIONI, Enquiries, Information Bureau

DEPOSITO BAGAGLIO, Left Luggage

SALA D'ASPETTO, Waiting-room

Chiuso alla domenica, Closed on Sunday

C = caldo, hot tap.   **F = freddo,** cold tap

Acqua Potabile, drinking-water

15   I PROMESSI SPOSI

Portava un bel busto di broccato a fiori,[1] con le maniche
She wore a beautiful bodice of brocade with flowers, with the cuffs

separate e allacciate da bei nastri: una corta gonnella di
open   and   laced   with   pretty   ribbons;   a   short   dress   of
filaticcio di seta, a pieghe fitte e minute, due calze ver-
coarse   silk,   with   close,   minute   pleats,   a   pair   of   red   stockings,
miglie, due pianelle, di seta anch'esse, a ricami. Oltre a
a pair of slippers, of silk also these, embroidered.   Apart from
questo, ch'era l'ornamento particolare del giorno delle
(all)   this,   which   was   the   adornment   for   her   wedding
nozze, Lucia aveva quello quotidiano d'una modesta
day,   Lucia   had   that   daily   one   of   a   (her)   modest
bellezza, rilevata allora e accresciuta dalle varie affezioni
beauty,   now   brought   out   and   increased   by   the   various   emotions
che le si dipingevan sul viso: una gioia temperata da un
which   were   depicted   on   her   face: a   joy   tempered   by   a
turbamento leggiero, quel placido accoramento che si
slight   agitation,   that   placid   melancholy   which   shows
mostra di quand'in quando sul volto delle spose, e, senza
itself from time to time on the face of brides, and, without
scompor la bellezza, le dà un carattere particolare. La
disturbing   beauty,   gives   them   a   particular   character.
piccola Bettina si cacciò nel crocchio, s'accostò a Lucia,
Little Bettina thrust herself into the group, sidled up to Lucia,
le fece intendere accortamente che aveva qualcosa di
made   her   understand   cautiously   that   she   had   something   to
comunicarle, e le disse la sua parolina all'orecchio.
communicate to her, and said her little word in her ear.

«Vo [2] un momento, e torno,» disse Lucia alle donne; e
" I'm going (out) a moment, and I'll be back," said Lucia to the
scese in fretta. Al veder la faccia mutata, e il portamento
women; and went down hurriedly.   On seeing the changed face, and
inquieto di Renzo, «cosa c'è?» disse, non senza un presenti-
uneasy bearing of Renzo, " What is it? " she said, not without a
mento di terrore.
presentiment of terror.

«Lucia!» rispose Renzo, «per oggi, tutto è a monte; [3] e
" Lucia! " replied Renzo, " for today, everything's in the air; and
Dio sa quando potremo esser marito e moglie.»
God knows when we can be husband and wife."

«Che?» disse Lucia, tutta smarrita. Renzo le raccontò
" What? " said Lucia, all dismayed. Renzo told her
brevemente la storia di quella mattina: ella ascoltava con
briefly the story of that morning: she listened in
angoscia: e quando udì il nome di don Rodrigo, «ah!»
anguish: and when she heard the name of Don Rodrigo, " ah! "
esclamò arrossendo e tremando, «fino a questo segno!»
she exclaimed blushing and trembling, " (So) it's got so far! "

«Dunque voi sapevate?» disse Renzo.
" Then you knew? " said Renzo.

«Pur troppo!» rispose Lucia; «ma a questo segno!» [4]
" Only too (well)! " replied Lucia. " But to (come to) this! "

«Che cosa sapevate?»
" What did you know? "

«Non mi fate ora parlare, non mi fate piangere. Corro
" Don't make me speak now, don't make me weep. I'm running
a chiamar mia madre, e licenziar le donne: bisogna che
to call my mother, and send away the women: it's necessary for us
siamo soli.»
to be alone."

Mentre ella partiva, Renzo susurrò: «non m'avete mai
While she was leaving, Renzo muttered, " you had never told
detto niente.»
me anything."

NOTES

[1] **broccato a fiori,** flowered brocade.
[2] **vo = vado,** I go.
[3] *essere a monte, idiom:* to be in the air.
[4] **a questo signo,** to this point, sign = To come to this!

LESSON VIII

§ 1. *Present Participle and Gerund—The Italian Gerund— Italian Infinitive and Past Participle for English* **-ing**—**I Promessi Sposi 16**

THERE is often some confusion in the minds of English-speaking learners of Italian in regard to distinguishing between the Italian Present Participle and the Gerund and their correct use, and this is chiefly due to the fact that in Italian they have different forms, whereas in English the same form is used for both. Thus, in English both Present Participle and Gerund end in *-ing* as in *singing, speaking, writing*, etc. So one must be clear, first of all, about the meanings—the two distinct meanings—which each can have. Take the following sentences:

(1) I am singing; I was speaking; I shall be writing.

(2) The singing lady; the speaking representative; the writing machine.

(3) Fond of singing; fond of singing songs; fond of writing letters.

It will be seen that in (1), (2), and (3) the words *singing, speaking, writing* have different meanings, and in each case the *-ing* word has a different grammatical function. Thus:

In (1) they are used as part of a tense-form, known as the " Continuous ", because it represents continuous action.

In (2) they are used as Adjectives to describe the nature of a Noun.

In (3) *Fond of singing*, here *singing* has a Noun function. *Fond of singing songs, fond of writing letters*, here the words *singing, writing* represent a Noun-and-Verb function combined.

So much for the English words ending in *-ing*. Now let us look at Italian and we find *two* endings for our *-ing*:

Infinitives	Present Participles	Gerunds
-ARE	-ante	-ando
-ERE	-ente	-endo
-IRE	-ente	-endo

You may now consider the Italian Present Participle and Gerund in their own right and, if you do this, forgetting for a time the English values outlined above, their use is not difficult.

The Italian Present Participle is now rarely used with its *verbal* value. You need not learn at this stage the verbs which still occasionally use it, because you can do without it and turn your sentences in some other way with a relative. **avere, contenere, formare, indicare, comandare, rappresentare, attestare,** and **eccedere** are sometimes found in reading in the Present Participle form, though modern writers use it less and less. The general use of the Present Participle can be stated quite briefly:

The Italian Present Participle is a *verbal adjective* which can sometimes be used as a Noun. Thus:

(1) As a verbal adjective:

il lavoro andante, everyday work
è una stoffa di qualità andante, a stuff (material) of everyday quality
il mio fratello, tremante, aspettava, my brother, trembling, was waiting
i venditori ambulanti di Roma, the pedlars of Rome. (*Note the agreement, like an adjective, with* **venditori.**)

(2) As a Noun:

un amante, a lover
un rappresentante, a representative

THE ITALIAN GERUND: Broadly speaking, the Italian Gerund corresponds to our Present Participle, but *it tends more to have the force of a verb than of an adjective.*

K

(1) It usually indicates an action contemporary with or parallel to that of the principal verb in a sentence. Thus:

> **uscendo ho chiuso la porta,** (while) going out I shut the door (**mentre,** while, *is understood*)
>
> **uscendo Lei deve chiudere la porta,** going out, you must shut the door
>
> **scendendo le scale caddi,** coming down the stairs, I fell

(2) The Italian Gerund is combined with the verbs **stare, andare,** and **venire** to indicate duration or persistence of an action:

(*a*) stare—

> **sto cercando la stazione,** I'm looking for the station

This makes our " Continuous Present " and other tenses.

> **egli stava parlando,** he was speaking
> **io stetti leggendo,** I was reading
> **starà cantando,** she will be singing, etc.

(*b*) andare—

> **vado meditando,** I go on meditating

(*c*) venire—

> **vengo scrivendo,** I am just writing

(3) The Gerund can be used in an absolute sense with its own subject:

> **La mia prigione essendo così alta, gli uomini laggiù mi parevano fanciulli.** My prison being so high, the men down there seemed to me small boys.

(4) Most English phrases of *condition*, *time*, *cause*, *means*, *manner*, can in Italian be conveniently rendered by the Gerund. Thus:

> **facendo così,** so doing . . .
> **essendo povero,** being poor
> **andando lesto lesto,** going, walking quickly
> **vedendo che il giuoco,** seeing that the game
> **ottenendo il passaporto,** obtaining the passport

—such phrases being introductory to a statement which follows them. For example: **ottenendo il passaporto, potrebbe partire il mese prossimo,** (*by*) *obtaining the passport, you might be able to leave next month.*

This is a convenient, simple formula which can be used in everyday speech, and should be mastered with—

(5) Personal Pronouns, but note: (*a*) When the Personal Pronoun subject is in the First or Second Person (**io, tu, noi, voi**) these pronouns are used. (*b*) But, with the Third Person, **lui** and **lei** are the more usual forms:

> **Essendo io a letto, hanno dovuto sostituirmi all'ufficio.**
> (I) being in bed, they had to replace me at the office.
> **Avendo messo mano lui, le cose sono state rimesse in ordine.** (He) having put (his) hand to it, things were put back in order.

(6) In the list of musical terms on page 133 you will notice the high proportion of Gerunds used, **andante** is about the only Present Participle. (Also notice the large number of Past Participles similarly used.)

ITALIAN INFINITIVE FOR ENGLISH *-ing*: This is a common and useful form, in which the definite article is usually placed before the Italian Infinitive. Thus:

> **Non mi piace lo studiare, il leggere.** I don't like studying, reading
> **ma mi piace il dormire,** but I like sleeping

ITALIAN PAST PARTICIPLE FOR ENGLISH *-ing*: The Italian Past Participle is often used (with **essere**) to indicate a state where in English we would use the Present Participle—especially for such states as *sitting, kneeling, leaning, growing, emerging*. Of these verbs the most useful is **sedere,** to sit.

inginocchiarsi: Il sacerdote si era inginocchiato davanti l'altare maggiore. The priest was kneeling before the high altar.

SEDERE: La vecchia è seduta in una poltrona. The old woman is sitting in an armchair.

It would not be incorrect to use **stare** with the Gerund in such cases. Thus:

Il sacerdote si stava inginocchiando, etc.
La vecchia sta sedendo, etc.

16 I PROMESSI SPOSI

«**Ah, Renzo!**» **rispose Lucia, rivolgendosi un momento,**
" *Ah Renzo!* " *answered Lucia, turning a moment,*
senza fermarsi. Renzo intese benissimo che il suo nome
without stopping. Renzo understood very well that his name
pronunziato in quel momento, con quel tono da Lucia
pronounced in that moment, with Lucia's tone of
voleva dire: potete voi dubitare ch'io abbia taciuto se non
voice meant: can you doubt that I had kept silent only
per motivi giusti e puri?
for just and pure motives?

Intanto la buona Agnese (così si chiamava la madre di
Meanwhile the good Agnese (Lucia's mother was so called)
Lucia), messa in sospetto e in curiosità dalla parolina
put into suspicion and curiosity by the (little) word
all'orecchio, e dallo sparir della figlia, era discesa a veder
in the ear, and the disappearance of her daughter, had come down to
cosa c'era di nuovo. La figlia la lasciò con Renzo, tornò
see what news there was. Her daughter left her with Renzo,
alle donne radunate, e, accomodando l'aspetto e la voce,
turned to the grouped women, and, accommodating look and voice,
come potè meglio, disse: «il signor curato è ammalato;
as best she could, said: " The priest is ill;
e oggi non si fa nulla.»   Ciò detto, le salutò tutte in fretta
and to-day nothing will be done."   That said she took leave of all
e scese di nuovo.
hurriedly and came downstairs again.

Le donne sfilarono, e si sparsero a raccontar l'accaduto.
The women filed out, and dispersed to tell (of) the happening.
Due o tre andaron fin all'uscio del curato, per verificar se
Two or three went right to the priest's gate, to verify whether he
era ammalato davvero.
was really ill.

«Un febbrone,» rispose Perpetua dalla finestra; e la
" A bad fever," replied Perpetua from the window; and the
triste parola, riportata all'altre, troncò le congetture che
sad word, reported to the others, cut short the conjectures which
già cominciavano a brulicar ne' loro cervelli, e ad an-
already were beginning to crawl (stir) in their minds, and to emerge
nunziarsi tronche e misteriose ne' loro discorsi.
broken short and mysterious in their talk.

* * *

Lucia entrò nella stanza terrena, mentre Renzo stava
Lucia went into the downstairs room, while Renzo was
angosciosamente informando Agnese, la quale angosciosa-
anxiously informing Agnese, who anxiously was listening
mente lo ascoltava. Tutt'e due si volsero a chi ne sapeva
to him. Both of them turned to (the one) who knew more
più di loro, e da cui aspettavano uno schiarimento, il
of it than they did, and from whom they were expecting a clarification,
quale non poteva essere che doloroso: tutt'e due, lasciando
which could only be painful: both (of them), allowing
travedere, in mezzo al dolore, e con l'amore diverso che
to be seen, amid their grief, and with the differing love which
ognun d'essi portava a Lucia, un cruccio pur diverso
each bore (towards) Lucia, an anxiety, also differing,
perchè avesse taciuto loro qualche cosa, e una tal cosa.
because she had kept something back from them, and such a thing.
Agnese, benchè ansiosa di sentir parlare la figlia, non
Agnese, although anxious to hear her daughter speak,
potè tenersi di non fare un rimprovero. «A tua madre
could not refrain from reproving her. " To your mother
non dir niente d'una cosa simile!»
not to say anything about such a thing! "

§ 2. *Italian Use of Moods and Tenses: Present, Imperfect, Past
Definite, and Future—The Conditional—Compound Tenses
—I Promessi Sposi 17*

In the treatment of verbs, auxiliary, regular, and irregular,
general indications of meanings have been given and, if you feel

that you know those verbs fairly well, you may now proceed to learn the Italian use of moods and tenses, the sequence of tenses, and their dependence. First, we shall deal briefly with the Italian uses of tenses when these uses differ from English:

PRESENT TENSE INDICATIVE: (1) Used in Italian for our Future, to indicate determination, certainty, and immediacy. Thus:

> **Vado subito a casa.** I'll go home immediately.
>
> **Partiamo per Italia il mese prossimo.** We shall leave for Italy next month.
>
> **Egli viene a trovarvi la settimana prossima.** He'll come to (find) see you next week.

(2) Used in Italian when the action started in the past and *still continues*. Thus:

> **Studio l'italiano da sei mesi.** I have been studying Italian for six months. (*Here* **da** = from, since.)
>
> **Sono in Italia da un anno.** I have been a year in Italy.

IMPERFECT AND PAST DEFINITE: The Imperfect is used to express:

> (1) Incomplete, continuous, or habitual action in the past.
> (2) As a descriptive tense for the past.
> (3) As a tense for contemporary events, that is, when something happened simultaneously with another.

Thus:

> (1) **Noi andavamo ogni giorno.** We used to go every day.
> (2) **Il mare era azzuro.** The sea was blue.
>   **La mia sorella aveva ventisette anni.** My sister was twenty-seven years of age.
> (3) See (3) below:

The Past Definite is used to express:

> (1) Narrative of events which took place quite definitely in the past (and were not repeated).
> (2) With (1) the Imperfect is used when the second or other event(s) happened at the same time as (1). Thus:

(3) **Quando la mia madre morì, io avevo soltanto due anni.** When my mother died I was only two years of age.

In everyday speech the compound past (**avere** with a Past Participle) is more often used than the Past Definite.

Io ho parlato l'italiano colla ragazza. I spoke Italian with the girl.

THE FUTURE: The Italian Future is often used to express uncertainty, especially that kind of uncertainty which is mixed with probability. Thus:

Quanti anni avrà la signorina Rubini? Avrà vent'anni. How old might Miss Rubini be? (Probably) twenty years of age.

Diranno che ella ha trenta anni. They'll (probably) be saying that she's thirty.

Chi è la signora? Sarà la madre della signorina Rubini. Who is the lady? She's (probably) Miss Rubini's mother.

Lei crederà che io ho torto. You'll (probably) think I'm wrong.

And also as an equivalent for the English continuous Present Tense when, in fact, this indicates a future event:

Loro partiranno il primo (di) dicembre. They are leaving on the 1st of December.

THE CONDITIONAL: The Italian Conditional is often used where we would use another tense. For example:

(1) For politeness. **vorrei** has often already been met in " Situation Material " to express *I want, I should like.* Thus: **vorrei parlare col direttore**, *I want to speak to the manager.* Or, one could equally well say: **Potrei parlare col direttore?** Can I speak to the manager? **Non saprei** is a useful, polite way of saying *I don't know.*

(2) To indicate an uncertainty or mere possibility, when we should use a more definite tense. Thus: **Dove sta Guiglelmo? Sarebbe in Londra.** Where's William? He's in London (though this is doubtful). And also to indicate something not done, or to cast doubt on a claim: **Disse che sarebbe andato alla stazione.** He says that he went to the station (but he did not go).

COMPOUND TENSES: Revise Lesson VI, § 1, which covers most instances that are likely to arise.

17   I PROMESSI SPOSI

«Ora vi dirò tutto,» rispose Lucia, asciugandosi gli occhi
" Now I'll tell everything," replied Lucia, drying her eyes
col grembiule.
with her apron.

«Parla, parla! — Parlate, parlate!» gridarono a un tratto
" Speak, speak! — Speak, speak! " [1] cried of a sudden
la madre e lo sposo.
the mother and the bridegroom.

«Santissima Vergine!» esclamò Lucia: «chi avrebbe
" Most holy Virgin! " [2] exclaimed Lucia: " who would have
creduto che le cose potessero arrivare a questo segno!»
believed that things could come to this mark (pass)! "
E, con voce rotta dal pianto, raccontò come, pochi giorni
And, in a voice broken in weeping, she told how, a few days
prima, mentre tornava dalla filanda, ed era rimasta
before, when she returned from the silk-factory, and had remained
indietro dalle sue compagne, le era passato innanzi don
behind her companions, she was passed by Don
Rodrigo, in compagnia d'un altro signore; che il primo
Rodrigo, in company with another gentleman; that the first
aveva cercato di trattenerla con chiacchere, com'ella
had tried to accost her with gossip (prattle), as she

diceva, non punto belle; ma essa, senza dargli retta,
said, not at all nice; but she, without giving him ear,
aveva affrettato il passo, e raggiunte le compagne; e in-
had quickened her step, and joined her companions; and mean-
tanto aveva sentito quell'altro signore rider forte, e don
time had heard that other gentleman laugh loudly, and Don
Rodrigo dire: scommettiamo. Il giorno dopo, coloro
Rodrigo say: let's bet (have a bet).   The day after, they
s'eran trovati ancora sulla strada; ma Lucia era nel mezzo
found themselves again on the road; but Lucia was amidst
delle compagne, con gli occhi bassi; e l'altro signore
her companions, with her eyes (cast) down; and the other gentleman
sghignazzava, e don Rodrigo diceva: vedremo, vedremo.
guffawed and Don Rodrigo was saying: we'll see, we'll see.
«Per grazia del cielo,» continuò Lucia, «quel giorno era
"By grace of heaven," continued Lucia, "that day was
l'ultimo della filanda. Io raccontai subito. . . .»
the last of the spinning. I told at once. . . ."

    «A chi hai raccontato?» domandò Agnese, andando in
    " To whom did you tell? " asked Agnese, challenging her,
contro, non senza un po' di sdegno, al nome del con-
not without a little indignation, the name of her preferred
fidente preferito.
confidant.

    «Al padre Cristoforo, in confessione, mamma,» rispose
    " To Father Cristoforo, in confession, mamma," replied
Lucia, con un accento soave di scusa. «Gli raccontai
Lucia, with a suave tone of apology. "I told him
tutto, l'ultima volta che siamo andate insieme alla chiesa
everything, the last time that we went together to the convent
del convento: e, se vi ricordate, quella mattina, io andava
church: and, if you remember, that morning, I kept
mettendo mano ora a una cosa, ora a un'altra, per in-
putting a hand now to one thing and then to another, in order
dugiare, tanto che passasse altra gente del paese avviata
to delay, while other people from the locality passed
a quella volta, e far la strada in compagnia con loro;
in that direction, and to make the road in company with them;

perchè, doppo quell'incontro, le strade mi facevan tanta
because, after that encounter, the roads frightened me so
paura . . .»
much."

Al nome riverito del padre Cristoforo, lo sdegno d'Agnese
At the revered name of Father Cristoforo, Agnese's
si raddolcì. «Hai fatto bene,» disse. «Ma perchè non
irritation softened. "You did well," she said. "But why not
raccontar tutto anche a tua madre?»
tell everything also to your mother?"

NOTES

[1] **Parla,** Second Person Singular, the mother speaking; **parlate,**
Second Person Plural, the bridegroom.
[2] " Holy Mother of God " is more usual in English.

---

§ 3. *The Subjunctive Mood—To Avoid Using the Italian Sub-
      junctive—The Italian Subjunctive and its Uses—Conjunctions
      followed by Subjunctive: List—*I Promessi Sposi 18

As the Subjunctive Mood has almost disappeared from modern
English, the use of this Mood, which strongly survives in the
Latin languages, including Italian, is often a bugbear to English-
speaking learners. They may take comfort from one fact: *it
can be avoided when speaking or writing Italian.* But there is one
equally important fact which should be read with the first: *good
Italian speakers often use it in speech, and it is constantly used in
both Italian prose and verse.*

All learners should be able to *recognize* an Italian Subjunctive
form and its approximate meaning. For this reason those parts
of the general treatment of verbs in Lessons V and VI should
be revised. Only those learners who wish to have a closer
knowledge of the uses of the Subjunctive need study what is
given below. First come those who wish to avoid the Subjunctive.

I. TO AVOID USING THE ITALIAN SUBJUNCTIVE: Turn your
statements so that some other form is possible. This may mean
a complete paraphrase of what you intend to say. Thus:

Say: **È inutile dire quello.** It's useless to say that.

Instead of: **È inutile che Lei dica quello.** It's useless for you to say (that you say) that.

Or:

La segretaria che io cerco deve sapere l'italiano. The secretary I'm looking for must know Italian.

Instead of: **Io cerco una segretaria che sappia l'italiano.**

It will be seen that the Infinitive is a useful form for such paraphrases. But the Italian Gerund can also often be used:

(Lei) avendo fatto ⎱ **così, sono contento.**
　　　　facendo ⎰

Instead of: **Sono contento che Lei abbia fatto così**

to express: I'm glad that you have done that.

Those who wish to avoid using the Subjunctive by such ingenuity should be warned that the paraphrase can seldom express the exact meaning or delicacy of the Italian Subjunctive. But, for practical purposes, it should work well enough. You must regard the method as a makeshift. The alternative is to take the Italian Subjunctive more seriously and master the principles and rules which govern its correct use.

II. THE SUBJUNCTIVE AND ITS USES:

Definition: The Italian Subjunctive is the mood of—

> DOUBT
> UNCERTAINTY
> FEELING
> WILL, WISH, or DESIRE

It expresses something which is rarely a hard fact.

The straightforward simple sentence of affirmation, negation, or interrogation—by far the most useful kind of sentence for everyday use—is in the Indicative Mood. Thus:

(1) The sun shines by day and the moon by night.
John always keeps his promise.
William is a very bad boy.
He did not arrive in time.
Are you going to the opera this evening?

But a sentence can consist of an affirmation, a negation, or an interrogation followed by another sentence which qualifies it in some way. Thus:

(2) I'm keeping you a place, so that you may be near me.
I wish that he were as smart as his sister.
If I had his wealth, I should pay the money.
I won't come, unless you ask me.

You will see that these statements consist of affirmations, of which each one has another statement to qualify it. *Doubt* of some sort is raised by the two statements read together.

As far as possible, in writing and speaking, you should use sentences such as those given under (1), because when in Italian you use sentences such as those under (2) you are probably committed to the Subjunctive, the Mood of doubt, etc. Here, your main or principle Verb is followed by one in some way dependent on it.

When you understand this, you may begin to learn some principles which govern the use of the Subjunctive in Italian.

The Subjunctive is used:

I. After those ideas expressed in the definition given above: They include *opinion, necessity, hope, fear, surprise, wonder, command, consent.* Thus:

Credo che Lei non possa farlo.   I think you can't do it.
Credo che Lei non venga.   I think you won't come.
Voglio che Lei sia buono.   I wish you to be good.
Desidero che Lei venga con me.   I want you to come with me.
Siamo contenti che Loro siano arrivati.   We're glad you've arrived.
Permetta che io lodi suo fratello.   Allow me to praise your brother.
Dubito che egli abbia parlato l'italiano.   I doubt whether he has spoken Italian.
È possibile che sia contento.   It's possible that he may be pleased, content.
È inutile che mi dica così.   It's useless to tell me so.

When the main verb is in either the past or conditional, the verb in the Subjunctive is in the Past or Pluperfect Subjunctive:

Credei che loro partirono ieri. I believed that they left yesterday.

Vorrei che loro venissero oggi. I wished them to come to-day.

Pensai che Lei ebbe dimenticato il mio nome. I thought (that) you had forgotten my name.

A main verb in the Past Definite is followed by one in the Present or Past Subjunctive, according to the meaning or intention:

Egli ha detto che Lei venga. He said that you would come (*meaning* NOW).

Loro hanno detto che Lei venisse. They said that you would come (THEN).

The Subjunctive is used:

II. After the Conjunction **SE,** *if*, when it expresses a condition that is merely imagined or impossible to realize. Thus:

Se suo fratello agisse sempre così, io sarei contento. If your brother would always act thus, I'd be glad.

Se fosse un uomo ricco, avrebbe pagato. If he were a rich man, he'd have paid.

Se avessi il danaro, ve lo darei. If I had the money, I'd give it to you.

SE translates the English *if I were, if I had been*, etc. and then **se** is followed by the Subjunctive:

se io fossi, if I were
se loro fossero, if they were
se io fossi stato, if I had been
se noi fossimo stati, if we had been, etc.

Note: when the condition is an accepted fact, or merely formal, then **se** is followed by the Indicative:

Se Lei ha delle forti ragioni, verrà. If you have any strong reasons, you'll come.

Se Lei studierà bene, le farò un regalo. If you study well, I'll give you a present.

Se lo fece, Lei sarà punito. If you did it, you'll be punished.

The Subjunctive is used:

III. (1) After a superlative or a negative expression and certain words listed below:

   (1) **È la più bella donna cheio *a*bbia mai vista.** She's the most beautiful woman I have ever seen.

   Non c'è nessuno in questa università che possa leggerlo. There's nobody in this university who can read it.

   (2) after—

chiunque, whoever	**qualunque,** whatever
il sole che, the only one who	**il primo che,** the first who
l'*u*ltimo che, the last that	

The above is a summary of the principal and commonest uses of the Subjunctive. The remainder may be dealt with briefly. The Subjunctive is used:

   (1) To form the polite and other Imperatives, see page 172 *et seq.*

   (2) In certain Indirect questions.

   (3) After—

      (i) Impersonal Verbs, see page 267.

      (ii) After Certain Conjunctions, see pages 116–117.

      (iii) Indirect questions in the past tense.

      (iv) For polite imperative: always Present Subjunctive Third Person Singular and Plural.

Of these, you already know about (*iv*)—for which see pages 171–173 *et seq.*

As regards (*i*), it is only among the Miscellaneous Impersonal Verbs listed on page 172 that there are verbs which *may* take the Subjunctive to follow.   But even this can be avoided, as you will see.   For when a verb following an Impersonal Verb gives the sense clearly you must use the Infinitive.   Thus:

Le bisogna comprare un biglietto alla stazione.

It is necessary for you to
You must } buy a ticket at the station.

But when the impersonal **bisogna** is used and it does not indicate the person precisely, when it is necessary to do so, the Subjunctive will clarify:

Bisogna che ella esca.   She must go out.

—for, it is obvious that, if you say or write **bisogna uscire**, this means *It is necessary to go out* without regard to person.
Similarly:

Basta che loro parlino.   It is enough for them to speak.
Basta parlare.   It's enough to speak.

In speech, because of the situation and the context, it will seldom be necessary to use the Subjunctive.   Thus, in general, you may safely use the Infinitive after those Impersonal Verbs which are followed by another verb.

As regards (*ii*) it is when a conjunction or a conjunctional phrase (see pages 116–117) implies a condition precedent that the Subjunctive follows it.   Here is a list of such Conjunctions:

CONJUNCTIONS FOLLOWED BY THE SUBJUNCTIVE:

AFFINCHÈ, in order that
POSTO CHE, supposing that
A MENO CHE (NON), unless
PRIMA CHE, before
BENCHÈ, although
PURCHÈ, provided that

DATO CHE, given, granted that
QUALUNQUE, whatever
QUANTUNQUE, although
DOVUNQUE, whenever
SE, if (*see page* 285)

NON OSTANTE CHE, notwithstanding that
SEBBENE, although
SENZA CHE, without
PER QUANTO, however *

SOLO CHE, unless, except
POICHÈ, since †
SUPPOSTO CHE, supposing that

  * Before an Adjective.　　　　† Indicating cause.

Thus:

Dobbiamo andare a vedere il mio cugino prima che faccia così. We must go and see my cousin before he acts so (does so).

Per quanto povero Lei sia. However poor you may be.

Non compro senza che io abbia prima veduto. I don't buy without first having seen.

Non si può dire che sia primavera prima che vengano le rondini. One can't say it's spring before the swallows come.

Verrò a meno che non sia possibile. I'll come unless it's not possible.

18　　　　I PROMESSI SPOSI

Lucia aveva avute due buoni ragioni: l'una, di non
Lucia had had two good reasons: (the) one, not

contristare nè spaventare la buona donna, per cosa alla
to sadden or alarm the good woman, for a thing for

quale essa non avrebbe potuto trovar rimedio; l'altra, di
which she could not have been able to find a remedy; the other, not

non metter a rischio di viaggiar per molte bocche una
to (put in) risk travelling by many mouths a

storia che voleva essere gelosamente sepolta: tanto più
story which she wished to be jealously buried; all the more

che Lucia sperava che le sue nozze avrebber troncata, sul
as Lucia hoped that her marriage would have cut short, at the

principiare, quall'abbominata persecuzione. Di queste
beginning, that hateful persecution. Of these two reasons, never-

due ragioni però, non allegò che la prima.
theless, she put forward only the first.

«E a voi,» disse poi, rivolgendosi a Renzo, con quella
" And you," she said then, turning to Renzo, in that
voce che vuol far riconoscere a un amico che ha avuto
tone in which she wishes to make a friend recognize that he has been
torto: «e a voi doveva io parlar di questo? Pur troppo lo
wrong, "and to you ought I to speak of this? Anyhow you
sapete ora!»
know (it) now! "

«E che t'ha detto il padre?» domandò Agnese.
" And what did the Father say to you? " asked Agnese.

«M'ha detto che cercassi d'affrettar le nozze il più che
" He told me that I should try to hasten the wedding as much as
potessi, e intanto stessi rinchiusa; che pregassi bene il
I could, and meanwhile that I should stay closed up (indoors); that
Signore; e che sperava che colui, non vedendomi, non
I pray well to the Lord; and that he hoped that man, not seeing me,
si curerebbe più di me. E fu allora che mi sforzai,»
would not care more about me. And it was now that I forced my-
proseguì, rivolgendosi di nuovo a Renzo, senza alzargli
self," she went on, turning again to Renzo, without raising
però gli occhi in viso, e arrossendo tutta, «fu allora che
however her eyes to his face, and all blushing, " it was now
feci la sfacciata, e che vi pregai io che procuraste di far
that I strained things, and I begged you to try to make
presto, e di concludere prima del tempo che s'era stabilito.
haste, and get it concluded before the time that had been set.
Chi sa cosa avete pensato di me! Ma io faceva per bene,
Who knows what you have thought of me! I was doing it for well
ed ero stata consigliata, e tenevo per certo . . . e questa
(the best), and I had been advised, and held for certain . . . and this
mattina, ero tanto lontana da pensare . . .»
morning, was far from thinking . . ."

Qui le parole furon troncate da un violento scoppio di
Here the words were cut short by a violet fit of
pianto.
weeping.

«Ah birbone! ah dannato! ah assassino!» gridava Renzo,
" Ah (the) villain! Ah the damned (villain)! Ah the assassin!"

correndo innanzi e indietro per la stanza, e stringendo di
Renzo was shouting, running up and down the room, and pressing
tanto in tanto il manico del suo coltello.
from time to time the handle of his knife (dagger).

«**Oh che imbroglio, per amor di Dio,**» **esclamava Agnese.**
"*Oh what a muddle, for love of God,*" *exclaimed Agnese.*
Il giovine si fermò d'improvviso davanti a Lucia che
The young man stopped suddenly in front of Lucia who
piangeva; la guardò con un atto di tenerezza mesta e
was weeping; looked at her with an attitude of mixed tenderness and
rabbiosa, e disse: «questa è la ultima che fa quell'assas-
rage, and said: "this is the last thing that assassin
sino.»
will do."

§ 4. *Interjections and Exclamations—Exclamations Which Are*
Mere Sounds—Exclamations Which Are Short Words—
Other Exclamatory Expressions—Stationery: Books and
Periodicals—**I Promessi Sposi 19**

Interjections (that is, exclamations) are words or sounds that
can be regarded as necessary and common parts of everyday
speech. Thus: *hello! alas! help! oh! ah!* They usually
express surprise, grief, wonderment, disdain, desire, a wish, or
some other sentiment. It will be appreciated that such exclamations can be very useful to the learner of a foreign language, and
it is not difficult to acquire a vocabulary of them in Italian which
will meet most requirements of everyday life. For purposes of
learning, they may be conveniently classified as follows:

I. EXCLAMATIONS WHICH ARE MERE SOUNDS

ah! eh! ih! oh! uh! ahi! ehi! ohi! uhi!

ah! = surprise, interest grief
eh! = surprise, a query or doubt
ih! = pained surprise (not much used)
oh! = our *oh!*

uh! = fear
ahi! = surprise or pain
ehi! Hello!
ohe, ohi! Hello there!
uhi! How unpleasant!

II. EXCLAMATIONS WHICH ARE SHORT WORDS

ahimè }
ohimè } Alas! How terrible! Awful!

aiuto! Help!
animo! Courage! Cheer up!
benone! Well done! Fine! Excellent!
bravo! Bravo! Well done! Well played! Well sung!
deh! Really? (*a surprised* oh!)
guai! Woe! What a tragedy!
magari! Certainly!
mah! (*expresses doubt*)
oh bella! Well, really?
oibò! Fie! How disgusting!
orsù! Well, then! Come, now!
olà! Look out!
peccato! What a pity!
piano! Gently! Go easy!
piano, piano! Very gently, now! Softly!
povero me! Unhappy me!
pst! Hush!
su! Up! Get up!
vergogna! Shame!
via! Away! Get out!
viva! Long live! (*expresses joy*)
zitto! Silence! Shut up!

These exclamations are usually invariable, except those formed with an adjective. Thus: **povero!** *Poor man!* **Povera!** *Poor woman!* And: **povero me! povera me! poveri loro!** etc. **zitto! zitta!** hush, *be quiet!* in accordance with the gender of the person addressed.

III. Other Exclamatory Expressions

ECCO, *here is*, and its compounds with pronouns:

eccomi!	Here I am!
eccolo!	Here he is! Here it (*m.*) is!
eccola!	Here she is! Here it (*f.*) is!
eccoci!	Here we are!
eccone!	Here are some!
eccoli!	Here they (*m.*) are!
eccole!	Here they (*f.*) are!

The word **ecco** has in it the sense of *Look!   Behold!*

CHE, *what*, can be used with nouns or adjectives to form exclamatory phrases, or by itself:

Che! Che?	What! How so?
che vergogna!	What a shame!
che povero!	What a poor man!
che ragazza!	What a girl!
che uomo!	What a man!

What is given above will cover most requirements, but there are many essentially Italian expressions in everyday use for which there is not even approximate equivalent.   For example: **Per Bacco!** *By Bacchus!* or **Corpo di Bacco!** *Body of Bacchus!* Of course, we should not say this literal equivalent. **Bacco,** *Bacchus*, was the old Roman god of wine, and his name survives to this day in these hearty exclamations, which can be used in all sorts of ways to express pleasure, surprise, contempt, and other feelings in accordance with the context.   **Bacco** is mentioned merely by way of example.   Many more of these popular (and often vulgar) exclamations can be learnt by experience, the only way, for few of them are to be found in reference books.

You will have noticed that in **I Promessi Sposi** interjections and exclamations occur fairly frequently.   It will serve a double purpose—general revision and special—if you look back through some of the reading matter and see what exclamations are used and how they are used.   In general, their use can be learnt only by experience: by listening to speech and by reading.

Stationery: Books and Periodicals

la cartoleria, stationer's shop

la cartolina postale, post-card

la cartolina illustrata, picture post-card

le buste, envelopes

la carta da scrivere, writing-paper

la penna stilografica, fountain pen

la matita, pencil

la matita automatica, propelling pencil

la gomma, rubber, eraser

le mine, leads (refills)

la etichetta, label

le etichette di bagaglio, baggage labels

la carta topografica, map

una carta della città, map of the city

il cartolaio, stationer

la bottiglia d'inchiostro, bottle of ink

una guida della città, a guide (book) to the city

un dizionario, a dictionary

il libro, book

un libraio, a bookseller

una libreria, bookshop

un romanzo, novel

un romanzo di, a novel by . . .

una carta della regione, a map of the district

il giornale, newspaper

la rivista, review

il taccuino, notebook

un'agenda, pocket diary

la funicella, string

la carta assorbente, blotting-paper

Dove si trova una cartoleria? Where is there a stationer's?

Vorrei delle cartoline illustrate. I want some picture post-cards.

Ha un dizionario italiano–inglese? Have you an Italian–English dictionary?

Ha giornali inglesi? Have you any English newspapers?

Mi bisogna carta per macchina per scrivere. Una risma. I want some typing paper. A ream (500 sheets).

Non troppo sottile e di buona qualità. Not too thin and of good quality.

Può riempire questa penna stilografica? Can you fill this fountain pen?

Desidero un romanzo in italiano, non troppo difficile a leggere. I'd like a novel in Italian, not too difficult to read.

Ha il più recente libro di . . .? Have you the latest book by . . .?

Ha libri inglesi? Have you English books?

Desidero una guida tascabile di Firenze, con piante. I want a pocket guide to Florence, with plans.

Questo è troppo grande, troppo caro. This one is too big, too dear.

Non ha una guida più piccola? Haven't you a smaller guide?

Ha riviste inglese od americane? Have you any English or American magazines?

Note: From now onwards the translation of Reading Matter will be given separately from the text and not interlinearly as hitherto. You should now by this time have a good idea of the " run " of Italian prose, and not require such close help as is provided by interlinear translation. The translations given from now onwards will still be almost literal, though sometimes a little freer than up to now. Proceed as directed on pages 158–159.

19   I PROMESSI SPOSI

«Ah! No, Renzo, per amor del cielo!» gridò Lucia. «No, no, per amor del cielo! Il Signore c'è anche per i poveri; e come volete che ci aiuti, se facciam del male?»

«No, no per amor del cielo!» ripeteva Agnese.

«Renzo,» disse Lucia, con un'aria di speranza e di risoluzione più tranquilla: «voi avete un mestiere, e io so lavorare: andiamo tanto lontano, che colui non senta più parlar di noi.»

«Ah Lucia, e poi? Non siamo ancora marito e moglie! Il curato vorrà farci la fede di stato libero? Un uomo come quello? Se fossimo maritati, oh allora . . .!»

Lucia rimise a piangere: e tutt'e tre rimasero in silenzio, e in un abbattimento che faceva un tristo contrapposto alla pompa festiva de' loro abiti.

«Sentite, figliuoli; date retta a me,» disse, dopo qualche momento, Agnese. «Io son venuta al mondo prima di voi; e il mondo lo conosco un poco. Non bisogna poi spaventarsi tanto:

il diavolo non è brutto quanto si dipinge. A noi poverelli le matasse paion più imbrogliate, perchè non sappiam trovarne il bandolo; ma alle volte un parere, una parolina d'un uomo che abbia studiato . . . so ben io quel che voglio dire. Fate a mio modo, Renzo; andate a Lecco; cercate del dottor Azzecca-garbugli, raccontategli . . . Ma non lo chiamate così, per amor del cielo: 'è un soprannome. Bisogna dire il signor dottor . . . Come si chiama, ora? Oh to'! non lo so il nome vero: lo chiaman tutti a quel modo. Basta, cercate di quel dottore alto, asciutto, pelato, col naso rosso, e una voglia di lampone sulla guancia.

TRANSLATION: "Ah! No, Renzo, for heaven's sake!" cried Lucia. "No, no, for heaven's sake! The Lord is also for the poor; and how do you wish (expect) him to help us, if we do evil?"

"No, no, for heaven's sake!" repeated Agnese.

"Renzo," said Lucia, with a more tranquil air of hope and resolution, "you have your trade, and I can work: let's go so far (from here) that that fellow will not any more hear tell of us."

"Ah, Lucia, and then? We aren't yet husband and wife! Will the priest wish to vouch for us our unmarried state?[1] A man like that? If (only) we were married, well then . . .!"

Lucia began weeping again: and all three fell back into silence, in a (state of) depression which made a sad contrast to the festive pomp of their clothes.

"Listen, children; pay attention to me," (Agnese) said after some moments. "I came into the world before you; and I know the world a little. There's no need then to get so frightened: the devil's not so ugly as he's painted. To us poor folk the tangles appear more mixed, because we don't know how to find the end of the skein (of wool); but at times an opinion, a little word (talk) from a man who has studied . . . I know well what I mean. Do in my way, Renzo;[2] go to Lecco; find Doctor Hit-Trouble, tell it (all) to him . . . But don't call him that, for heaven's sake: it's a nickname. You must say Doctor . . . What's his name, now? Oh, dear! I don't know his real name; everybody calls him that. However, seek out that doctor (who is) tall, thin, bald, with a red nose, and a mole of raspberry[3] on his cheek.

NOTES

[1] put up our banns.
[2] Do as I say, Renzo.
[3] a mole like a raspberry.

§ 5. *Taking Stock—Revision—Keeping Notebooks—Idioms: List of Examples—*I Promessi Sposi 20

At this point it may be useful to pause and take stock of what has been achieved so far. You have covered the essentials of Italian grammar and, in the reading, you have seen how it works. You should also have acquired a useful vocabulary of words and phrases. In fact, you are already equipped to deal with straightforward Italian.

From now onwards your task will be to fill in gaps and to expand your knowledge. But meanwhile you should glance backwards, beginning at Lesson I, and note down everything of which you are doubtful. Keep a notebook in which difficulties are jotted down, and another for all new words and phrases. Such notebooks save much time in revision.

IDIOMS: For definition see page 212. It has been said that Italian is not a difficult language to speak in a grammatically correct manner, but that it is difficult to speak it *idiomatically*. In speaking with Italians the learner finds that, especially in familiar conversation, they tend to use many phrases and turns of phrase which cannot be translated literally. Here is a simple example: we say *That may be* or *It might be so* or simple *Maybe* or *Maybe so*. An Italian would say for any of these: **Può darsi,** literally *It can give itself*. The number of such idiomatic phrases is almost infinite; each city, town, and locality always has some of its own. Here it is possible to give only some examples of idioms. Others will be found on pages 213–214 and in the Reading Matter. But what follows will indicate the nature of these useful phrases, all of which are best learnt by experience rather than from lists or dictionaries.

IDIOMS: LIST OF EXAMPLES

What is it about? **Di che si tratta?**
My teeth ache. **Mi dolgono i denti.**
He makes no fuss about it. **Non se ne fa caso.**
From day to day. **Di giorno in giorno.**
How old is he? **Quanti anni ha?**
Agreed! **Siamo intesi. Convenuto!**

He gets angry for nothing. **Va in collera per nulla.**
It won't do. **Così non va.**
How are you? **Come sta Lei?**
Pretty well, thanks. **Non c'è male, grazie.**
I'm astonished at it. **Ne sono stupito.**
What use is it? **A che serve?**
I'm fully aware of it. **Lo so benissimo.**
When will you be back? **Quando sarà Lei di ritorno?**
It must be so. **Bisogna essere così.**
I'll be with you at once. **Sono subito da Lei.**
He was beside himself with rage. **Era fuor(i) di sè dalla rabbia.**
Not a bit. **Punto punto.**
She has the blues. **Ella ha i nervi.**
Don't breathe a word! **Acqua in bocca!**
He speaks broken Italian. **Parla un cattivo italiano.**
In plain (civilian) clothes. **Vestito da borghese.**
For all that. **Con tutto ciò.**
And so on. **E così di seguito.**
A friend of mine. **Un amico mio.**
The fun of it is . . . **La cosa buffa è . . .**
I feel giddy. **Mi gira la testa.**

The above are fairly simple idioms, worth learning because they help in conversation. Others will be met as the Course proceeds.

20   I PROMESSI SPOSI

«Lo conosco di vista,» disse Renzo.

«Bene,» continuò Agnese: «quello è una cima d'uomo! Ho visto io più d'uno ch'era più impicciato che un pulcin nella stoppa, e non sapeva dove batter la testa, e, dopo essere stato un'ora a quattr'occhi col dottor Azzecca-garbugli (badate bene di non chiamarlo così), l'ho visto, dico, ridersene. Pigliate quei quattro capponi, poveretti! a cui dovevo tirare il collo, per il banchetto di domenica, e portateglieli; perchè non bisogna mai andar con le mani vote da que' signori. Raccontategli tutto l'accaduto; e vedrete che vi dirà, su due piedi, di quelle cose che a noi non verrebbero in testa, a pensarci un anno.»

Renzo abbracciò molto volontieri questo parere; Lucia l'approvò; e Agnese, superba d'averlo dato, levò, a una a una, le povere bestie dalla stia, riunì le loro otto gambe, come se facesse un mazzetto di fiori, le avvolse e le strinse con uno spago, e le consegnò in mano a Renzo; il quale, date e ricevute parole di speranza, uscì dalla parte dell'orto, per non esser veduto da' ragazzi, che gli correbber dietro, gridando: lo sposo! lo sposo! Così attraversando i campi o, come dicon colà, i luoghi, se n'andò per viottole, fremendo, ripensando alla sua disgrazia, e ruminando il discorso da fare al dottor Azzecca-garbugli. Lascio poi pensare al lettore, come dovessero stare in viaggio quelle povere bestie, così legate e tenute per le zampe, a capo all'in giù, nella mano d'un uomo il quale, agitato da tante passioni, accompagnava col gesto i pensieri che gli passavan a tumulto per la mente. Ora stendeva il braccio per collera, ora l'alzava per disperazione, ora lo dibateva in aria, come per minaccia . . .

TRANSLATION: " *I know him by sight,*" said Renzo.
" *Good,*" continued Agnese: " *that's a tip-top man!* [1] *I (myself) have seen more than one who was more embarrassed than a chicken in (the) oakum, and didn't know where to beat their head,* [2] *and, after being an hour in private* [3] *with Doctor Hit-Trouble (take good care not to call him that), I've seen (them), I say, laughing about it. Take those four capons, poor little things! I was going to wring their necks for Sunday's feast, and take them to him; because you must never go with empty hands to those gentlemen. Tell him all that's happened; and you'll see that he'll tell you, squarely,* [4] *(of) such things that would not come into our heads, thinking of it (for) a year.*
Renzo very willingly accepted (embraced) this counsel; Lucia approved of it; and Agnese, proud of having given it, lifted, one by one, the poor creatures from the coop, put together their eight legs, as if she was making a little bunch of flowers, wound round and tightened (tied) them with a (piece of) string, and delivered them to Renzo's hand; who, having given and received words of hope, went out by the way of the kitchen-garden, so as not to be seen by the children, who would run after him shouting: " the bridegroom! the bridegroom! " So crossing the fields or, as they call them there, the " places ", he went off by by-paths, raging, thinking over his misfortune, and turning over the speech he would make to Doctor Hit-Trouble. I leave then the reader to think how they must have travelled those poor chickens (beasts) thus tied and held by their claws, head(s) downwards, in the hands of a man who, agitated (excited) by so many passions (emotions), accompanied with gesture(s) the thoughts which were passing in (a)

tumult through his mind. Now he held out his arm in anger, now he raised it in desperation, now he brandished it in the air, as if in (like) a threat.

NOTES

[1] **un cima d'uomo,** a top of (a) man = a tip-top man.

[2] **battere la testa,** to beat one's head = which way to turn.

[3] **a quattr'occhi,** with four eyes (together) = in private (or, *tête-à-tête*).

[4] **su due piedi,** on two feet = squarely, frankly.

Note: All these four are idioms.

LESSON IX

§ 1. *Word Formation: by Prefixes, Suffixes, and by Putting Words Together—List of Common Prefixes with Examples— Tobacco and Cigarettes—***MACCHIAVELLI: Il Principe 1,** *with Notes and Translation*

THE whole of this Lesson is devoted to word formation. In Italian this is achieved:

(1) By Prefixes—a prefix is a word-element placed at the beginning of a word to make it into another word. This happens in English when we place the element *counter* before *act* to make *counteract.*

(2) By Suffixes—which, similarly, are word-elements placed at the end of a word to make it into another. We have them in English: *farm, farmer*; *tour, tourist*; *ignore, ignorance*; and so forth.

(3) By putting two words together to make a third. We do this in English also. For example: *station* and *master* make *stationmaster*, often written *station master* or *station-master*, but always a compound of two elements, however it is written. (There are differences between British and American spelling.)

As the English language in general is partly derived from Latin, which might be described as " old Italian ", there are innumerable parallels in the two languages. This is often a guide to the English-speaking learner of Italian, and it is to help him that the subject of word formation in Italian is treated here.

Let us begin with the Prefixes which are constantly being met in Italian.

Turn back to Verbs, regular and irregular, and you will see that, allowing for the three verbal endings **-are, -ere,** and **-ere,** there are not only Italian verbs which closely resemble their

English equivalents—**rispondere**, *to respond*, *reply* **affliggere**, *to afflict*—but these and many other verbs have prefixes which correspond almost exactly to our English ones. Thus we have **corrispondere**, *to correspond*, and **infliggere**, *to inflict*. The warning must be given that sometimes the Italian prefix does *not* give the verb quite the same meaning that we would immediately expect. For example, **prendere** means *to take*, but **rapprendere** means *to congeal*. In the List of Prefixes which follows, the usual indication of each one is given, and this covers many of the words in which it is used.

LIST OF COMMON PREFIXES WITH EXAMPLES

a = *to*, as in **accorrere**, *to run to*, and **affondare**, *to sink*, from **fondo**, *bottom*. (Note that the **f** of **fondo** is doubled.) **affondare** means *to send to the bottom*. **forca** = *wooden hay-fork*, *pole*, and *gallows*. Hence **afforcare**, *to hang*.

a = *without*, as in English *amoral*, *apolitical*: **apolitico**, *apolitical*.

ante } = *before*.
anti }

        anteguerra, pre-war
        antidiluviano, antidiluvian

anti- = usually *against*.

        antipapa, against the pope
        anticristiano, anti-Christian

arci- = our *arch* in archbishop.

        vescovo, bishop; **arcivescovo**, archbishop
        arciprete, archpriest, a dignitary in some Italian cathedrals
        fallito, bankrupt; **arcifallito**, utterly bankrupt
        arcibeato, supremely happy
        arciduca, archduke

con- }
(com- } = *with*, *between*.
  before }
p, b, m) }

dividere, to divide; condividere, to divide between, among

piangere, to weep; compiangere, to pity, to regret

Before r and l, con = cor, col. Thus:

lato, side; collaterale, collateral

regione, region; corregionale, one from the same " region ", district

correligionario, co-religionist

contro-
contra- } = *against.*

segno, sign; contrassegno, countersign

senso, sense; controsenso, nonsense

stimolante, stimulant; controstimolante, sedative

The list of these words is a long one, but remember that contr- (-o or -a) nearly always means *against, opposite to.*

de-
di- } = *away from, arising from.*

porre, to put; deporre, to depose, lay down, give evidence

vincolo, bond; divincolarsi, to free oneself (from bonds)

de often equals our *de*:

crescere, to grow; decrescere, decrease

grado, grade, rank; degradare, to degrade

Again, the list of these words is a long one. But remember that de- usually indicates something *from, away from,* often something completely negative.

extra-
estra- } = *above, outside of.*
stra-

legale, legal; extralegale, extra-legal

la dote, dowery; dotale, of a dowery; stradotale = estradotale, married woman's own property

fra-
tra- } = *between, among.*

> **porre,** to put; **frapporre,** to interpose
> **correre,** to run; **traccorrere,** to outrun
> **lucere,** to shine; **tralucere,** to shine through
> **mischiare,** to mix; **frammischiare,** to mix
> up

in-
im- } = our *in-* and also intensification of an action.

> **cero,** wax; **incerare,** to wax
> **chiudere,** to shut; **inchiudere,** to shut in
> **in-** = *in-*, *un-* as negative.
> **fedele,** faithful; **infedele,** unfaithful
> **condotta,** conduct, behaviour; **incondotta,**
> misbehaviour

mis-   a negative like English *mis-*.

> **fatto,** fact, action; **misfatto,** misdeed

pre-   = English *pre-*, usually with the idea of *before*.

> **correre,** to run; **precorrere,** to anticipate
> **precipitare,** to rush, precipitate; **pre-**
> **conoscere,** to know beforehand
> **preavviso,** notice beforehand

re-
       } = a repeated action; or an action in response to
       another; or the beginning of a new situation.
ri-   Often corresponds to English *re-*.

> **cantare,** to sing; **ricantare,** to sing again,
> afresh
> **conoscere,** to know; **riconoscere,** to
> recognize

s-   = the contrary; an important prefix.

> **caricare,** to load, charge; **scaricare,** to
> unload, discharge

Also indicates intensity of action.

> **pettegolo,** gossiping, gossipy; **spettegolare,**
> to gossip (constantly)

sopra-   = *above, upon, beyond, super-.*

> **abbondante,** abundant; **sopra-abbondante,**
> superabundant

sopraddetto, aforesaid
sopracorrente, upstream
soprascarpa, overshoe

sotto- = *under, below.*

sottobibliotecario, under-librarian
porre, to put; **sottoporre,** to put under, to subject
sottoscrivere, to subscribe

In many words it is exactly equivalent to Eng. *sub-*. But **sub-** also appears in Italian:

affitto, lease; **subaffitto,** sub-lease

trans-
tras- } = Eng. *trans.*

continente, continent; **transcontinentale,** transcontinental
trasbordo, transhipment
trascrivere, to transcribe
portare, to carry; **trasportare,** to transport

Note: In most of the examples given above the forms and meanings are easily recognizable. The frequently recurring Italian prefixes **e-** and **es-** are not included in the list, because although they often mean *out of, from,* as in **evadere,** *to go out of, escape from,* or **espellere,** *to expel, drive out* (English and Italian prefixes derived from Latin *ex*) there are too many Italian words beginning with **e-** or **es-** for derivation only to be a safe guide. This is unfortunately, for the learner, also true of some of the other prefixes, but to a much lesser degree. One has to learn many words with prefixes as vocabulary.

Tobacco and Cigarettes

la tabaccheria, tobacconist
il pacchetto, packet
la sigaretta } cigarette(s)
le sigarette
il pacchetto di sigarette, packet of cigarettes

il tabacco virginia, virginia tobacco
il sigaro } cigar(s)
i sigari
la pipa, pipe
la borsa, pouch

l'accendisigaro, lighter
un pacchetto di tabacco, packet of tobacco
il bocchino, holder
i cerini, matches
la scatola, box
il portacenere, ash-tray
la vetrina, window
le cartine, cigarette papers
il portasigarette, cigarette case
il tabacco del paese, home grown tobacco

il sigaro avana, Havana cigar
più grande, bigger
più piccolo, smaller
il nettapipe, pipe cleaner
il tabacco da pipa, pipe tobacco
lo stoppino, wick
la capsula di benzina, lighter fuel (capsule of)
il temperino, pocket-knife

Un pacchetto di sigarette, per favore.   A packet of cigarettes, please.

Lei vuole tabacco biondo o nero?   Do you want light or dark tobacco?

Vorrei un pacchetto di tabacco per la pipa.   I want a packet of pipe tobacco.

Voglio tabacco inglese, americano.   I want English, American tobacco.

Desidero un sigaro avana.   I want a Havana cigar.

La marca mi è indifferente, ma ne voglio uno buono.   The brand does not matter, but I want a good one (cigar).

Vorrei anche una scatola di cerini.   I'd like a box of matches also.

Voglio provare le sigarette Macedonia.   I want to try Macedonia(n) cigarettes.

Può darmi un poco di fuoco, per favore.   Could you give me a light, please?

Queste sigarette sono troppo forti.   These cigarettes are too strong.

Voglio qualche cosa non tanto forte.   I want something not so strong.

Abbiamo anche tabacco da naso, se vuole.   We have some snuff also, if you wish.

Grazie. Preferisco fumare il tabacco.   Thank you. I prefer to smoke tobacco.

L

MACCHIAVELLI: IL PRINCIPE

Niccolò Macchiavelli (1469–1527), Florentine statesman and
writer, immortalized by his remarkable work **Il Principe**, *The
Prince*, has given the English language the words Macchivellian,
and Macchiavellianism, which we take to have sinister meanings.
But Macchiavelli, in *The Prince*, merely set out with great
lucidity the political doctrines which he thought must be followed
in order to maintain the power of the ruler and the State; he did
this at a time of stress and difficulty.   It is not safe to epitomize
his doctrines, for he has to be read with his background and objects always in mind.   But one may say, briefly, that he advocates
expediency and cunning where these serve best, and force where
it serves best.   If one reads " ruler " or " statesman " or " head of
state " for Prince, it is not difficult to appreciate why his doctrines
have so greatly appealed to so many statesmen since his time.
His style is simple and direct, the meaning rarely in doubt.   The
passage which follows is from a chapter of **Il Principe**.

1. *In che modo i principi debbano osservare la fede*

Quanto sia laudabile in un principe mantenere la fede,[1] vivere
con integrità e non con astuzia, ciascuno lo intende.   Nondimanco
si vede per esperienza ne' nostri tempi, quelli principi aver fatto
gran cose, che della fede hanno tenuto poco conto, e che hanno
saputo con l'astuzia aggirare [2] i cervelli degli uomini, ed alla
fine hanno superato quelli che si sono fondati in su la lealtà.

Dovete adunque sapere come sono due generazioni di combattere: l'una con le leggi, l'altra con la forza; quel primo (modo)
è proprio del uomo, quel secondo delle bestie; ma perchè il
primo spesse volte non basta, conviene ricorrere al secondo.
Pertanto, ad un principe è necessario saper bene usare la bestia
e l'uomo . . .[3]

Essendo adunque un principe necessitato sapere bene usare la
bestia, debbe di quella pigliare [4] la volpe e il lione; perchè il
lione non si difende da' lacci, la volpe non si difende da' lupi.
Bisogna adunque essere volpe a conoscere i lacci, e lione a
spigottire i lupi.

Coloro che stanno semplicemente in sul lione, non se ne

intendono. Non può pertanto un signore prudente, nè debbe, osservare la fede, quando tale osservanza gli torni contro, e che sono spente le cagioni che la facero promettere.

NOTES

[1] **la fede,** faith, *here* good faith.
[2] **aggirare,** to move in a circle = to confound, deceive.
[3] **usare la bestia e l'uomo,** to use (the qualities of) the beast and (of) man.
[4] **pigliare,** to take (on) the qualities of.

TRANSLATION:

In What Way Princes Must Observe Good Faith

However laudable it may be in a prince to maintain good faith, to live with (by) integrity and not by cunning, everyone understands. Nevertheless it is seen by experience in our times, (that) those princes have done great things, who for good faith have held small esteem, and who have known (how) by trickery to confound men's brains (minds), and in the end have overcome those who have based themselves on loyalty (rectitude).

You must know then that there are two kinds of fighting: one with (the aid of) the laws, the other with force; that first (way) is proper to man, the second to the beasts; but because the first very often is not enough, it is expedient to (have) recourse to the second. On that account, for a prince it is necessary to know well (how) to use (the qualities of) beast and man . . .

A prince then being obliged to know well (how) to use the beast, he must from that take on (the qualities of) the fox and the lion; because the lion does not defend himself from snares, the fox does not defend itself from wolves. He must therefore be (a) fox to know snares, and lion to frighten (away) wolves.

Those who (take their) stand simply on the lion, do not understand this. In fact a prudent gentleman cannot, nor ought he to, keep faith when such observance may turn against him, and when the causes are extinguished which made him pledge (promise) it.

§ 2. *Italian Suffixes: Augmentatives and Diminutives—General List of Suffixes: Nouns*—Nations' and Cities' Inhabitants, *Endings for—Wines: Word List—Italian Wines:* **di Piemonte; Toscana; Roma; Napoli** and **Sicilia—Il Principe 2**

There are many suffixes in Italian, and they are important because they enrich the language with innumerable words that are not difficult to recognize if the basic or elemental word is known. Some of these suffixes can be classified in groups, of which augmentatives and diminutives are the most important. The others are best learnt from lists with examples.

I. Nouns: (1) *Augmentatives:* these add to or intensify the original meaning as to *size, degree, or quality.* Thus:

(*a*) -one—
　　il libro, book; **il librone,** the big book
(*b*) -occio—
　　il frate, monk; **il fratoccio,** great 'ass of a monk'
(*c*) -ozzo—
　　la predica, sermon; **il predicozzo,** long-winded sermon

(*a*) merely increases. (*b*) and (*c*) increase, usually in a derogatory sense.

(2) *Diminutives:* indicate *smallness,* sometimes with a sense of endearment, sometimes of contempt or commiseration:

(*a*) -ino—
　　il ragazzo, boy; **il ragazzino,** the (dear) little boy
　　la cesta, basket; **il cestino,** (nice) little basket
　　il podere, farm; **il poderino,** little farm
(*b*) -etto—
　　il podere, farm; **il poderetto,** miserable little farm
　　-ello—
　　la cesta, basket; **la cestella,** small basket, hamper
(*c*) -accio—
　　il libro, book; **il libraccio,** horrid book
　　-accio + -one = unpleasant + size. Thus—
　　il libraccione, horrid great (big) book
　　-astro—
　　il poeta, poet; **il poetastro,** rotten poet
　　-uccio—
　　il libro, book; **il libruccio,** paltry little book
　　-ucolo—
　　il poeta, poet; **il poetucolo,** poor little poet

Two diminutives are often added to the same word:

il giovane, youth; **il giovanotto,** strong youth; **il giovanottino,** (fine strong) young fellow

Italian makes much use of augmentatives and diminutives, and it is interesting to take at random from the dictionary a basic word, say **il padre,** *father,* and list its derivatives:

il padrino, little friar, godfather
il padrone, master, owner, landlord
il padronaccio, disagreeable master, etc.
il padroncino, little master
il padroncione, important master, etc.
la padronanza, ownership (*see below,* **-anza**)
il padronato, large property, estate, business (*see* **-ato**)

Adjectives: **padronale,** belonging to the master; **padronesco,** patronizing

Verb: **padroneggiare,** to rule

The learner should make a point of being able to recognize the indications of all these suffixes, learning the derivatives and their meanings as he goes along. But he should be wary of experimenting with words of his *own* make-up! They may not always convey the meaning he intends, and could easily convey an utterly undesirable meaning. So, beware!

But what the learner must note is this: Here is just *one* word, the noun **padre,** and from it no less than TEN other words are made! Think of the possibilities dependent on these suffixes!

You will already realize the importance of suffixes and, with the prefixes, the importance of both in helping to build up your vocabulary. In the " All-purposes " vocabulary at the end of the book very few of the possible derivatives are listed, though some of the commonest will be found there. You must resort to a good dictionary for the remainder, as and when they are met.

GENERAL LIST OF SUFFIXES: NOUNS

-aglia: collective, or disparaging sense
  bosco, wood, forest; **boscaglia,** forest district
  gente, people; **gentaglia,** rabble
-aia: **fungo,** fungus, mushroom; **fungaia,** mushroom-bed

-aio: occupation or vocation
    libro, book; **libraio,** bookseller
    forno, oven; **fornaio,** baker

-aiolo
-aiuolo } related occupation
    cencio, rag; **cenciaiolo,** rag-picker
    legno, wood, timber; **legnaiolo,** carpenter, cabinet-maker

-ante: participle as noun
    villeggiare, to stay (in the country); **villeggiante,** country-dweller

-anza: **ignorare,** to be ignorant of; **ignoranza,** ignorance

-ario: often for our *-ary*
    visione, vision; **visionario,** visionary

-ato: Past Participle as Noun
    gelare, to freeze; **gelato,** ice for consumption, ice-cream

-enza: **convenire,** to come together, be advantageous; **convenienza,** convenience

-ezza: abstract = *-ess*
    debole, weak; **debolezza,** weakness

-ia: **trattore,** keeper of eating-house; **trattoria,** eating-house, small restaurant

-iera: **il sale,** salt; **la saliera,** salt-cellar

-ismo: *-ism*
    scettico, sceptic; **scetticismo,** scepticism
    comunismo, communism
    socialismo, socialism

-ista: *-ist*, *-ian*
    musica, music; **musicista,** composer (**musicante,** music player, performer)

-IONE: a wide range corresponding to our *-ion*
    evadere, to escape; **evasione,** escape
    posizione, position, etc.

-mento: **cambiare,** to change; **cambiamento,** change

-sore: **incidere,** to incise, cut; **incisore,** engraver

-tà: *-ty*
    università, university; **facoltà,** faculty
    Note: **vile,** vile, cheap; **viltà,** vileness

-tore: feminine **-tora** or **-trice**
          attore, actor; **attrice,** actress
          lodatore, -atrice, praiser, flatterer
-tura: **tingere,** to dip, dye; **tintura,** dyeing, tinting

NATIONS' AND CITIES' INHABITANTS: Endings **-ano, -ese,
-ino, -otto** and some others. See pages 41–42 and now consider
the following short list of examples:

Country	*Inhabitant*
Italia, Italy	**Italiano,** Italian
Roma, Rome	**Romano,** Roman
Genova, Genoa	**Genovese,** Genoese
Imola, Imola	**Imolese,** Imolese
Reggio (Emilia)	**Reggiano,** a man from Reggio-Emilia
Reggio (Calabria)	**Reggino,** a man from Reggio-Calabria
Chioggia	**Chioggiotto,** a man from Chioggia
Spagna, Spain	**Spagnolo,** Spaniard

As it is not possible to give a full list, the above are intended
to indicate that one must pay attention to the Italian words for
inhabitants of countries, cities, and towns. They do not always
follow straightforward rules.

WINES: Word List

il vino, wine in general
asciutto, rough, poor
stagionato, matured
vinetto, very light
vecchio, old
del paese *or* **nazionale** } from the district of that town, usually on draught
acerbo, harsh, sour
nuovo, new

generoso, generous, full, strong
maccherone } **di molto corpo** } strong, full-bodied
leggiero, light
sincero, sound
dolce, sweet
mosto, not fermented, very new
tagliato, very weak
raspante, bitter, tart (bad)

del barile, from the cask, on draught

bottiglia, bottle

fiasco, flask, much used in Italy

in bottiglia, in bottle

la cantina, cellar

il sciampagna, champagne

nostrano, -ale, home-grown

vini nostrali, home-grown wines

da dessert, dessert

vino pastoso, sweet wine

della Mosella, Moselle

moscadello, muscatel

del Reno, Rhine (= Hock)

nero, rosso, red (wine)

bianco, white

spumante, sparkling

da pasto, table wine

barbaresco ⎫ Piedmontese
barbera   ⎭ wines

VINI NOSTRALI: *Italian Wines*

I. di Piemonte

Asti spumante, a sparkling wine, " Italian Champagne "
Barbera (sparkling)
Barolo
Nebbiolo

II. Toscana

Chianti, resembles Burgundy
Pomino, an ordinary table wine
Aleatico, dark red, sweet (from Florence and Elba)
Moscadello di Montepulciano
Vino santo, excellent straw-coloured dessert wine
Malvasia, Malvagia, strong, sweet, Malmsey wine
Vernaccia, sweet white wine

III. Roma

i vini dei Castelli Romani (These are among the most pleasant of the everyday local wines made in Italy. They come from Grotto Ferrata, Frascati, Marino, Monte Porzio, Velletri, and other places.)
Orvieto, light, white, and good
Est Est, light white wine from Montefiascone.

IV. Napoli e Sicilia

Lagrima Christi (" Tears of Christ "), a wine from Vesuvius
Falerno, Falernian wine (dating from classical times, not to

be drunk when new. That often served is the colour of
brimstone, which disconcerts the uninitiated.)

The list does not exhaust Italian wines, many of which are
really excellent and unknown outside the country. When not in
a city or large town you will generally drink **il vino del paese,**
often called **il vino nostrale** or **nazionale.** The wine-bottle
usually seen is **il fiasco,** unless you are in a hotel, where **la
bottiglia** is considered more polite and may contain either a
choice Italian or a foreign wine at a higher price. In Rome you
may decide, like many good judges, that **il vino dei Castelli
Romani,** served from the barrel, is highly satisfactory. Many
Italian wines do not do themselves justice after they have travelled,
so do not judge them finally until you have sampled them in their
own locality. *Vermouth* (**il vermut, Vermutte**) is, however,
almost universally known. **Un americano,** an essentially
Italian **aperitivo** (*appetiser*) not greatly patronized by foreigners,
helps to create the right kind of appetite for Italian food and the
wine which goes with it. If you want some good wine and don't
know where to find it, use the word **sincero.** Thus: **Dove si
beve del vino sincero?** Or, stronger: **Dove si può bere
del vino sincero sincero?**

2. *Il Principe*

E se gli uomini fussero tutti buoni, questo precetto non sarebbe
buono; ma perchè sono tristi,[1] e non la osserverebbero a te, tu
ancora non l'hai da osservare a loro. Nè mai ad un principe
mancheranno cagioni legittime di colorare la inosservanza. Di
questo se ne potrebbe dare infiniti esempi moderni, e mostrare
quante paci, quante promesse sono state fatte irrite e vane per la
infedeltà dei principi; e quello che ha saputo meglio usare la
volpe, è meglio capitato.

Ma è necessario questa natura saperla bene colorire, ed essere
gran simulatore e dissimulatore, e sono tanto semplici gli uomini,
e tanto ubbidiscono alle necessità presenti, che colui che inganna
troverà sempre chi si lascerà ingannare. . . .

Ad un principe adunque non è necessario avere in fatto tutte
le soprascritte qualità, ma è ben necessario parer di averle.

Anzi ardirò di dire questo, che avendole ed osservandole sempre,
sono dannose; e parendo d'averle, sono utili; come parer
pietoso, fidele, umano, religioso, intero, ed essere; ma stare in
modo edificato con l'animo che bisognando non essere, tu possa
e sappia mutare il contrario.

NOTE

[1] **tristi.** There are two words: **triste** and **tristo.** The first nearly
always means *sad*. But **tristo-, -a, -i, -e** (here **tristi**) means *morally bad*,
which is Macchiavelli's meaning.

TRANSLATION: *And if men were all good this precept would not
be good (valid); but because they are morally bad, and would not
observe good faith towards (to) you, you also have not to keep it with
them. Nor to a prince will there ever lack (legitimate) reasons for
colouring (disguising) the non-observance. Of this it is possible to
give infinite modern examples, and to show how many peaces, how
many pledges, have been made null and void by the faithlessness of
princes; and that one who has known best (how) to use the fox meets
with best fortune.*

*But it is necessary to know well how to colour (camouflage) this
nature (character), and to be a great hypocrite and dissembler, and
men are so simple-minded, and so greatly obey (respond to) present
necessities, that he who deceives will always find one who allows
himself to be duped. . . .*

*For a prince, then, it is not necessary to have in fact all the above-
mentioned qualities, but it is very necessary to seem to have them.
On the contrary, I will go (so far as) to say this, that having them
and always observing them, they are harmful; and seeming to have
them, they are useful: so that to appear compassionate, faithful,
humane, religious, sincere, and to be so; but to be so constituted in
mind that not needing (to be so), you can and know (how) to change
(to) the opposite.*

3. *Word Formation: Derivatives from Adjectives—List of
Suffixes: Adjectives—from* **-ARE** *Verbs—Nouns Made from
All Verbs—Alcoholic Drinks—***Il Principe** 3

Adjectives as well as Nouns form derivatives with augmentatives and diminutives, using the same endings. You will note,
however, that the augmentative **-one** (*f.* **-ona**), and the disparaging **-astro,** give the Adjective the character of a noun:

stupido, uno stupidone, stupid, a very stupid man
giovane, giovinastro, young, young scamp

Diminutives are frequently in **-ino (-ina), -etto, (-etta)**:

> **bello,** beautiful; **bellino,** pretty
> **capriccioso,** fickle, capricious; **una capricciosetta,** a fickle hussy

-uccio is coaxing, endearing, and **-occio** is slightly augmentative in a jocular sense. **belloccio,** *darling beauty, beautiful one.* Note that **caro,** *dear,* has **carino,** for *pretty* and **caretto** in the sense of *rather costly,* whereas **caruccio** can mean either.

The suffixes **-iccio** and **-ognolo** are used with adjectives of colour:

> **bianco,** white; **bianchiccio,** whitish
> **azzurro,** blue; **azzurrognolo,** bluish

List of Suffixes: Adjectives

-abile: *-ble,* possible to, or to be

> **cantare,** to sing; **cantabile,** melodious, possible to sing
> **papa,** pope; **papabile,** capable of being pope

-ace: **preda,** booty; **predace,** predacious

-ale: **natura,** nature; **naturale,** natural

-ando: **laurea,** laurel crown, doctor's degree; **laureando,** candidate for doctor's degree (*from* **laureare,** to confer a degree)

-ario: **leggenda,** legend; **leggendario,** legendary

-ato: The Past Participle easily takes the quality of adjective.

> **(buon) senso,** (good) sense; **sensato,** sensible

-esco: **Petrarca,** Italian poet; **petrarchesco,** like Petrarch

> **Dante, dantesco**

-evole: **lodare,** to praise; **lodevole,** praiseworthy

-iano: **Cristo,** Christ; **cristiano,** Christian

-iccio: **massa,** mass, heap; **massiccio,** massive

-ico: **cono,** cone; **conico,** conical

-iero: **mattina,** morning; **mattiniero,** early rising

-ino: **Alpi,** Alps; **alpino,** Alpine

-istico: **carattere,** character: **caratteristico,** characteristic

-ivo: **offendere,** to offend; **offensivo,** offensive
         ricreare, to recreate, refresh; **ricreativo,** recreative, amusing

-izio: **natale,** birth (*adj.*); **natalizio (giorno-),** birthday

-oso: **gotta,** gout; **gottoso,** gouty

As with nouns and adjectives, Italian has suffixes for Verbs to add to or alter their meaning. These are perhaps the most important:

    -acchiare   **-icchiare**   **-ucchiare**   **-ellare**
    -eggiare   **-icare**   **-izzare**

You will note that they all end in **-are.** Take the first four:

-acchiare: **rubare,** to rob, steal, **rubacchiare = rubare un poco =** to pilfer

-icchiare: **cantare,** to sing, **canticchiare = cantare sottovoce =** to sing softly

-ucchiare: **leggere,** to read, **leggiucchiare = leggere un poco, svogliatamente,** to read a little, unwillingly (**svogliato =** unwilling, loath)

The **-cchiare** endings *tone down* or modify the meaning of the original verb, and are easily recognizable.

The next three suffixes serve for the derivation of Verbs from Nouns or Adjectives. Thus:

-eggiare: **passo,** step; **passeggiare,** to go for a walk (*also* to cross streets)

-icare: **zoppo,** limping; **zoppicare,** to limp (*also* to be shaky—in health or otherwise)

-izzare: **carbone,** charcoal, coal; **carbonizzare,** to carbonize

-ARE VERBS: The **-are** Verbs have been emphasized for their large number and their few irregular Verbs. It was also stated that all new Verbs added to the language end in **-are.** But the largest category of **-are** verbs consists of those which simply add this ending in order to make a verb of a word in another grammatical category. For example:

From an Adjective:

assente, absent; **assentarsi,** to absent oneself

From a Noun:

capitano, captain; **capitanare,** to captain
catalogo, catalogue; **catalogare,** to catalogue

Sometimes it is not possible to tell whether a verb is made from a noun, or a noun from a verb. For example: **la scomunica,** *excommunication*; **scomunicare,** *to excommunicate.* But one is always recognizable from the other, the greater possibility being that the **-are** verb is made from the noun.

NOUNS MADE FROM ALL VERBS: It is relevant here to remind the learner that nouns can be made from most verbs. Thus:

il bere, drinking   **il vivere,** living
l'andare, walking   **il venire,** coming

Alcoholic Drinks

l'aperitivo, aperitif, appetizer
l'acquavite, brandy
il cognac, Cognac
il gin, gin
secco, dry
dolce, sweet
il liquore, liqueur
il rhum, rum
il whisky, whisky
whisky al seltz, whisky and soda
la birra, beer
la birra scura, dark beer
la birra chiara, light beer
la birra a spina, draught beer
i vini, wines
il vino di botte, from the cask
il vino rosso, red wine
il vino bianco, white wine

il Porto, port wine
Sherry, sherry
la bibita fredda, ghiacciata, cold, iced drink
lo spaccio di vino, wine-shop
la birreria, bar or place where beer is sold
osteria, inn, little drinking-place
il bicchiere, glass
un bicchiere di vino, a glass of wine
un bicchierino di liquore, a (little) glass of liqueur
la caraffa, carafe, bottle for draft wine
una caraffa di vino, a carafe of wine
la carta dei vini, wine list

una bottiglia di vino, a bottle of wine
la mancia, tip

dare la mancia, to give a tip
le bevande, drinks (in general)

Cameriere! vorremo bere qualche cosa. Waiter! We'd like something to drink.

Che c'è da bere? What is there to drink?

Vuol bere vino o birra? Would you like to drink wine or beer?

Mi porti una bottiglia di vino rosso e due bicchieri. Bring me a bottle of red wine and two glasses.

Le piace il vermouth? Do you like Vermouth?

Alla sua salute! Sua salute! To your health.

Che gusto ha? How does it taste?

È molto piacevole, forte, insipido. It's very pleasant, strong, insipid.

Finisca il suo vino. Finish your wine.

Cameriere, il conto! Waiter, the bill.

Vorremo due whisky al seltz (or whisky-soda). We'd like two whiskies and soda.

For Italian Wines, see pages 312–313.

3. *Il Principe*

Ed hassi [1] ad intendere questo, che un principe, e massime un principe nuovo, non può osservare tutte quelle cose per le quale gli uomini sono tenuti buoni, essendo spesso necessitato per mantenere lo stato operare contro alla fede, contro alla carità, contro alla umanità, contro alla religione.

E però bisogna che egli abbia un animo disposto a volgersi secondo che i venti e le variazioni della fortuna gli commandono; e come di sopra dissi, non partirsi dal bene potendo, ma sapere entrare nel mal necessitato . . .

Faccia adunque un principe conto di vincere e mantenere lo stato, i mezzi saranno sempre giudicati onorevoli, e da ciascuno lodati; perchè il vulgo ne va sempre preso con quello che pare e con l'evento della cosa, e nel mondo non è se non vulgo; e i pochi ci hanno luogo, quando gli assai non hanno dove appoggiarsi.

Alcuno principe dei presenti tempi, quale non è bene nominare, e, non predica mai altro che pace e fede; e dell'una e dell'altra è inimicissimo; e l'una e l'altra, quando e' [2] l'avesse osservata, gli arrebe più volte tolto o la riputazione o lo stato.

* * *

These extracts are from the text edited by Mario Casella in modernized spelling. Considering the early period in which **Il Principe** was written, the student may be surprised to find not only how modern Macchiavelli is in his thought, but in the language in which he expresses it. There are few archaisms.

TRANSLATION: *And you have to understand this, that a prince, and most of all a new prince, cannot observe all those things by which men are held to be good, being often driven in order to maintain the State to act (operate) against good faith, against charity, against humanity, against religion.*

And on that account it behoves him to have a mind disposed to turn according as the winds and the fluctuations of fortune command him; and as I said above, not to go away from the good being able to, but to know how to enter into the necessitated evil. . . .

Then let a prince take care to conquer (difficulties) and to maintain the State, (and) the means will always be judged honourable, and by everybody praised; because the rabble is always taken in by what appears (seems) and by the outcome of the thing, and in the world there is nothing if not rabble (only rabble); and the few have place there, while the many have not anywhere to support themselves (to lean against).

A certain (some) prince of the present times, whom it is not well (desirable) to name, and never preaches anything else but peace and good faith; and to both he is most hostile; and of either had he observed it, he would many times have had his reputation or the State taken away.

NOTES

[1] **hassi,** old form for **hai.**
[2] **e'** = **egli.**

§ 4. *Word Formation: Other Methods—With Prepositions* **A,** **DI, DA,** *and* **IN**—*Compound Words—Various Combinations of Words—Alpine Sports: Mountaineering—Railway Timetable:* **ORARIO**

In addition to the system of making new words by prefixes and suffixes, Italian has other methods. The simplest and most obvious is by using a preposition to establish a relationship of such a nature between two Nouns that they will make what is often a Compound Noun in English, or one that is in effect a Compound Noun. Thus:

(1) The Preposition **A** is used to connect two Nouns, the first being the principal one, the second being the *agency* by which it acts:

una nave a vela, a sailing-ship
una macchina a vapore, a steam-engine

Another word, not a noun, can be the first or principal word, as in:

scritto a macchina, typewritten (*the second is still the agency or means*)

(2) The Preposition **DI** is used to connect two Nouns, making them an adjectival compound, and the first is the principal, the second the *material* of which it is made, as in:

il vestito di lana, the woollen dress
la statua di marmo, the marble statue

As in (1) above, **di** can also be used with a word not a Noun (usually a Past Participle) to show what material something is made of:

una casa costruita di cemento, a cement house

(3) the preposition **DA** is similarly placed between two nouns, the first being the principal, the second to indicate the *purpose* or *suitability* of the first, as in:

la sala da pranzo, the dining-room
la camera da letto, the bedroom

(4) **IN** is often used for *material*, so that one often hears or sees:

la statua in marmo, as well as **di marmo** (2, above)

All these are in everyday use and should be known. They do not present any difficulties, but this cannot be said of true compounds in Italian. One has to be careful of genders and plurals. You have already met some compound nouns such as **passaporto,** *passport*; **capostazione,** *stationmaster*; and **ferrovia,** *railway,* but now we shall look at some more and examine the principles which govern them. They may be classified under headings in accordance with their composition, which determines their plurals:

(1) *Adjective + Noun,* the plural is that of the noun:

francobollo, postage-stamp; **francobolli,** postage-stamps

pianoforte, piano; **pianoforti,** pianos

chiaroscuro, monochrome picture; **chiaroscuri,** monochrome pictures

bassorilievo, bas-relief; **bassorilievi,** bas-reliefs

But note:

mezzelune, half-moons

mezzetinte, mezzotints

mezzenotti, midnights

(2) *Two Nouns of the same gender,* only the second changes for the plural. Thus:

capoluogo, chief town; **capoluoghi,** chief towns

capolavoro, masterpiece; **capolavori,** masterpieces

(3) *Two Nouns of different gender,* only the first changes for the plural:

capostazione, stationmaster; **capistazione,** station-masters

(4) *Verbal form + plural Noun,* usually remain invariable, as in:

il lustrascarpe, i lustrascarpe, shoeblack(s)

il portalettere, i portalettere, postman, postmen

(5) *Verbal form or Adverb + masculine singular Noun;* these take the normal endings for the plural, that is, the plural of the noun, as in:

passaporto, passport; **passaporti,** passports
battimano, applause; **battimani** (*more common*)
battibecco, wordy battle; **battibecchi,** wordy battles
grattacapo, troublesome thought; **grattacapi,** troublesome thoughts
passatempo, pastime; **passatempi,** pastimes
asciugamano, towel; **asciugamani,** towels

(6) *Verbal form or adverb + singular feminine Noun,* when they make masculine compound nouns, these do not change in the plural:

il portabandiera, flag-bearer; **i portabandiera**
il guardaroba, linen cupboard *or* cloakroom; **i guardaroba**
il cavalcavia, bridgeway; **i cavalcavia**

(7) Sometimes the compound nouns under (6) are by their nature feminine, and then they take the feminine plural endings:

la portabandiera, female standard *or* flag-bearer; **le portabandiere**
la guardaroba, cupboard *or* cloakroom keeper, feminine; *pl.* **le guardarobe**

Unless the learner intends to pursue his studies of Italian to a much higher standard than is aimed at in this book, he may, at all events at this stage, be content to treat all the above words as vocabulary, without mastering the principles. Or he may deal with these on a second perusal.

THE MAIN POINT IS TO BE ABLE TO RECOGNIZE COMPOUND NOUNS — ESPECIALLY THOSE GIVEN ABOVE—AND KNOW THEIR MEANINGS.

Alpine Sports: Mountaineering

l'alpinismo, mountaineering

gli sci, skis

lo sciatore, skier

i bastoncini, sticks (for skiing)

il pattinaggio, skating

la discesa in toboggan, tobogganing

la discesa in bob, bob-sleighing

il pattinaggio artistico, figure skating

il salto (cogli sci), ski-jumping

la corsa, race

la corsa in discesa, race downhill

la gara di pattinaggio, skating race

le scarpe da montagna, mountain boots

con ramponi, with studs

le scarpe chiodate, spiked boots

la salita, climb, climbing

lo stato della neve, the condition of the snow

i pattini, skates

sciare, to ski

il pattinatore, skater

le racchette, snow shoes

§ 5. *Word Formation: Compound Words* contd.—*Compound Words: Some Examples—Endings: Their Meanings—Italian and English Words from Latin and Greek*

We can go one stage farther in making compound words in Italian. You will already have realized that sometimes the Italians are imaginative or poetical in their word-building, of which a better example can hardly be found than:

il pomodoro = il pomo d'oro = the golden apple = tomato (*plural* i pomodori)

(*Note:* the word is often written pomidoro, pomidori.) and that:

la ferrovia = la via di ferro = iron way = railway

and similarly:

lo spazzacamino = colui che spazza il camino = he who cleans, sweeps the stove, chimney = chimney-sweep

il portafoglio = oggetto che porta fogli = an object for carrying " sheets of paper ", that is, documents = portfolio, brief-case

il paravento = oggetto che para il vento = an object which " parries ", keeps off the wind = screen

—and innumerable others, mostly recognizable, could be given.

It is convenient here to list a number of words which are made of elements, many of which have a corresponding element in English, some of the Italian words (because of their Latin origin) being more easily understood in Italian than in English. Take, for example, **la piscicoltura.** You know **il pesce**, *fish*, and **la coltura**, *culture* (also *refinement*). Hence, you should be able to work out that **la piscicoltura =** *the culture or breeding and rearing of fishes* = our *pisciculture*, a word which you may never have met! Here is a useful short list of such words in Italian:

COMPOUND WORDS: SOME EXAMPLES *

ambidestro, ambidextrous
arboricoltura, arboriculture
benefico, beneficent
calorifero, calorific
cappellificio, hat-factory
carnivoro, carnivorous (meat-eating)
centrifugo, centrifugal
cruciforme, cruciform
cuneiforme, cuneiform
equidistante, equidistant
fiammifero, match (for lighting)
locomotiva, locomotive
mortifero, death-dealing
onnivoro, omnivorous
quadrupede, quadroped
radiografia, radiography
radiografista, radio-operator
radiogramma, radio (tele-)gram
rettilineo, rectilinear
sanguifero, sanguinary
unisono, unison
verificare, to verify, confirm

Note that some Italian endings have a definite meaning:

-fico = chi fa = making or giving, *as in* **benefico**
-ficare = rendere = giving back: **verificare**
-ficio = luogo dove si fa = place where made: **cappellificio**

* From Latin, with a similar or recognizable word in Italian and English.

-forme = che ha una certa forma = with a certain
form: **cuneiforme, cruciforme,** etc.

-fugo = che fugge = which flees from: **centrifugo**

-gero = che porta: armigero, arms-bearing

-voro = che divora = which eats, devours: **carnivoro**

All of the above is of some importance for the serious student,
because each item is an example of a certain parallelism between
Italian and English. The original Latin word (with which the
practical student is not deeply concerned) provides the Italian
and a similar equivalent in English.

It would not be difficult to extend the parallels to include
English and Italian words that are derived from a common Greek
original. But Italian is a *Latin* language, Greek is not. And
we need not be concerned with Italian words derived from Greek
more than to say that many of them have equivalents in English,
of which just a few simple examples may be given to illustrate
the word-building in Italian and English:

antropologia, anthropology

cinematografo, cinemato-
graph

farmacista, pharmacist,
chemist, druggist

microscopio, microscope

olografo, holograph (will)

tecnologia, technology

germanofilia, sympathy for
the Germans

francofobo, dislike, hatred of
the French

stenografo, stenographer

telegramma, telegram

chirurgo, surgeon (chirurgeon
was the old word)

There are in Italian hundreds of these words of Greek origin,
and there are thousands of words of Latin origin, which both
have in English approximately similar equivalents. This brief
excursion into derivation is merely to show that the subject is
not entirely an unpractical one. But we cannot afford in such
a book as this the space which it deserves.

LESSON X

§ 1. *Requirements for Practical Use of Italian—The Sentence—*
*The Simple Sentence—The Compound Sentence—*IL VESU-
VIO—*Cartoons:* Per rinfrancar lo spirito

IF the learner has up to this point followed instructions, memorized most of the material (words and phrases), mastered the
grammar, and worked carefully through all the reading matter so
as to drive home the necessary material and mechanism of the
language, he should have in his head what is required for most
of the practical purposes of everyday life. If he has had oppor-
tunities of listening to spoken Italian he should be able to understand most of it. If he has practised speaking with Italians his
own fluency in speaking will depend largely on the amount of
practice he has had. All these are fundamental requirements of
an essentially practical nature.

It is hardly likely that, up to now, he will have needed to
write, to *compose* very much Italian, apart from making up
phrases or putting down for memorizing such separate items as
he may think necessary. Yet there is one form of writing which,
almost from the beginning and certainly from now onwards, will
be useful: letter-writing. The forms for opening and ending a
letter are quite simple, and will be found on page 330. The
body of the letter and, in fact, any other form of writing is another
matter. But this can be simplified down so that he or she who
has absorbed what has gone before ought not to have any great
difficulty about composing a simple letter in Italian. Practice
will perfect the learner in this. And, once a good letter can be
written, if it is desired to go further and be able to write more
complex narrative or descriptive matter, or a composition for
examination purposes, a work on Italian Syntax will be required.
What is given here should, if known, carry him a long way.

The basis of all writing—and speaking—is the simple sentence.
Let us begin with this.

For our purpose here, sentences may be simple or compound.

I. THE SIMPLE SENTENCE: This consists of a single proposition or statement, which can be a direct statement (affirmative or negative), a command or request, or a question. Thus:

(1) *Direct Statement*—

John is a good boy. (*Affirmative.*)
John is not a good boy. (*Negative.*)

(2) *Command*—

Tell John to come here.

(3) *Request*—

Please reserve two corner seats for us.

(4) *Question*—

Will you be coming with us?

II. THE COMPOUND SENTENCE: The compound sentence consists of two or more simple sentences. Thus:

(1) John is a good boy, but he doesn't like work.
(2) Tell John to come here and bring his camera.
(3) Please reserve a room and send for my baggage.
(4) Will you come with us and help us to win a prize?

Strictly, there is another kind of sentence, usually called the " complex "—and it can be very complex!—but, as you can avoid such sentences completely in writing letters or almost anything else, they will not be dealt with here. You will have met many such in the reading, with their principal and subordinate clauses, their principal verbs in the indicative, the subordinate in the subjunctive, and so forth. You know enough to be able to recognize them and know their meaning: and that suffices for practical purposes.

It should be clear from what has been said that the learner should for some time rely upon his ability to make good *simple* sentences. These are not only the commonest in speaking, but they can cover an immense range. For example:

(1) **I grandi magazzini hanno un gran assortimento di cravatte.** The big stores have a great variety of neckties.

(2) **Mi metta i francobolli in questa lettera, per favore.**
Put the stamps on this letter for me, please.

(3) **Si fermi un momento qui perchè io vorrei fare qualche fotografie.** Let's stop here a moment because I want to take some photographs.

(4) **Lei può mettermi ad un piccolo tavolo vicino al parete?** Can you put me at a little table near the side?

But if it should be necessary to say or write something more elaborate, then two or more simple sentences can be joined together by conjunctions (see page 116). Thus:

Le spiagge più frequentate in Italia sono la Riviera, il Tirreno e l'Adriatico e l'autunno è più stabile che la primavera, ma in generale a partire dall'aprile il tempo è mite fuorchè luglio ed agasto quando fa molto caldo.

The most frequented beaches in Italy are the Riviera, the Tyrrhenian, and the Adriatic, and (in) autumn (the weather) is more settled than spring, but generally from April (onwards) the weather is pleasant except in July and August when it's very hot.

You will soon find that quite long compound sentences of this nature can be made without great difficulty. You will also in fact find that simple and compound sentences are the warp and woof in the texture of some of the best Italian prose and poetry, and that nearly all other kinds of sentences are used for variation, elegance, or subtility of expression. Take, for example, the opening sentence of the first instalment of **I Promessi Sposi** on page 160, in which there is only one subordinate clause with the verb in the subjunctive. Glance back at almost any passage of **I Promessi Sposi** and you may be surprised to find how much of it all is simple, direct statement.

This is your clue to speaking and writing Italian. Letter-writing need not go outside it. First master the formulae for openings and endings of letters, and make the body of your letter as simple as possible.

Il Vesuvio Ai Margini del Cratere

All'Osservatorio ci attende il direttore Imbò che ha visto concludersi l'ultimo periodo effusivo ed esplosivo nella deflagrazione del marzo 1944, un'eruzione che, nella letteratura del Settecento, sarebbe stato un incendio spettacolare con nubi ardenti, archi luminosi, fontane di lava e un cono cipressoide in luogo della comune forma del pino pliniano.

Ma, dopo quella tremenda convulsione, il vulcano, vinto dalla sua stessa mostruosa violenza, è diventato un malato difficile, fa di tutto per nascondere il suo vero stato di salute, respira e rifiata quel tanto che occorre a mantenerlo in vita ed a recuperare le forze perdute. E intanto all'Osservatorio si moltiplicano e si affinano gli strumenti di osservazione: sismografi ultrasensibili da vibrare al distacco e al tonfo di una pietra nel cratere; gravimetri e clinometri da misurare il campo magnetico; si va in giro con gli apparecchi intorno al cratere per una più diretta auscultazione dell'apparato respiratorio e per la misurazione termica delle fumarole nell'attesa di un rialzo di temperatura e di un'auspicata e benefica decongestione. «Non è letargo»; mi dice sorridendo e quasi a rassicurarmi Imbò, mostrandomi le linee tremule dei diagrammi, «è il dinamico riposo del Vesuvio».

AMEDEO MAIURI

Agosto 1956

---

la deflagrazione = il deflagrare, the rapid burning away.
il Settecento = il secolo XVIII, the eighteenth century.
cipressoide, cypressoid, resembling the shape of the cypress tree.
il pino, pine tree. **pliniano,** Plinian.
è diventato, has become, *from* **diventare,** to become.
rifiata, breathes again, *from* **rifiatare,** to breathe again.
quel tanto, that quantity, as much, as long as.
si affinano, *from* **affinare,** to refine.
il sismografo (-i), seismograph.
il distacco, detachment.
il tonfo, the fall.
il cratere, crater.
il gravimetro, gravimeter, an instrument for measuring the weight of bodies.
il clinometro, clinometer, an instrument for determining slope.
l'auscultazione (ascultare, to listen), auscultation, act of listening.
termico, thermic, relating to heat.

la fumarola (-uola), emanation of gas from a volcano.
l'attesa, expectation.
il rialzo, rise, *from* **rialzare,** to rise *or* rise again.
il dinamico riposo, dynamic rest, quietness.

§ 2. *Letter Writing—Formal Openings—Formal Endings—Familiar and Friendly Endings—Examples of Letters:* (1) *Private Letters;* (2) *A Commercial Letter—***Avviso:** *Advertisement.*

FORMAL OPENING OF A LETTER: When the name of the person is not known or is omitted, open your letter with the words:

Egregio Signore (egregio, famous, distinguished)
Pregiato Signore (pregiato, honoured)
or
Stimato Signore (stimato, esteemed)

If the surname is used, then:

Egregio Signor Locatelli
Pregiato Signor Locatelli
or
Stimato Signor Locatelli

To a firm (**una ditta**), this opening is usually omitted. One simply starts the letter with some polite phrase. It is common in formal business letters to use the Second Person Plural throughout: **Voi,** not **Lei** or **Loro.**

On the envelope to a private person, one puts: **All' Egregio Signor Locatelli.**

To a firm: **Alla Spettabile Ditta,** followed by the name (**spettabile,** *respectable, eminent*).

To a lady one usually writes: **Gentilissima Signora** or **Signorina,** and if she is known to you, add her name: **Gentilissima Signora Locatelli.** On the envelope put: **Gentilissima Signora Locatelli.** *Or:* **Gentma, Sig.a.**

A FAMILIAR OPENING: **Caro mio** or **Cara mia:**

Mio caro amico or **Cara amica mia**
or
Caro Giovanni

Per rinfrancar lo spirito

— Dimmi, caro, che cosa debbo fare?

— Veramente le belle donne non mi hanno mai attirato, vero, cara?

— Gelsomina! E la macchina?

— Prova un'altra volta, e se non ci riuscirai apriremo una scatola di sardine.

rinfrancare, to give new courage

FORMAL ENDINGS:

> **Colla massima stima, vi saluto,** followed by signature
> **Con distinti saluti**
> *or*
> **Ben distintamente (vi** or **La) saluto**

FAMILIAR AND FRIENDLY ENDINGS: One has to be a little careful, and make the ending suit the relationship. Here are some formulae:

> **Distinti saluti,** Kind regards
> **Con i più distinti saluti,** With kindest regards
> **Mi creda** (*polite*) *or* **credimi** (*familiar*) *followed by* **devotissimo suo,** Yours very sincerely
> **Affettuosi saluti,** With best wishes
> **Suo affezionatissimo (sua -a),** Yours with best regards
> **Con amichevoli saluti,** With friendly greetings
> **Con amicizia,** With friendship (*a safe, friendly ending*)

When writing (*a*) to a hotel or (*b*) to a boarding-house, you address yourself to (*a*) **Al Signor Direttore** and (*b*) **Al Signor Proprietario,** and, as it is safe to be polite, open with **Gentilissimo Signore** in each case and end with **Colla massima stima, vi saluto** or **Con saluti distinti.**

'**Carissimo** and **carissima** in the opening of a letter should be reserved for intimate relationships. Also second person singular.

The letters which follow were written by a teacher of Italian in reply to letters written by one of her pupils, an adult student of the language. They may be treated as models of the sort of correspondence which you might have with an Italian teacher or friend. A translation is not given, because from now onwards you should be able to puzzle out the meaning with little difficulty apart from an occasional word. If you cannot do so, this means that you will have to turn back and revise grammar, or go back over some passages of reading matter. Note the simple, straightforward style of these letters.

Examples of Letters

I.

Gentilissimo Signor Maxwell,

Solo poche righe [1] stamane per ringraziarla per la sua cortese lettera—che le rimando corretta.

Vedo con piacere che fa meno sbagli e che ha fatto anche molto progresso nella costruzione delle frasi.

Le mando accluso un libro con dei bozzetti [2] adatti per traduzione essendo sicura che le saranno molto utili. Sono graduati, perciò incominci dal primo sebbene, naturalmente, lo troverà molto facile.

Che strana coincidenza! Anch'io sto studiando lo spagnuolo! Ma, disgraziatamente, non ho molto tempo. Trovo però della difficoltà nella pronuncia.

Con distinti saluti,
Lucia Vittorini.

[1] **rigo,** line.   [2] **bozzetto,** short passage.

Egregio Signor Maxwell,

Torno or ora [1] dalla scuola ove mi hanno detto che la lezione che dovevo dare giovedì mattina è stata rimandata al pomeriggio dello stesso giorno. Essendo una classe, mi è difficile cambiare l'ora.

Le sarebbe perciò possibile di venire giovedì mattina (sono libera durante tutta la mattinata) invece dell'ora che avevamo stabilità.

Scusi tanto e grazie. Non mi scriva a meno che non potesse venire, ed io l'aspetterò giovedì in mattinata, invece del pomeriggio.

In fretta, tanti saluti,
L. V.

[1] **or ora,** this very moment.

Gentilissimo Signor Maxwell,

Mi scusi tanto se non Le ho inviato primo le sue correzioni, ma son stata molto occupata in questi ultimi giorni e, come accade quando non si fanno le cose immediatamente, esse vengono rimandate di giorno in giorno—Avevo quasi dimenticata la sua lettera nel mio cassetto [1] e, proprio per caso,[2] l'ho ritrovata questa sera.

Fortunatamente abbiamo avuto diverse nottate tranquille; ne son tanto contenta, poichè godo immensamente la quiete intorno al lume, la sera; sola, nella mia cameretta, occupandomi di qualcosa che eleva e unite la mente e l'animo: questi sono i più bei momenti della giornata, quando si prova un certo senso di profonda soddisfazione spirituale, che nasce dall'aver fatto il proprio dovere, e dall'attività della mente e del pensiero.

Ieri lessi nel giornale che una bomba era caduta a " X "! Ho fede però, che Lei non ne abbia risentito nessun danno.

Tanti distinti saluti,
L. V.

[1] cabinet drawer.   [2] by chance.

Gentilissimo Signore,

Ecco finalmente la sua traduzione corretta di ritorno. Non gliel'ho mandata prima perchè l'avevo smarrita [1] fra altre carte e perciò mi scuso se ho tardato tanto.

Davvero che per tutti questi termini tecnici di guerra moderna ci vorrebbe veramente un buon dizionario militare, poichè io ignoro moltissime nuove espressioni del genere, e non sono in istato di assisterla convenevolmente [2] in questo genere di traduzioni. Le potrò però sempre correggere il suo italiano, e ciò con vivo piacere.

Sono tanto lieta [3] di sentire il buon esito del suo esame, sebbene non lo avessi mai dubitato.

Gradisca [4] le mie congratulazioni.

In questi ultimi tempi abbiamo avuto una sequela di nottate pacifiche e tranquille, che sarà, molto probabilmente, interrotta da un'incursione delle più accanite [5] ed intense! Senza dubbio si vogliono preparare per qualche importante nuovo attacco su di noi—o forse sono troppo occupati in Creta?

Quando ha tempo e voglia, mi mandi nuovamente qualche sua traduzione.

Con i miei più distinti saluti,
L. V.

[1] lost, misplaced.   [2] conveniently, suitably.   [3] glad, happy.
[4] accept, please accept.   [5] furious, mad.

II. *Answer to an Inquiry.*

Con riferimento alla Sua richiesta
relativa ai nostri programmi per
l'estero in lingua italiana, La
informiamo che Le abbiamo inviato
con plico a parte, un volumetto di
recente pubblicazione, dal quale Lei
potrà ricavare tutti i dati che La
interessano.

Le precisiamo inoltre che sarà
nostra cura farLe avere periodi-
camente il volumetto stesso.

Con i migliori saluti.

R A I
Radiotelevisione Italiana
Le Direzione Generale

§ 3. *Proverbs*—**I PROVERBI ITALIANI E INGLESI**—*Cartoons
Illustrating Proverbs*

Italian is rich in proverbs and proverbial sayings, both in its
literature and in the everyday speech of the people, especially
the peasants. A comparison of Italian and English proverbs
shows that many of them are, literally, the same and present no
difficulties, and that still more are almost the same or quite
easily grasped. For example:

> **A chi è affamato,**
> **Ogni cibo è grato.**
> To whom is hungry,
> Every (kind of) food is pleasing.

avviso   Advert.

—where we would say *Hunger is the best sauce*. This is a matter of perceiving the association, assuming that one knows the English proverb. But some Italian proverbs and sayings are not so easily associated with their English counterparts. For example, we often say, *I know what I know*, but an Italian would say, **So da che parte vien il vento**, *I know from which part (direction) the wind comes*, which is closer to *I know the way the wind blows*.

Many proverbs are also idioms and of quite frequent use in everyday life. **Ridere sotto i baffi**, literally *To laugh under the moustache* (plural in Italian) is our *To laugh up one's sleeve*.

Enough has been said for the learner to realize that the only way to learn Italian proverbs is to memorize them, but always making sure that he knows the custom to which they refer, as in *Good wine needs no bush*. It may be argued that a learner has no need of proverbs, and perhaps that is true at this stage. But it can truthfully be said that every language is rich in proverbs, thoughts, and expressions that are entirely its own, and that, well used, they can help to give grace to conversation. If they are dealt with briefly here, it is because there is no end to them in Italian, but a knowledge and appreciation of a few will help the foreigner towards an appreciation of the subject, and perhaps towards a desire to enlarge his knowledge of it.

I Proverbi Italiani e Inglesi

Alcuni dei nostri proverbi vantano una traduzione quasi esatta in inglese. Per esempio:

> —*Non c'è rosa senza spina:*
> There's no rose without a thorn.
> —*Al bisogno si conosce l'amico:*
> A friend in need is a friend indeed.
> —*Lontan dagli occhi, lontan dal cuore:*
> Out of sight, out of mind.
> —*In burrasca ogni porto è rifugio:*
> Any port in a storm.
> —*Il tempo sana ogni cosa:*
> Time heals everything.

Darsi delle arie

To ride a high horse.

Prendere due piccioni con
una fava.

To kill two birds with
one stone.

Mettere il bastone tra le ruote.

To put spanners in the wheels.

Ridere sotto i baffi.

To laugh up one's sleeve.

—Buon vino non ha bisogno di frasca:
Good wine needs no bush.
—Chi s'aiuta, Dio l'aiuta:
God helps him who helps himself.
—I primi amori sono i migliori:
First love, best love.
—I genii s'incontrano:
Great brains think alike.

Tuttavia ci sono molti altri proverbi che possono essere tradotti in inglese esattamente, come senso e come valore, ma che hanno in inglese forma loro propria, diversa da l'Italiano. Così, il nostro detto " *Non menare il can per l'aia* " che vuol dire: " Non fate tanti discorsi inutili " viene reso in inglese con l'espressione in uso comune di tutti i giorni: " Don't beat about the bush ". Come pure il nostro proverbio così aggraziato " *A ogni uccello il suo nido è bello* " si ritrova in inglese sotto la forma " East, west, home's best ".

E così via di seguito, e vediamo come " *Tutto il mondo è paese* " (The whole world is kin) e come le vicende di tutti i giorni, le stesse speranze, gli stessi affetti e gli stessi pensieri ci vincolano tutti. Finisco con una traduzione curiosa. " *Paese che vai, usanze che trovi* " si dice in Italia, savio consiglio e ammonimento sano e sereno. In Inglese c'è un vecchio proverbio che dice " When you are in Rome do as the Romans do ". Un proverbio assai antico che forse data dai giorni quando ognuno sognava di andare a Roma in pellegrinaggio, e in questo come in tante altre cose si sente il riavvicinamento di due terre.

R. T.

(With the cartoons from **La Voci degli Italiani.**)

---

vantano, *boasts,* from **vantare. la burrasca,** *squall.* **la frasca,** *bush*—in this proverb the word is used for *advertisement,* and in this sense comes from an old custom of putting a branch or small " bush " outside a vintner's or tavern to advertise its wares. The coloured barber's pole is still similarly used in many countries.

Non menare il cane (il can) per l'aia, literally *Don't lead the dog to the threshing-floor*—because the dog cannot tread out grain. The proverb is used when there's too much talk without specific result, when it leads nowhere.

così **via di seguito**, *so on successively*. **la vicenda,** *vicissitude*. **riavvicinamento,** Noun, akin to **vicino**, *near, neighbourly*, and here meaning *closeness, neighbourliness* because of **il pellegrinaggio,** *the pilgrimage(s)* to Rome. **vincolar (si),** *to bind, join together*.

The cartoons on pages 338–339 illustrate proverbs of which the fundamental meaning is the same, although expressed in quite different words —not uncommon in proverbial sayings in all languages.

§ 4. *Abbreviations in Italian: List*—CRUCIVERBA A DOPPIA LETTURA: Un Grande " Motel " a Roma

SOME COMMON ITALIAN ABBREVIATIONS

Abbreviation	*Explanation*	*English Equivalent*
AASS.	Azienda Autonoma Statale della Strada	State Road Board
a.C.	avanti Cristo	B.C. Before Christ
d.C.	dopo Cristo	After Christ, A.D.
A.C.I.	Azione Cattolica Italiana Automobile Club Italiano	Italian Catholic Action Italian Automobile Club
ALI.	Aviolinee Italiane	Italian Air Lines
C.	numerazione romana	Roman numeral for 100 $\overline{C} = 1000$
C.A.I.	Club Alpino Italiano	Italian Alpine Club
Card.	Cardinale	Cardinal
cav.	cavaliere	a title, *chevalier*, knight
C.D.	Comitato Direttivo Corpo Diplomatico	Directive Committee car-sign: Diplomatic Corps
C.G.I.L.	Confederazione Generale Italiana del Lavoro	Italian General Confederation of Labour
C.N.R.	Consiglio Nazionale delle Ricerche	National Council of Research
com.	comandante	commander, major
comm.	commendatore	a title: commendor
C.R.I.	Croce Rossa Italiana	Italian Red Cross
C.V.	cavallo vapore	horse-power, H.P.
D.	numerazione romana	Roman numeral for 500. $\overline{D}. = 5000.$
dal.	decalitro	decalitre
dam.	decametro	decametre
D.L.	Decreto Legge	Decree Law
dott.	dottore	doctor, Dr.
Egr.	egregio	distinguished, *see page* 330
Em.mo.	Eminentissimo	Most Eminent
ENTE	institution, society	Usually followed by word or abbreviation. *See* **R.A.I.**
F.N.M.	Ferrovie Nord di Milano	Northern Milan Railway
F.S.	Ferrovie dello Stato	State Railways
G.B.	Gran Bretagna	Great Britain (car mark)

342 ITALIAN FOR ADULTS

Abbreviation	*Explanation*	*English Equivalent*
G.U.	Gazzetta Ufficiale	Official Gazette
ICS	Istituto Centrale di Statistica	Central Institute of Statistics
Ill.mo.	illustrissimo	most illustrious
Kg.	chilogrammo	kilogram, Kilo.
Km.	chilometro	kilometre, Km.
Kmq.	chilometro quadrato	square kilometre, sq. Km.
LL.EE.	Loro Eccellenze	Your Excellencies
LL.EEm.	Loro Eminenze	Your Eminences
LL.PP.	Lavori Pubblici	Public Works
L.st.	lire sterline	pounds sterling
M.	numerazione romana	Roman numeral for 1,000
M.E.	Medio Evo	Middle (period) Age, Ages
M.R.	molto reverendo	Very Reverend
ms., MS.	manoscritto	Manuscript, MS.
N.	numero	Number, No.
N.T.	Nuovo Testamento	New Testament
O.N.U.	Organizzazione delle Nazioni Unite	United Nations Organization, U.N.O.
OO.PP.	Opere Pubbliche	Public Works
P.	padre	father, of priests
P.I.	Pubblica Istruzione	Public (national) education
PP.	padri; porto pagato	priests; carriage, postage paid
P.S.	Pubblica Sicurezza	Public Security (force), Police
P.S.I.	Partito Socialista Italiano	Italian Socialist Party
P.T.	Poste e Telegrafi / Polizia del Traffico	Posts and Telegraphs / Traffic Police
P.V.	Piccola Velocità	small velocity, slow (of trains)
q.	quadrato	square, of measures
Ra.	radio	radius, radio
R.A.I.	Radio Audizione Italiana	ENTE R.A.I., Italian Broadcasting organization
S.	santo	Holy, St., Saint
S.A.	Società Anonima	Limited Company
S.C.V.	Stato della Città del Vaticano	Vatican City State
S.I.A.E.	Società Italiana degli Autori ed Editori	Italian Authors' and Publishers' Society
sig., sig.a., sig.na.	signore, signora, signorina	Mr., Mrs., Miss
S.P.	Santo Padre	Holy Father; the Pope
Spett.	spettabile	" respectable " before the name of a firm
S.S.	Sua Santità / Santa Sede	His Holiness (the Pope) / Holy See
S.U.A.	Stati Uniti d'America	United States of America, U.S.A.

Abbreviation	*Explanation*	*English Equivalent*
V.E.	**Vostra Eccellenza**	Your Excellency
	Vostra Eminenza	Your Eminence
X	**numerazione romana**	Roman numeral 10. $\overline{X} =$
		10,000
W.C.	**(latrina)**	water closet

Note: The list is not exhaustive. Any good Italian dictionary will provide many more.

CORRIERE ITALIANO

Un Grande "Motel" a Roma
come un Piccolo Villaggio

In Italia esiste una rete di 25 " motels ", che offrono una comoda e conveniente ospitalità ai turisti motorizzati; la prossima primavera, la rete sarà arricchita da un nuovo esercizio, che sorgerà presso Roma, al 18.o chilometro della via Cassia.

Situato sulla corrente del traffico proveniente da Firenze, l'autostello domani si presenterà al turista come un piccolo villaggio, immerso nel verde di una collina e isolato dai rumori della strada consolare da un viale lungo poco più di 500 metri.

Il complesso alberghiero unico nella sua forma in Italia comprenderà 32 casette, allineate su otto file e disposte orizzontalmente al pendio della collina. Vi sarà poi un edificio centrale provvisto di ristorante, di due piscine, di due campi da tennis ed uno da golf, mentre un'intera ala sarà destinata agli uffici, ai servizi, ed agli alloggi del personale e degli autisti. Una rete di stradine ghiaiose, lungo il pendio, allaccerà fra loro le 32 casette, internamente divise in due stanze, nelle quali potranno essere ospitate 128 persone. La costruzione dell'autostello, che si chiamerà Belamotel, importerà una spesa di 160 milioni di lire.

Nel Belamotel romano le formalità per l'affitto saranno ridotte alla forma semplice. I prezzi saranno contenuti al di sotto delle tariffe di un albergo di prima categoria e il cliente avrà a disposizione una stanza di 5 metri per 4, un bagno e ogni conforto.

CRUCIVERBA A DOPPIA LETTURA

Questo cruciverba ha la specialità di ripetere le parole orizzontalmente e verticalmente. Ecco perché le definizioni sono tanto poche...

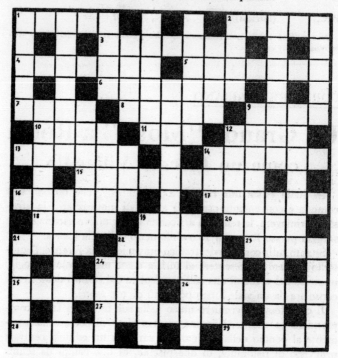

Definizioni

1. Vi si trova molta gente... di lettere e... di vaglia - 2. E' contro l'ubiquità - 3. Spostati - 4. Respiro più forte - 5. Sta in Germania - 6. Trampoliere - 7. Nome di un eresiarca - 8. Discendente di un re d'Argo e di Micene - 9. Animale che ride - 10. Irsuta - 11. Nome femminile - 12. Respiro difficile - 13. Frana - 14. Cavaliere ungherese - 15. Imprese di chi ha coraggio - 16. Dea della Giustizia - 17. Alpi bergamasche - 18. Residenze - 19. Primo fra infiniti - 20. Nome femminile - 21. Opera - 22. Stelle - 23. Poema di grandi gesta - 24. Re dei Làpiti, fulminato da Giove - 25. Con - 26. Abbreviativo maschile - 27. Il vanitoso per eccellenza - 28. Immagine sacra - 29. Ripassa il filo nell'ordito.

Solution on p. 346

Per le vetture verranno ricavati piccoli garage sfruttando la pendenza della collina.

UNA MONETA DA 500 LIRE ALLO STUDIO IN ITALIA

Quanto prima verranno messe in circolazione in Italia monete metalliche da 500 lire, che sostituiranno gli equivalenti biglietti di banca. Le caratteristiche ed il nome della nuova moneta sono attualmente oggetto di particolari studi. Si ritiene che il contenuto in argento della nuova moneta sarà particolarmente elevato e proporzionato al suo importo, anche perchè è risaputo che uno dei sistemi più efficaci per scoraggiare la falsificazione della monetazione metallica è quello di rapportare il contenuto in metallo al valore intrinseco della moneta.

DUE MILIONI DI ABITANTI A ROMA ENTRO IL 1959

La popolazione romana è aumentata di 48.983 unità, dal giugno 1956 alla data del 30 giugno 1957 infatti risultavano presenti a Roma 1.908.319 persone di cui 1.835.135 in possesso della cittadinanza. La media della immigrazione, che si credeva lievemente flessa in questi ultimi tempi, ha invece dimostrato di essersi mantenuta ai livelli costanti degli anni precedenti e forse di aver subito un ulteriore aumento, aggirandosi attorno alle 45 mila unità annue la immigrazione media registrata negli anni del 1946 al 1956.

In tal modo è facile ritenere che entro il 1959 nella Capitale si saranno effettivamente raggiunti i due milioni di abitanti come popolazione permanente e residente.

La Voce degli Italiani, LONDRA

---

una rete, a network. **i turisti motorizzati,** motoring tourists. **arrichito,** enriched. **sorgere,** to rise. **proveniente da,** coming from. **autostello,** motel. **strada consolare,** much used road. **la piscina,** swimming-pool (*also* fish pond). **autista,** motorist. **complesso alberghiero,** entity of inns. **stradine ghiaiose,** gravelled paths. **il pendio,** slope. **allaccerà,** will link up, *from* **allacciare.**

N

stanza, room. **una spesa,** amount, income. **l'affitto,** lease, letting. **ricavato,** dug out. **sfruttando,** taking advantage of. **la pendenza,** gradient.

§ 5. *The Next Steps—Books to Read—Reference Books: Dictionaries and Grammars—Newspapers and Magazines—*Per scrivere e parlar bene

When the student has satisfied himself (and his teacher, if he has had one) that he has worked through this book to good effect, his next steps must lead towards the perfecting and expansion of what he has learnt here. How to set about this must depend on his circumstances, but it can safely be said that he will learn more in a holiday of weeks than he will learn by months of study from books. So, if it is at all possible, have a holiday in Italy, however short it may be. If he is working for an examination he will know the standard of knowledge required and adjust his studies accordingly, taking account of any texts that may be prescribed. Apart from these, he must never miss an opportunity of speaking Italian with Italians or of listening to radio broadcasts as often as possible. Another thing he can do without labour, and that is to read as many books in English as possible about Italy, whether they be novels, history, biography, or literature in general. This provides a background of knowledge which will be useful for reading books by Italian authors in their original language, a stage which should quickly be achieved if this course has been worked through carefully.

The first book in Italian to be read should without doubt be *I Promessi Sposi*, to which the learner has been introduced here. There are many editions, but that published by Le Monnier, Florence, is a good one for this purpose, being well supplied with explanatory notes and commentary by the editor, Enrico Bianchi. There is an excellent translation in English by Archibald Colquhoun (No. 999 in Everyman's Library, published by J. M. Dent & Sons, Ltd., London); a great stand-by for the student. Another suitable and delightful book is *Le Avventure di Pinocchio*, by C. Collodi; the dialogue in it is particularly good for the foreign student. It is in its class a masterpiece, having something of the reverse quality of Swift's *Gullivers Travels* in that, being originally written for children, it is greatly enjoyed by adults.

Pinocchio is published in the inexpensive Biblioteca Moderna Mondatori, Milan, which also publishes the following books that can be recommended:

> *Il chiodo rosso*, by Alessandro Varaldo
> *L'immorale*, by T. Antongini
> *Come le foglie*, by Giuseppi Giacosa
> *Tempo di marzo*, by Francesco Chiesa
> *Tutta Frusaglia*, by F. Tombari
> *I divoratori*, by Annie Vivanti
> *Il Principe*, by Niccolò Machiavelli

The list of books could be extended indefinitely, but those mentioned above are chosen as suitable for this purpose.

Another important asset of the language-learner lies in the fact that since the end of the Second World War many modern English and American books are being translated into Italian. The list grows every year. Why not, then, read some of them in Italian, even if you have read them before in English? Mondatori publish Joseph Conrad's *The Nigger of the Narcissus* under the title *Il nero del " Narciso "* and Raymond Chandler's *The Great Sleep* as *Il grande sonno*. Any bookseller who specializes in Italian books should be able to supply many more.

A good dictionary has now become essential. The Italian–English and English–Italian dictionaries (large and small) by

Alfred Hoare, published by Cambridge University Press, fulfil most requirements. But, for several reasons, I would advise the serious student to make himself accustomed as soon as possible to the use of a dictionary in Italian for Italians. There is a truly admirable biggish one: *Novissimo Dizionario della Lingua Italiana*, by Fernando Palazzi, published by Ceschina Principato, Milan. And, possibly more attractive, and eminently serviceable for most students, is the smaller version of the same work: *Il Piccolo Palazzi*, from the same publishers. The *Pocket Langenscheidt's Universal Dictionary—English–Italian and Italian–English* (1955) really can be carried in the pocket or in a lady's handbag and it is good (London Agents: Methuen & Co., W.C.2).

There is no Italian Grammar in English that is comparable to many grammars of other languages, and I think that the student who wishes to fill in and expand his knowledge of Italian grammar should turn to, say, *La Lingua Nazionale*, by Bruno Migliorini (published by Le Monnier, Florence), or to the *Grammatica Illustrata della Lingua Italiana*, by Vincenzo Palumbo (published by Signorelli, Rome), both of which are esteemed in Italy.

All students of Italian in Great Britain will find it advantageous and pleasant to become a member of The Italian Institute, 39 Belgrave Square, London, S.W.1. This Institute provides Courses in the Language and Literature, lectures by eminent Italians and others, concerts, film-shows, and there is an excellent Library from which books can be borrowed. The cost of membership is small in comparison with the facilities offered. Italian daily newspapers and weeklies, some of the latter illustrated, provide topical reading. Dailies: *Corriere della Sera*, Milan; *La Stampa*, Turin; *Il Messaggero*, Rome; and *Il Mattino*, Naples. There are several weeklies: *OGGI* can be recommended.

Those persons living outside Italy who wish to subscribe to Italian periodicals and magazines, or wish to purchase books in Italy, may write directly to the respective publishing house or a bookseller who supplies overseas readers. Two excellent examples are *Libreria Hoepli* of Rome (Largo Chigi, 15) and

Milan (Via Mameli, 13), and *Libreria Dedalo* of Rome (Via Barberini, 75). On receiving the order, the publisher or book-seller concerned will send the book or magazine required, together with the bill, which must be paid in accordance with present currency regulations governing either the dollar or sterling areas. *La Voce degli Italiani*, a London weekly (6*d*.), can be obtained through a newsagent or direct from: La Voce degli Italiani, 29 Beauchamp Place, London, S.W.3.

Every student who has a hobby or speciality, or is for some reason interested in any particular subject, should endeavour to find books in Italian on that subject. Hoepli of Milan publishes a series of popular books covering a wide range of subjects; and there are others. Here a bookseller can help, and in London there is: Alec Tiranti Ltd., 72 Charlotte Street, W.1; although their speciality is works on fine art, they stock a good range of other books, and can obtain from Italy any book in print. But there is another useful source of information which can pro-vide information not always available to booksellers. This is: *Il Centro Nazionale di Informazioni Bibliografiche*, which has been established in Rome, corresponds with all the libraries and cultural institutes in Italy and various centres belonging to other nations. It gives oral and written information to those persons desirous of widening their knowledge of Italy and Italian affairs and furnishes lists of useful publications on a wide range of subjects. It does not pretend, however, that the in-formation it supplies is exhaustive. Bibliographical items are furnished free of charge. A small payment is required for:

Typed copies of newspaper and magazine articles and extracts from books.

Photographic reproduction (this work is carried out by an expert).

Inquiries to: *Il Direttore della Biblioteca Nazionale Centrale* " Vittorio Emanuele II "—Via del Collegio Romano 27, Rome, Italy.

per scrivere e parlar bene

DIZIONARIO LINGUISTICO MODERNO

Per gentile concessione dell'Editore Mondadori pubblichiamo questa " guida pratica per scrivere e parlare bene " che è ricavata dal " Dizionario Linguistico Moderno " di Aldo Gabrielli. Lo scopo che ci proponiamo è lo stesso che si è proposto l'autore del dizionario: **" di insegnare a chi mal la conosce e di ricordare a chi trascurandola l'ha dimenticata, la buona lingua italiana."**

ADEMPIRE. Meno comune **adempiere**, è verbo transitivo e si costruisce con il complemento oggetto: **adempiere un dovere, adempiere una promessa** e sim. Non è quindi corretto usarlo come intransitivo e con la preposizione **a**, e dire " adempire a un dovere, a una promessa ".

ADIBIRE. Neologismo, dal latino **adhibere;** dal linguaggio burocratico è passato oggi nell'uso; certo è pendantesco e la sua coniugazione faticosa. Meglio si useranno i verbi **adoperare, usare, assegnare, affidare** (meno bene **destinare**), secondo i casi.

ADORARE. Dal latino **adorare** (composto di **ad,** verso, e **orare,** pregare), vuol dir propriamente: " rivolgersi a uno con la preghiera ", e quindi tributare il culto ad una divinità. E' il verbo da usare propriamente per il culto a Dio.

Oggi però si adora un poco ogni cosa. Così si adorano gli sport del calcio e degli sci, si adora il mare, si adora se stesso, si adorano la pizza napoletana e gli spaghetti con le vongole. E' la stessa elefantiasi dell'immagine, per cui oggi c'è chi " va pazzo " per i marroni canditi, per il ballo e per la canasta. Gonfiezza ed esagerazioni tutte fr. Con maggior misura e con uguale efficacia, si dirà **mi piace moltissimo, sono ghiotto, sono avido, sono ingordo, amo soprattutto, preferisco specialmente, ho un debole per,** e sim., secondo il bisogno.

ADOTTARE. Propriamente " prendere alcuno per figlio secondo la legge ", si usa bene anche in senso figurato, quando significa far proprio, approvare, accettare un pensiero altrui: **adottare un'opinione, un metodo, una dottrina.** Si usa male invece riferito a decisioni, deliberazioni, pensieri personali; in questi casi si dirà **prendere** una decisione, **scegliere** un partito, **attuare** un provvedimento, e simili.

AERODROMO. Neologismo, campo d'aviazione; foggiato su **ippodromo (aero** e gr. **dròmos,** campo per le corse, arena); oggi tuttavia è molto più raro di **AEROPORTO,** che sa meno di esperimento, di spettacolo.

La Voce degli Italiani, LONDRA.

" ALL PURPOSES " VOCABULARY

This list contains some 2500 words by means of which all others except technical words can be defined or explained. In this sense it can claim to be useful for " all purposes ". But it does not contain all the words which have appeared in the body of the text; those not in the Vocabulary have been explained in their place. Furthermore, there are here words which have not appeared in the reading but which it is advisable to know. The more unusual irregular Verbs are omitted, also numerals, pronouns, and geographical names given on pages 41-42.

A

A, ad, to, at
abbandonare, to abandon
abbasso, downstairs
abbastanza, enough
abbondanza, abundance
abile, skilful, clever
abilità, skill
abitante, inhabitant
abito, coat, dress
  gli abiti, clothes
abitudine, habit
accadere (*irr.*), to happen
accanto, -a, near to
accendisigaro, lighter (cigarette)
accettare, to accept
accoglienza, welcome, greeting
accogliere, to welcome
accompagnare, to accompany
accusare, to accuse
aceto, vinegar
acqua, water
— minerale, mineral water
— di Seltz, soda-water
acquarello, water-colour
acquisto, purchase
adagio, slowly
adettato, adapted
addio! good-bye

adesso, now
aerodromo, aerodrome
aeroplano, aeroplane
aeroporto, airport
affamato, hungry
affare, affair, transaction
affari, business, commerce
affatto, quite, at all
affetto, affection
affezionato, affectionate
affinchè, in order that
affisso, affixed (a, to)
affondato, sunk
agente, agent
  di polizia, policeman
aggiungere, to add
agiatezza, comfort, leisure
agnello, lamb
ago, needle
agricoltura, agriculture
agro, -a, sour
aiutare, to help
aiuto, help
ala, wing
albergo, inn, hotel
albero, tree
alcool, alcohol
— denaturato, methylated spirit
alcuno, -a, any, anybody, some,
  somebody

allegro, gay, merry
alloggiare, to lodge
allora, then
  d'allora, since then
  d'allora in poi, from then on
almeno, at least
altare, altar
altezza, height
alto, high, tall
altrimenti, otherwise
altro, -a, other
altrove, elsewhere
amabilità, kindness
amare, to love
amaro, bitter
ambasciata, embassy
ambasciatore (-trice), ambassador (-ess)
ambedue, both
ambizione, ambition
amicizia, friendship
amico, friend (*pl.* **amici**)
ammalarsi, to get sick, ill
ammalato, -a, ill, sick
amministrazione, administration, management
ammobiliato, furnished
amore, love
  per amore di, for sake of
analisi, analysis
anche, also
ancora, yet, still
andare (*irr.*), to go
  — **a cavallo,** to ride on horseback
  — **a male,** to go bad
  — **a piedi,** to go on foot
  — **a prendere,** to fetch
  — **a spasso,** to go for a walk
  — **in carrozza,** to ride in a carriage
andato, -a, gone
anello, ring
andito, passage, corridor
angolo, angle, corner
anima, soul, spirit
animale (*m.*), animal
animo, mind
animo! courage!
annali (*m.*), annals
annata, year (the whole)
anniversario (*m.*), anniversary

anno, year
anticamente, formerly
anticamera, entrance, hall
antico, -a, ancient
antipasto, hors d'œuvres
antipatico, -a, unattractive
anzi, rather (more)
aperitivo, aperitif
aperto, -a, open, opened
apparecchio, apparatus
  — **radio,** radio set
  — **fotografico,** camera
appartamento, apartment, flat
appassire, to wither, to fade
appena, as soon as, hardly
applaudito, -a, applauded
applauso (*m.*), applause
applicazione (*f.*), application
apposta, on purpose, expressly
approvazione, approbation, approval
appunto, just
aprire, to open
arancia, orange
arco, arch
ardere (*irr.*), to burn
arena, sand
argento, silver
aria, air
arioso, -a, airy
armadio (*m.*), cupboard, wardrobe
armata, navy, fleet
arme, arma (*f.*), weapon
armonia, harmony
arrendersi (*irr.*), to surrender
arrivare, to arrive
arrivato, -a, arrived
arrivederci! good-bye, au revoir!
arrivo, arrival
arrosto, roast (-beef)
arte, art
artiglieria, artillery
artista (*m. & f.*), artist
ascensore (*m.*), lift, elevator
asciugamano, towel
asciutto, -a, dry
ascoltare, to listen
asino, ass
aspettare, to wait, expect
aspettato, -a, waited for, expected
aspetto, aspect

assaggiare, to taste, to try
assai, enough
assalire (*irr.*), to attack
assetato, thirsty
assicurato, -a, assured
assistenza, assistance, help
assistere (*irr.*), to assist, attend
astenersi (*irr.*), to abstain
astuccio, case, cover
attento, -a, attentive
attenzione (*f.*), attention
attirato, -a, attracted, won
atto, act
attraversare, to cross
attraverso, across
attribuito, -a, attributed
augurio, good wish
autobus, bus
automobile (*f.*), motor-car. Also
  l'auto
autunno, autumn
avere, to have
— **aver . . . anni . . .** to be . . .
  years old
— **bisogno,** to want to need
— **caldo,** to be warm
— **da fare,** to have to do
— **a mano,** to have at hand
— **in uggia,** to have a dislike for
— **fame,** to be hungry
— **fretta,** to be in a hurry
— **freddo,** to be cold
— **molto piacere,** to be delighted
— **paura,** to be afraid
— **premura,** to take care
— **ragione,** to be right
— **sete,** to be thirsty
— **sonno,** to be sleepy
— **torto,** to be wrong
— **vergogna,** to be ashamed
aviazione, aviation, flying
avvertimento, warning
avvezzo, accustomed
avvocato, lawyer
azione, action
azzurro, blue

B

Bacio, kiss
bagaglio, luggage
bagnarsi, to bathe

bagnato, wet
bagno, bath
— **fare il —,** to take a —
ballare, to dance
ballo, ball, dance
bambino, child, baby
banca, bank
banchetto, banquet
banchiere, banker
banco (di mostra), counter
banchina, platform (railway),
  quay *banquette quai*
bandiera, flag
barba, beard
barbiere, barber
barca, boat
basso, -a, low
bastare, to be enough
basta! That's enough!
bastone (*m.*), stick
battaglia, battle
battere, to beat
batteria, battery
baule (*m.*), trunk, box
bellezza, beauty
bello, -a, beautiful
benchè, although
benedire (*irr.*), to bless
bene, well
beneficenza, charity
benino! good! well done!
benzina, petrol, gasoline
bere (*irr.*)   } to drink
bevere (*irr.*)   }
bevanda, drink
bevuto, drunk
biancheria, laundry
bianco, white
biancone (*m.*), luggage counter
biblioteca, library
bicchiere (*m.*), glass
bicicletta, bicycle
biennio, two-year period
biglietto, ticket
bimestre, two-months period
birra, beer
biscotto, biscuit
bisognare, to be necessary, to
  want
bocca, mouth
bock (*m.*), **di birra,** " pint " of beer
bollo, stamp (**francobollo**)

bontà, goodness
bordo, ship's side
  a bordo, on board
borsa, purse, handbag; Stock Exchange
bosco, wood
bottega, shop
bottiglia, bottle
bottone (*m.*), button
bove, ox
braccio, arm
bravo! bravo! excellent!
bravo (*m.*), cut-throat
bretelle (le), braces
brina, hoar frost
brocca, jug
bruciato, burned
brutto, ugly
buca delle lettere, letter-box
bucato, washing, laundry
bue, ox
bugia, story, falsehood
buio, dark
buonissimo, very good
buono, -a, good
burro, butter
busta, envelope

C

cabina, cabin
— telefonica, telephone box
caccia, hunt, hunting
cacciatore, hunter
cadere (*irr.*), to fall
caduto, fallen
caffè, coffee, café
caffettiera, coffee-pot
cagna, bitch
calamaio, inkstand
calcio, football
calcolato, calculated
caldo, -a, warm, hot
calore (*m.*), heat
calpestio, tramping, hiking
calzature (le), footwear, shoes
calze, stockings
calzette (le), socks
calzolaio, shoemaker
cambiare, to change
cambiato, -a, changed, exchanged
camera, Parliament

camera, room
cameriera, maid-servant, waitress
cameriere, waiter
camicia, shirt
caminetto, mantelpiece, fire-place
camminare, to walk
campagna, country, countryside
campanello, bell
campanile (*m.*), bell-tower
campo, field
campo d'atterraggio, landing ground
cancello, gate *la grille*
candela, candle, sparking plug
candeliere, candlestick
cane (*m.*), dog
cantare, to sing
cantina, cellar
canto, singing, song
canzone (*f.*), song
capanna, cottage
capace, capable
capelli (*m.pl.*), hair
capire, to understand
capitale (*f.*), capital
capitano, captain
capo, head, chief
capo cameriere, head waiter
Capodanno, New Year's day
capolavoro, masterpiece
capostazione, stationmaster
cappa, wrap, cloak
cappella, chapel
cappellaio (*m.*), hatter
capellino, hair
cappello, hat
capriccio, caprice
carabiniere, civil guard
caraffa, carafe
carbone (*m.*), coal
carattere, character
carburatore (*m.*), carburettor
carestia, famine
caricare, to charge, scarcity
carne (*f.*), meat, flesh
— di montone, mutton
— maiale, pork
caro, -a, dear, expensive
carrozza, carriage
carta, paper, card, map
— da lettere, writing-paper
— asciugante, blotting —

cartellone, poster
cartolaio (*m.*), stationer
cartolina postale, post card
casa, house
a casa, at home
caserma, barrack(s)
caso, case
cassa, cash desk
cassetta, drawer, cash box
cassettone (*m.*), chest of drawers
cassiere, cashier
castello, castle
castigo, punishment
catena, chain
catinella, basin
cattivo, -a, bad, naughty
causa, cause
a — di, on account of
cavaliere, cavalier, knight
cavalleria, cavalry
cavallo, horse
— da corsa, race-horse
— a cavallo, on horseback
cavatappi (*m.*), corkscrew
cavolo, cabbage
c'è, there is
cedere, to yield, to leave
ceduto, -a, yielded
celebre, celebrated
cena, supper
centinaio (*m.*), hundred
cento, hundred
cera, wax
cercare, to seek, to look for, to try
cercato, -a, sought, looked for
certamente, certainly
certo, -a, certain
lo chauffeur, chauffeur (Fr.)
che, than, that, which, who
  che? che cosa? what?
  che cos' ha? what's the matter?
chi, he who; chi? who?
  chi . . . chi, one . . . another, the one . . . the other
  di chi, whose
chi sa? who knows? heaven knows!
chiamare, to call
  si chiama, is called
chiamato, -a, called, named
chiaro, -a, clear, light (in colour)

chiasso, uproar
chiave (*f.*), key
chiedere (*irr.*), to ask, beg
chiesa, church
chiesto, asked
chilometro, kilometre
chiosco, kiosk (newspapers)
chiudere (*irr.*), to shut
chiunque (*invar.*), whoever
chiuso, shut
ci, there, to, us
ci sono, there are
ciabattino, cobbler
ciascuno, -a, each one, everybody
cibo, food
cicatrice (*f.*), scar
cielo, sky, heaven
ciglio, brow, eye-brow   *le sourcil*
cinematografo, cinema
cinghia, strap
cioccolata, chocolate
ciò, that, it
circa, about
città (*f.*), city, town
cittadino, -a (*m. & f.*), citizen
classe (*f.*), class
cliente (*m. & f.*), customer
clima, climate
cocktail (*m.*), cocktail
codesto, -a, that (over there)
cogliere (*irr.*), together
  cognac (*m.*), brandy
cognato, -a, brother-, sister-in-law
cognome, family name, surname
colazione, breakfast, luncheon
  la prima —, breakfast
  la seconda —, lunch
collega (*m. & f.*), colleague
colletto, collar
collina, hill
collo, neck
colonna, column
colore (*m.*), colour
colpa, fault, blame
colpevole, guilty, culpable
coltello, knife
colui, colei, coloro, he, she, those
combattere, to fight
combattimento, combat, fight
combattuto, fought
come, as, like, how

cominciare, to begin
  cominciato, begun
comandante, commander, chief
comandare, to command, order
comandato, ordered
commedia, comedy
commerciale, commercial
commerciante, merchant
commercio, commerce
commesso, salesman
comodo, comfortable, convenient
commozione, emotion, perturbation
compagnia, company
  in — di, in — with
compagno, companion
compenso, compensation
compito, task, job
complicato, complicated
complimento, compliment
composto, composed
comprare, to buy
  comprato, bought
compratore, buyer, customer
compromettere (*irr.*), to compromise
con, with
concedere (*irr.*), to grant
concerto, concert
condannato, condemned
condizione, condition
condotta, conduct
conduttore, conductor
conferma, confirmation
confidare, to confide
confondere (*irr.*), to confuse, mix
conoscere (*irr.*), to know, recognize
conosciuto, known
conoscenza, knowledge, acquaintance
consegnato, consigned
conseguenza, consequence
consenso, consent
considerato, considered
consiglio, advice, council
consistere (*irr.*), to consist
consolare, to console, comfort
consolato, consulate
console, consul

contadino, -a, peasant
conte, count
contento, -a, content, glad, pleased
contessa, countess
conto, bill, account
contraddire (*irr.*), to contradict
contrario, -a, contrary
contro, against
conveniente, convenient
convenire (*irr.*), to suit, agree
convento, convent
conversazione, conversation
convincere (*irr.*), to convince
coperta, cover, blanket, rug
coperto, -a, covered
copia, copy
copiare, to copy
copiato, copied
coppia, couple, married couple
coprire (*irr.*), to cover
coraggio, courage
coraggioso, courageous
corallo, coral
corda, cord, string
cornice, frame
coro, choir
corona, crown
correre (*irr.*), to run
corretto, correct(ed)
corridoio, corridor
corrispondere (*irr.*), to correspond
corsa, race
corso, course, avenue, main street
cortese, polite
cortile (*m.*), courtyard
corto, short
cosa, thing
  Che cosa? What?
così, so. **così . . . come,** as . . . as
costa, coast
costare, to cost
costretto, obliged, compelled
costringere (*irr.*), to compel
costui, costei, he, she; that
costume, custom, costume
cotesto, -a, that
cotoletta (di), cutlet (of)
cotone, cotton, thread
cotto, cooked

cravatta, necktie
creatura, creature
credere, to believe
crema, cream
crescere (irr.), to grow
  cresciuto, grown, increased
crisi (f.), crisis
critica (f.), censure, criticism
cuccetta, sleeping berth
cucchiaio, spoon (large)
cucchiaino, teaspoon, spoonful
cucina, kitchen
cucire, to sew
cucito, -a, sewn
cugino, -a, cousin
cui, whom
cuocere, to cook
cuoco, -a, cook
cuore (m.), heart; senza cuore,
  heartless
cura, cure, care, treatment (med.)
curiosità (f.), curiosity
cuscino, cushion

D

da, by, from
dacchè, since
danaro, money
danno, damage
dappertutto, everywhere
dare (irr.), to give
— disturbo, to give trouble
— la mano, to shake hands
— pensiero, to worry
darsena, dock
darsi, to happen
dato, -a, given
dattero, date
davanti(a), before
davvero, indeed, truly
debito, debt
debole, weak
debolezza, weakness
decimo, -a, tenth
decimo, -a, primo, -a, eleventh
decimo, -a, secondo, -a, twelfth
decimo, -a, terzo, -a, thirteenth
delusione (f.), disappointment,
  delusion
denaro, money
dente (m.), tooth

dentifricio, toothpaste
dentista (m. & f.), dentist
dentro, in, into
  dentro a, inside the
deposito, cloakroom
deputato, deputy
desiderare, to wish
desiderio (m.), desire
desinare (m.), (family) dinner
desistere (irr.), to desist
desolato, -a, desolate
destra, right
  a destra, on to the right
dettato, -a, dictated
detto, -a, said, told
deve, he must
devono, they must
di, of, any, some
dialogo, dialogue
diamante (m.), diamond
dichiarato, -a, declared
diciannovesimo, -a, nineteenth
diciassettesimo, -a, seventeenth
diciottesimo, -a, eighteenth
diecina, half a score
dietro, -a, behind
difesa, defence
difetto, defect, fault, lack
differenza, difference
difficile, difficult
difficoltà, difficulty
diffidenza, distrust
di là (da), that side (of)
diligente, diligent
dimenticanza (f.), forgetfulness
dimenticare, to forget
dimenticato, -a, forgotten
dimostrato, -a, demonstrated,
  shown
dinanzi (-a), before, in the presence (of)
dintorno (m.), outskirt
Dio, God
dipingere (irr.), to paint
dipinto, -a, painted
di qua (da), this side (of)
di rado, seldom
dire (irr.), to say, to tell
diretto, -a, direct
direttore, manager
direzione, direction, manager's
  office

dirigere, to direct
dirimpetto, -a, opposite
diritto (*m.*), right
discorrere (*irr.*), to speak, discourse
discorso, speech, discourse
disegno, drawing, scheme
disgrazia, misfortune
disperazione, despair
dispiacente, sorry
dispiacere (*m.*), regret, sorrow
  dispiacere (*irr.*), to be sorry
disposizione, disposition, inclination
disposto, inclined
disprezzabile, despicable
disprezzare, to despise
distanza, distance
distinguere (*irr.*), to distinguish
distribuzione, distribution
disturbo, trouble
disubbidire, to disobey
dito, finger
diventare, to become
divertente, amusing
divertimento, amusement
divertirsi, to enjoy oneself
dividere, to divide
diviso, divided
dizionario, dictionary
doccia, shower bath
documento, document
dogana, customs (house)
doganiere, customs officer
dollaro, dollar
dolce, sweet
dolere, to pain
dolere (*m.*), pain, sorrow
mi duole, it pains me
— **i denti,** to have toothache
dolersi, to complain
doloroso, painful, sorrowful
domanda, question
domandare, to ask
domani, to-morrow
— **l'altro,** day after to-morrow
domestica, servant
domicilio, domicile, residence
dominare, to dominate, overlook
donde, whence
donna, woman, lady
dopo, after

doppio, double
dormire, to sleep
dote, dowery
dottore (*m.*), doctor
dottoressa, lady doctor
dove, where
dovere (*m.*), duty
dovere (*irr.*), to have to, must, to owe
dozzina, dozen
dubbio, doubt
dubbioso, doubtful
dubitare, to doubt
duca, duke
duce, leader
duetto }
duo } duet
duomo, cathedral
duplice, double
durante, during
duro, hard

E

E, ed, and
è, is
eccellente, excellent
eccellenza, excellence, excellency
eccetto, except
eccezione, exception
ecco, here is, here it is
eccola, here she, it is
eccole, here they are (*f.*)
eccolo, here he, it is
eccoli, here they are (*m.*)
eccomi, here I am
  eccoci, here we are
eclissi, eclipse
eco (echi), echo(s)
educare, to educate
educazione, education
effetto, effect
efficacia, efficacy
eguale, equal
elenco, list, catalogue
elettrico, electric
enciclopedia, encyclopaedia
enfasi, emphasis
entrare, to enter
entrata, entrance
erba, grass
erede, heir, -ess

eroe, hero
eroina, heroine
esagerazione, exaggeration
esame, examination
esatto, -a, exact
esempio, example
esercito, army
esigenza, exigency, compulsion
esistere, to exist
esortazione, exhortation
esperienza, experience
esposizione, exhibition
esposto, -a, exposed
espressione (*f.*), expression
essere (*irr.*), to be
— **all' ordine,** to be ready
— **al verde,** to be penniless
— **d'accordo,** to agree
— **da più di . . .,** to be better than . . .
— **di buon umore,** to be in high spirits
— **in forse,** to hesitate
— **in procinto di . . .,** to be on the point of . . .
esso, he *or* it, **essa,** she, **essi, esse,** they
estate (*f.*), summer
è stato, has been
est, east
estero, -a, foreign
   all' estero, abroad
estorcere (*irr.*), to extort, to wrest
estremo, -a, extreme
età, age
etichetta, label
evitare, to avoid

F

fa (*in reference to time*), ago
fa (si), fanno (si), it is made, they are made
fabbricato, -a, built
faccenda, affair
   faccende di casa (*f.pl.*), household matters
facchino, porter
faccia (*f.*), face
facile, easy
fagiuoli, French beans
falegname (*m.*), carpenter

fallire, to fail
falso, -a, false
fame (*f.*), hunger
famiglia, family
famoso, -a, famous
fanale (*m.*), lantern
fanciullo, -a, small boy, little girl
far(e) (*irr.*), to do, to make
— **a tempo,** to be in time
— **fare il . . .** (*with a noun of profession*) to be . . .
— **il broncio,** to be cross
— **il piacere di,** to be so kind as
— **il sordo,** to turn a deaf ear
— **male,** to hurt
— **meglio a,** to have better
— **mostra,** to make a show
— **presto,** to make haste
— **una passeggiata,** to take a walk
— **le valigie,** to pack (trunks)
— **una visita,** to pay a visit
farfalla, butterfly
farina, meal, flour
farmacia, chemists', druggists'
farmacista, chemist
faro, lighthouse, traffic light
fatica, labour, hard work
— **per . . .,** suited to . . .
fatto, -a, made, done
fatto, fact
fattoria, farm
favola, fable
favore (*m.*), favour
— **a favore di,** in favour of
— **per favore,** please
fazzoletto, handkerchief
fede (*f.*), faith
fedele, faithful
felice, happy
felicità, happiness
femmina, female
ferita, wound
ferito, -a, wounded
fermare, to stop
fermo, -a, still
feroce, ferocious
ferro, iron
ferrovia, railway
fertile, fertile
festa, feast, holiday, festival
fiamma, flame

fiammifero, match
fiasco, flask (2·3 litres of wine)
fico, fig, fig-tree
fiducia, trust, confidence
figlio, figliuolo, son
  figlia, figliuola, daughter
filo, thread, wire
finalmente, finally, at last
finestra, window
finchè, till
fin da, since; **fin d'ora,** from now
  on
fine (*f.*), end
  alla fine, at last, after all
finestra, window
finire, to finish
finito, -a, finished
fino a . . ., until, up to . . .
fioraia, flower stand, stall
fiore (*m.*), flower, blossom
fiorire, to blossom, to bloom
firma, signature
firmare, to sign
fissato, -a, fixed
fitto, -a, thick
fiume (*m.*), river
foglia, leaf
foglio, sheet of paper
fondo (in) a . . ., at the bottom
  of . . .
fontana, fountain
(le) forbici, scissors
forchetta, fork
foresta, forest
forestiero, foreigner, stranger
forma, form
formaggio, cheese
formato, formed
forse, perhaps
forte, strong
fortuna, fortune
fortunatamente, fortunately
forza, strength
  a — di, by dint of
fosso, ditch
fotografia, photograph
fra, between, among
franchezza, boldness
francobollo, postage stamp
fratello, brother
freddo, -a, cold
freno, brake

fresco, fresh, cool
  al fresco, in the open air
fretta, haste
frittata, omelette
fritto, fried
fronte (*f.*), forehead
frontiera, frontier
frutta, dessert, a single fruit
frutto, fruit (in general)
fucilata, gun-shot
fucilato, shot
fucile (*m.*), gun
fuggire, to run away, escape
fumare, to smoke
fuoco, fire
fuori, outside
furgone (*m.*), luggage van
furore, fury, rage

G

Gabbia, cage
gabinetto, lavatory, W.C.
galleria, gallery
gallina, hen
gallo, cock
gamba, leg
garage (*m.*), garage
gatto, cat
gelato, ice-cream
gelosia, jealousy
generale, general
genere (*m.*), gender, genus, kind,
  sort
genero, son-in-law
generoso, generous
genio, genius
genitore, parent
gente, people
gentile, kind, gentle
gentilezza, kindness
gentilmente, kindly
geografia, geography
ghiaccio, ice
già, already
giacca, coat, jacket
giallo, yellow
giardiniere, gardener
giardino, garden
gilè (*m.*), waistcoat
giocattolo, plaything, toy

gioia, joy, precious stone
gioie, jewels
giornale (*m.*), newspaper
giornata, (whole) day
giorno, day
giovane, young
giovane (*m. & f.*), youth
giovanotto, young man
gioventù, youthfulness
giovinezza, youth, young people
gita, trip, excursion
giù, down
giudice, judge
giudizio, judgment
giungere (*irr.*), to arrive, overtake, reach
giuoco, game
giusto, right, correct
glorioso, glorious
gloria, glory
goccia, drop
godere, to enjoy
gola, throat
gomma, india-rubber, *also* tyre
gonnella, skirt
governatore, governor
governo, government
gradire, to like
gradito, -a, agreeable, pleasing
grammatica, grammar
grammofono, gramophone
grande, big, great, grown up
grandinare, to hail
grano (*m.*), corn
gratitudine (*f.*), gratitude
grave, grave
grazia, pardon, grace
grazie, thank you, thanks
grazioso, -a, pretty, nice
gridare, to cry, to shout
grigio, -a, grey
guadagnare, to gain, to earn
guadagno, gain
guai! woe!
guanciale (*m.*), pillow, cushion
guanto, glove
guardare, to look at
guardia (*f.*), policeman
guarire, to recover
guerra, war
guida (*f.*), guide, guide-book
gusto, taste

H

ha, he has
ha avuto, he has had
hai, thou hast
hanno, they have
ho, I have

I

Iddio, God
idea (*f.*), idea
ieri, yesterday
ieri l' altro, the day before
yesterday
inchiostro, ink
indifferenza, indifference
indulgente, indulgent
illuminare, to illuminate
immenso, -a, immense
immergere (*irr.*), to plunge
impadronirsi di . . ., to take
possession of . . .
imparare, to learn
imparato, -a, learned, learnt
impazienza, impatience
impedire, to prevent
impegno, engagement
imperatore, emperor
imperatrice, empress
impiegato, -a, employee, employed, clerk
impiego, employment
importante, important
importanza, importance
importare, to mind
non importa, it doesn't matter
impossibile, impossible
impresa, undertaking
impressione, impression
imprudenza, imprudence
in, in, into
incaricare, to charge, entrust
incaricato, a person entrusted
incarico, charge, office
incerto, -a, uncertain
inchiostro, ink
incitamento, incitement
incominciare, to start
incontrare, to meet
incontrato, -a, met

indicato, -a, indicated, shown
indirizzo, address
indovinare, to guess
infatti, in fact
infelice, unhappy
inferiore, inferior, lower
informazione, information
infreddatura, a cold
ingannare, to deceive, to cheat
ingegnere, engineer
ingegno, talent, genius
ingresso, entrance
in mezzo a . . ., in the midst of . . .
innamorato, a(di) . . ., in love (with)
innocente, innocent
innocenza, innocence
insalata, salad
insegnare, to teach
insetto, insect
insieme (con), with, together
insistere (*irr.*), to insist
insopportabile, unbearable
intelligente, intelligent
intelligenza, intelligence
intenzione (*f.*), intention
interessante, interesting
interpretare, to interpret
inteso, -a, understood
intitolato, -a, entitled
intorno, around
intrigo, intrigue
inutile, useless
invadere (*irr.*), to invade
invece di . . ., instead of . . .
inverno, winter
invidia, envy
invitare, to invite
invitato, invited, guest
invito, invitation
ira, anger, ire
isola, island
istitutrice, governess

L

là, there
labbro (*m.*), lip, edge
  (*pl. m. or f.*) **i labbri** or **le labbra,** edges, lips
lacrima, tear

ladro, thief
laggiù, down there
lagnarsi, to complain
lago, lake
lampada, lamp
lampeggiare, to lighten
lampo, lightening
lana, wool
lapis (*m.*), pencil
larghezza, breadth
largo, broad, large
lasciare, to leave (behind), abandon; to leave a place
lasciato, left
lassù, up there
lato, side
latte (*m.*), milk
latteria, diary
lattiera, milk-jug
lavabo (*m.*), wash-basin
lavandaia, laundress
lavare, to wash
lavarsi, to wash oneself
lavorare, to work
lavoro, work
legazione (*f.*), legation
legge (*f.*), law
leggere, to read
  letto, read (*p.p.*)
leggiero, light
legna, wood, fuel
legno, wood, timber
legumi(i), vegetables
Lei, you
lente, eye-glass, lens
lento, slow
lenzuolo, sheet (bed)
leone, lion
  -essa, -ess
lesso, boiled meat
lettera, letter
letteratura, literature
letto, bed
lettura, reading, lecture
lezione, lesson
lì, there (*more precise than* **là**)
  Esce di lì! Get out!
liberare, to deliver, free
liberazione, delivery, liberation
libero, free
libertà, liberty
libraio, bookseller

libreria, bookshop
libro, book
limonata, lemonade
limone, lemon
lingua, tongue, language
lira, unit of currency
lira sterlina, pound sterling
lista, list, menu
litro, litre
locanda, lodging-house, inn
locandiera, innkeeper's wife
locandiere, innkeeper
lodare, to praise
lodato, praised
lode (f.), praise
lontano, far
Loro, you
  (il) loro, their(s)
luce (f.), light
lucido, shining
lume, light, enlightenment
luna, moon
lunghezza, length
lungo, long
lupo, wolf

M

ma, but
macchina, machine
macchina fotografica, camera
madre, mother
maestà, majesty
maestro, master, teacher
magazzino, warehouse
  il grande —, big store
maggiore, greater, older
magistrato, magistrate
maglia, vest (woollen)
magnano, blacksmith
magnifico, magnificent
mai, ever
maiale (m.), pig, pork
malato, sick
malattia, sickness
male, bad, evil, disease
  mal di capo, headache
  — denti, toothache
  — gola, sore throat, etc.
malizia, mischief, trick
mamma, mamma
mancanza, want

mancare, to miss, lack
mancia, tip, gratuity
mandare, to send
mandato, -a, sent
mandra, flock
mangiare, to eat
mangiato, -a, eaten
manica, sleeve
manifattura, manufactory
maniglia, handle, knob
mano (f.), hand
mantenere, to maintain, to keep,
  to support
mantenuto, -a, maintained, kept
manzo, beef
mappa, map
marca, mark
marchese, marquis; marchesa,
  marchioness
marciapiedi (m.), pavement
mare (m.), sea
marinaio, seaman
marito, husband
marmellata, jam
marmo (m.), marble
marrone, brown
maschio, male
massimo, -a, greatest
materasso, mattress
matrimonio, marriage
mattina, morning
maturo, -a, ripe
meccanico, mechanic
medesimo, -a, same, self
medicamento, medicine, remedy
medicina, medicine
medico, doctor
mediocre, neither good nor bad,
  medium
meglio, better
mela, apple
melo, apple-tree
memoria, memory
  a memoria, by heart
meno, less. meno . . . che,
  meno . . . di, less . . . than
mentre, while
meravigliarsi (di) . . ., to wonder, to be astonished (at)
meraviglioso, marvellous
mercanzia, goods
mercante, merchant

mercato, market
a buon mercato, cheap
merce, wares
mercè, thanks to
meritato, -a, deserved
merito, merit
mese (m.), month
messo, -a, put
metà, half
metallo, metal
metro, metre. Also, underground railway
mettere (irr.), to put
— poco, or troppo tempo, to
take too little or too much time
mezzanotte (f.), midnight
mezzo (m.), half, means, middle
per — di, by means of
mezzogiorno, noon
mi, me, me, to me
migliaio, a thousand
migliorato, -a, improved
migliore, better
milione (m.), million
mille (sing.), thousand
millesimo, -a, a thousandth
minestra, soup
miniera, mine
minimo, -a, least
minore, smaller, younger
minuto, minute
mio, -a, my, mine
miseria, misery
misura, measure
misurare, to measure
mite, mild
mobilia, furniture
moda, fashion
modellato, -a, modelled
modello (m.), model
moderno, -a, modern
modestia, modesty
modificato, -a, modified
modista, milliner
modo (m.), manner, way
moglie (f.), wife, woman
molto, -a, -i, -e, much, many
momento, moment
monaco, -a, monk, nun
monarca (m.), monarch
monastero, monastery
mondo, world

moneta, money. la piccola —,
change
montagna, mountain
montone (m.), ram, mutton
monumento, monument
morbido, -a, soft
mordere (irr.), to bite
morire (irr.), to die
mortale, mortal
morte (f.), death
morto, dead
mosca, fly
mostarda, mustard
mostrare, to show
motivo, motive
motocicleta, motor-cycle
motoscafo, motor boat
mucchio, heap
municipio, town hall
mura, city walls
muro, wall (of house)
museo, museum
musica, music
mutande (le), drawers (garment)

N

nascere (irr.), to be born
nascita, birth
nascondere (irr.), to hide
nascosto, hidden
naso, nose
Natale, Christmas
natalizio, birthday
nato, born, arisen
natura, nature
navata, nave
nave (f.), ship
nazionale, national
nazionalità, nationality
nazione, nation
ne, of him, of them, of her, it
nè . . . nè, neither . . . nor
nebbia, fog
necessario, necessary
necessità, necessity
negare, to deny, refuse
negozio, shop, business
nemico, enemy
neppure, not even
nero, black
nessuno, nobody, not any

neve (*f.*), snow
nevicare, to snow
nido, nest
niente, nothing
nipote, nephew
no, no
nobiltà, nobility
noce, (*m.*) walnut tree, (*f.*) walnut
nocivo, harmful
nodo, knot
noia, annoyance, bore
noioso, tiresome, boring
nome, name, noun
non, not
non importa, it doesn't matter
non . . . mai, never
nonno, -a, grandfather, -mother
nonstante, in spite of
— che, although
nord, north
nota, note
notato, noted, noticed
notizia, -e, news
notte (*f.*), night
nozze (*f.pl.*), wedding
nulla, nothing
numero, number
nuora, daughter-in-law
nuotare, to swim
nuovo, new
  di nuovo, again
nutrimento, nourishment
nutrire, to feed, nourish

O

O, od, or
obbediente, obedient
obbedienza, obedience
obbedire, to obey
occasione, occasion
  d'—, second hand
occhiali, spectacles, glasses
occhio, eye
occupare, to occupy
occupato, busy
oceano, ocean
odio, hatred
odorato, sense of smell
odore, odour, fragrance
offerta, offer
offrire, to offer

oggetto, object, thing
oggi, to-day
ognicosa, everything
ognuno, each, every(body)
olio, oil
oltre, beyond
ombra, shade
ombrello, umbrella
omnibus, omnibus
onda, wave
onestà (*m.*), honesty
onesto, honest
onomastico, saint's day
onore (*m.*), honour
opera, work
operaio, workman
operoso, -a, hardworking
opinione, opinion
opposto, opposite
ora (*f.*), hour
ora (*adv.*), now
  d'ora innanzi, from now on
orario, time-table
orecchio, ear
ordinare, to order
ordinato, -a, ordered
orgoglio, pride
ordine (*m.*), order
originale, original
ormai, now, by this time
oro, gold
  d'oro, golden
orologeria, watchmaker's
orologio, watch
ornamento, ornament, accomplishment
ospite, host
osservare, to watch, observe
osservazione, observation
osso, bone
ostacolo, obstacle
ottavo, -a, eighth
ottenere (*irr.*), to obtain
ottenuto, -a, obtained, produced
ottimo, -a, best, very good
ovest (*m.*), west
ozio (*m.*), idleness

P

pacchetto, packet (of cigarettes, etc.)

pacco, parcel, package
pace (f.), peace
padre, father
padrona (f.), owner
  di locanda (f.), inn-keeper
padrone, master, owner
paesaggio, landscape
paese (m.), country, village
pagare, to pay
pagato, -a, paid, paid for
pagina, page
paio (m.), pair; paia (f.pl.), pairs
palazzo, palace
palco, box (in a theatre)
pallone (m.), ball, football
palma, palm-tree
pane (m.), bread
paniera, basket
panino, roll
panna, cream
pantaloni, trousers
Papa (m.), pope
paravento, screen
parco, park
pare (mi—), it seems to me
  mi pareva, it seemed to me
  mi parrebbe, it would seem to
  me
parecchio, -i, some, (pl.) several
parente, relation
parere (irr.), to seem, to look like
parete (f.), wall (inside)
parlare, to speak
parlato, -a, spoken
parola, word
parroco, parish priest
parruchiere (m.), hairdresser
parte (f.), part, side
particolare, particular
particolarmente, particularly
partire, to depart, to leave, to go
partito, -a, departed, gone, started
Pasqua, Easter
passaporto, passport
passare, to pass
passato, -a, past, passed
passeggiero, passenger
passeggiata, walk
passero, sparrow
passione (f.), passion
passo, step
pasta, paste

past'asciutta, dry paste (food)
pastore (m.), shepherd
  (le) patate, potatoes
patria, native land
patrimonio, patrimony, fortune
patrono, patron; patronessa,
  patroness
pavimento, floor
pazienza, patience
pazzia, craze, madness
pazzo, -a, foolish, crazy
peccato! what a pity!
pecora, ewe, sheep
pedone (m.), pedestrian, passer-
  by
peggio (il), the worst
peggiore, worse
pelle (f.), skin, leather
pelliccia (f.), furs
pellicola, film
penna, pen, feather
pennello, paint-brush
pennino, steel pen
pensare, to think
pensatore, thinker
pensiero, thought
pensione (f.), boarding-house
pentimento (m.), repentance
pentirsi, to repent
pentito, -a, repented
pepe (m.), pepper
per, for; through; by; in order to
pera, pear
perchè, because
—? why?
perciò, therefore
perdere, to lose
per, by
— di là, on that side, by that way
— di qua, on this side, by this
  way
perdita, loss
perdonato, pardoned
perdono, pardon
perduto, lost
pericolo, danger
pericoloso, dangerous
perla, pearl
permesso, permission
permesso, permitted
permettere, to permit
pero, pear-tree

però, but, however
persistere (irr.), to persist
persona, person
persuadere (irr.), to persuade
perverso, depraved
pesante, heavy
pescatore, fisherman
pesce, fish
peso, weight
— lordo, gross weight
pessimo, worst
pettine (m.), comb
pezzo, piece
piace, (it) pleases
   mi piace, it pleases me
piacere, pleasure
   per piacere, please
piacere (irr.), to like
piacevole, agreeable, pleasing
piaciuto, liked
piangere (irr.), to cry, weep
piano (n), floor; also plan, map
   (of city)
piano, softly, slowly
piano! easy!
pianoforte, piano
pianta, plant
piantato, planted
pianterreno, ground floor
pianura, plain
piatto, dish
piatto, -a, flat
piazza, square
piccolo, small, little
piede (m.), foot
a piedi, on foot
piega, fold
pieno (di), full (of)
pietà, pity
pietanza, dish
pietra, stone
— pigiama (m.), pyjamas
pigione (f.), house-rent
pilota, pilot
pioggia, rain
piove, it's raining
piovere (irr.), to rain
piovoso, raining, rainy
pipa, pipe
piroscafo, steamer
pittore, painter
pittura, painting

più, more
— che, — di, more than
   il — delle volte, in most cases
piuttosto (che), rather (than)
poco, little; pochi, few
   a poco a poco, little by little
   un poco(po') di, a little of
poesia, poetry, poem
poichè, since
politica, politics
polizia, police
pollo, chicken
polvere, dust, powder
polso, wrist, pulse
poltrona, arm-chair
pomeriggio, afternoon
ponte, bridge
pontefice, pontiff, Pope
popolazione, population
porta, door
portacenere (m.), ashtray
portafoglio, pocket-book, attaché-
   case
portamoneta (m.), ladies handbag
portare, to take, carry
portasigarette, cigarette-case
portato, carried, brought
portico, porch
portiere ⎱ doorkeeper, janitor,
portinaio ⎰   hall-porter
posato, placed
possesso, possession, property
possibile, possible
posta, post office
   a bella posta, on purpose
postero (-i), descendant(s)
posto, place, seat (in a car, etc.)
potente, powerful
potere (m.), power, influence
potere (irr.), to be able
povero, poor
— me! Poor me!
pranzare, to dine
pranzo, dinner
prato, meadow
predire (irr.), predict
preferire, to prefer
pregare, to beg, pray
prego, please
pregevole, valuable
preghiera, prayer, request
premio, prize, reward

premura, attentions
prendere (*irr.*), to take
— **fuoco,** to burn
preparare, to prepare
preparativo, preparation
preparato, -a, prepared
presentare, to introduce, to present
presentato, -a, introduced, presented
presidente, president, chairman
preso, -a, taken
presso, near
prestare, to lend
prestato, -a, lent
presto, fast, soon, early
presto o tardi, sooner or later
presumere (*irr.*), to presume
prete, priest
pretendere (*irr.*), to pretend
prevenire (*irr.*), to prevent
prezioso, -a, precious
prezzo, price, cost
prigione (*f.*), prison
prima che (*with verb*), before
prima di (*ref. to time*), before
primavera, spring
prime (sulle), at first
primo, -a, first
principe, prince
principessa, princess
principio, beginning
privato, private
procedere, to proceed
procurare, to procure, to try
procurato, -a, procured
prodotto, -a, produced
professione, profession
professore (*m.*), professor
profondo, -a, deep
poco profondo, shallow
profumo, perfume
programma (*m.*), program, prospectus
proibire, to forbid
prole (*f.*), offspring
promessa, promise
promesso, -a, promitted
promettere (*irr.*), to promise
pronto, -a, ready, prompt
pronunzia, pronunciation
proposito (a), speaking of, apropos
proprio, really, actual

prosciutto, ham
prosperità (*f.*), prosperity
prossimo, -a, next
protettore, protector
protezione (*f.*), protection
sala di —, fitting room
prova, proof
provato, -a, proved, tried, tried on, felt
prudente, prudent
prugna, plum
pubblicare, to publish
pubblicato, -a, published
pubblico, -a, public
pubblico (*m.*), the public
pulcino (*m.*), chicken
pulire, to clean
pulito, -a, clean
punito, -a, punished
punta, point, zero
punto, point, moment
punto, -a, not any, no
puntura, puncture
purchè, provided
pure, yet

Q

qua, here
quaderno, copy-book
quadro, picture
qualche, some
qualcuno, -a, some one
quale, which. **il** *or* **la quale,** who, whom
qualità, quality
qualunque, whatever
quando, when
quand' anche, even if
quantità, quantity
quanto, as
quanto? How much?
quanto tempo? How long?
quanto meno, the less
quanto più, the more
quanto, -a, all that which, how many, how much
quanto, -a . . ., tanto, -a, as much . . . as, so much . . . as
per quanto, however
in quanto a, as to

quantunque, though
quartiere (*m.*), quarters, apartment
quarto, -a, forth
quasi, almost
  quasi che, as if
quello, -a, that
questo, -a, this
qui, here
qui dentro, in here
  di qui, hence
quindicesimo, -a, fifteenth
quindicina, about fifteen

R

raccomandato, -a, recommended, registered (of a letter)
raccomandazione (*f.*), recommendation
raccontato, -a, related
radere, to shave
radio (*f.*), radio
ragazzo, -a, boy, girl
raggio (*m.*), ray
— di sole, sunbeam
ragione (*f.*), reason
ragionevole, reasonable
rame (*m.*), copper
ramo, branch
rappresentazione, performance
raramente, rarely
razza, race, breed
re, king
redini (*pl.*), reins
regalare, to make a present
regalato, presented, given
regalo, present
reggimento, regiment
regina, queen
registro, register (hotel)
regola, rule
repubblica, republic
resistere (*irr.*), to resist
restare, to remain
restaurato, restored
restituire, to return, give back
restituito, returned
revisione (*f.*), examination (of luggage)

ricamo, embroidery, *also* advertisement
ricchezza, riches
ricco, rich
ricevere, to receive
ricevuta, receipt
ricevuto, received
ricezione, reception (hotel)
ricompensa, reward
riconoscente, grateful
riconosciuto, recognized, acknowledged
ricordare, to remind
ricordarsi, to remember
ricordo, remembrance
ricusare, to refuse
ridente, smiling
ridere (*irr.*), to laugh
ridicolo, ridiculous
ridire (*irr.*), to tell again
riempire, to fill
riflettere (*irr.*), to reflect
riga, ruler
rilegatura, binding
rimandare, to send back
rimandato, postponed
rimanere, to remain
rimasto, left over, remained
rimborso, reimbursement
rimedio, remedy
rimprovero, reproach
rincrescere (*irr.*), to regret
rinfusa (alla), confusedly
ringraziare, to thank
riparare, to repair
riparo, repair
ripartato, repaired, sheltered
ripetere, to repeat
ripetuto, repeated
ripido, steep
riportare, to carry back
riposare, to rest
riscontrato, met with
riscontro, draught (of air)
risentirsi (di), to be angry
riservare, to reserve
riservato, reserved
risoluzione, resolution
risparmiare, to spare, save
rispettabile, respectable
rispettare, to respect
rispetto, respect

rispondere (*irr.*), to reply
risposta, reply
ristorante (*m.*), restaurant
ritardato, delayed
ritardo, delay
  in ritardo, late
ritorno, return
  di —, back again
ritratto, portrait
riuscire (*irr.*), to succeed
riva, bank
  — del mare, coast
riviera, sea-coast
rivista, review, magazine
roba, things, stuff
rodere (*irr.*), to gnaw, corrode
romanzo, novel
rompere (*irr.*), to break
rosa, rose
rosolio, liqueur, cordial
rossetto (per le labbra), lipstick
rosso, red
rotolo, roll (e.g., film)
rovina, ruin
rubato, stolen
rubinetto, tap
rumore (*m.*), noise
ruota, wheel

S

sabbia, sand
sacrifizio, sacrifice
sagrestano, sacristan
sala, hall
— da pranzo, dining-room
sale (*m.*), salt
salire (*irr.*), to go up, climb
salotto, sitting-room
salsiccia, sausage
saltare, to jump
saltato, jumped
salutare, to greet
salute (*f.*), health
saluto, greeting
salvato, saved
salvo (*adj.*), saved
sandwich (*m.*), sandwich
sangue (*m.*), blood
sano, -a, healthy, wholesome
santo, -a, saint. holy (*adj.*)
sapere (*irr.*), to know (things)

sapone (*m.*), soap
sapore (*m.*), taste, flavour
sarto, -a, tailor, dress-maker
savio, -a, wise
sbaglio (*m.*), mistake, fault
sbarcato, -a, landed
scaffale (*m.*), shelf
scala, stairs, ladder
scambiato, -a, exchanged
scarpa, shoe
scatola, box
scegliere (*irr.*), to choose
scelta, choice
scelto, -a, chosen
scena (*f.*), scene, scenery
scendere (*irr.*), to go down
sceso, -a, descended, gone down
scherzo, joke, pleasantry
schiavitù (*f.*), slavery
schioppo, gun
sciarpa, scarf
scienza, science
sciupare, to spoil, to waste
sciupato, -a, spoiled
scontrino, voucher
  lo scontrino del bagaglio, luggage ticket
scritto, -a, written
scrittoio, desk
scrittore (*m.*), writer
scrittrice (*f.*), writer
scrittura, writing, hand-writing
scrivere (*irr.*), to write
scolaro, scholar
scommessa, bet
scompartimento, compartment
scoppiato, -a, broken, burst, exploded
scuderia, stable
scudo, shield. *Also* five-lire piece
scultore, sculptor
scultura (*f.*), sculpture
scuola, school
scuro, dark, brown
scusa, excuse
scusare, to excuse
se, if, whether
sè, oneself, himself, herself, itself, themselves
sebbene, though
secco, dry
secolo, century

secondo, -a, second
  secondo, according
sedere (*irr.*), to sit
sedia, chair
segno, sign
segretario, -a, secretary
seguire, to happen, to follow
seguito, -a, followed
sembrare, to seem
  sembra, it seems
seme (*m.*), seed
semplice, simple
sempre, always
  sempre diretto, straight on
senapa, mustard
sentenza, sentence
sentiero, footpath
sentimento, feeling, sentiment
sentire, to feel, to hear
senza, senza che (*with a verb*),
  without
separato, -a, separate
sera, evening
serata, evening (the whole)
serva, maid, servant
servire, to serve
servizio, service
servitore (*m.*), servant
seta (*f.*), silk
sete (*f.*), thirst
settimana, week
severamente, severely
severità, severity
severo, -a, severe
sfortunato, -a, unfortunate
si, one, people; *ref. pron.*
sì, yes
sicchè, so that
sicurezza, safety
sicuro, -a, sure, of course
siete, you are
sigaretta (*f.*), cigarette
sigaro (*m.*), cigar
sigillo (*m.*), seal
significare, to mean
signora, lady, madam, Mrs.
signor(e), Mr., sir, gentleman
signoria (*f.*), lordship
signorina, Miss, young lady
silenzio, silence
simbolo, symbol
simpatia, sympathy

simpatico, attractive, sympathetic
sincerità, sincerity
sincero, sincere
sinistra, left
  a — on, to the left
sistema (*m.*), system
smarrito, mislaid, lost
smeraldo, emerald
smoking, dinner-jacket
soccorrere (*irr.*), to help, succour
società, society
soddisfazione, satisfaction
soffitto, ceiling
soffrire (*irr.*), to bear, suffer
soggetto, subject
soggiorno, stay, sojourn
sogno, dream
soldato, soldier
sole (*m.*), sun
solito, usual
  per il —, usually
solitudine, solitude
solo, alone
soltanto, only
somigliare, to resemble
somma, sum
sonare, to sound, play (music),
  ring, strike (of clock)
sonato, rung, played, struck
sonno, sleep
sopra, on, upon
  di —, upstairs
soprabito, overcoat
soprannome, surname
sorella, sister
sorgente (*f.*), spring, source
sorgere (*irr.*), to arise, dawn
sorprendere (*irr.*), to surprise
sorriso, smile
sottana, petticoat
sottile, thin
sotto, under
sottoveste, waistcoat
sovente, often
spada, sword
spago, string
spalla, shoulder
spargere (*irr.*), to shed, spread
sparito, disappeared
spazio, space
spazzola, brush, clothes-brush
spazzolato, brushed

spazzolino per i denti, tooth-brush

specchio, mirror

specie (f.), kind

spedire, to despatch, forward, register luggage

spedito, forwarded

spendere, to spend

spengere (irr.), to extinguish

spento, extinguished

speranza, hope

sperare, to hope

spesa, expense

speso, spent

spesso, -a, thick

spettacolo, spectacle, perform-ance

spiacevole, disagreeable

spiaggia, seaside

spiegare, to explain

spillo, pin

splendere, to shine

splendido, splendid

spogliarsi, to undress

sporco, -a, dirty

sport, sport

sportello, window (ticket —, etc.)

sposare, to marry

sposato, married

sposo, bridegroom (-a, bride)

spremere, to squeeze out

spugna, sponge

spumante, foaming
   vino —, sparkling wine

squadrone (m.), squadron

squallidezza, squalor

stadio, lo, stadium

stagione (f.), season

stamani, this morning

stanco, tired

stanotte, to-night

stanza, room

star bene, to be well

— di buon animo, to be of good spirit, courage

— di casa, to live, be in

stare (irr.), to stay, live, be

stare a disagio, to be uncomfort-able

— in forse, to be in doubt

— in pensiero, to be anxious

— in piedi, to stand

stare male, to be bad ill

— meglio, peggio, better, worse

— sull'intesa, to be on the look-out

stasera, this evening

stato (n.), state

stato, been

statua, statue

stazione (f.), station

stecchino, toothpick

stella, star

stesso, same

stilografica, fountain pen

stima, esteem

stivale, boot

stoffa, stuff, material

stomaco, stomach

storia, history

strada, street

straniero, foreigner

strano, -a, strange

straordinario, -a, extraordinary

strappato, -a, torn

stretto, -a, narrow

studente, student

studiare, to study

studio, study, studio

stupendo, -a, stupendous

su, on, upon. su! up!

subito, at once

sud, south

sudicio, -a, dirty

suo, -a, his, her, its

suocero, -a, father-in-law, mother-in-law

suono, sound

superato, -a, surpassed, sur-mounted

superiore, superior, upper

supporre (irr.), to suppose

supposto che, granted

supremo, -a, supreme

sussidio, subsidy

sussistere (irr.), to subsist

sveglia, alarm-clock

svegliare, to awaken

sventura, misfortune

T

tabacco, tobacco

tabarin (m.), night club

taccuino (*m.*), notebook
tagliare, to cut, trim (hair)
tagliato, -a, cut
tale, such a one
   tale . . . quale, like . . . like
tal dei tali (*m. & f.*), So-and-so
talvolta, sometimes
tanto, so
— **meglio,** so much the better
— **meno,** the less
— **peggio,** so much the worse
— **più,** the more
— **. . . quanto . . .,** as . . . as,
    so . . . as
— **-a,** so much
— **-a, . . . quanto, -a,** as much
   . . . as, so much . . . as
tappeto, carpet, table-cover
tardare, to delay
tardi, late
tasca, pocket
tassa, tax
tatto, sense of touch
tavola (-o), table
taxi (*m.*), taxi
tazza, cup
tè (*m.*), tea
teatro, theatre
telefonare, to telephone
telefono, telephone
telegramma (*m.*), telegram
tema (*m.*), theme
temere, to fear
temperino, penknife
tempo, time, weather
temporale (*m.*), storm
tenda, curtain, tent
tenebre (*f. pl.*), darkness
tenente, lieutenant
tenere (*irr.*), to keep, hold
tennis (*m.*), tennis
tentativo, attempt
termometro, thermometer
terra, earth
terrazzo, terrace
terribile, terrible
terzetto, trio
tesoreria, treasury
tesoro (*m.*), treasure
testa, head
tetto, roof
ti, thee, to thee

toccare, to touch
— **a . . .,** to be one's turn
tocco (il), one o'clock
tolto, -a, taken out, off, away
tomba, tomb
torcere (*irr.*), to twist
torlo (*m.*), yolk
tornato, -a, come back
torre (*f.*), tower
torta, cake
torto, wrong
tosto, soon
tovagliuolo, napkin, serviette
tra, between, among
tradotto, -a, translated
tradurre (*irr.*), to translate
traduzione, translation
tragedia, tragedy
tram (*m.*), tram, tramcar
tramonto, sunset
tranne, except
transatlantico (*m.*), liner
tranvai (*m.*), tramway
trarre (*irr.*), to draw, pull
trascorrere (*irr.*), to pass, to
   elapse
trascorso, -a, passed
trasmesso, -a, transmitted
trasmettere (*irr.*), to transmit
traversato, -a, crossed
tremendo, -a, tremendous
treno, train
tribù (*f.*), tribe
tribunale (*m.*), tribunal
triennio, period of three years
trimestre (*m.*), period of three
    months, quarter
trina, lace
trio, trio
triplice, triple, threefold
triplo, -a, triple
triste, sad
troppo, too, too much (*adj. & adv.*)
trovare, to find
trovato, -a, found
tuono, thunder
turchino, -a, blue
turismo, tourism
turista, tourist
turistico, touristi
tuttavia, however, yet
tutti e due (*m.*), both

tutti e tre, all three
tutto, -a, all
— ad un tratto, all at once

U

uccello, bird
uccidere (irr.), to kill
udire (irr.), to hear
udito, sense of hearing
— -a, heard
ufficio, office
l'ufficio postale, post office
— biglietti, ticket —
ultimo, -a, last
umido, -a, damp
un, -a, a, an, one
una volta, once
unità (f.), unity, union
università (f.), university
uno, -a, a, an, one
  a — a —, one by one
  — per volta, one by one
uomo, man; pl. uomini, men
uovo, egg; pl. uova, eggs
usanza, custom
usato, -a, used
uscire (irr.), to go out
uscita, exit
uscito, -a, gone out
utile, useful
  l'—, the utility
uva (f.), grape; pl. le uve

V

vacca, cow
vagone (m.), carriage (railway)
valigetta, hold-all, suit-case
valigia, trunk
valle (f.), valley
valore (m.), valour, value, worth
vapore (m.), steam, steamboat
vaso da notte, chamber-pot
vasto, -a, wide
Vaticano, Vatican
vecchiaia, old age
vecchio, -a, old
  il —, the old man
  la vecchia, the old woman
vedere (irr.), to see
vedovo (-a), widower, widow

veduto, -a, seen
veleno, poison
velluto, velvet
vendere, to sell
vendicato, -a, avenged
venditore (m.), seller, salesman
— di frutta, etc., fruit, etc., seller
venditrice (f.), seller, saleswoman
venduto, -a, sold
venerazione, veneration
venire (irr.), to come
ventaglio, fan
venticello, light breeze
ventina, a score
vento, wind
venuta, arrival, coming
venuto, -a, come
verde, green
vergogna, shame. Shame!
vergognarsi, to be ashamed
verità, truth
vernice, paint, varnish
vero, -a, true
verso, towards
vescovo, bishop
vestibolo, hall, lounge
vestirsi, to dress oneself
vettura, cab
vetturino, cabman
vi, you, to you; adv., there
via (f.), street, way, path
—, away
—! come now!
viaggiare, to travel
viaggio, voyage, journey
vicino, -a, neighbour
—, -a, near to (adj.)
vicolo, lane
vietare, to forbid
vietato, forbidden
vigile urbano, traffic policeman
villa, villa
villaggio, village
vincere (irr.), to vanquish, to
  win
vino, wine
vinto, -a, vanquished, won
violino, violin
violoncello (m.), cello
virtù (f.), virtue
visita, visit
visitare, to visit

viso, face
vissuto, -a, lived
vista, sight, view
vita, life
vitello, veal
vittima, victim
vittoria, victory
viva! long live!
vivace, lively, bright
vivere (*irr.*), to live
vivo, alive
vizio, vice
voce (*f.*), voice
voglia, will
volare, to fly
volentieri, willingly, with pleasure
volere (*irr.*), to want, wish
   voglio, I want

volta, time
   una —, due —, once, twice, etc.
   più di una —, more than once
   il più delle volte, in most cases
volubilità, fickleness
vulcano, volcano
vuoto, empty

Z

zaffiro, sapphire
zaino, knapsack, rucksack
zanzara, mosquito
zio, -a, uncle, aunt
zitto, silent
   —! hush! shut up!
zuccheriera, sugar-basin
zucchero, sugar